Masks and Masking

Masks and Masking

Faces of Tradition and Belief Worldwide

GARY EDSON

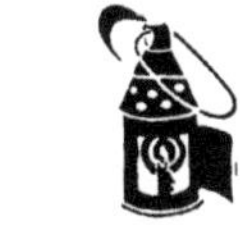

McFarland & Company, Inc., Publishers
Jefferson, North Carolina, and London

LIBRARY OF CONGRESS CATALOGUING-IN-PUBLICATION DATA

Edson, Gary, 1937–
Masks and masking : faces of tradition and
belief worldwide / Gary Edson.
p.   cm.
Includes bibliographical references and index.

ISBN 978-0-7864-4578-3
softcover : 50# alkaline paper ∞

1. Masks—Social aspects.   2. Masks—Symbolic aspects.
3. Masks—Psychological aspects.   4. Masks—Religious aspects.   I. Title.
GN419.5.E36   2009   2005010585

British Library cataloguing data are available

Cover photograph ©2009 PhotoSpin

Manufactured in the United States of America

*McFarland & Company, Inc., Publishers
Box 611, Jefferson, North Carolina 28640
www.mcfarlandpub.com*

To M

A sign for water that is related
to the Egyptian hieroglyph, the
Greek *mu*, and the Goddess in
her life-giving function.

Contents

Preface

As indicated by the extensive bibliography, a large number of excellent books and articles have been written that relate to various aspects of the present work. Each of the authors has made a significant contribution to the scholarly study of their particular topic. Considering the vast amount of information, it is obvious that the present work can offer but a limited overview of the related material.

One concern I have is that because of its brevity, this book may appear to deal with masking in a superficial manner. This is not so. The seriousness and concern for the topic should be apparent to those willing to read the book from beginning to end.

A second concern is that the material in this book might appear to be in some way ethnocentric or inconsiderate of today's nomenclatural and perspective norms. Every effort has been made to present the material without bias or prejudice. Unavoidably when I am quoting from other scholars' work gender-specific references are sometimes made. No references have been included in this text that use racially derogatory terminology. Precautions aside, there are undoubtedly terms, expressions, or references that will disturb someone's sensibilities. For those unintentional moments I accept responsibility. Ultimately I am answerable for the contents of this book.

Is this work to be the quintessential chronicle on masks and masking? No. It is to assist interested people in gaining a greater appreciation of masks and the collective role they play in the saga of human life. For some it will be inadequately academic and for some too narrow in scope, but perhaps for others it will trigger an interest that will cause them to reconsider masks as meaningful symbols of cultural and social evolution.

Comments About This Book

No one book can adequately describe, define, explain, and detail the importance of the mask as a part of the history of humankind. It was only in recent years that major interest has focused on masks and masking. Early researchers were few, and their fieldwork was often limited to one geographic location or one indigenous group. Nevertheless, a wealth of information has been accumulated out of those pioneering activities, although there was an isolation of the mask in many of those books that placed it in either an academic or historical context without consideration of its larger meaning.

Much of the earlier material written about masks was based on three types of information. First, there were the data generated by persons striving to place every act, ritual, or cultural undertaking into a quasi-scientific mode based on preestablished and often extra-cultural practices. The second methodology involved a social assessment based on contemporary issues that decontextualized the objects. The third form of inquiry was predisposed to determining the authenticity of particular masks and masking traditions and cross-cultural influences. All these approaches provided valuable information; however, they were not particularly illuminating as explanations of the general significance of masks and masking.

One of the difficulties often encountered when discussing traditional masks is that they were viewed as ends unto themselves rather than means to an end as they were originally conceived. It is in this context that the concept of "art" is frequently introduced. As objects without apparent application in most "modern" circumstances, masks are assigned a niche in the plastic arts category with an aesthetic value. In this way, they can be enjoyed and appreciated out of context. This perspective denies the "wholeness" of the mask and restricts the viewer's ability to see and understand its complete nature. The true genius of expression is lost.

In the study of masks and masking, it is likely that too little attention has been given to the activities associated with the maskers and too much is inferred based on contemporary assumptions. The significance of masks often has been appraised from a single perspective without consideration of the collective influences that defined their production, meaning, and use. There was in the masking practice a relationship that defined the role of the maker, user, and viewer.

This book is arranged to give substance to some of the interesting issues about masks and masking. However, it does not presume to be an all-inclusive general history of this subject, nor does it propose a radical hypothesis regarding the origin or use of masks. Its purpose is to bring together the various aspects of masks and masking in a way to provide relevant information, stimulate interest, and provoke further investigation of these special objects of cultural patrimony. Undoubtedly, this is a topic of study to which a strong emotional response may be anticipated as masks are primary elements in many sentinel aspects of social and cultural life. Because of the expressive power of masks, it is very likely that certain of my own personal preferences have found their way into the ideas expressed in this book. Nevertheless, no attempt has been made to interpret the material presented from a particular point of view. There is no preestablished artistic, religious, historical, or anthropological agenda to be given preference over another. If a particular bias is demonstrated, it is the result of personal interest and was unavoidable.

There are a number of reasons for writing this book, and two are of particular importance. One reason is directly connected with the notion of creative expression as it relates to the socio-cultural environment. Often, the study of art and art history has been represented as a series of events isolated from the societies in which those activities occurred and the images were produced. In reality, all art forms are firmly fixed within the social framework of their origination. The second reason is less complicated: Masks are interesting as examples of culturally integrated objects of unique merit. They combine the best of art, ethnology, and anthropology.

The challenge for this book is to consider the spirit of the mask and its influence on the ontological status of the mask wearer rather than simply describing the appearance of masks. Its purpose is to provide a clarified perspective of masks and the activities associated with masking.

Finally, this book was written, for the most part, in the past tense not because the cultures are "dead" but because the masking practices have changed and continue to change.

A Note About the Illustrations

A decision was made to use drawings rather than photographs to illustrate this book. The drawings are to show both the similarities and differences between masks in distinct cultures.

The section at the back of the book "About the Drawings," beginning on page 249, describes my model(s) for each drawing. The pieces illustrated were chosen to allegorize fundamental emotional and spiritual perspectives as well as to document different styles, shapes, and designs. However, they do not present the true "face" of the masks in the same way as photographs. The drawings are a representation of the mask without the color, texture, and real image of the piece. The spiritual representations present in the masks are therefore undisturbed.

There are three compelling reasons for using drawings rather than photographs.

(1) Drawings provide a referential illustration for the reader but do not transmit the exact likeness of the mask or head. Many masks are considered to be sacred or culturally revered objects that have a "life." Some pieces are to be maintained in a place and manner to allow spiritual "feeding" and to facilitate delivery of the appropriate attention and veneration. Others examples such as the Maori *mokamoka*, although not masks, are protected by the Policy on Human Remains and Ethical Concern. The Policy does not forbid pictures of these tattooed heads; however, reason, respect, and good judgment raise questions of proper conduct when dealing with human remains as objects of cultural heritage.

(2) Drawings reduce the images to black and white patterns that eliminate the emotional and psychological influences of color whether viewed from a personal or cultural perspective. They (the drawings) simplify the mask's appearance to the most significant elements, and in that way convey more of their meaning.

(3) The availability of good quality, highly descriptive photographs is limited.

Although all the masks illustrated in the book have been photographed and exhibited at some time, they are a part of the cultural and spiritual heritage of a particular people. It is proper for objects that have spiritual significance to be recognized for their special attributes and given the appropriate consideration. That is what this book attempts to achieve.

The superscipt letters (a, b, c, and so on) in the captions refer to the Notes to the Captions beginning on page 221.

The primary resource for this book is literary as only a small portion of the material is drawn from direct field investigation. However scrupulous my attention to resources and factual representation of available information, the choice of data and images in the text is mine. I was attracted by the idea of the "mask" and its influence on people and vice versa. In part because of time and distance, the spirit behind masks must involve some degree of speculation and occasionally the related research can be confusing. It is very easy to make assumptions based on unrecognized ethnocentrism, and such errors are difficult to discover. In general, the crux of the book is that multiple cultural realities are socially facilitated through individual and collective definitions of phenomenological occurrences and that this supposition connects the realities of early peoples with a commonly shared expression — the mask.

Gary Edson
Lubbock, Texas

Introduction

The sight of the masked figure, as a purely aesthetic experience, carries us beyond "ordinary life" into a world where something other than daylight reigns; it carries us back to the world of the savage, the child and the poet, which is the world of play....[1]

This book is about people and the masks they wore to survive the elements, acknowledge and confirm their identity, celebrate the important events of their lives, and venerate their personal and collective gods. The book is not about one people but many peoples emotionally, culturally, and physiologically immersed in their distinctive environments. It endorses the reality that "The mind of man is capable of anything — because everything is in it, all the past as well as all the future. What was there after all? Joy, fear, sorrow, devotion, valour, rage — who can tell? — but truth — truth stripped of its cloak of time."[2]

Why did people make masks? When was the first mask made? Who made the first mask? It is possible that there will never be factual answers for these questions. Masking began at a distant time before written records were maintained; therefore, it is impossible to know the whole truth of their origin. However, it is fair to say that there are aspects of culture that continue today as verification of the historical significance of masks and masking. Comprehending the relationship between masks and their socio-cultural role is essential if they are to be viewed as complex visual stimulators in their appropriate patrimonial context.

A person encountering masks for the first time often wonders what they mean. Why were they made? How were they used? For the viewer to find answers to these questions, masks must be considered as an occurrence that was present in almost every culture of the world. An analysis of the forms assigned to masks and masking in different cultural applications gives insight into their purposes and supports the assumption that they had a definable socio-cultural meaning.

Because of their expansiveness, there was a wide range of beliefs and practices associated with the making and using of masks; however, there were persistent themes that provided theoretically useful generalizations about masking as a form of social communication. Masks, in a few cultures, continue to have an important role as conveyers of spiritual significance connected with traditional beliefs, rituals, and ceremonies. The mask, for some peoples, serves as a melding device that links the activities of daily life with the spirit world of their ancestors and the forces of nature. For other persons, masks have special roles in the enactment of myths and historical dramas that were fundamental to maintaining traditions and continuing social order.

The masking tradition in many cultures was a tool that people fashioned and used to fulfill their needs. It was a declaration of identity as well as an expression of time that began with the society's earliest recollections and extended beyond the present and far into the future. Masking was an information process, a school of applied philosophical thinking, and a convergence of practical thoughts and sacred beliefs. Each aspect of the masking tradition identified a broadly defined cultural formation seeking to communicate its dignity and sense of purpose.

The Undeniable Presence of Masks and Masking

Masks have often been viewed as elements of culture that were unrelated to other socio-cultural or magico-religious elements. Frequently, they were understood or presented as ancillary paraphernalia of ritual events. This perspective failed to consider the time, place, and circumstances of the people that made and used the masks. The masks were about belief and were the faces of the cultures in which they were made. They told the stories of the people — their history and traditions; life and death; and the past, present, and future. In addition, they made myths seem real, eased the pains of child birth, facilitated intergenerational cultural continuity, and added humor to untenable and often unacceptable situations. It is not possible to grasp the structure and function of masks in a given society unless the culture is considered in its entirety.

The mask was often a disguise. It was a method of hiding the identity of an individual for purposes of spiritual transformation or supernatural communication. If identity is "the collective aspect of the set of characteristics by which a thing [or a person] is definitively recognizable or known,"[3] then the use of a mask altered identity in a way that was "magical." The mask did not always hide the features of the wearer; however, it offered a different and sometimes special appearance that stimulated and maintained cultural cognition.

Masks in recent history became so associated with particular activities that they often became symbolic and eventually were discontinued because of the strong connotations. For instance, in seventeenth-century Europe many persons wore masks to disguise their identity and to facilitate the pursuit of clandestine activities. Lovers wore masks to avoid discovery. Prostitutes wore masks to disguise their true identity, and members of society wore masks so they might indulge in socially deviant behavior. So many people wore masks that the act of masking was associated with some form of disreputable activity and thereby lost its surreptitious purpose.[4]

The unusual appearance of masks often was used to attract and direct attention. It was nature for the uninformed to view masks as exotic objects from unfamiliar places because few individuals were prepared to appreciate the fascinating creations of people with customs and practices different from theirs. This attitude was marginally reduced by greater exposure to distant lands and people, and gradually the unknown cultures became more familiar as objects appeared in theaters and festivals. However, the vicarious interaction with people and places hardly acquainted the viewer with the conditions, beliefs, and traditions that influence daily existence in the mask-making society. Seldom was the viewer made aware of the activities and emotions that made the unknown image makers or their cultures constituents of the human community. By nature and purpose, much of the worldview transmitted to, and from, divergent societies focused on the eccentricities of a people rather than the similarities.

Mask making was a complex undertaking that combined form and content to evoke both visual and emotional values. The primary factors of human existence placed masks within a social context to address the life ways and attitudes governing daily behavior toward those "things" that occupied the invisible space between humans and the cosmos. Three describable forces in this often-contesting environment were of paramount importance to all people. The first was physiological, and it dealt with the life functions of birth, puberty, illness, and death. The second was ethereal, and it recognized human contact with the forces of nature. The third was sociological, and it referred to human interaction with other humans. Each of these essential forces included an element of anxiety because they were associated with the strivings of life. It was the uncertainty of life (and death) that generated an indispensable need for supernatural intervention.

There were beliefs, customs, and recollections within all human societies that were vestiges of the past. They were a part of the social inheritance of a particular group of people, and they were perpetuated by habit and tradition.[5] Included in this patrimonial record were tales of the activities, deeds, and adventures of all genus of supernatural or superhuman beings. The masks were a part of the psychosymbolic structure of human existence that gave recognition to exceptional beings. One of the reasons masks are studied is because they retain that association and they are different from image observed in other forms of socio-cultural expression. By their unusual nature, they arouse curiosity, stimulate the imagination, and transport the viewer from the seemingly mundane activities of daily life to a different, often mystical, time.

A system of masking activities depended on being connected with human exigencies and their satisfaction. Such events were believed to be instrumental in satisfying essential needs whether physiological, sociological, or spiritual. When those activities ceased to be useful they were discontinued, and the related masks were reassigned to other societal priorities.

The First Masks

Research has shown that because of the relatively sparse human population in the early centuries of the recent epoch of the Quaternary Period (Cenozoic Era), ancient people were a minority in the sequence of related elements. The activities of life were interconnected in that unregulated and often overwhelming environment. There was likely no clear differentiation between the various manifestations of existence. Food gathering and preparation, interpersonal relationships, procreation, hostility, death, beliefs, symbols, and myths were constant and overlapping factors of survival in this primordial setting. That which early people did not possess in materiality, they sought to acquire mystically with the assistance of magic.[6] The mask aided in this process by providing the appropriate guise for spiritual interaction.

Masks probably evolved in several places simultaneously. They might have been for protection against the elements as some have proposed or protection for combatants in times of war as others have speculated. They might have served as disguises to confuse animals being hunted or to deceive unwelcome spirits. Most masking activities had a historic catharsis that went beyond known records whether the fountainhead was a few centuries or thousands of years ago extending into prehistoric times.

Imaginably, the first masks might have been used to frighten the enemy, disguise the wearer, appease the gods, or attract a spouse. The range of possibilities for the use of masks is only limited by the information available through contemporary reference and conjecture based on the archaeological record. Mircea Eliade in *Symbolism, the Sacred, and the Arts* called attention to the mystic role of masks with the statement: "Ceremonial nakedness greatly increases the magico-religious power of woman.... Man, on the contrary, increases his magico-religious possibilities by hiding his face and concealing his body."[7]

Throughout history, the first impression of a person is determined by visual scrutiny, and the anatomical feature that attracts the greatest attention is the face. An amount of study has been conducted to determine why people respond to certain facial types, and while the shape, size, color, and texture cannot be overlooked, the arrangement, including the alignment of the features (eyes, nose, mouth, and ears), appears to have a primary influence on viewer response. Although the reactions often are subconsciously motivated or culturally altered, people respond to familiar configurations and assigned values based on accepted norms. This harmonious arrangement of facial features is commonly described as beauty.

The concern for an orderly arrangement of features often is applied when visualizing masks, and the image that comes to mind is a carved, modeled, or woven object that was worn on the face or head. However, the viewer's understanding of masks frequently is restricted due to the perplexities caused by ethnocentrism. Although the viewer may seek to understand the mask, there is a pattern of thinking below the level of conscious perception that is culturally formed. Therefore, it is extremely difficult not to impose those perceptions upon the nature and purpose of masks from unfamiliar socio-cultural systems. Thus, another people not endorsing the same values and beliefs may view the significance a particular mask has for one culture differently.

A similar complication can occur when studying masks isolated by time and space. It is impossible for today's viewers to transport themselves to the time in which a particular mask was conceived, made, and used. Contemporary investigation allows minimal access to the transcendental aspects of ancient masks and the associated beliefs. It is normally the elucidation of others that influences our thinking, and those perspectives may project erroneous ideas. It is equally probable that the mask-associated myths and rituals have been altered over time by the influence of extra-cultural forces.

To better comprehend the meaning of masks, it is preferable to eliminate preconceptions about how or why a particular mask was made and to concentrate on the "message responsibility" assigned to the object. The messages encoded in some masks appear to support literal translation, whereas in others the information is less obvious and may be a part of the initiating society's secret knowledge that was intended for those inducted into the magico-religious order. This approach set aside the "effort" of making the mask in consideration of the socio-cultural "effect" of the mask.

Although obscured by the shadows of the past, some aspects of masking history are not based on conjecture. Cave paintings from about twenty thousand years ago depict figures with animal masks, early Egyptians left images of humans with animal "heads" (masks), and Incan burial chambers contained masks of gold to cover the faces of the dead. These masking occurrences and many others are a part of the record of human existence, and they appear to confirm the use of masks for at least twenty thousand years. Furthermore, the way the masks were utilized infers an early association between masking and some type of pietistic practice.

Every society reaches a particular level of magico-religious sophistication within the context of their beliefs and institutions. The motivations in most cultures that lead to the creation and use of masks stemmed from the processes developed to fulfill the basic needs of society through the implementation of traditional beliefs. The physical manifestation of the belief-associated images, the technical skill of the image maker, and the availability of materials contributed to the diversity of mask images found around the world. Masking, from this perspective, was a culturally inclusive practice because it was a form of socio-cultural (or magico-religious) experience shared by most peoples for many of the same reasons.

Campbell wrote in *Myth and Mythmaking*, "The mask [was] revered as an apparition of the mythical being that it represent[ed], yet everyone [knew] that a man made the mask and that a man [was] wearing it."[8] The fact that the masked person was a composite of mask, person, and myth was disregarded in the minds of the viewers. A new paradigm was formulated in their imagination to support that thinking that deviated from the logical patterns of understanding to a theatrical realm of "make-believe." In that mental attitude, reason was not allowed to intrude upon established belief, and the viewer was seized by a sentiment of emotional identification.[9]

Masks as Socio-Cultural Prototypes

Nations of people were not founded on desire and reason alone. The first priority of all social structures was a system of beliefs and the associated rituals to ensure the perpetuation of an established ideology and dogma. Inevitably, knowledge and reason had secondary roles in furthering social and material objectives. When there were conflicts between reason and belief, the typical human inclination was to endorse those tenets that were a part of their tradition. Early people reacted according to the examples assigned to them by their history and to the characteristics of their social order. This persistence was true for the economic, social, political, and cultural life of a people. Ceremonies, rituals, and magic were a part of maintaining a belief system, and the significance of each of these factors depended upon those practices and beliefs transmitted from the preceding generation.

The foundation of a belief system resided with the people. When imposed by external forces, such systems lacked truth and had little meaning. However, masks often illustrated outside influences. In early times those forces were usually singular in nature and spaced over extended periods of time. This allowed a gradual adaptation of the foreign influences into the local culture. As examples of this process, many masks made in Bali and Java for use in the dramatic enactment of historic epics demonstrate the influence of India. The masks and the dramas were often based on the *Ramayana* and the *Mahabharata*, traditional Indian narratives.[10] Moreover, masks made in West Africa and along the Northwest coast of North America were adorned with mirrors, nails, fabric, and paint acquired as trade goods from extra-cultural sources. As social interaction increased and multicultural influences were brought to bear, patrimonial integrity was diluted. Partly for that reason and partly due to the great diversity of masks used among the cultures of the world, concepts about masking origins and purposes are nonspecific.

Beyond the historic records of masks and human behavior, there is the question of whether masks were originally objects of necessity for early peoples or elements of choice that were freely selected to fulfill a preestablished objective. Current literature suggests that early peoples carefully and thoughtfully formed and used masks as necessary elements of individual and social existence. However, more recent masking activities appear to be based on the notion of free choice, as there may be little connection between the necessities of societal existence and mask selection and use. Early masking activities were normally intended to promote the beliefs of a people, whereas contemporary masking often asserts the psyche of an individual.

Current information indicates that many early cultures had complex belief systems requiring equally complex practices of veneration. However, as the record of prehistoric rituals and beliefs is very limited, verification of those theories is highly speculative. As a means of establishing cultural patterns, scholars, beginning in the seventeenth century, visited and studied socio-cultural groups in different parts of the world. The study focused primarily on non–European peoples as a possible resource for information about the origins of the human belief system and the associated social institutions.[11] The study of human consciousness has expanded and become more inclusive as anthropological activities have become closely linked with the social sciences. The investigation, in this context, has focused on urban settings and so-called "peasant communities" in different parts of the world with a primary concern for developing countries. In addition, anthropologists also have divided the field into various forms of study dealing with religious beliefs and practices to the interplay of biology and social systems.

Masks continue to have an exotic quality that speaks of distant cultures for most people. The masks generate a special kind of admiration and empathy as interestingly beautiful but unusual objects. As reflective faces of humanity, masks show a perspective that is introspective and self-realizing. The mask was witness to the historical and cultural evolution of the human race just as all related imagery expressed the beliefs and values of society in which they were made. They performed an important function unlike other symbols that ingeniously reflect the human spirit.

Masks are a type of mystical expression. They are forms of communication that have primary meaning to their makers and users and secondary significance to persons outside their original cultural milieu. Although they were created to fulfill a function, they can be viewed as an integral and perhaps primary element in the evolutionary symbology of humanity.

1

Symbolic Mutilation

Masks are universal. In cultures all over the world masks [were] worn to protect, to provoke fear, to symbolize social status, to exalt, to mock, to amuse. They transport[ed] the wearer from the world of the mundane to one which [was] otherwise out of reach. Masks serve[ed] as vehicles through which tensions [were] relaxed, dilemmas resolved, social taboos bridged, and communications established.[1]

Indelible Marks of Membership

The body is a form of social and personal expression. It has been altered, transformed, mutilated, and subjected to all forms of modification and victimization for the sake of social or religious acceptance. Those practices "sacrificed" the body and made it sacred within its social surroundings. The human body has been a source of pleasure and pain according to the dictates of cultural beliefs. The customs that prompted those practices were too complex in their inception to be considered at the psychological level without knowledge of their history. However, masks and masking appear to be a response to many of the same social and cultural stimuli. Their common use suggests that, at least under certain conditions, archaic peoples everywhere responded to socio-cultural causes in a relatively similar way.

Tattooing and scarifying as alterations of the skin and methods of changing a person's appearance were forms of physical masking. Among some peoples, such as the Polynesians, tattooing replaced some of the more traditional types of physical mutilation. As examples, a Samoan male child was in his minority until tattooed, and in the Marquises Islands tattooing was a principal initiatory rite that was undergone by every male youth at puberty.[2] Those practices replaced circumcision and other phallus-oriented initiatory ceremonies. Body modifications including circumcision; infibulation; clitoridectomy; and breast, foot, and face lacerations were indications of status and rank in many societies. The mutilation altered the physical appearance of the individual to conform to established social customs.

Similarly, it was common for initiates to receive a permanent mark, or marks, denoting their group membership. That practice appears to have been associated with mystic and secret organizations from the earliest times. The markings included tattoos, scars, brands (shaped scarification applied with hot needles or tools), or some form of anatomical modification such as teeth extraction or shaping; lip, nose, ear, or tongue perforation; or head, neck, arm, or foot deformation.

The simple tattooed lines radiating from her lower lip and down her chin identified a Yukon-Kushokwim woman. She represented but one of the many cultural groups that mark their members in a distinct way. Face alteration or beautification by tattooing in different forms was known to have been a part of cultural tradition in Africa, the Americas, and Asia. Tattooing was so pervasive in Europe that it had to be prohibited by the Scottish church council in 787 CE.[3]

Because various peoples used tattooing, it had many manifestations. Most facial markings were a configuration of dots and lines used to exaggerate or extend certain facial features. The eyes, nose, and mouth were accentuated in that way as were the forehead and chin (see drawing 1.1). The designs were both simple and complex with one of the most ornate being the cuneiform pattern of the New Zealand Maori (see drawing 1.2).

The early inhabitants in Siberia practiced a method of tattooing described as "needle-and-thread." A thread covered with soot was pulled under the skin to create a colored pattern in this method of tattooing.[4] Those body marks were to enhance individual appearance and reinforce group identity. Magic tattoos—those consisting of mystic symbols and signs—were thought to give special powers including the ability to manipulate the minds of people and to make them see events or beings that did not exist.

A second commonly practiced method of face and body modification was scarification. That practice possibly originated as a form of self-mutilation administered in response to anger, frustration, fear, or guilt.[5] Whatever the reason for its origination, scarification was a practice that evolved

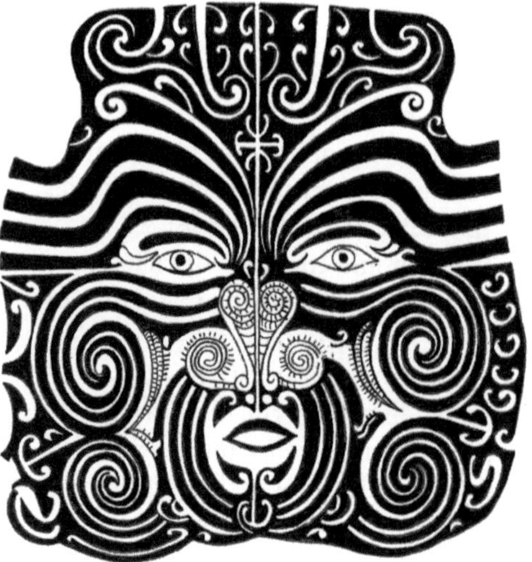

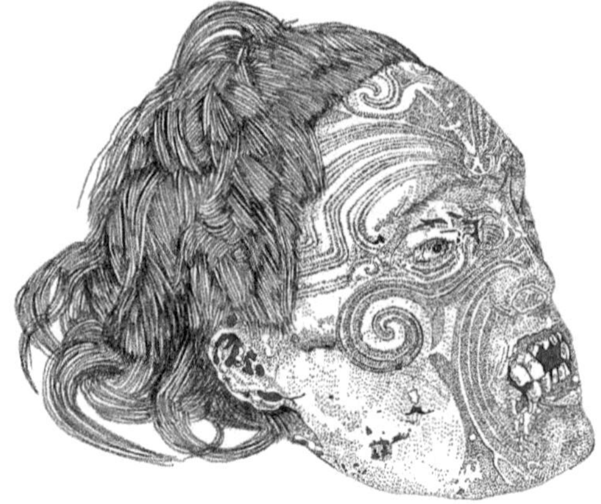

Drawing 1.1 (*left*) Tattooed Maori face illustrating one of the unique features of Maori tattoo art, the use of the spiral as exemplified by the pattern on the cheeks. The openwork spirals were also a favored pattern used on the prows of Maori war canoes. Drawing 1.2 (*right*) Tattooed mummified head (*Makomokai*) revered by the Maori. This ancestral object is from New Zealand. The dried and preserved head of an ancestor was retained to bestow honor on the deceased.

into a custom associated with beliefs as well as forms of magic and ritual observance. Scars were made by cutting or scratching the skin of the face, back, chest, or arms with shells, knives, or stones and rubbing clay or ash into the wound. The process was repeated until the desired raised patterns of fibrous tissue were achieved. Due partly to the simplicity and directness of that method of mutilation, it was practiced from ancient times.

Two psychogenic aspects of humans appear to be universal — they fear the unknown and have a limitless capacity for belief. Pursuing that sentiment, transformation of the flesh by scarification was a plausible practice. Self-mutilation was considered a form of symbolic power to enhance people's lives by "altering the contours of nature."[6] Some methods of alteration including distention were common to many cultural groups. The ear lobes and lips were distended several inches to accommodate ear and lip plugs, and some peoples found special charm in the results of neck extending. Constricting was also a commonly practiced form of body modification as witnessed by the Chinese custom of binding women's feet by preventing normal development. Another body-modifying technique was cranial alteration as practiced in various regions of Africa and the Americas.

From the practice of body modification, it was an easy step to the act of alteration by sacrificing body parts. The front teeth were excised or shaped to demonstrate a cultural tradition and to meet established ideals of beauty. Both the Crow and Sioux people are known to have cut off fingers to demonstrate dedication and commitment.[7] Apparently, all parts of the human body were believed to have special qualities especially after death. The wearing of necklaces or bands of human fingers, teeth, and hands was practiced in many parts of the world from North America to the South Pacific, and in some locations, a whole human arm was an element of special adornment.

The "hand of glory" epitomized the notion of body parts providing special magical power. It was believed that by holding the mummified hand of an executed murderer in which was placed a candle made of the fat of a hanged man, the person was invisible. That superstition was common throughout France, Germany, Spain, and Great Britain and was reportedly[8] being utilized as late as 1831 by burglars in Ireland.

Fascination with the human body and the concern for retaining the essence of ancestors and enemy might have resulted in cannibalism — the eating of human flesh. Scholars have challenged the existence of cannibalistic societies, but stories abound about the practice often associated with magico-ritual activities. Cannibalism probably began in the time of the Neanderthal and was practiced by people in various locations of the world.[9]

Reportedly, the eating of human flesh included mothers consuming their stillborn children to regain their spirits, the eating of a dead person to absorb their qualities and to ward off accusations of sorcery, and in Melanesia the feasting on the body of a convicted criminal as a final gesture of punishment. Masks were an element of the "recognition" of cannibalism although not a part of the practice. The giant maneating bird spirit masks of the Hamatsa Society (cannibal society) guarded against the cannibal spirit. The Kwakiutl (Northwest Coast) masks join the images of a raven and a human — "Cannibal-at-North-End-of-the World"[10] (see drawing 3.9). The members of the Hamatsa Society assemble to symbolically consume the body of the cannibal woman, a mythical predator and eater of children. That ritual event was similar to those found in other societies.

Obvious association can be drawn between tattoos and scars and the concepts associated with the use of masks. Facial tattoos as practiced in many parts of the world, North Africa to the South Pacific, altered the recognizable features of the individual (see drawing 1.2). The designs often were inspired by a mystical source and imparted special meaning. Similarly, scarification was often spirit- or ancestor-based and devised to convey special meaning associated with membership in an organization or secret order. Both methods of physical transformation (tattoos and scarification) were commonly applied during or at the conclusion of a ritualistic ceremony in which the person receiving the marks was the subject of initiation rites.

Those identification marks were human inspired and had no association with the so-called "devil's mark"—the supposed mark of a witch in sixteenth- and seventeenth-century Europe. The mark of uncertain design or location was believed to be applied by the devil as a sign of collaboration. The unusual "mark" or protuberance was thought to be easily recognizable because it would not bleed and was insensitive to pain. It was thought in some cultures to be a teat "from which the familiar [helper spirit in the shape of a bat, rat, or frog] could suck the witch's blood as a form of nourishment."[11] As verification of that belief, a method used to trap unresponsive witches was to isolate them and wait for a suspicious animal to appear. When the mark was found on the body of a suspected witch, it was a certain sign of a diabolical pact and a death warrant by the hands of the Holy Inquisitor for those suspect of being in an alliance with Satan.[12] The search for the "devil's mark" was a common feature in witch trials.

By deforming, tattooing, scaring, or painting their bodies, people were attempting to improve upon their appearance and following a practice that was believed to unite humans with the spirit world. The transformational practices within a particular culture could be viewed as a collective act of veneration or atonement that expurgated critical aspects of the life process. Consistent with that practice and in lieu of physical modification, a mask, as a transformer of the actual and imagined image of a person, gained acceptability as a medium for influencing and accommodating relevant spirit forces. The mask provided a spirit helper that could shift to different planes of the physical and metaphysical worlds.

Masks and the Metaphysical Understanding of Life

Because most human activities do not occur in a social vacuum, it is reasonable to believe that neither did masking. Masking and other types of social practices in their earliest forms placed primary importance on meeting survival needs, and as a part of that fundamental equation, masks had both psychological and physiological manifestations. This concept is both simple and complex. It is simple in that the basic needs were easily defined — adequate food, shelter, and protection and the ability to procreate. Fulfilling those needs was often a complex (difficult) process due to the severity of the living conditions and the marginal expertise of humankind. (Probably, the difficulty was not intellectual but practical.) The technological plateau of early people often made them powerless when faced with the "mysterious things" that influenced the requirements of daily life, and masking in different societies had a role in addressing one or all these exigencies.

There was a physical and metaphysical understanding of life based on reciprocity in many cultures—the concept of giving and receiving. The pressures of survival-related needs tended to broaden the range of stimuli to which the individual or society responded, but a lack of practical knowledge about those activities undoubtedly caused unique responses. The most expedient means for meeting a social need was bound to the ways of the group's antecedents. There was little flexibility in the methods for satisfying basic needs in most tradition-based social structures. The system lacked the capacity to undergo spontaneous change.[13] Concepts of reality in that environment were based on historic patterns that served as previews and projections of the future.

Ancient people perpetuated a world that embodied their traditional beliefs, values, attitudes, and assumptions. Those characteristics shaped and explained their view of themselves and their surroundings. Due, partly, to the complicated and unpredictable nature of this system of survival, a dominate/subordinate relationship was maintained between humans and the environment and natural and supernatural experience. Those elementary features of human existence were thought to be universal[14] and influential to individuals and groups alike.

The educational system in many traditional societies included the teaching of respect for parents, ancestors, and spirit/deities. Both the traditions and the methods of veneration were probably passed from generation to generation. The substance of social and spiritual continuity was maintained. Many socially transmitted activities, locations, and symbols had the purpose of identifying and gaining power. They brought together the material and spiritual worlds within the human context, and masks were an element of that process that played an important role in maintaining social continuity. They were a part of the internal mechanism of community control. Because masked organizations (secret societies and clubs) had regulatory authority within a particular group by giving directions, providing instructions, resolving disputes, and divining the appropriate times of special events, they were granted "power" by the community for the common good (see drawing 1.3). Those group-based decisions reflected traditional patterns of sociocultural interaction.

Besides facilitating social stability

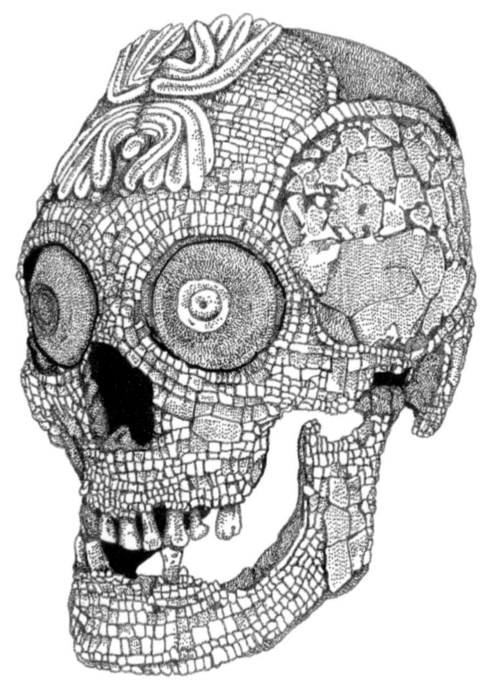

Drawing 1.3 Human skull with mosaic inlay made in Southwest Chiapas, Mexico. It dates from the Late Postclassical Period and is inlaid with turquoise, shell, and gold-copper alloy. The circular pattern of each side of the head is characteristic of the death-god figures shown in the codices. Human skulls with mosaic inlays are among the most recognized pieces of the Puebla Mixtec.

and order, power was a form of inner (individual and communal) strength. Power was also a spiritual energy or life force that enabled an individual or group to interact with the forces of the natural and supernatural world.[15] Once obtained, the power gave the "receiver" the ability to influence certain aspects of nature. The receivers of power were responsible to determine whether it was to be used in a beneficial or harmful way.

The lack of a single system of supernatural observance subjected early people to numerous seemingly disconnected and ostensible arbitrary rules and regulations. Religio-magical practices were important, if not primary, to daily life whether hunting, gathering, fighting, or procreating.[16] It was likely that the practical and mystical elements involved in a particular activity were inseparable in the minds and actions of early people. The laws of participation and perception regulated their collective activities, and to survive they shared their world with a profusion of spirit beings whose presence was reflected in every aspect of daily life.

Masking and the Human Spirit

Although various parts of the human anatomy were assigned importance from earliest times, the head was associated with the essence of life. Many cultures believed the "spirit" was located in the head and resided in the breath. Perhaps for that reason the head was revered and masks, as head or face covers, were associated with the identity of mystical beings. With that belief came the notion of gaining power or strength from acquiring the head of an enemy or ancestor. Headhunting has been viewed as symptomatic of a "primitive" or preliterate society; however, the mummified heads of dead heroes or valued ancestors were often preserved as oracles by relatively advanced social systems. Possessing the head of a worthy enemy was a sign of recognition of martial prowess, just as preserving the head of a relative signified familial respect and reverence. Real and symbolic beheading in various cultures was performed as a ritual of deification.[17]

Seemingly, early people associated the spirit with breath because breathing ceases at death. It was thought that the spirit left the body or could be drawn from the body by the air passing outward. A traditional technique used to harm a person was to steal their breath — to take their spirit away. That act of supernatural mayhem was performed in different ways in different locations. Sorcerers in the Pacific Northwest used a long pole with cedar bark wrapped around the end. The pole was held below the victim's nose at night, and the bark captured the person's breath (spirit).

At some time in ancient history, humans inspired by magical foretelling began to believe that the possession of a skull brought the protection and help of the dead.[18] The human skull, based on that conceptualization, became a primary symbol of mortality found in many localities of the world. It was a part of two very prevalent beliefs: (1) bones were centers of psychic energy, and (2) the head was the dwelling place of the spirit. The skull was also assigned great importance in medicine and magic. Various diseases were treated with concoctions made from or served in human skulls. The so-called "Spirit of the Human Skull" was such an elixir prepared from the unburied skull of a criminal.[19]

Skulls played an important role in various representations of belief. They were associated with the cult of the dead, ancestor worship, warfare, magic, and the rites of survival. The mystical significance of the human head was not restricted to one region or culture. Reportedly, the Persians consigned the top of the head to their deities, and early Germanic peoples preserved heads by fastening them to trees. The Celts hung the heads of slain enemies from house rafters to gain protection from the dead person's spirits, and Greeks, Jews, Semites, and Norsemen kept human heads so they might serve as oracles.[20]

The Mochica culture of Peru observed a ritual practice of decapitation, and elsewhere in the world headhunting and various forms of head taking and human sacrifice were used to appease the deities or transfer evil. In Mexico, Aztecs adorned temples with skulls of sacrificial victims, and people of the Southern Pacific covered

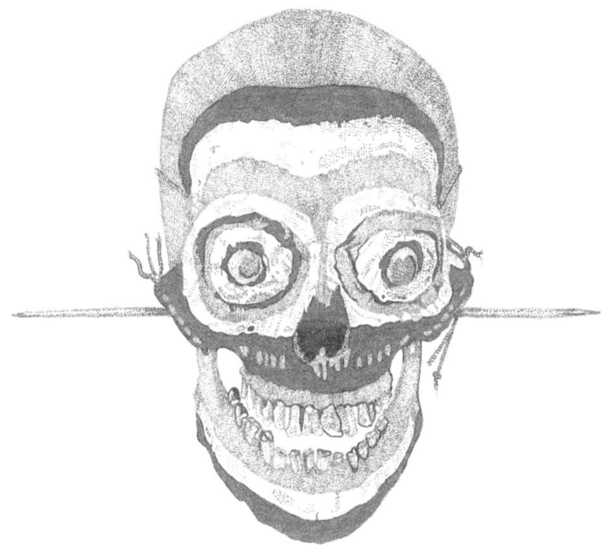

Drawing 1.4 New Britain skull from the Gazelle Peninsula. The eye sockets of the skull are ringed and the openings filled with shells to give an appearance of life. A symbolic spear is thrust through the neck. Because the ancestors governed the living world, their skulls were preserved as reminders of their constant presence. The retention of skulls was practiced in Australia, New Guinea, the Solomon Islands, New Britain, New Ireland, New Hebrides, Marquesas Islands, Mexico, and numerous locations in Africa and South America.

skulls with a mixture of clay and oil and modeled the surface to a likeness of the deceased (see drawings 1.4, 2.3 and 7.2). The Hindu Goddess Kali wore a garland of skulls, and Tibetan Buddhists shaped containers from skulls. In West Africa, the skull of the deceased was set on a pole on the grave. Eventually carved skulls (masks) affixed to poles replaced this grave-marking practice.

The belief in spirit occupancy extended to the keratinized filaments that grew from the epidermis of humans. Peoples in New Guinea believed their ancestral spirits lived in their hair and their presence made it grow. The males of those societies darkened their faces with charcoal to emphasize the beard area and to give themselves an unearthly disguise. In this altered condition, their ancestors "came to their faces." The people transformed themselves through the shaded elements of their self-decoration — a mask. However, the obscured features were not to represent another person, spirit, or animal; rather they were to imbue the individual with exemplary qualities.[21]

Masks and masking practices based on the skull were common in many cultures. Skull masks were generally painted white and had the bared teeth and empty eye sockets of the fleshless human skull (see drawing 1.5). The fetishistic fixation on the head gives added insight into the use of masks that transformed the masked persons into ethereal beings. The transformation achieved by masking was not a distortion of human form but a symbolic representation of spirit images.[22] The living portrayed their dead ancestors, as well as persons, animals, and other animate and inanimate objects from the spirit world in the quintessential masquerade.

Masking to Reveal Manifestations of Divine Beings

Because the face was a primary means of distinguishing one person from another, it was the practice of early people to represent their gods by making masks to show how a particular deity was envisioned. The wearing of a mask in the socially prescribed manner transformed the human into a superior being. The masked person was identified with the associated deity and allotted superhuman traits. Moreover, because masks often had standardized features, the onlookers immediately knew which spirit being was represented. They also understood the purpose of the masquerade and anticipated the required response. That principle extended to some forms of theatre

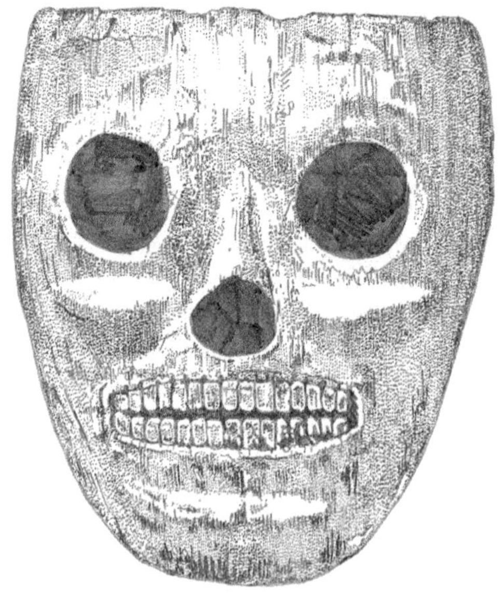

Drawing 1.5 A skull mask made of wood and pigment from Costa Rica. Male dancers wore masks of this type at New Year ceremonies and to commemorate the deceased one year after their death. Masks based on the skull had high brows, closed eyes (or open eye sockets), bared teeth, and ethereal natures that represent the spirit of the dead. Similar masks of clay have been found in the Guanacaste region of Costa Rica dating from pre–Hispanic times. The anthropomorphic masks were very realistic. Some examples had the appearance of including an inner figure, that is, a mask over a face similar to the image of the Aztec deity Xipe Totec, the Flayed God, draped in the skin of a sacrificial victim.

where the actor changed character by putting on different masks. The role of the actor was defined by the mask substitutions, and the audience was visually informed of the character change.

Honoring the head as the seat of the spirit and preserving the skulls of ancestors and adversaries demonstrated the importance attached to that part of the human anatomy. Therefore, it was both reasonable and understandable that facial covers—masks—had a significant role in magico-religious activities. The visual representation of human, animal, and spirit forces played an important role in the material as well as the spiritual lives of people.

An example of the social regulatory role of masks is found among the Hopi people of North America. Each year masked figures visited the homes of the Hopi people to inquire about the behavior of the children. The carved and painted wood masks the visitors wore had big teeth and powerful jaws. The masked visitors asked at each home whether the children had been good and obeyed their parents. It was customary for the children's mother to explain that they had not been too bad and that they were trying to do better. The masked figures explained that disobedient behavior was not socially acceptable and that one or more of the errant children might be eaten. The mother respectfully proposed a gift of corn if the visitors gave the children another chance to improve. The masked visitors reluctantly agreed and departed with a promise to return and to be watching in case corrective measures were required.

Another example of the socio-cultural influence of masking was found in Bali, where masks were the media through which the deities expressed themselves. The people of Bali, as in many other societies, turned to the god figures for assistance and protection. The most popular protective image mask was that of the Borang. Those masks were of various colors representing different deities. As the manifestation of *banaspati raja*, the God of the Forest, they were most often red. The Borang costume had four legs and was worn by two people, and as the *banaspati raja*, the deity of everything that had four legs was beastly in appearance. A folkloric manifestation of that belief was the story that witches were thought to go about on all fours. For that reason young children were carried and not allowed to crawl.[23]

Mask-related lore was often naive when observed from beyond the originating culture. However, when viewed by persons within the initiating society, seemingly esoteric masks motivated an appreciation that, unless intentionally altered, resulted in an instinctively appropriate action — the response to a social or cultural need. Although much of human life was composed of natural (instinctive) reactions to emotion-charged objects, humankind also had the added capability of imagination. Prompted by that ability, humans remembered past events and imagined the repetition of those experiences. People with that ability were capable of a dual existence — one real (earthly) and the other ethereal. They reacted to instinctive stimuli in the "real" life while the ethereal life had a different set of values and a different kind of perception — a spiritual integrity.[24]

Masks were a blending of these two separate life ways — the real and the imaginary. They were activated by the conditions or circumstances in which they were produced. The making of masks was an expression of the imagination and drawn from traditional designs rather than a representation of reality. The concept of "a different kind of perception" allowed the representation of images freedom from the limitations imposed by life. Masks were an expression of an impression that responded to a time, place, and need.

The Outward Appearance of Masks

Masks presented many "faces." They resembled humans, animals, plants, spirits, the elements, and deities. Masks were worn by the living and the dead, and they were differentiated by their use and structure. According to Eliade,[25] masks had three defined roles: They were used for ritual, war, and observances. Structurally, there were masks that were held in front of the face and those that covered the front of the face, covered part of the face, covered the entire head, rested on top of the head, or positioned on a superstructure high above the head. There were half masks, both upper and lower, and masks as separate symbolic insignia such as pendants, amulets, and badges.

Masks were an objectification of life. They concealed the face of the wearer, either actually or symbolically, and presented a "new" face to the viewer. They served different purposes in society. Often, as with the ancient peoples of the Andean cultures, they established and recognized the qualities of a deceased person, a practice associated with monarch-centered cultures.[26] Masks also identified the power or energy of significant persons in dramatic enactment (see drawing 1.6).

Masks were used to conceal the identity of persons fulfilling a roll as enforcer of social control such as the Shebe Malula mask of West Africa (see drawing 1.7). Masks in some areas of the world were used to give the masked person a temporary release from social control as exemplified by the Fool's Dance mask of the Assiniboin Indians of North America (see drawing 1.8). The raven mask of the Hamatsa Society, as a further representation of social authority, embodied the power of the

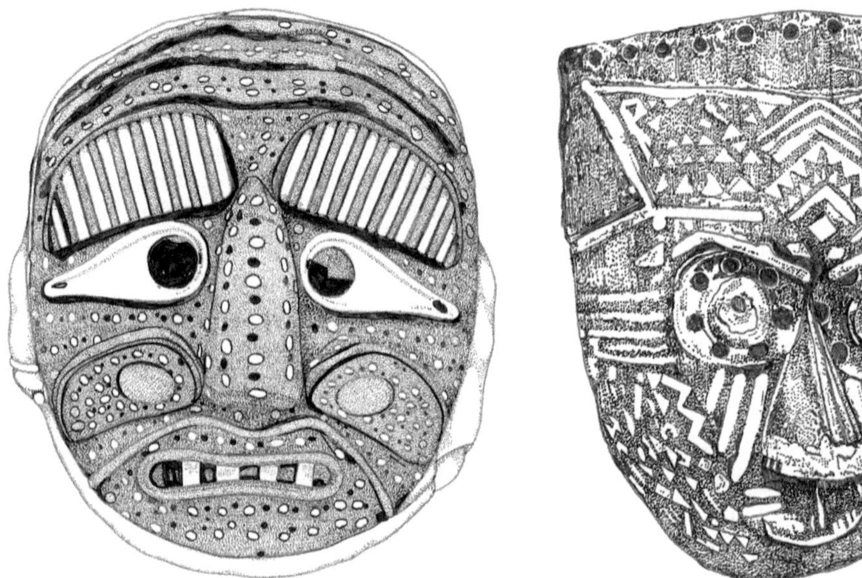

Drawing 1.6 (*left*) Malttugi (servant of a *yangban*) masks were worn for the Yangju Pyol Sandae Nori. These Korean masks were made of gourd, pine bark, string, fur, and paint. The Pyol Sandae Nori of Yangju was first performed about two hundred years ago "by a group of officials of the magistrate's office."[a] All Korean masks made of gourds were produced in about the same way. The gourd of a size to fit the actor's face was selected and cut in half. Holes were cut for the eyes and mouth. The nose and lips were formed from pine bark and attached with glue. String or animal fur was added to form eyebrows or facial hair and the masks were painted according to the specific designs for the drama. Drawing 1.7 (*right*) BaKuba Shebe Malula "police mask" associated with the Babende Society. This painted mask of carved wood is from Zaire. It has holes around the bulging eyes and incised patterns. Masks often had multiple meanings depending on the ceremony. The purpose of many masking activities was to uphold the moral codes, social relations, and cohesion of the group.

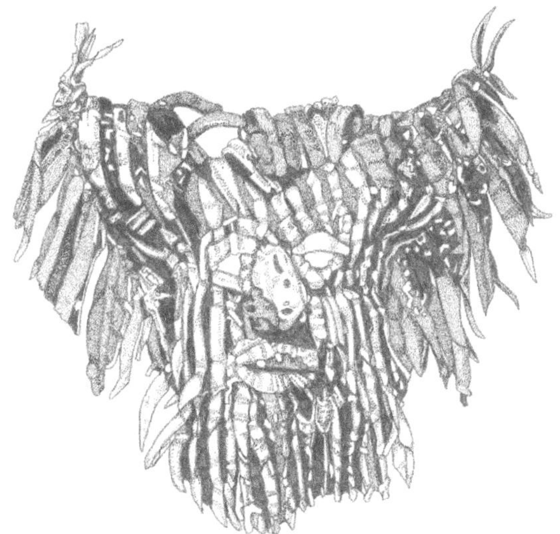

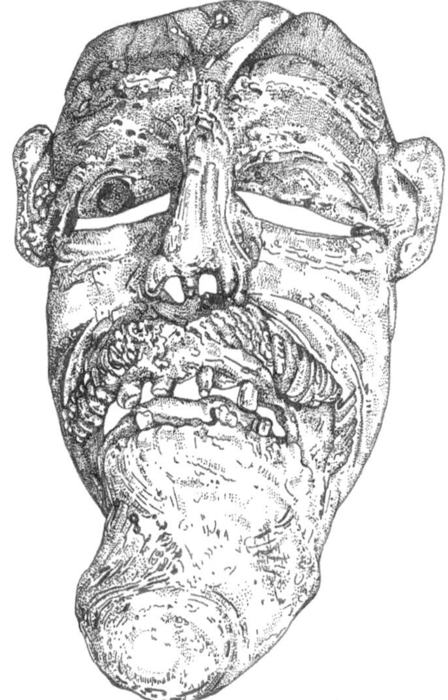

Drawing 1.8 (*left*) Assiniboin fool's dance mask made of cloth. Participants in the dance wore clownish attire including masks of shredded cloth. Indigenous peoples inhabiting the plains of North America often wore masks made of cloth and leather as well as animal heads such as bison, bear, and deer. Unlike their neighbors to the west, they were not inclined to carve masks from wood. Drawing 1.9 (*right*) A *viejo* mask made of wood from Guerrero, Mexico. This well-carved wooden mask was used in the *danza de los viejos*. The performance of *los viejitos* (little old men) was connected to the system of village governance in which the elders paid tribute to patron saints. The dance, dating to pre–Hispanic time, was originally dedicated to Huehueteotl, the god of fire.[b]

totem figure. In contrast, masks such as the *viejo* mask from Mexico (see drawing 1.9) have a very sensitive grandfatherly demeanor. Those masks evoked an emotional response and gave the viewer an enhanced sense of identity.

Few masks were, by design, intended to portray a particular animal, human, or deity realistically. "When people wish[ed] to associate themselves with powerful forces in their cosmos—birds, for example—they [did] not make realistic masks but instead [took] parts of birds such as bones and feathers, and [wore] these."[27]That idea of communicating the whole through a part explained the "characterizing" quality of many masks as predominant features were exaggerated and lesser attributes ignored (see drawings 1.10, 9.8, and 10.7).

A further example of emphasizing predominant features was the use of the eyes as a primary expressive element. Almost without exception, masks had predominant eyes that were parallel, equidistant from the frontal centerline, and had a penetrating gaze. The eyes of many masks served as the dominant facial organ for demonstrating and signaling states of emotion. Sometimes the bulging, nucleated eyes had a phallic character or metaphoric and symbolic relationships with other organs of the body.[28] The eyes of almost all masks were open, and the pupils were dilated in emotional arousal. The eye imagery exaggerated the whites (of the eyes) and froze an expression of fear, surprise, anger, or confrontation. Seldom was the countenance submissive. The eyes, beyond the obvious role of identification, were intended to arrest the onlooker both physically and emotionally.

The expressions of most masks, beyond the fixation of the eyes, were emotion charged — regardless of the intended reaction. The message transmitted did not invite a response; it declared a presence without direct communication of its intention.

Masks as Integral Elements of Social Maintenance

Masks had an important role in many cultures that caused them to be treated with special consideration. In Africa, they were often nourished as living beings and given offerings of food and drink, and in some cultures they were sprinkled with animal's blood. Secret societies, of which men, women, and children formed different groups, venerated societal masks. It

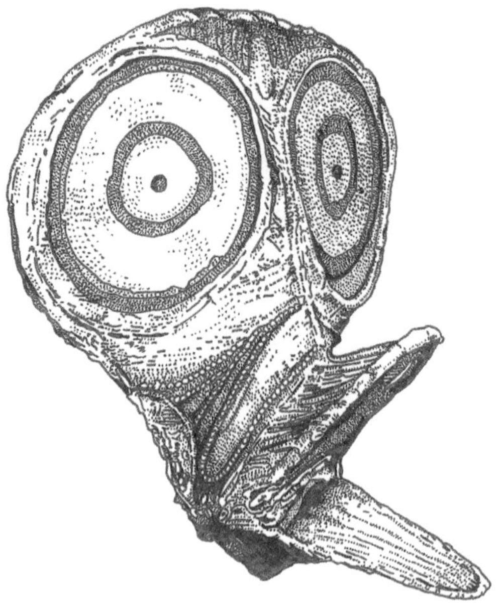

Drawing 1.10 Bird-form mask from New Britain made by stretching bark cloth over a palm-wood form. The masks were used for social and secular occasions but most likely were originally used for strictly religious purposes. They represented supernatural spirits and often had bizarre and asymmetrical shapes. The large eyes were said to represent those of an owl.

was the secret society (and its associated masks) that was the foundation of many communities. Those social arrangements were found in cultures around the world, and the qualities associated with that lifestyle remained as a guide for generations.

Because the face was the dominant feature for visual recognition, it was a logical first choice for modification or transformation. However, the materials of which the earliest face covers (masks) were made are not available for study today, nor is it possible to know why they were made. Surviving masks were configured in many different shapes and styles. They were made of a variety of materials depending on the natural resources of their originating locations. Gourds were a favorite material used for making drama masks in Korea[29] (see drawing 1.6). Other cultures used other materials including paper, wood, cloth, wool, metal, plant fiber, leather, clay, and bamboo to make masks. A "mask" in some locations was an entire costume that altered the body as well as the face.

When the mask makers fabricated a mask, they did not make what they saw; rather they represented what they envisioned or remembered. A part of the fabrication process was influenced by a retinal introduced image, but a larger part of the design was derived from tradition, imagination, and myth. Masks as three-dimensional images did not depict the world as it was but as idealized images filtered by the faculties of visual perception and mental alteration. It was the world as the image maker imagined it to be.

When making masks, the imager employed a number of standard visual forms to represent concepts known to the particular culture.[30] A mask was made by an individual (sometimes the user), inherited from a relative, or acquired from an image maker depending on the social structure and circumstance. In some societies a shaman, priest, or elder authorized the making of a mask and in the process assigned its spiritual role. Usually, masks were considered personal property as they were closely linked to the wearer and the assigned supernatural connection. When the owner died, a mask might be transferred to a son (normally a male heir), and in that way, the power of several generations could be accumulated in one mask.[31] In contrast to that practice, certain masking activities required the masks to be destroyed once the particular event was concluded.

An element of most belief systems was some form of regalia, implement, or medium. Masks fell into that classification. Masks were assigned different purposes in different societies. Some of those uses reflected conditions that influenced the creation of the masks, and although there were similarities in masks made by different peoples, each culture conveyed the unique characteristics of their belief system through the images they produced.

Early mask makers were generally restricted by the traditionalism of the training process and the requirements of the group. They were obligated to follow the "rules" that governed shape, form, and pattern. However, it was in the interpretation of those models that individual means of expression were allowed. Undoubtedly, the creative process found an outlet in the invention of new or different ways of expressing traditional styles (images) just as improved technical skill supported a refinement of details. In mask making as in all forms of individual expression, there were examples of superior and inferior workmanship. The best examples were finely

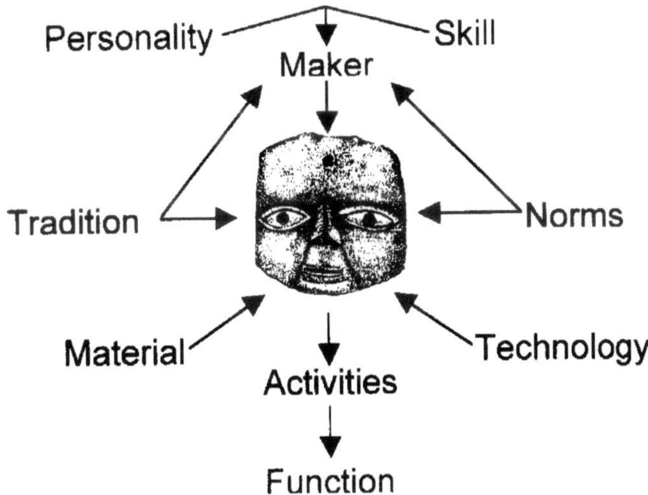

Figure 1.1 Influences altering the making and use of masks.

crafted with extraordinary attention to detail and surface treatment. The least effective examples were crudely formed with little concern for tradition; however, an unfinished appearance did not always reflect a lack of skill.

The act of mask making was expressionistic because much of the inspiration was drawn from the traditions of the people rather than an imitation of nature. The masks expressed ideas associated with beliefs or magic. They were often tied to "its function of mediation between the supernatural world and the natural world."[32] The mask makers among certain cultural groups were "professionals." They inherited the image-making role from family members who had attained an elevated rank within the group, tribe, or clan. The "imagers" in other areas of the world were selected because of special talent and trained through an apprenticeship in the methods and techniques of mask making. "But it was the professional artist who was held in high esteem, particularly in Africa, where, in some areas, he [normally a male] also had religious and political status."[33]

The images, colors, and designs were transferred from mask maker to apprentice during the training process. That control perpetuated traditional mask styles and maintained the identity of the group. The traditions of representation and expression common to a particular image maker, village, and cultural entity were preserved in that way. The proportions of masks, the details of the design, and the arrangement of features were taught as the "right" way to depict certain spirits or deities. "It is certain that the inherent conservatism so fundamental to preliterate cultures perpetuated throughout long periods of time the basic essentials of their art style."[34]

The color of masks was influenced by a number of factors from personal choice to tradition. The predominant colors were white, black, and red, and in some cultures yellow and green were added to the palette depending on the availability of the pigment. In Korea, China, and Japan the color red was used to repulse evil while white and black represented something holy. In many cultures white denotes purity and was often the color associated with mourning. Equally often, black conveyed a sense of nefarious behavior and was associated with the night and hostile spirits. Some have suggested[35] that the colors represented "products of the human body" (white, black, and red) and were associated with emotion and power.

In mask making certain visual and emotional associations might have been illogical but psychologically primal because the outcome of the mask making process was frequently determined by preexisting ideas. The mask did not express one emotion at a precise time; it was the essence of all emotions about a specific activity. It was the ability to understand, assimilate, and project a particular activity from a communal perspective that made the mask an effective instrument of society and a part of the human life cycle from birth to death.

Masks and other ritual regalia were made from a range of organic and inorganic materials, each of which was subject to different forms of deterioration. Wood and other cellulose-formed materials such as grass, reeds, plant fiber, and cotton deteriorate due to moisture, insects, fungi, light, and rough treatment. The other most common elements used in mask making were proteinaceous and occur in all living matter — animal tissue. Proteins are basic structural units of animal skins, silk, hair, feathers, horns, and visceral matter used for sewing, joining, or fabricating mask parts. Masks also included bone, antlers, teeth, and shells that are defined as organic/inorganic combinations—a compound of proteins (collagen) and calcium phosphate.

In those locations where masks were carved, the wood was often worked in a green or wet state. That practice was particularly true when the wood used was of an especially dense variety. After the basic shape of the mask was formed, the carved surface was smoothed and refined with rough plant fiber or a stone. The mask was then coated with oil or fat and smoked or allowed to dry. The covering of oil or fat reduced the rapid rate of dehydration and minimized the cracking of the green wood. Often the masks were stored in the rafters as far as possible from insects and ground water that could cause the wood to rot.

Notwithstanding the nature of the material from which they were made, masks were regarded as having magical properties; therefore they were often destroyed after they were used in ritual activities. Societies occasionally placed great importance in preserving, refurbishing, and reusing masks. Considerable attention was given to storing those masks in a safe location away from insects, moisture, and rodents as well as mortal or spiritual enemies. The masks were assessed for damage before each use and restored to acceptable condition. They were reconsecrated to ensure approval by the appropriate deities.

The masks created by the early image makers were more than objects of aesthetic pleasure. They were "requisite forms made for the economic, social, and/or political needs of the community, from materials thought to contain a vital force of their own."[36] The mask maker, as well as the mask, was an integral element in the social and ceremonial functions of the group. The image makers perpetuating the masking practices were guided by tradition, and the validity of that tradition was of primary concern for the host society. Consistent with societal practices, not all masks were intended to have smooth or refined surfaces; some were rough or irregular by design and had crudely formed features. Those masks were often devoid of details and lacked all aesthetic refinement.

Masks for personal or special purposes were often made by the user and were based on a design inspired by a dream or vision. Such masks normally were not intended for public display. They were symbols of personal communication between the inner and outer beings—the natural world of humans and the world of spirits. Masks of this type were for use during the lifetime of the maker and were either destroyed at the time of the maker's death or buried with the person to facilitate their passage to the next life.

The Purpose and Use of Masks

Because the origin of masking traditions extends into the most distant periods of human history, many of the associated practices undoubtedly evolved from survival-related rituals. Masks, like rituals, were to attain a given purpose — one that served the interests of the person or people. "There has never been a primitive culture that did not possess a highly developed system of secret teaching, a body of lore concerning the things that lie beyond man's earthly existence, and of wise rules of conduct."[37] Although Jung references "primitive" cultures, all peoples have had methods of communicating societal teachings to the next generation, and very often, masks and other forms of adornment were a part of the transfer process.

Although no one can describe with absolute certainty the "purpose" of masks among early people, that they existed has been verified from many sources. Generally, the uses assigned to individual masks or groups of masks are subject to interpretation, and no matter how logical or reasonable the concept, the opinions are speculative. The same can be said of much of preliterate magico-religious history, but beliefs, myths, and practices appear to validate many suppositions about the lives and lifestyles of ancient people.

The belief systems of early peoples have been subjected to substantial review and analysis by present day scholars. That ingredient of human existence might be ignored except for the fact that it has a direct relationship to residual cultural evidence including masks and masking and gives the contemporary reviewer insight into the heritage of modern society. That evidence seems to verify the idea that in archaic times masks were associated with certain ceremonies. For instance, the contents of early graves in various parts of the world included masks that were placed there at the time of burial for a particular reason. The precise purpose of the masks is unclear, but the associations are undeniable. As with many historical objects, once purpose or intention is removed from the contextual affiliation, the original meanings are obscured and subject to speculation.

Even though imposing contemporary standards on the beliefs and the related masking practices of early people lacks empirical validation, certain assumptions can be made. Commonly held beliefs mirror historical patterns that evolved from the earliest times of human existence. Primary among those socially purposeful activities is the belief in a "higher being." All cultures from time immemorial have held such beliefs, and there appears to be no distinction between prelogical and logical behavior in that practice. Luck is generally considered part of that belief schema, and integral to good fortune were charms, amulets, power words, and magical symbols. These practices, like that of masks and masking, were "purpose" oriented, and it is reasonable to assume that many disunited people have shared in this approach to interaction with their gods.

Masking and the Concept of Human Need

It is human nature to be attracted and distracted by the unusual or unknown, and one of the conditions inherent in such encounters is the urge (or need) to relate the unique to the commonplace. There is a tendency to analyze the unknown in the terms of the familiar. The usual outcome of this process is often misunderstanding and confusion whether dealing with objects, customs, or practices. The seemingly comic, grotesque, or odious images, activities, or customs may be more easily understood when viewed from a culturally aware vantage point. As an example, one of the reasons contemporary societies may find masks "unusual" relates to the manipulation of human features. This lack of acceptance of dissimilar facial traits is an attitude that has persisted for generations. Human appearance attributed to particular objects may receive positive assessment, but the same consideration may not be extended to other objects lacking those characteristics (see drawing 1.11). The

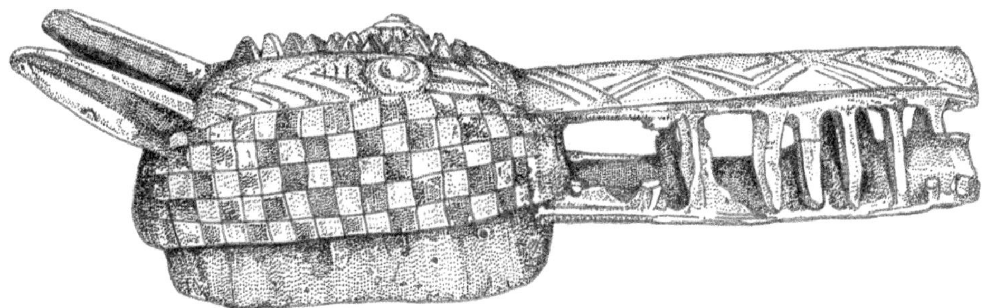

Drawing 1.11 Nunuma (?) mask from Burkina Faso made of carved and painted wood. This mask fuses the jaws of a crocodile with the head of a dog or fox. It is an excellent example of the concept of visual perception and the exaggeration of the dominant facial element.

unknown and the unidentifiable remain a cause for apprehension for many people, and the most commonly applied defense against those feelings is avoidance.

Masking and the associated activities were a cultural, historical, and ethnological phenomenon, but they also had a psychological purpose that must be considered. As an integral part of the "concept of human need," they are best explained as functionally interrelated elements that contributed to the survival or well being of a particular group of people. The "need" in this equation is considered as "something required" for the satisfactory functioning of humanity, and as these people were intrinsically social beings, those needs are organized and addressed through cultural activities.[38]

> The notion of "need" exists at the point where we can no longer distinguish between ourselves as incarnations of a species and ourselves as "individuals" in the usual sense of the word: endowed with certain capacities for self-differentiation from other members of the species.[39]

Human need changed according to the requirement of the individual as well as the society in which that person existed. Needs were connected to the "real" world. They were inclined to be associated with the inner nature of things rather than their surface appearance. Often, there was an overlapping of the "needs" and "wants" (preferences) of individuals, and both aspects of social survival related to masking activities.

Understanding the masking tradition is restricted by existing cultural limitations. In attempting to comprehend those "things" that existed beyond that limiting intellectual horizon, recognizable references are used. That manipulation allows the viewer to create a context in which to place the unfamiliar objects (masks and other magico-religious accoutrements) because it is that adjustment that facilitates understanding. The human mind is inclined to isolate phenomena, and it is often difficult to assign cultural relationships to unfamiliar or disassociated elements. That tendency is particularly complex when dealing with belief systems and the way those beliefs are integrated into the social structure. Masks, rituals, ceremonies, and symbols are often viewed as separate and seldom are considered as equal activities bounded by ethnic unity.

Much of the thinking about masks and masking has followed a path of assigning object-based (material) psychological assumptions to concept-based (ethereal) cultural activities. While that is not a universal truth, the influences are difficult to deny. Traditional field research has approached masks as interesting phenomena of a group's reality rather than an integral part of a cultural whole.

Masks can be viewed as having two distinct identities. One view relates to the physical shape or the outer surface, that is, the visual manifestation of the individual mask. That aspect identifies it with a particular entity whether animal, human, or spirit. It also gives information about the reason for the particular mask being worn for a particular event. The second identity of the mask is its inner contents or "spirit." That element of the mask relates to its force — its purpose for being. When the mask was worn, the masked person might have assumed the outward identity but only rarely the "spirit" of the mask. The "face" was more easily transformed than the inner being or "soul." "Masks, therefore, can be said to be a form of soul-catcher."[40]

The significance of that duality, the inner and outer aspects of the mask, cannot be overstated. This Janus element — the two faces, the seen and the unseen — is a key part of many mythological traditions and, therefore, a primary image source for masks and masking. The outer reality — the world of humans and nature — is a manifestation of the inner reality, the realm of the spirits.[41] When applied to humans, the Janus concept referred to "the person with a double image." That pronouncement identified a person who gained an advantage by use of wizardry or magic (see drawing 3.1).

The "otherness" of many masks has been lost as they have been assigned a role as decorative objects. In that transformation, they lost both their primary role as objects of power and their secondary position as elements of cultural heritage. Masks, in a traditional role, held a well-defined position that kept them at a proper distance from other objects. The associations were clearly delineated and there was order and harmony in their relationship with each other and with humankind. As traditional patterns changed, the associations became chaotic and in many ways irrelevant. Societies lost their unity, and patrimonial patterns were displaced.

Masking and the Physical and Metaphysical Worlds

Historians, missionaries, ethnologists, and anthropologists who have studied and reported extensively on primitive societies, ranging from those of the Stone Age in Europe to those of our present time, record[ed] the fact that even though developed in widely scattered parts of the world, they have this in common: masks and magic, fetish and ritual, totem and ceremony, superstition and taboo....[42]

There are many Paleolithic representations of human figures with animal masks. Probably the most interesting and most often described is the so-called "sorcerer" figures of Les Trois Frères cave in France[43] (see drawing 1.12). The sorcerer was drawn with antlers, canine ears, a long beard, a horse's tail, and bear paws instead of hands. In the same cave is another figure with a bison headpiece and holding bison (bovine) hooves. The figures are nude males with their genitals exposed, both appear to be robed in animal skins, and both have a dance-like posture.

A similar, though much later, representation of "dancing" figures with antlers is found at the Hixon site in Hamilton County, Tennessee. An incised shell gorget dating to the Mississippian Period (ca. 1300–1500 CE) shows two male figures with bird-like wings and antler headpieces. Additionally, across the western United States, figures with antlers were represented in petroglyphs and pictographs. It is assumed that these linear representations are shamanistic figures associated with hunting magic.

The significance of horns (antlers) has many explanations. One theory suggests that the deer (any of various hoofed ruminant mammals of the family *Cervidae*) had mythical affiliation among early people and that the affinity continued as the cultures evolved. That notion may be reflected in the Indo-European word "deer" that is the basis of a wide variety of derivatives meaning "to rise in a cloud," as dust, vapor, or smoke, and is related to semantic notions of breath.[44] These associations suggest a connection with the spirit world and have global manifestations. For instance, the deer and "deer park" have special meaning in Buddhism, and horns (antlers) are a prominent part of Siberian shamanism as a link to the spirit world (see drawings 6.3 and 6.4).

The physical world in which a people existed was composed of the various substances that were contin-

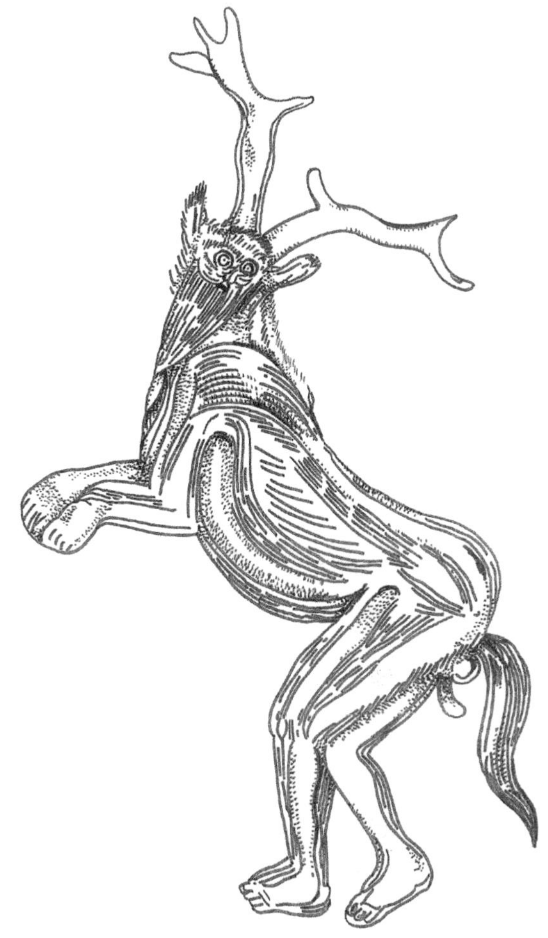

Drawing 1.12 "Sorcerer" figure found in the subterranean chamber of Les Trois Frères, France. This Middle Magdalenian figure dates from ca. 14,000 BCE and is an early depiction of a masked figure in a ritual (dance) posture. The cave painting combined human and animal shapes that probably had shamanistic significance. The nude male figure was drawn wearing a mask with antlers, a long beard, and wolf ears. The animal disguise might have been a way of identifying with helping spirits that were imagined in animal shapes.

ually mingled and transformed. It was a world regulated by organic laws that maintain the unity of substances in all their forms. Human interaction with the physical world was tempered by physical and psychic prowess that manifested itself as "spirits." Human understanding was extended into that amalgamation through sensation, knowledge, judgment, and will. "Sensation [was] the affirmation of life; knowledge distinguishe[d] the forms of that life; judgment compare[d] them; will act[ed] upon them, and suffer[ed] or link[ed] their reactions."[45] The magico-religious world, in its ethereal form, embodies both physical and psychological elements, and as the fountainhead of knowledge and wisdom, it was believed to be the source of all life.

In dealing with conditions beyond the normal bounds of human experience, people sought assistance from ethereal beings. That practice allowed spirits to manifest themselves in various ways and to be perceived as fulfilling different functions. They were a source of power, and everything responded to power. Realizing that concept to be relative to social and environmental conditions, as well as intellectual qualification, it is understandable why and how the belief in spirit beings and the efforts to manipulate their activities had such an important and pervasive role among early peoples.

The regulation of power was associated with the mask and infused into the act of mask making. The subjective (belief) and objective (practical) influences came together to form a whole conceptualization. The reality of the mask subsisted where the physical and metaphysical met in common unity with the symbol. It was in that unification that the true meaning of the mask was revealed.

There are a great number of similarities in all belief systems. All include a "greater force" that controlled or manipulated the universe no matter how large or small that space. In all parts of the world, the human mind reacted to the basic conditions of existence in much the same way. Included in the pursuit of survival whether economic, ritual, or emotional, for the living or the dead, masks held a significant role. Contemporary needs have not changed substantially from those of early humans. However, many concerns motivated by superstition and metaphysical reasoning have been denied and replaced by rules of order designed to regulate the subconscious according to the more manageable laws of society.

2

Substitute Faces

On a purely physical level, masks [were] made to hide the real faces of their wearers and to substitute artificial faces drawn from tradition and from the imaginations of mask makers. However, the act of covering the face [was] far more profound than a simple disguise, for the face itself [had] a far greater significance than one's features.[1]

Masks were a ubiquitous element of world culture and a window on society. The image maker who fashioned the masks functioned within the societies where they produced their work, and they reflect the values of that society. Therefore, masks must be placed in a broad socio-economic context that allowed a greater understanding of the culture and society of which they were a product. Whether being used in conducting rituals or as part of a hunting expedition, masks had a role in religious, economic, and social activities from the earliest times. Although the face cover had a significant role in human activities, seldom was the human face represented in the mask-making activities of early people. It was not until the Neolithic Age (in Europe and Western Asia 6000–3000 BCE) that "masks appear to take on even minimal human attributes."[2]

The Masking Practices of Early Humans

It is likely that archaic humans gave primary attention to self-preservation. It can be assumed that inhabitants of the Stone Age, being without the knowledge or technology to shape the most rudimentary tools and weapons, placed survival first on their instinctive agenda. The notion of survival in these circumstances undoubtedly manifested itself in many ways. Probably high on the list of concerns were defense against carnivorous animals, guardianship of territory, acquisition of an adequate food supply, protection against the elements, and perpetuation of the group. Those activities were instinct driven and inherent in most humans.

The research has shown that Neolithic society, from its incipient phase beginning in ca. 6500 BCE, used masks in rituals.[3] This practice is evidenced by the mask images found in conjunction with elevated shrine-like platforms in the dwellings of the culture that evolved in southwest Europe. The masked images were painted on various objects and surfaces, formed of clay, or served as decorative motifs on ceramic vessels.[4] Of particular interest are conical shapes made of clay with detached mask forms modeled to slide onto a tapered pillar or phallus form. The uses of the masks of this period are unclear, but undoubtedly some, if not all, represented deities. That some have a bird, snake, and other animal shapes suggest they were symbolic of those deities that had control over the life and subsequent death of the peoples inhabiting the region.

Masks attributed to Neolithic peoples support the assumption that in the beginning, face covers had fundamental magico-religious significance. Earlier people of the Paleolithic Period (ending in Europe ca. 8000 BCE) painted and incised images of what appeared to be masked dancers on the walls of their dwellings. In China, as early as the Chou dynasty (ca. 1122–249 BCE), bronze masks were worn, and in Tibet, masks have been used to represent gods and demons in mystery plays for centuries. Grotesque masks representing various deities relating to different cultural beliefs were found in Mesoamerica. Masks of wood or gold were used in numerous rituals in South America. Masks were a part of the cultural heritage of most indigenous peoples across North America, and in Africa, pictographs from prehistoric times include paintings of masked figures. Zoomorphic and anthropomorphic masks were used to represent deities and to cover the faces of the deceased in dynastic Egypt. The aboriginal peoples of Australia used masks and face painting, and on the numerous islands of the Pacific, masks were a part of the practice of ancestor worship.[5]

The history of early humans continues to be discovered in the symbols, images, and myths that have survived, and masks are an important part of the examination process. These symbols reflect the social, intellectual, and philosophical attitudes of thepre-literate inhabitants of the earth. Masks demonstrate that similar symbolic paradigms can be found at various locations and among disparate peoples at differing levels of socio-cultural development. These symbolic representations of myths, dreams, and the supernatural help contemporary investigators to better understand the attitudes, beliefs, and psychological complexities of early humans.

The research acknowledges that much of early human existence was a precarious process of survival so demanding that little time and energy remained for the appreciation of aesthetic achievements. Ornamentation of the human body developed in imaginative ways in all societies. Where clothing was worn as protective cover, anatomical adornment was less abundant and decoration was applied to garments. However, in warmer areas, there was hardly a part of the body that was exempt from some form of ornamentation, manipulation, or deformation. In comparison with many commonly practiced body distortions, masking was an extraordinarily conservative practice.

The mask as a means of individual transformation was of primary importance in most cultures of the world whether it was made of carved and painted wood as in Africa, Bali, Japan, and Tibet; of animal skin and horns as shaped by the Yaqui in northern Mexico and the Cucama in Peru; or constructed of paper as in China and Indochina. Masks in all instances preserve the cultural heritage of the people they represented regardless of the material of which they were made.

Masks for Transformation and Veneration

The mask in all its manifestations changed the face or head of the wearer, the most visually specific part of a human. The head is the principal source of expression. The eyes and mouth communicate fear, surprise, anger, and most other emotions associated with human action or reaction. The head is also associated with wisdom or chicanery—the diabolical application of wisdom.

Worship of the head has been described as a primary reason for the importance of the mask in African cultures.[6] While this idea may be correct in some cultural groups, it can also be argued that the mask was only a part of the representational process in Africa as well as other parts of the world. Body cover, movement, associated implements, and sometimes music accompanied the practice of representing cultural events as well as spirit beings. It is also true that much of the world gives greater attention to adorning the head or face for ritual purposes than other parts of the human body. Consequently, the altering practice begins with the head or face to make the greatest change in appearance.

Undoubtedly, the first "masks" were dabs of fat or dirt followed by types of face painting. Such adornment was the most common and practical method of concealing the individual. From the powder white foundation cosmetics used by Japanese geisha to the societal markings of the Ecuadorian aborigines, the stage make-up of Chinese actors, the exotic face painting of the Huli tribesmen, and the lip gloss and eye shadow used by Nubian women, face painting was a common and accepted practice. This social custom extended from the indigenous peoples in South America who paint themselves before approaching the dead to the peoples of the Northwest Coastal region of North America who painted their faces before starting a journey. Their purpose, in those instances, was to gain metaphysical assistance and emotional support for the task at hand.[7]

> ... African masks, with rare exceptions, [were] a male prerogative, from which women [were] kept rigidly excluded. In a number of societies, myth attributes the invention of masks to a woman who [stole] the disguises abandoned by demons; the men-folk then proceed[ed] to seize them, regarding the masks—the symbols of power — as the sole means of enabling them to exert over their wives the superiority essential to the maintenance of social order.[8]

Masking appears to have originated in the hunting societies and a belief in being spiritually linked with animals. It is equally probable that masks in some cultures were social control devices in that they were used to frighten people into initiating or rejecting certain actions or reactions. As examples: An unfaithful wife might expect a visit from a hideous, often malformed, creature to "scare" her into fidelity. This character took different forms in different societies. It was a gnome-like character with a long rope-like penis in Paraguay, and in Japan, the nocturnal visitor was described as a "frog" with an oversized human phallus. In Java the lion-faced demon figure Kirttimukha was appointed by Shiva as "door-keeper" against all wicked people—an image to ward off evil.[9] The mask in this social role was closely associated with mystic reference and magic in some form (belief or behavior) as a part of all cultural life. Belief in chthonian beings (deities and demons from the underworld) shaped many social customs that promoted masking practices.

Lommel postulates that animal masks were among the first to be used.[10] The logic behind this supposition is that the early hunter needed a means for approaching prey. When stealth proved inadequate, the hunter resorted to disguise and imitation. The skin and movements of the animal being hunted were used to make the human less noticeable. Sometimes the head of the animal was included as part of the disguise to give a more realistic appearance. After the successful "kill," the story of the hunt had to be told and the skin provided a perfect "costume" to aid in demonstrating the events. It is possible that the mask came to embody the "spirit" of the animal and served not only to tell the story after the conquest but also to call for spiritual assistance before the hunt. The animal mask allowed the human to act the part of both the hunter and the hunted. It was a symbolic joining of the two elements—life and death (see drawing 2.1).

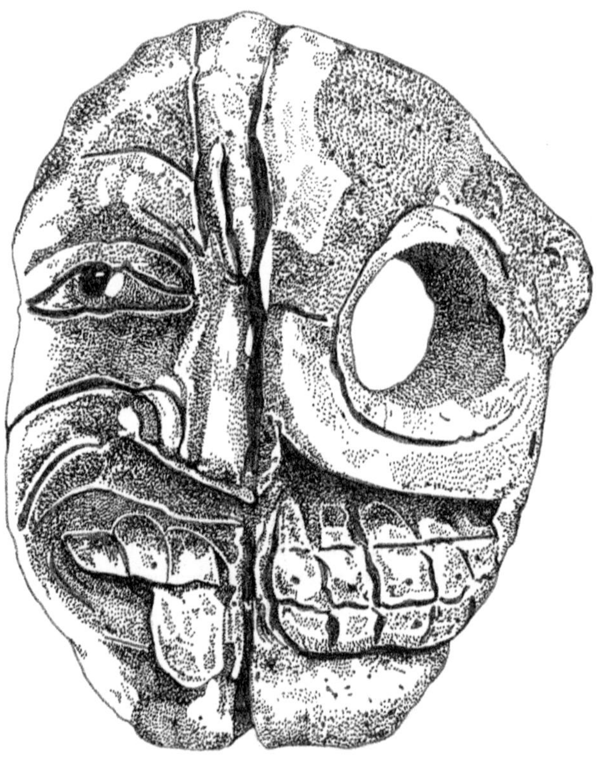

Drawing 2.1 Life and death mask made of clay from the middle preclassic culture of Mexico (ca. 900–300 BCE). This mask from Tlatilco exemplifies the concept of duality that was a central part of the indigenous cultures of Mexico. The two elements of the mask are combined to make a single statement. They are the dual aspects of life whether male and female, good and bad, or the creator and destroyer. The Janus mask (two faces) of the Romans represented the same notion— the dual nature of humans and deities.

If the first mask were a hood of bark or the skin of an animal, this connection was possibly the source of a totem to serve as the emblem of a clan or family by virtue of an asserted ancestral relationship. The clans might have evolved into totemic secret societies within the larger social order. This application of totemic identification altered the purpose of masquerade and gave new meaning to imitating the movements and gestures of the animal. "As civilisation advanced the skin of the animal was replaced by a mask, and the roaring which originally was to imitate the noise of the totem animal was replaced by the use of an instrument."[11]

As social requirements changed, the mask replaced previously accepted methods of transformation.[12] The deer dance of the Yaqui and Mayo of northern Mexico was an example of the dynamic force of masks and the associated activity (see drawing 2.2). In *La danza del venado*, the deer

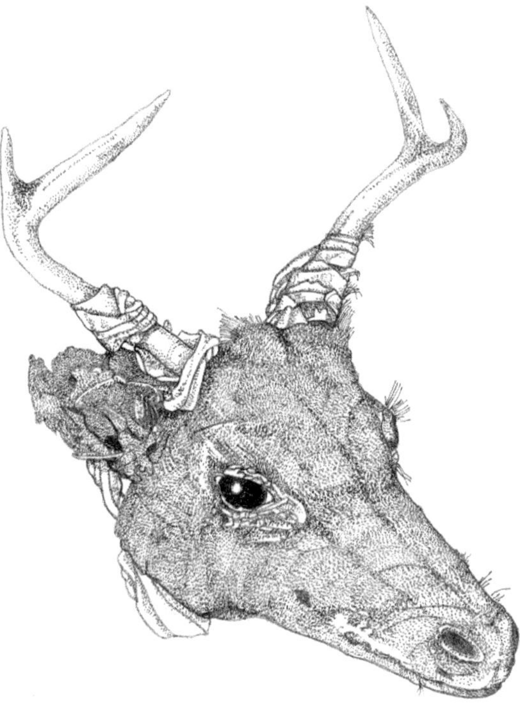

Drawing 2.2 Deer dance mask collected in northern Mexico in 1934 by Dr. W. Curry Holden while doing research among the Yaqui and Mayo. This extraordinary mask, made of a stuffed deer head with the horns attached, was used in *la danza del venado*, a popular *pascolas* dance. It was worn on top of the dancer's head and secured with leather thongs tied under the chin. Streamers of red ribbon were tied to each horn to accentuate the dance movements and represented the blood of Christ. Performers simulated the hunt that ends in the killing of the deer. It was a dance that celebrated the deer and asked forgiveness for taking its life.

dancer was bare to the waist and wore a skirt of woven cloth. On the dancer's head was fastened the head of a deer complete with antlers. A belt of deer hooves was wound around the dancer's waist and cocoon rattles were attached to each leg. The dance told the deer that the people needed food and mimicked the movements of the animal as it ate, drank, sniffed the air, and fled.[13] The dancer celebrated the deer and asked forgiveness for taking its life. The mask (deer's head) aroused memory by its emotional appeal and reinforced the experience of stalking and killing the animal. Simultaneously, it allowed the hunter/viewer to rationalize the hunt and validate the killing of the deer. The balance between humans and nature was maintained.

The mask of the totemic deity represented the animal, and imitating the movements and noises of the animal facilitated the referencing maneuver. The symbolic metamorphosis embodied the characteristics of humans and animals (or sometimes plants or inanimate objects) established a ritual pattern that was resident in most early cultures. The word "totem" was derived from the language of the Ojibwa people of North America, but the application of the concept varies from culture to culture. Totemism among the Polynesians usually involved spirit beings that were internal to particular animals. A commonly recognized materialization of totemism was the "totem poles" of the Haida, Tlingit, and Tsimshian peoples of the Northwest Coast of North America. Those carvings were erected to memorialize important events.[14]

Masks That Defined the Identity of a People

Assessment of masking must consider the philosophical question about identity. The elaborate masks and costumes in some cultures were passed to succeeding generations to give a sense of continuity. Other cultures were less formal in the transfer of "objects" but share myths and ritual practices intended to verify the group identity and to ensure its future. Myths, legends, rituals, and masks taught the history of a people beginning with the creation of the world, the origin of the first people, and the foundation of their survival-related belief system.

It is probable that masks and masking evolved as a form of sympathetic magic from a very practical origin. This approach reflected the requirements of the hunter/warrior lifestyle. To sustain themselves on a primary diet of animal flesh, early hunters encountered ferocious beasts that were as often the hunter as the hunted. The hunter (humans) believed that by controlling the image (spirit) of the animals it was possible to be safe and successful in the hunt. The quarry being pursued probably was drawn or scratched on the cave wall (or in the dirt) to attain control of the "image," and as the hunters' confidence grew, they mimicked the animal's movements and sounds. They enhanced the believability of the movements by wearing a skin or holding the head or skull of a slaughtered animal. The carving of masks to portray the representative beast, deity, or omnipresent being was a reasonable progression from this beginning. If the image aided in the hunt, there was reason to believe it could provide the same assistance with other dangerous elements in the lives of the people.

Masking and the socio-cultural context within which it is placed had significant societal relevance. A cultural tradition such as masking was aligned with a body of information shared among the members of a particular group or culture. As time passed and the context of the masking activity changed, masks and the related practices became less applicable to the needs of the people. Consequently, new rituals were initiated and used for the purposes previously associated with the masks, and in that process, cultural patterns were modified. The symbolic activities associated with masks and the masking traditions differed from the action of other rigid survival techniques. Masks borrowed from the sacred beliefs of the past where they were used to help the group to think and act and, as culturally amplified objects, they empowered the people through historic associations.

Masks in the various manifestations are what they are — masks— and simultaneously, they were more. The mask disguised the appearance of a person by presenting an artificial or substitute face — a face that represented another entity. They were also mnemonic elements shaped and used to provide cues for retrieving pertinent cultural information. The memories stimulated by a mask were linked to other autonomous psychological processes including perception and belief. However, comprehension of the messages remembered depended on an individual's or group's prior knowledge of the image (mask) and the circumstances the memory defined. Myths, legends, and rituals were integral elements of the mnemonical schema.

Masks of Traditional Transformation

At some forgotten time early in the history of humankind, something happened to convince people that portraying the human form in effigy was dangerous. If it were as Lissner[15] speculated, this condition grew out of the hunting cultures that relied on sympathetic magic to transfer the premise of danger or death through graphic representations of the animal world. The animal was, by extension, put under a spell through the medium of its effigy,[16] and eventually the effigy could be ceremonially killed according to acceptable custom and ritual. A similar reference can be found in "black" magic rituals that use human effigy to transfer pain or death to the person represented.

The belief that effigies captured the souls of the persons or animals they represented could have been a factor in the design and use of the first masks. It is equally possible that mask making related, in some unique way, to the archaic practice of remodeling human skulls with clay and paint and that both evolved from a supernatural genesis. The earliest example of a skull remodeling technique dates from around 5000 BCE and was found in the Middle East near the town of Jericho. However, the practice of embellishing skulls is found in various parts of the world including the remote regions of Oceania and could have been practiced at an earlier time (see drawing 2.3). The connections between the two forms of face or head transformation are both physiological and spiritual.

Entrenched practice views the past in terms of current ideas, beliefs, and standards.

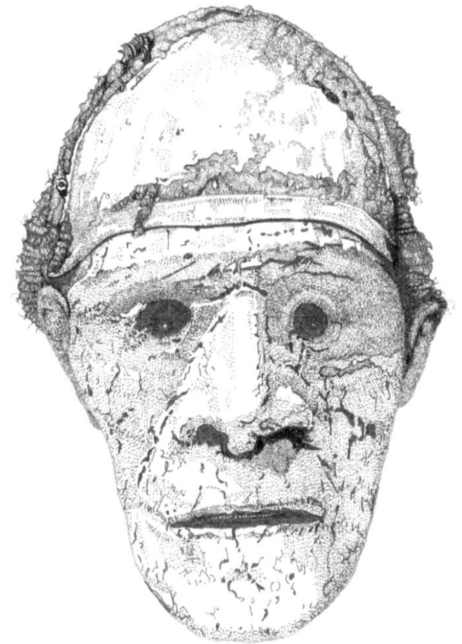

Drawing 2.3 New Hebrides skull with molded face made from a mixture of earth and fiber. This head came from the island of Toman that lies to the south of Malekula. The elongated (dolichocephalus) skull is painted with red and black colorants and has a fringe of hair.

This perspective is an "interpretation" that permits historians, anthropologists, ethnologists, and others to impose a learned value on objects, beliefs, and rituals. It also provides a venue for cultural cleansing that is the elaboration of certain acceptable ideas and attitudes and the devaluation of those attributes that are viewed as unacceptable by accepted standards. A different view occurs when objects (including masks) are considered in the context of their time of origination and utilization.

In early studies of masks and the people who used them, too often the people were viewed as curiosities and the masks were considered a "primitive" art form. Those attitudes reflected a singular perspective of the world and the traditions of indigenous peoples. As luminous fragments of culture, masks were invested with social meaning and that meaning cannot be separated from the associated activity. They were an entry into the private realm of a society as well as a protective device against physical or mental encroachment. The role of masks in most societies was as a connecting element that linked a complicated web of relations between the various parts of tradition into a unified whole.[17]

As early socio-cultural phenomena, masks were undoubtedly probes into the impenetrable vastness of the universe. They had a special place in the traditions of many people. The person who wore a mask had an obligation to comply with the practices of the group and not allow unacceptable acts—taboos—to interfere with the effectiveness of the masking activity. For example, tradition required that the masked persons performing the Nightway healing ritual of the Navajo not speak. Consequently, if a performer spoke, that person was believed to be a likely candidate to lose their eyesight, suffer throat problems including loss of speech, or become paralyzed[18] (see drawing 2.4).

As instruments of transformation, masks were endowed with a special quality that was both mysterious and ingenious. The recognition and understanding of the outward appearance of masks can be connected to the human conscious analogy and not necessarily by likeness to the associated being. Masks reflect the objective conditions by which a people were defined. These qualities were inherent in anything that was metamorphosed to become "something else" while remaining the same. Masks violated natural boundaries. They hid from view the magic character created by the mask. Juan Edwardo Cirlot equated the mask to the chrysalis, the third stage in the development of an insect when it is encased in a cocoon.[19] The emotion-producing objects were enveloped in the strictures of social continuance.

The imagery used in mask making represented the relationships between objects and events. Much of the information contained in masks was perceived in a linear manner: transmitter (mask) > message (myth or story) > receiver (viewer). In addition to this basic communicational alignment, there were messages that included or required understanding of symbolic language and psychology. The viewer, in this procedure, was the primal source of comprehension based on previous knowledge, attitudes, values, and symbolic references. These referential details were influenced by social, physical,

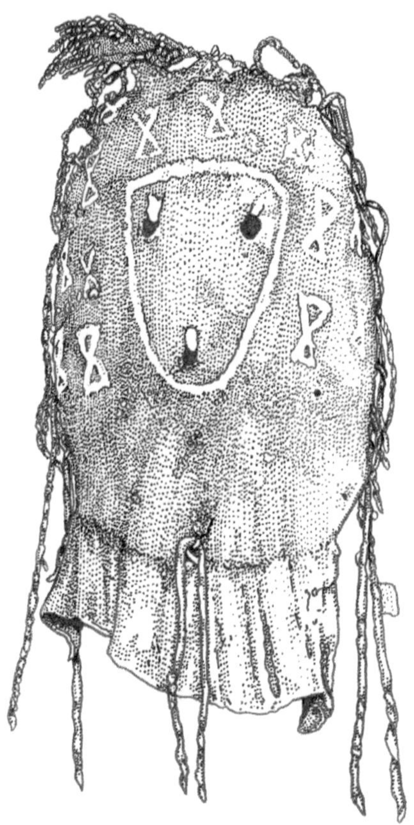

Drawing 2.4 Nightway masks (*ye'-i bichai*) used in the Navajo nine-day healing process were cut and sewn during a Nightway ceremonial and used at a subsequent ceremony. The buckskin masks were either head or face masks and had to be made in a public ceremony but could not be "induced" until the following ceremonial gathering. The singer who was to use them sewed the buckskin. The Nightway ceremonial included fourteen different masks representing twenty-four different gods. The masks were painted white, blue, red, or black according to the deity represented.

and personal factors, and they could be stimulated by both verbal and nonverbal factors.

Masks as Images of Self-recognition

The collective "memory" of a culture is of singular importance. It is the history of a people and a record of past practices. The use of images, including masks, to supply the references for the memory of words or deeds was essential for preliterate cultures. The images impressed upon the human mind the stories and acts that were the patrimony of the group, and masks were the cues that helped in remembering. They assisted in retrieving the appropriate information about a particular event, myth, or story. A single mask could promote the recollection of many words or an entire story when accompanied by music and dance in a ritual setting.

Memory of traditions is stimulated by two separate but interconnected systems. One is a verbal reminder associated with myths and legends delivered in abstract symbolic terms—a learned language. The other mechanism is the imagery system that makes use of masks and other forms of perceptual information.[20] Added to the memory equation is the fact that "experience is consistently reshaping recollection."[21] This factor suggests that the interchange between memory and experience is reciprocal. Experiences are modified by sympathetic recollection just as recollections are tempered by current experience.

Verbal transmission depended on vocabulary and commonality of word meaning including a level of fluency that may vary from person to person. In contrast, visual recognition and perception influences stored images regardless of the substance of which the image was formed. The memory of the viewers was defined by the visual information transmitted by the mask, and the learned image could be recalled and delivered as needed.[22] This notion assumed that memory was a dynamic process that enabled the transmission of visual information by the experience through which images were formed.[23]

All the so-called "civilized" peoples of the world evolved from an ancestry that could be described as "primitive." The term "primitive," in this use, refers to those peoples not adequately developed to construct a literature to convey their ideas and practices; that is, they were preliterate. Stories and myths aided in defining and describing fundamental social and spiritual concepts for those peoples leaving no written record.

Many preliterate cultures had semi-official "rememberers" entrusted with the task of memorizing the traditions and practices of the group. Consciousness of the past contributed to the maintenance of the integrity and continuity of the group and defined their "differences" from other peoples. Masks were mnemonic elements that awaken memories of activities and attitudes related to socio-cultural events. It was their role to transmit impulses that were strong enough and sufficiently stimulating to awaken memories appropriate to a particular occasion. Masks consolidated memory, experience, perception, and emotion into a visual (or visional) form.

The memory stimulated by the mask was socially formulated and to be effective, it (the mask) was conceived and constructed in a way to engender modes of recollections that were historically and culturally grounded. Masks were beautiful or hideous, comic or obscene, that is, a visage to stimulate an emotional response that reinforced the memorability of the image. Some masks were decorated with extraordinary designs or with mystical attachments, and others were stained with blood or red paint so the images were more unusual and, therefore, anchored in the memory of the people.[24] Those images were easy to recognize because they were realizations of the myths and beliefs of the people as well as the visualization of the image maker. They reflected a community's cognitive habits and enhanced the maintenance of social cohesion.

Excellent examples of masks as mnemonic images were those used in the Topeng dance of Bali. This dance was reported[25] to have originated in ca. 840 CE. It was a dramatic dance that presented the *Chronicles of the King* describing the early kingdoms of Bali and Java and served to preserve the history of Bali. The dance called upon the ancestors for help. Only fragments of these myth-based stories could be told in a performance; however, telling the entire tale was unnecessary because the people were familiar with the story and only needed reminding to recall the colorful events that illustrated the relationships between the past and present[26] (see drawing 2.5).

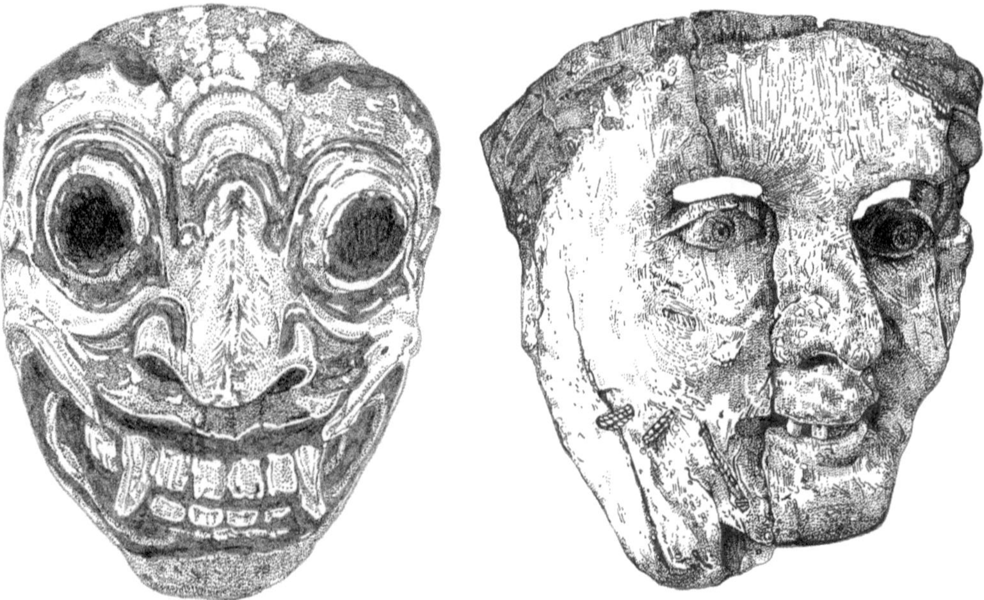

Drawing 2.5 (*left*) *Topeng* (mask) made of painted wood. This mask, held in place with a mouthpiece, is from Bali and was used in the *Topeng* dance. The word "topeng" means "mask" or "something pressed against the face," and the earliest examples of these masks are protected from being photographed as they are considered sacred. The *Topeng* is an ancient dance drama that related to the ancestral history of Bali Hindus. It combined music, dance, and mime to celebrate past heroes and to demonstrate their relevance to the contemporary world. Drawing 2.6 (*right*) Abuela Teresa (Grandmother Teresa) mask made of wood from Guerrero, Mexico. This old mask used in the Tenochtli dance is an excellent example of an anthropomorphic mask carved with great skill. It has traces of white paint and is repaired in several places. Eight dancers, one of whom played the part of Hernán Cortés, performed the dance. The enactment was based on the battle between the native people of Mexico City at the time of the Conquest.

From earliest times, masks had an important role in aligning and maintaining social order as people associate their activities, expressions, or attire with the masked ritualists. There was the joining factor of social identity and the role of purpose, and the individual was the part they played in the ritual. That role was made more real by the mask (see drawing 2.6).

The Cerebral Character of the Mask

Humans were thought to be influenced by two distinct forms of belief — one theoretical and the other practical. Theoretical values dealt with conditions or circumstances that were beyond commonly understood cause and effect. An example of this kind of belief was that if a person obeyed the appropriate rituals and avoided the social taboos, rain would come in the spring and crops would grow. The belief, in theory, was correct because proper actions normally generated desired results. In contrast, practical beliefs reinforced actions that were directly related to cause and effect. Those actions were the result of practice and generally represented training passed from father to son or mother to daughter. This kind of thinking was exemplified by observance of certain planting practices or dietary regimen. These beliefs often had an element of practical truth and exerted an amount of regulatory control.

For many early cultures, masks had a direct effect on daily life. At the same time, masks were influenced by factors of importance to the everyday undertakings of a people. As mythic symbols, they were entwined with human activities that far exceeded the realities of contemporary beliefs. There were at least seven factors that influenced the production and use of masks within any given society.

- Spiritual: acknowledging the dependence of humankind on powers beyond the scope and authority of the natural world
- Biological: referring to the genealogical affiliation of the people and referencing their traditional social and spiritual activities
- Territorial: giving attention to the geographic orientation of the people as well as their location in association with other cultural groups
- Physiological: considering the anatomical changes of the individual as well as the various other forms of social affiliation imposed upon the group, such as age, gender, and marital status
- Volitional: recognizing the willing decision to participate in secret societies, clubs, or organizations
- Occupational: defining the role of the particular occupation in the community or social structure
- Positional: pertaining to the rank and status of a person or group of people in a particular society, such as the elders, council, or peasantry

Included in these factors was a range of traditionally determined and sometimes highly complicated activities controlled by human behavior that were found either singularly or collectively in every culture. However, there was constant interaction between the elements that reflected the changing norms, customs, traditions, and rules that resulted from interaction between humanity and the natural and supernatural worlds. Masks were the manifestations of that invisible realm.

Masks and masking had a coherent logic as integral parts of cultural life that could be understood only in the total social context. They were a primary part of the process that provided explanations for coincidence and disaster guided by the "principle of uncertainty."[27] Masks were vehicles that enable people to project their hopes, fears, and disappointments across a wider spectrum of society by identifying and personalizing the forces of nature that afflict them. In this way, "fate" and "chance" could be regulated by direct social action. Masks, magic, and rituals were the means of filling the void between the known and the unknown.

Masks as the Essence of Socio-Cultural Life

Although masks acquired special meanings, the visual form could only be stimulated by what was perceptively understood; it could not be drawn precisely from observation.[28] The mask-making process did not start from the optical projection or an attempt to "copy" or reproduce an image from nature; rather, it was a manifestation of equivalent properties adapted to a particular medium and for a particular purpose. The mask became a representational form or model of the essential qualities of a selected spirit being, and it was often the "making" of the mask rather than the mask itself that was of primary importance.

The characteristics of a mask pertained to form, shape, subject, meaning, or purpose.

- How a mask was made defined the form and included the design, structure, pattern, or composition. The form was an embodiment of the techniques used because those processes influence the final product.
- Shape was the characteristic surface configuration of a mask.
- The subject identified by the mask was a materialization of a person, animal, plant, or imaginary being.
- The meaning of the mask addressed those realities that went beyond the physical appearance to include the magico-religious message such as a request for individual or group assistance.
- The purpose of the mask identified the projected outcome of the mask and masking event — the granting of a request or the control of a situation.

Describing masks as ritualistic objects denotes their pertinence to ritualism instead of being the result of an emotional response to individual expression. While they excited emotions in others, they were intended to follow a tradition, and in that way, tradition became the connecting factor along with the purpose for which the mask was to be used that determined the form, shape, subject, meaning, and purpose.

The mask as visual communication had to satisfy at least three criteria before it could be effective.

- Reference required the mask to fall within the tradition of the particular society or culture. Without this frame of reference, neither the transmission nor reception of the message was possible.
- Identity alluded to the symbolic understanding that was instilled in the mask. The mask, to function correctly, had to be properly shaped and colored to project a particular message from the transmitter to the receiver.
- Context required the mask to be understandable within the physiological and psychological fabric of the producing culture if the message was to be communicated.

Masks and the Traditional "Face"

The image that most often comes to mind when masks are considered is one of a full or partial face covering that altered the features of the person. In practice, many masks did not cover the face but were placed either on top of the head or elevated high above the head on a scaffold. Some masks covered the entire head as helmets, and others symbolically altered the persona of the wearer but did nothing to hide or disguise the person's facial features.

Masks were made in various shapes and forms. Some covered the face and had eye and mouth openings. Others were three-dimensional sculptures that fit over the head and were collectively called "helmet masks." These masks were often carved from a full tree trunk that was hollow. They covered the entire head and were carved on all surfaces. Another type of mask rested on top of the head and had a "cap-like" woven structure to hold it in place with ties that passed under the wearer's chin. These masks often were a part of an elaborate costume that obscured the entire body of the person. Small masks were sometimes carried as amulets and "passports." The

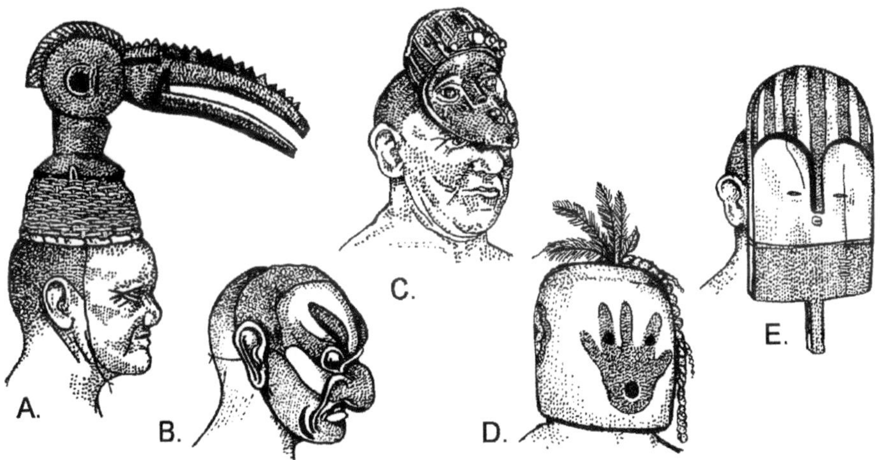

Drawing 2.1 The ways masks are worn: (A) a superstructure placing the mask above the head; (B) a face mask covering the entire face; (C) a forehead-mounted mask; (D) a helmet mask that completely covers the head; (E) a shield or plant mask held in front of the face.

passport masks identified the bearer with a particular people, society, or social order. They were credentials used to gain the assistance of fraternal organizations when traveling outside a familiar area.

The mask identified the wearer with the power, energy, and physical properties of animals or supernatural beings. They can be divided into image categories that were consistent worldwide although all did not appear in all locations. These categories are anthropomorphic (human form), zoomorphic (animal form), and fantastic (imaginary, expressionistic, and grotesque forms).

Masks should be viewed not as an objective rendering of a specific subject for the purposes of identification but as a subjective interpretation of the emotional response to a series of culturally and socially relevant conditions. The final image was often subject to a number of variables that existed beyond the cognition of the viewer.[29] However, it is reasonable to assume that a given group of people with the same or similar background responded to a mask or masking situation in a like manner even if they did not understand the complete meaning of the ceremony, drama, or ritual. "The mask [was] the medium of interpretation by which supernatural beings [could] show themselves and reveal to human vision scenes of a mystic world which they scarcely understood."[30]

The masking tradition and the associated rituals contributed to the cultural continuation of a people. The masks also provided symbolic protection for individuals and communities against disease and other forms of physical harm initiated by malevolent spirits. They aided in maintaining the balance between the various elements of the cultural unit by reinforcing the prescribed ceremonies and rituals and, ultimately, masks served as tangible symbols to illustrate the oral "literature" of the people.

Masks communicated the interdependence of the group and fulfilled the need for emotional security by establishing a group, tribe, clan, or family consciousness. Masks had a symbolic presence that represented the idealization and visual representation of the senses. They were an element of the cultural vocabulary of a particular people, although their complete meaning was generally understood or known only by the members of a secret society or clan. As an example of that special language, in New Ireland the clan-owned design vocabulary included a variety of naturalistic and geometric forms that were used singularly or arranged in fantastic combinations to form unusual human eyes, nose, or mouth elements.[31]

The symbolic reference had real meaning. "The passage from imagination to reality [brought] into play the material used and its laws, which impose[d] their own constrictions on the creative mind."[32] The link between the concept of "self" or "self-image" and "mask" was exemplified by the word "person" that was derived from the Latin noun *persona*, meaning "an actor's mask." Persona probably came from the Etruscan word *phersu* that meant "mask,"[33] and by the first century BCE, it had acquired a meaning that referred to the character or role in life assumed by a person. Persona continued to be associated with the mask as concealment or the alter ego at the beginning of the twentieth century. In Jungian philosophy, it referred to the identity assumed by a person adapting to the "outside" world, that is a mask (see drawing 2.7).

The persona and the appearance of the face related to the state of the mind. Certain ideas and emotions influence the movements of the muscles of the face to give a particular expression that characterizes different emotions. The mask was a perfect device to conceal or disguise that disposition. The mask functioned simultaneously to obscure a person's face and to create a new identity.[34] Various means were available to hide a person's facial features, but few other objects had the socio-cultural presence assigned to masks. The mask concealed and redefined. It transformed the appearance and thinking of the person by the meanings encoded in the image.

Masks were used to present a "face" to viewers and to save "face" for the wearer.[35] The mouth covers worn by various early peoples exemplify this idea. In Mesoamerican cultures (Tarascan, Aztec, Zapotec, Mixtec, Mayan, and into Central and South America) ornaments attached to the nose covered the mouth of the wearer, concealing that expressive facial feature (see drawing 2.8). Similarly, both men and women have worn veils to cover the lower part of the face, and facial tattoos disguise emotional signals. The teeth were shaped, removed, or blackened, and nose and lip plugs (labrets) were worn in various cultures to alter the shape or movement of the mouth. These devices masked or concealed mouth gestures and expressions.

The relationship between the public and private self was perhaps the reasoning behind the small pendent and nose masks found in Central and South America. These gold foil images were defined as "mouth masks" because they concealed the mouth of the wearer. These unique masks had an added significance as they were often found in burial sites associated with death masks.[36] It

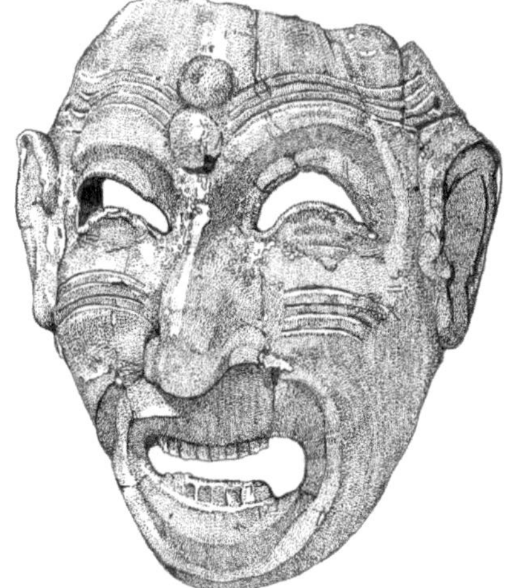
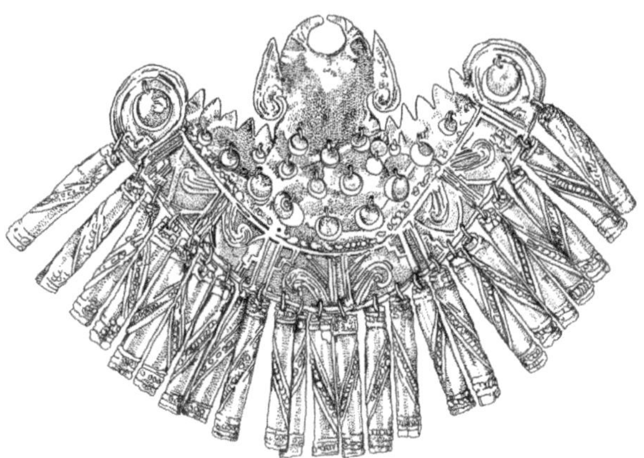

Drawing 2.7 (*left*) Demon mask made of terra cotta from the Punic Period (ninth century BCE to 146 BCE) in Carthage. This small mask has two bumps in the center of the forehead that are of particular interest as they may relate to images of the Gorgon. The forehead protuberances were common on Athenian representation of gorgons in the sixth century BC.[c] Similar lumps were found on figures representing leonine creatures. Masks of this type possibly had apotropaic significance — they were to ward off evil. Drawing 2.8 (*right*) A Calima style *Nariguera* (nose mask) made in Colombia. This shaped metal mask was attached to the nose and covered the mouth of the wearer. Persons with authority wore mouth masks when pronouncing judgments and for certain rites about death and war. The *nariguera* concealed the speaker's mouth and moved as the wearer's breath twirled the small metal disks and caused the cylindrical tubes at the lower edge of the mask to make a jingling sound.

was possible the mouth shields were intended to give an "other world" quality to the words spoken by persons of power or special privilege. On the other hand, perhaps it was not the sound but the gestures of the mouth that were being distorted.

Masks were often generic representations of humans (anthropomorphic forms) or animals (zoomorphic forms). They conveyed the primary characteristics of the image depicted with little attention given to personalized features. The shapes of heroes or villains and deities or demons were dictated by tradition and although the quality of the masks changed, the basic imagery remained the same. An example of this characteristic is the tiger masks of Mexico. All had very similar elements, but each mask was a unique creation presenting the mask maker's impression of a tiger (see drawing 2.9). In contrast, the Iroquois False Face Society masks were given to the people in the distant past by supernatural beings and those masks were shaped and painted in very specific ways. They were faces dictated by tradition.

In societies where members sought to attain different levels or grades of achievement or power, masks often represented important ancestors as memorial representations of past service to the group. The idea was that each person was to achieve the highest possible level of power or authority during his or her lifetime and to aid future generations to achieve or exceed that "grade." In that way, the family moved upward in the hierarchy of the society. Successful ancestors were called upon for assistance and a representative mask was a means of demonstrating the power of that person. The ancestors in this way aided the present generation and through their successes, they prepared the way for their progeny. Continuity was maintained.

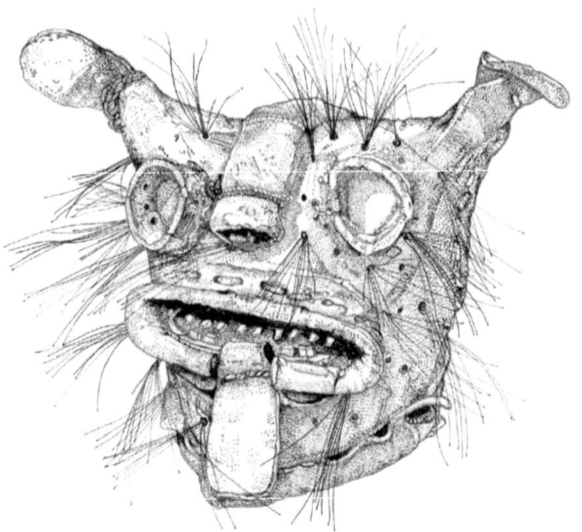

Drawing 2.9 *Tecuani* (tiger) mask made of thick leather with wild boar bristles and red painted accents. *Tecuani* translates to "people eaters,"[d] and masks of this type were worn in the tiger dance. This helmet mask from Zitlala in the state of Guerrero, Mexico, was formed of stout leather to withstand the pounding its wearer received from other dancers in the early May festival. Each dancer had a "tail" of knotted rope that was used to beat the other dancers. The deep-set eyes were customarily set with mirrors to give the tiger a feeling of life and movement.

Masks as Elements of Early Reverential Activities

It can be assumed that the essential parts of early reverential activities were practice and repetition rather than belief. Activities were associated with natural or physiological phenomena and thereby became the accepted practice in a particular circumstance. As the practice was passed from generation to generation, it became an essential part of social custom. Humans assigned their fears to the deities or demons, and with that transfer beliefs were formed. Because of a need to identify with ethereal beings, early peoples gave them human or animal shapes and attributes. In addition, they assigned human and animal characteristics to their deities. To further divine affiliation, selected members of the group wore the trappings of the deity and acted as intermediaries. The mask played a primary role in this enactment (see drawing 2.10).

One belief common to most early inhabitants was that of a separation of the physical elements of the human being and the inner self—the spirit or soul. There was the nearly universal belief that some part of a person survived beyond bodily death[37] Because of that belief, the idea of an afterlife was an important part of most magico-religious systems and the notion of a life after death was a necessary part of formulating and maintaining social order. The exact nature of the surviving element was viewed in various ways, but the word "soul" was commonly used to describe that part remaining after bodily death. The word "spirit" was also used but with no clear distinction between it and the concept of the soul. A person who followed the accepted social norms could expect their inner being to reside in comfort and peace or be reborn on a higher plane, whereas the spirit/soul of those who deviated from accepted practices was damned to unrest or was subject to rebirth in a lower life form.

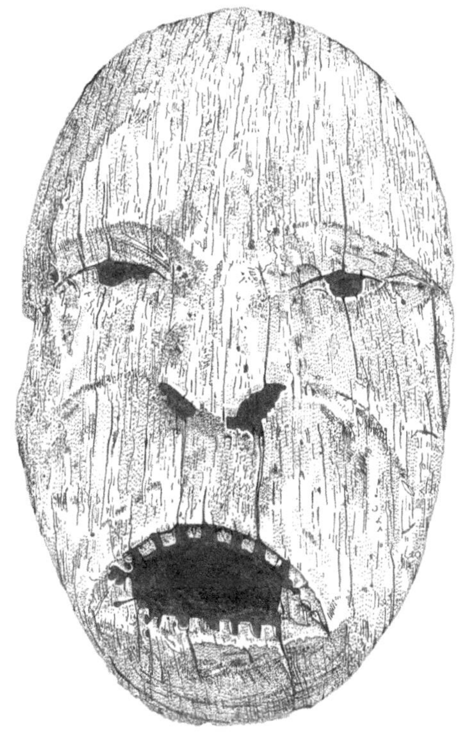

Drawing 2.10 "Helping spirit" mask from the Kuskokwim River region of Alaska made in the mid-nineteenth century. It is made of wood and originally painted but has faded. The "helping spirit" mask represented a trasformation of the shaman's psychic structure. These spirits were used to influence the people of the shaman's group and were associated with techniques of trance and ecstasy.

"Those who wore the masks in ritual thus entered a liminal realm in which the reality of the temporal, mundane world was simultaneously juxtaposed to and fused with the timeless world of the spirit."[38] However, not all peoples divided afterlife existence into positive and negative, although many did. The belief in an underworld place for the souls of "bad" people supported the notion of zombies, vampires, were-animals, and other forms of the living-dead. Those restless souls wandered among the living awaiting some extraordinary form of demise so they could find eternal rest. The beliefs or myths associated with those depraved beings served to further the regulatory practices of society. There was little reason to aspire for paradise without the threat of purgatory. Demons were the counterpart of benevolent deities. One without the other denied hope and reason. Masks were often a reminder of the negative aspects of life.

Early man placed the location of the spirit/soul in the skull rather than the heart. (The gender-specific designation is used because it was the male as the hunter/warrior and the organizer of secret societies that promoted most spiritually oriented concerns of the people.) This notion related to ancestor worship where the heads of ancestors were retained as objects of spiritual importance, head-hunting where the heads of enemies were taken to deny a resting place for the adversarial spirit, and the development of masks as symbolic head spirit locations. Skulls were often decorated or covered with clay to give a likeness of the deceased to ensure the retention of ancestral spirits (see drawings 1.2, 1.4, and 2.3). However, the skulls of enemies were normally left unadorned to be unattractive and unrecognizable to the potentially combative spirit.

How and why people believed in the presence of an inner being has been the subject of much speculation. The survival of the soul beyond bodily death may have its origin in dreams, memories, or fears. However, once the notion was conceived, it was self-perpetuating. Belief in the existence of a spirit/soul in humans allowed the same idea to be applied to animals, plants, and other natural objects. Some cultures believed that "spirits" animate everything found on the earth and in the earth. Spirits were always given consideration. The various beliefs whereby natural phenomena and things animate and inanimate were thought to possess an innate soul were described as "animism." This commonly held perspective gave credence to the use of animal masks for joining the element of human existence (see drawing 2.11).

"Each mask [was] a vehicle for movement between the present and the primordial worlds,

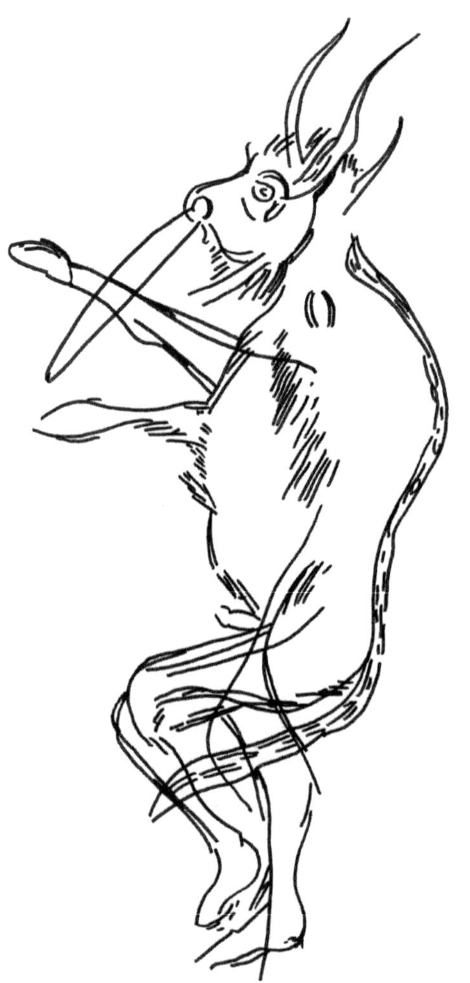

Drawing 2.11 A painted bison figure with mask from Les Trois Frères, France. This figure is a masked male holding a magical bow. (The bow shape extending from the bison muzzle may represent the animal's spirit escaping from its nostrils — the breath of life.) The figure has the back, legs, and penis of a human. The person appears to be wrapped in the skin of a bison.

and all the masks together [were] a means for the transfer of occult power from the latter to the former."[39] The basic concept behind many activities in which masks were worn emphasized the supposition of spiritual and/or physical transformation and demonstrated the act of symbolic death and rebirth — the losing and regaining of personal identity. Masking was a magico-religious act that transmitted a traditional message of transformation and renewal of life (see drawing 2.12).

Masks in all societies were the reflected faces of the socio-cultural environment in which they evolved. The gradual variation of form and use can be attributed to the evolution of production techniques and the availability of diverse materials. Masks were altered further due to the loss of belief in the ceremonies with which they were originally associated. As masks were transformed from sacred objects to dramatic and comic forms, they developed along lines that are more diverse.[40] The cultural significance of masks and the masking tradition was diluted by contact with "outsiders" that did not share a similar system of beliefs.

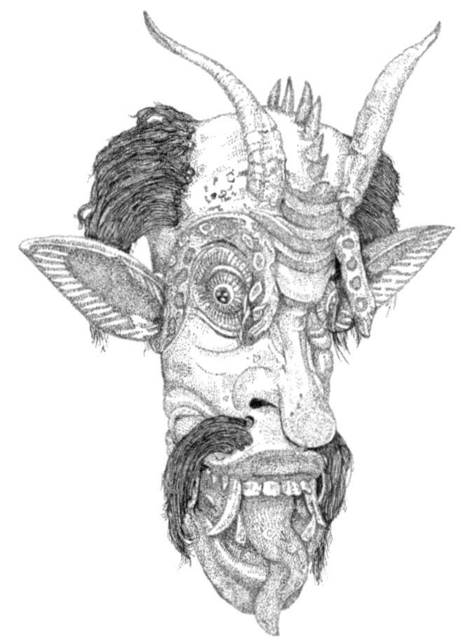

Drawing 2.12 Devil mask made of wood, horn, and hair from the state of Guerrero, Mexico. This fantastic mask was made of carved wood with goat horns, animal hair, boar's teeth, and paint. The serpent shapes that wrap around the eyes and the ears add to the sinister appearance of the mask. This piece is an excellent example of the classic devil image associated with many festival events in Mexico and might have been associated with rain-petitioning activities. The serpent forms are an agricultural symbol and like the extended tongue have phallic connotations suggesting fertility and procreation. This mask reflects the pre–Hispanic tradition of depicting the devil with a grotesque face covered with "unpleasant" creatures. The later, European-style devil masks have an evil-looking face painted red.[c]

3

Cultural Signs

"Culture" is essentially "human"— it is manifested in the social order as is the life of the individual; these are not dichotomous but integrally related entities.[1]

The meaning of the word "culture" is not self-evident. It is often used to express the notion of superior, elite, or relating exclusively to intellectual and artistic activity. Culture in the reality of human existence includes a variety of connotations with particular reference to the functional sense of cultivating "something." From this perspective, it can be applied to the cultivation of everything from crops to intellectual capacity. It can be said that although culture came to be associated with the concept of "style of life," it should not be separated from the idea of development and the "betterment of the human condition."[2]

Culture as social behavior is often a confusing concept with a variety of inferred meanings. Malinowski described culture as being "partly material, partly human and partly spiritual."[3] It was a concept that allowed humans to deal with the problems that confront society both individually and collectively. It "exists in the same way that beliefs, values, customs, forms of social and economic organization exist, for culture is the organized total of such things."[4] It represents "the totality of socially transmitted behavior patterns" and all other products of "human work and thought characteristic of a community or population."[5]

Encompassed in the pattern of human existence are many elements subsumed under the notion of culture that are intangible and evade direct observation, including magic and mysticism. Whatever the composition of culture may be, the elements of individual achievement must be formulated into a tradition that can be communicated with other members of the group and passed to future generations.[6] In the process of transmission, every member of the group becomes aware of the meaning of socio-cultural activities; they become culturally centered.

Masks and masking were significant components of the deity structure (the spirituality) of cultures. The beliefs of a society are formulated at its inception and are rarely altered throughout its existence.[7] If culture is viewed as the widest context of human behavior and inclusive of all forms of knowledge, belief, morals, laws, and customs,[8] then it references learned conduct by members of society. Masks contribute to that learning as part of the cultural process in a particular society and as long as they fulfill that need, they are of value to that society.

The issues related to culture and masks were complex. Because culture shaped the thinking, imaging, and behavior of early people, the transmission of those attitudes was a dynamic source of social change. It was that process that was the energy and inspiration for cultural evolution and the advancement of informational exchange. In the socializing process, communication was one of the most significant achievements of early people. That they developed methods for expressing their beliefs as well as the basics of daily existence is extraordinary. Masks, pantomime, music, and ceremony were ways of transmitting cognitive insight.[9] They were the symbolic voices of the community.

Cultural evolution was the result of people pursuing those aspects of life they had reason to value and that reflected a conditioned perspective of economic as well as social progress. It was culture that connected the elements of human existence and gave those activities meaning. Culture also determined how a people related to their physical environment, the earth, the cosmos, and their belief in other forms of life.

One of the greatest changes in human existence was the extraordinary revelation of self-awareness.[10] People became aware of themselves and their relationship with the wholeness of nature, and they began to transform that vastness to meet their purposes. Out of that consciousness came the understanding that human existence was predicated on numerous factors, many of which were beyond the control of mortals. This realization carried the seeds of hope and fear and laid the foundation for systems of belief. The phenomenon of self-awareness was also the beginning of imitation and probably led to the first masked activities.

Due, at least partly, to the lack of technology and an inclusive understanding of the universe in which they lived, early people experienced a disconnection between their desires and needs and the insurmountable diversity of the environment. Because of the unknown forces that constantly altered their lives, people needed a greater force than themselves to whom it was possible to petition for assistance or malfeasance could be assigned. If a superior power was not contrived, the people had to be responsible for their own faults, failures, and inabilities. As people became aware of the possibilities of external intervention, activities were devised to influence supernatural forces, and persons within the group assumed the role of intermediary.

The intermediary position in that fragile milieu was often claimed by a person professing divine right, and he or she relied on masks and rituals to reinforce that assertion. Evidence indicates that in early times, persons who discharged priestly duties and enjoyed sacred recognition as descendants of deities ruled numerous cultures. This condition was reported in parts of Europe; the Middle East; and regions of China, Africa, and South America. The priest-kings were vested with temporal as well as spiritual authority. They were persons claiming royal rights as incarnates of a particular deity and as that deity's earthly representative. These earthbound gods were expected to perform the appropriate rituals to bring into union the natural and supernatural worlds for the benefit of the people.

As part of the growing sense of self-awareness and group consciousness, cultures developed a body of practices or standards that regulated behavior by which an individual was determined to be socialized or acceptable. That process of encul-

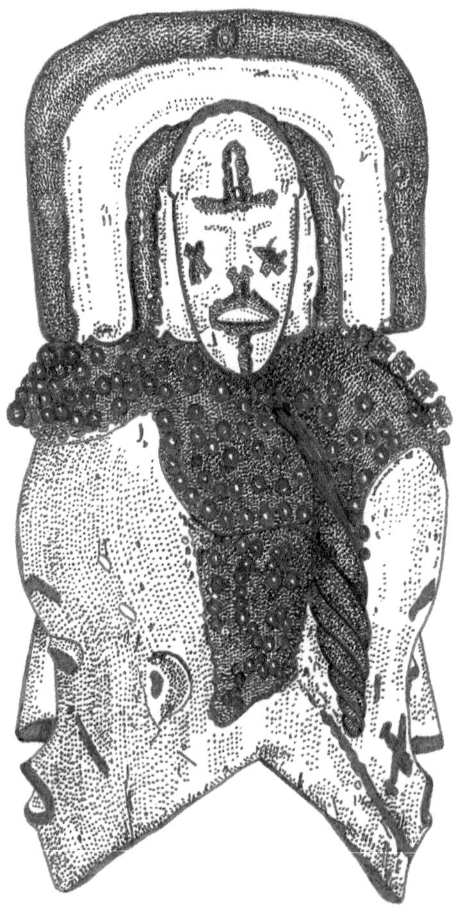

Drawing 3.1 Igbo *Janus* mask from West Africa made of painted wood with faces looking in opposite directions. One face may be giving attention to the past and the other to the future, or the elements may be acknowledging the masculine/feminie qualities that are essential to human existence. The joining of opposites is a recurring theme in many societies. The light and dark, good and bad, and life and death are aspects of life that could not be ignored; therefore, they had to be manipulated by ceremonies and group observances. Masks were a necessary part of that practice. The two small masks attached to the structure that rises from the top of this mask link the images and the viewer as elements of the present.

turation commenced at birth and included attitudes toward everyday life, such as interpersonal relationships, as well as the more refined beliefs and practices of a society. Considering the pervasiveness of the concept of the deified ruler, there is little wonder why people believed in the power of the supernatural and why masks and other regalia were worn to integrate the material life with the cosmic world.

Part of that psychic amalgam was the emotive power of the mask on the activities of people. Masks were a synthesizing force that stimulated the imagination and beliefs of the people and allowed them to alleviate or focus their fears. Masks and masked events satisfied the human need for integration of the diverse activities of life by facilitating communication and survival. Masks offered at the same time a perspective of both sides of the cosmic spectrum — the sacred and the mundane (see drawing 3.1).

The Mask as a Sacred Emblem

Most observations about masks are descriptive rather than explanatory. The observer relates the "look" of the mask and defines the material of which it was made, but gives scant attention to its purpose or use. This attitude is easily validated as the contemporary viewer can only speculate about the genesis of a particular mask and its role in a society.[11] However, there are factors common to many people in different places that provide insight into the motivations of early image makers and the masks they produced.

It is accepted that humans have followed the dictates of a hunting lifestyle for the vast majority of their existence and, as hunters, they developed a special relationship with nature and the resident environment. Animals were a necessary part of their daily existence. Early humans in the struggle for survival embraced a basal respect for animals and their innate hunting ability. The hunters sought to acquire the prowess of animals and to share their skill, wisdom, and spiritual insight. In many cultures, animals were viewed as intermediaries or "friendly" spirits. Reflecting this human/animal symbiosis, family groups and clans established a special relationship with an animal totem. Totemic groups identified themselves with a specific totem[12] because they believed themselves related to that entity through mythical ancestry.[13] The totem, in some cultures, was also an animal through which the group's sorcerer was thought to gain assistance and an emblem of identity by virtue of ancestral relationships. The totem image, for that reason, was a part of the clan members' ritual activities, and was represented with masks and associated costumes (see drawing 3.2).

Early people gave different meanings and importance to animals depending on local beliefs. A specific creature might be viewed as a pest or a totem. However, all peoples are thought to have had a form of classification that identified the importance of each animal within the belief structure. Data suggest there were at least five classes or divi-

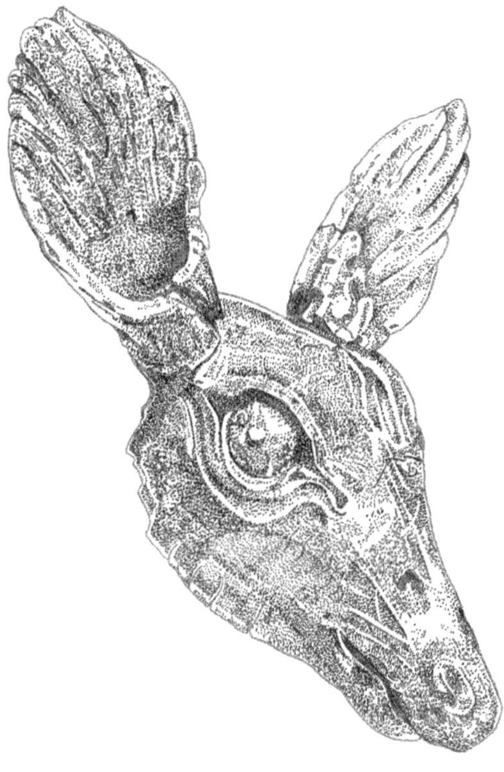

Drawing 3.2 Calusa deer mask uncovered near Key Marco, Florida. This small fifteenth-century mask is considered one of the most unique archaeological finds relating to this extinct indigenous culture. It was probably worn on the crown of the head and attached with leather thongs. As the dancer moved the ears could move, giving a feeling of the grace of a deer. Originally the mask was painted and probably had shell-inlaid eyes.

sions of animals corresponding to their primary habitation.[14] There were those that inhabited the land, water, the subaquatic world, the sky, and the highest reaches of the cosmos, a place believed to be of pure fire or light. It was not unusual for a mask to incorporate more than one of these components.

The various elements of a culture constituted the design for living used by a people, and no matter how unusual some of the activities might have appeared, they had a predefined relevance to the group's survival. Those practices provided acceptable ways of meeting situations that were a part of daily existence. For the particular culture, those solutions were often the foundations of their universe. Therefore, a people who had a system of values by which to live could not without courting inefficiency and chaos maintain a portion of their lives where they thought and acted according to a contrary set of values.[15]

Masks and the Socio-Cultural Continuum

In areas of the world where three-dimensional form flourished, the mask held a special place of importance.[16] For most peoples the mask was an imaginative representation of the likeness or image of a deity or spirit. While each mask had a unique quality as the result of the carver's representation of the spirit/deity, it was a part of the cultural continuum of the group. The mask, for that culture, was a symbolic entity embodying a measure of universal truth. The processes associated with mask making were not based on being "different" but on the imaginative blending of content and expression. Furthermore, the mask was not an idol but a representation of the deity or image pertaining to a particular act or event identified with the deity.

The mask, like other socio-cultural and magico-religious objects when viewed outside its originating environment, was only partly discernible beyond its obvious visual manifestations no matter how knowledgeable the viewer might have been. That obfuscation was because masks were not isolated products of spiritual or aesthetic invention but expressions of the vitality in which they were created. Masks transmitted their origins in ways that could not be conveyed by the ethnological facts or aesthetic theories and techniques. Even when the facts and theories were completely known they were poor substitutes for nourishing the emotions and imagination that initiated the masks.[17]

The mask was intended to make the viewer recall the related image or presence and, consequently, it (the mask) was a symbol that had to be deciphered. The masking tradition, "in contrast with social institutions, provide[ed] especially fruitful material for the study of creative expression, innovation, and cultural change."[18] Each culture had a set of traditional aesthetic standards, and image makers attempted to work within those norms. The creative process practiced in that way remained within accepted social patterns while incorporating new materials, technical advancements, and cerebral innovations. Cultural conventions limited the degree of change allowed imagemakers, but gradual variations in form, material, technique, or incentive were inevitable.

Despite the circumstances under which the masks were made, traditional images were a human product and seldom anonymous. The identities of the persons making the masks might have been lost to time or ignorance, but the fact remains that individuals produced the objects. In the maker's society his identity (most often, the image maker was a male although in some societies, such as the Iroquois, women fabricated masks) was well known.[19] In addition, while the name of the imager did not alter the importance of the mask, it is necessary to recognize the personal nature of the imaging statement.

Although the concepts behind masks in various cultures were modeled by tradition, the sociological and physiological forces often combined with new elements, creating a conglomeration of practices and beliefs. The "new" ideas were integrated into the coherent heritage of the people in extremely effective ways that generated their own provenance. This amalgamation reflects one of the most powerful causes for cultural change: the influence of one culture borrowing from another.[20]

Masks and Masking as Cultural Models

Culture is the sum of human mental and physical actions, reactions, and activities that exemplify the behavior of constituents of a social group both individually and collectively in relationship to their environment, to others, and to themselves as individuals.[21] It also supplied a people with derived potentialities, abilities, and powers. The complete manifestation of culture included the beliefs of the group, and part of that belief system was the concept of the supernatural in which animals and elements of nature were viewed as having perceived forms and superhuman powers. Similarly, objects were thought to possess beneficent or malevolent power (energy). It is plausible that certain of these cultural characteristics date to the beginning of human existence.

It is believed that the human conscience emerged as a social force less than five thousand years ago and that the most fundamentally important thing in the developing life of humankind was the rise of ideals of conduct.[22] It stands to reason that this attitude was also a measure of achievement for a people joined in a common pursuit. Early society, as a collective group effort, gathered intellectual stimulation through its senses. It modified that stimulation with experience and previously acquired information, and the resulting knowledge influenced the behavior and attitudes of its members (see drawing 3.3).

The individual, no matter his or her place in the social order, existed in the culture of the associated group. Correspondingly, that culture survived because it was incumbent within the individuals it embraced. The people were both the product and the proponent of their culture. This socio-psychological dynamic varied from group to group, but most synthesized groups were composed of persons with similar beliefs, expectations, and interests.

Early societies had a number of devices for promoting cultural integration and regulation. Certain aspects of abnormal behavior such as witchcraft and sorcery resulted in expulsion or death in Europe during the fourteenth and fifteenth centuries. Such "deviant" persons in other societies often were assigned a

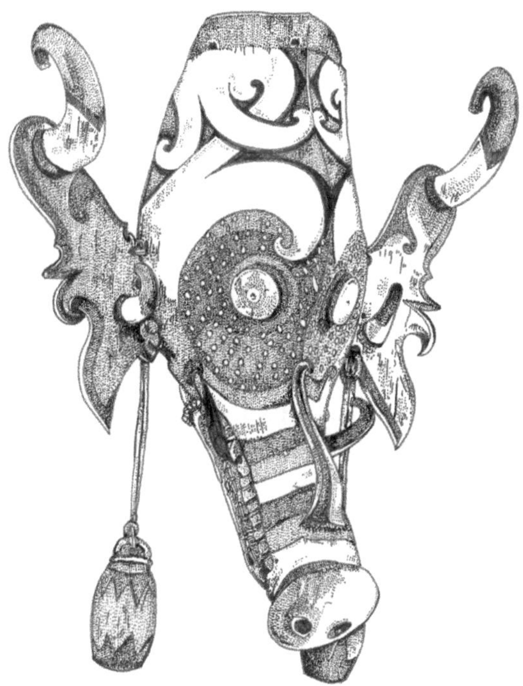

Drawing 3.3 *Hudo'* dance mask from Kayan, East Kalimantan, made of wood, pigment, and fiber. The mask represented the wild boar and was worn by dancers in agricultural rites intended to ensure a good rice crop. Shamans (**balian** in Borneo) also wore *Hudo'* masks in the process of caring for constituents afflicted with various diseases.

place or position of honor as with the seers, shamans, and mystics among the peoples of North America, Africa, or some parts of Asia. The range and scope of cultural practices, conventions, and values varied greatly, and they were shaped by many real and imagined forces.

Different belief systems evolved to express the fears and expectations of disparate people. Each system was satisfactory to those who were taught its values. Life in most early societies depended on the ability of the people to adapt to their surroundings and their aptness in coping with the unknown forces of nature. Beliefs arose, out of that process, about the causes and effects of certain natural occurrences. In turn, those beliefs prompted discrete ceremonies and rituals to assure a level of security in uncertain, arduous, and often-hostile times. That humankind might survive, the ancestors, supernatural beings, and deities were petitioned for the essentials of life. Culturally dictated rituals and observances were performed to ensure that the revered beings and the powers of the universe were sufficiently honored that they would not withhold from the people those things needed for survival.[23]

Masks and masking as part of the survival strategy were crucial to the idea and purpose of culture. "[T]he function of a cultural phenomenon always consist[ed] in showing how it function[ed]."[24] That was particularly true of masks. Just as certain ideals of conduct shape all societies and make them unique from all others, masks were a part of the traditions that have evolved to meet the needs of a particular group of people living under a particular set of circumstances. As dissimilar cultures reflected a range of traditions, they could not be assessed according to the standards of one people or tradition. In each culture, the techniques of manufacture and the shapes of the masks made over time varied significantly. However, there appears to have been a number of similarities in the utilization of masks as well as a commonality of socio-cultural purposes.

Masks and the Ordering of Society

All people reflect their history. They are a product of the society from which they emerged, and they have a natural as well as nurtured affinity for the myths, rituals, and superstitions of their ancestors. This attitude often supersedes intellect as it rests in the moral fiber of the person along with a number of other beliefs that identify the cultural heritage of the group. Such attributes go beyond commonly held beliefs and emphasize group and individual identity.

The concept of "identity" pertains to the behavioral or personal characteristics by which an individual or group is recognizable. It is a psychological pattern relating to perception, definition, and projection of self or group in relation to others that includes a cultural dimension. Identity reinforces self-esteem and empowerment for an individual or group and gives a sense of distinctiveness.

It was easier to distinguish those unique traits in persons or groups that were self-segregating because they rigorously initiated their progeny into the traditions and social customs they endorsed and maintained. Any deviation from the accepted paradigm was normally unacceptable and caused sanctions or eventual expulsion from the family or group. As world conditions changed, societies attempted to maintain ancestral traditions by transmitting them through various means both public and secret. Ancestor worship was one method of addressing these issues, and masks were an integral component of the process (see drawing 3.4).

Perhaps because of cross-culturalization, ambiguity was a reality for most social groups; due to that uncertainty people were influenced by a great number of forces that were beyond their control or understanding. They relied on "faith" and interpersonal dependence to survive the circumstances that altered every aspect of their lives. Archaic societies were often direct in resolving their "state of incertitude." They sought assistance from the powers of the unknown — those forces that were the least understood and the most responsible for the uncertainty.

Concern for the unknown aspects of existence was a consuming human condition, and one great fear was that no conscious experience exists after death. To address those concerns and to provide a measure of protection against the forces that constituted those dangers, humans sought comfort in the supernatural — the soul and spirits that existed beyond the biological limitations of the body. That concept, engaging the unknown to combat the unknown, was paradoxical. It was a strategy based on belief that could only be confirmed by survival. However, the spiritual pursuits of early people required no external justification or validation. The mask, as a manifestation of magico-religious belief, was respected as a symbol of the force it represented as well as a necessary ingredient in the social process that defined traditional belief. Each aspect of the mask was necessary in relation to other components to ensure the appropriate message was communicated (see drawing 3.5).

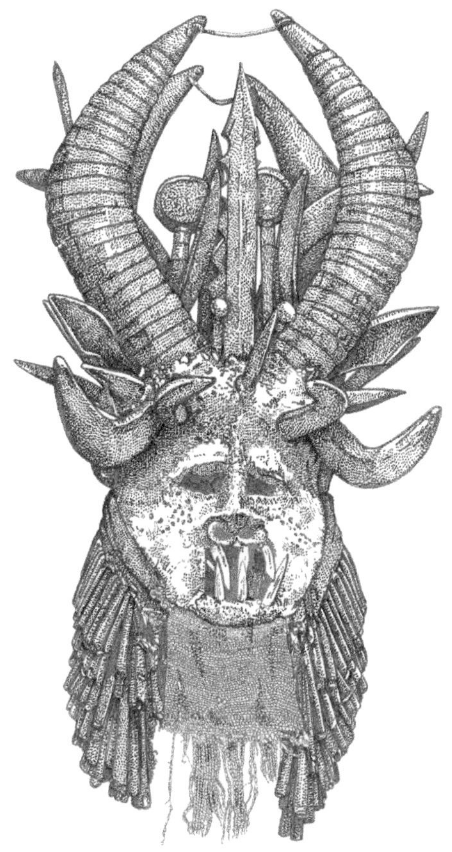

Drawing 3.4 *Mgbedike* mask made by the Igbo culture of Nigeria. This mask of wood, fibers, vegetal paste, and pigment was used to dramatize the interaction between the worlds of the living and the living dead. These masks called attention to the elders of the group as being living ancestors and illustrated the interchangeability of man and spirit. The underlying message addressed the duality of all things — life and death, youth and old age.

Images associated with certain ideas did not necessarily reside in the memories of a particular society. It was the perceptions of those images that existed as the impression of an emotional reality. Seldom was it known which considerations governed the decisions to configure a particular mask image, but it is reasonable to assume that they were of special symbolic importance to the people. It is also reasonable to believe that the images were considered beneficial and favorable according to the standards of the time and place.

Through the centuries, the human species has dedicated an extraordinary amount of energy to achieving stability. Early hunters joined in groups to stabilize hunting activities knowing that the coordinated hunt was more effective than the solitary stalker. Eventually, communities were formed, duties divided, regulatory systems organized, and a number of other steps were taken to reinforce the notion and reality of stability. The cultural process, in the quest for a stabilized society, imposed certain restrictions on human behavior, and masking had a specific role in those activities. Consequently, the origination of masking was defined by the duties the masks were expected to perform (see drawing 3.6).

Early peoples had little personal or group security, and no culture since the Paleolithic Era has existed without a level of dependence on mystical procedures to govern a range of social activities. Communication outside the family or clan was probably limited, and the influences of nature and the environment were often mysterious. The cycles of life were assigned to unknown forces, and for millennia people struggled to define and control the conditions that increased or decreased the likelihood of their survival as individuals and groups.

When the conditions of surviving or the requirements for achieving a particular goal became too difficult, it was human nature to alleviate the circumstances that blocked the way. Often that process included determining that the connection between the objective and accomplishment of that objective was not governed by reality but by the supernatural. Early people devised methods for dealing with the unknown, and since they could not change the world in which they lived, they changed themselves. They altered their bodies, wore masks, attained a state of ecstasy, or yielded to a condition of social euphoria that magically

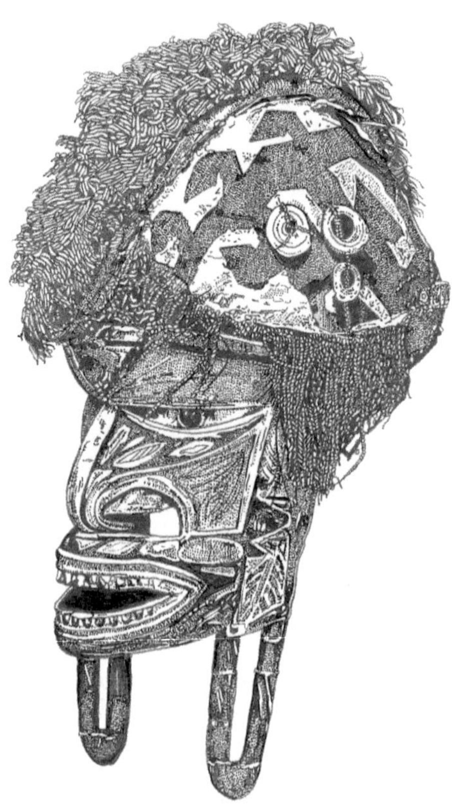

Drawing 3.5 *Tatanua* mask of Northern New Ireland made of vegetable fiber, parinarium fruit paste, lime, pigment, and other materials. Masks of this type were associated with one of the dances incorporated into the mortuary celebrations of central and northern New Ireland. The masks were found over a relatively wide area, causing a variation in their form and socio-cultural significance. The *tatanua* dance might have been a part of a celebration for members of a clan who had died since the last celebration. This was an exclusively male ritual associated with power. The masks were traditionally black, white, and red, but other colors were sometimes added. The hair crest was made from dried fiber and dyed yellow.

rearranged the world by abrogating their connection with it.

To address the inconsistencies of daily life, different beliefs were devised to deal with various comprehensible and incomprehensible situations. The belief that souls were quasi-physical and could exist outside the body in dreams and visions, could be transferred from one body to another, and persisted after the death of the body as ghosts or by reincarnation[25] was the dominant postulation of the time. In the process of spiritual consolidation, beliefs and deities were compressed and incorporated into forms that are more prescriptive. That transformation made the belief system more stable as it was collectively maintained, and in that permutation, it was formalized with a hierarchical structure, systematic rituals, and predictable practices. This transition was a gradual evolution that moved the people out of an age of acknowledged fear and ignorance into a time of presumed understanding based on unifying beliefs.

The process of spiritual consolidation varies from people to people and evolved at different rates in different locations. However, it can be assumed that not all people in all societies shared the same beliefs or levels

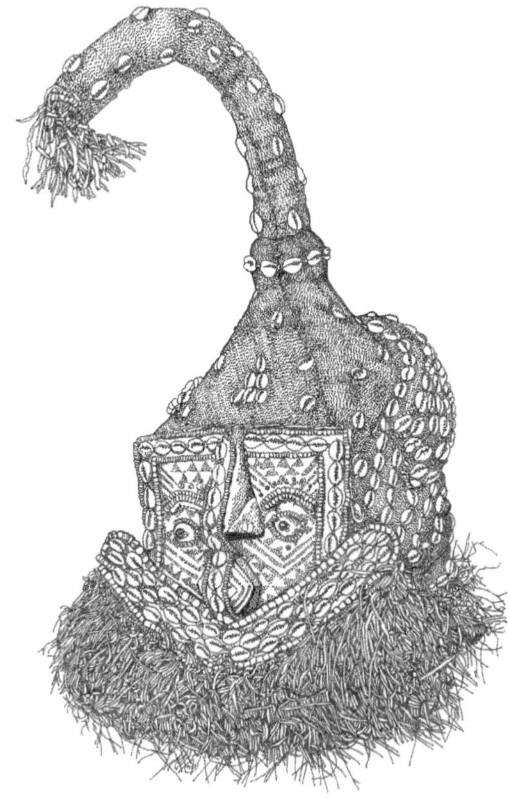

Drawing 3.6 A *Mukyeem* (or *mwaash ambooy*) helmet mask made of vegetable fiber, cowrie shells, paint, and beads. The Bakuba (Kuba people) of the Congo region of Africa made the mask. The trunk-like appendage extending from the top of the mask represents the trunk of an elephant and denoted royalty. The mask probably symbolized *Woot*, the mystical ancestor who originated royalty.

of belief. For example, it probably would be erroneous to think that all people in a particular group held common attitudes about supernatural beings or, for that matter, embraced the same level of sociological or intellectual development. Undoubtedly, some people were indifferent to the forces of the spirit world and added rituals to their routine only when required by social pressure or extreme need.

Although often considered intellectually exclusive, the relationships between the mystical and scientific conceptions of the world are closely aligned. The succession of events in both premises is regular, certain, and determined by immutable laws. The complexities of social consolidation took thousands of years and in many ways paralleled a broader sense of understanding of the sciences as they are defined today. The life forces from the earliest time to the Renaissance (ca. 1400 CE) were assigned to the gods. Humans were believed to have minimal influence over their personal destiny. Power, other than brute strength, rested outside the human sphere. The gods were appeased by various activities, but the outcome was always unpredictable. The earth was the center of the cosmos in that mode of thinking, and all action revolved around the known landmass. The gods occupied the ether space. Life was simple, but it was beyond human control.

The deities were the "givers" and "takers" that were called upon to fulfill social needs during that period of cultural evolution. The "gods" had to maintain a feeling of duality to remain accountable to their supporters or they had to have an alter ego or nemesis with which they were in constant struggle. Myths, rituals, and the associated masks often portrayed the mystical unity of opposites. They called attention to the contrasting merits of good/evil, youth/old age, feast/famine, or people/nature. There was often the direct confrontation between the protagonist and the antagonist that provided the basic "message" of the myth and the script for masked activities.

Portrayals of opposing forces were easily understood and emotionally pleasing. Good and evil were necessary elements of human existence because one could not be recognized without the other. Numerous stories, legends, and myths dramatized the discord in which the giver and taker of life were manifested in the single character transformed by magical or spiritual intervention. Masks offered the possibility of duality by giving a "different" face to the masked person. This impression of separation of the real from the unreal was an important element of masking and social liability. The two-faced Janus mask found in many cultures exhibited the duality as well as the juxtaposition of humans and spirits (see drawing 3.1).

Masks Defining Social Order as Power

Early people maintained family groups for protection and to acquire the necessities of daily existence. As a group, they hunted large animals, protected their encampments, gathered the grains and roots against the off season, and provided the necessary critical mass to establish and defend a fixed territory. For many of the same reasons, the family groups eventually joined with others with similar beliefs to form larger units. Over time, the groups grew larger and achieved an identity as a tribe or cultural entity. In those evolutionary steps, early people were communally oriented. The individual had minimal importance whereas the community or common "good" was paramount.

There was, as a part of the social structure, a collective desire to improve the lives of the people that could be greatly enhanced by familiarity with the regulatory spirits (deities) of nature. Therefore, the group organized festivals and other social events as community activities to secure assistance from the supernatural powers that influenced their daily existence. Members of the group performed ritualistic acts in these events, and although the enactments generally were performed by a small group of selected persons, the message projected represented the interests of the group. That is not to say that certain activities were not individually motivated; however, even the ostensibly self-serving endeavors were associated with social expectations.

The significance of supernatural intervention was of extraordinary importance because it was the adhesive that held the group together, and the rituals were the means of demonstrating that unity. Beliefs were the foundation for truth within the social order, and eventually those truths became the rules of the society. The identity of the group was formed out of that beginning and, subsequently, those beliefs became the rudiments of their cultural heritage.

The transfer of power to maintain cultural continuity was achieved in various ways according to the traditions and beliefs of the clan, group, tribe, or culture. The passing of social authority (power), for some peoples, required extensive training and ritual practice; for others, ascendancy was offered in a dream and could be declined. Spiritual endorsement often was for personal use as well as to serve the interests of the group. Personal power protected the individual, gave him or her success in the hunt, or assured the birth of a male child. Group oriented power aided in the bringing of rain during a drought, the return of agricultural crops or animals, and the recovery from a social or natural catastrophe (see drawing 3.7). Power used for the benefit of the group was considered more potent than that retained for personal use. The concept of power, in this occurrence, refers to the ability to "cause to happen" or to bring about a particular act, action, or sequence of events.

Ceremonies and rituals were most often associated with the transfer of knowledge, and knowledge was identified with power. The most commonly recognized ceremonies associated with that transference were those that marked

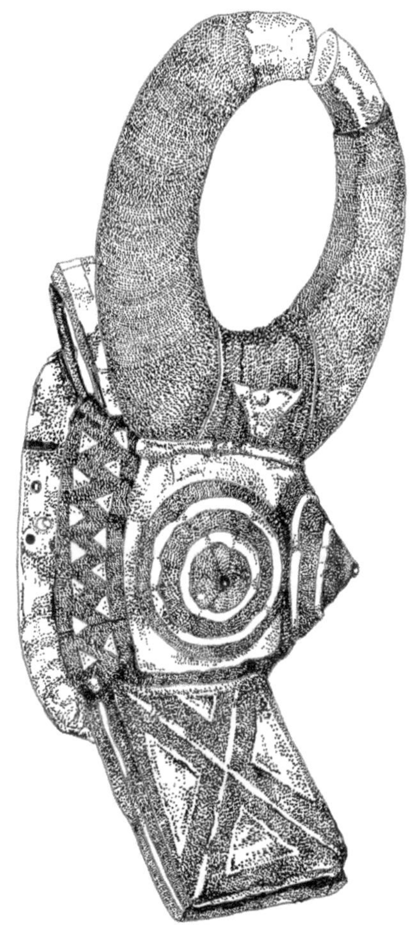

Drawing 3.7 *Bwa* mask representing a buffalo. This painted wood mask from Burkina Faso has prominent concentric rings for the eyes, a long snout, and circular horns. The mask was worn by the *Do Society* at festivals for the dead.

the passage of youth to adulthood — puberty. In that ceremony young people, male and female, were initiated into the adult activities of the group and instructed in the ways of adulthood. It was the transfer of knowledge necessary to gain social acceptability and, in many cultures, masks were used to "hide" the face of those participating in this transitional process. When the initiates emerged from behind the masks, they were given new names and entered life as a "new" person — one vested with socially endorsed knowledge.

For many social groups there was no authority greater than the power of the person who controlled the mask. The masked person could cure illnesses and overcome enemies. They were the purveyors of ambivalence that was the essence of social necessity — good and evil, life and death. The mask, for many peoples, was believed to be a container of the spiritual presence of both the wearer (the human) and the symbolized (the spirit being). The mask, in this context, purified the human spirit and placed it in a position for interaction with the supernatural — the spirit force (see drawing 3.8). Masks were agents of transformation, and those persons who received power, sometimes called "singers," or "jugglers" (in Native American cultures) were considered special and uniquely qualified for that responsibility. There was a distinction, in most groups, between those who sought power and those who received it by spiritual intervention. To be taken by the gods was a gift beyond the reach of most.

Masks and the Urgency of Essential Needs

Masks have been placed "high on the pinnacle of man's aesthetic accomplishment."[26] However, this recognition may be misleading because life or death urgencies caused early humans to produce masks to meet a basic need and seldom were they for artistic sensibility. Most often, it was the associated ritual and not the mask that had primary importance. Because of the life-related nature of rituals and masking, humans at all levels of the cultural and developmental scale were bound to the pursued parallel objective. One primary objective had relevance to the quantity of life. Fertility, virility, and prodigality rituals as well as other activities that ensured the continuity of the group exemplified that attitude. That element of societal necessity was considered the most urgent and demanding. Other objectives related to the quality of individual life and considered the successes of the person as hunter, warrior, progenitor, and leader. Obviously, the two motives were closely linked, and as the

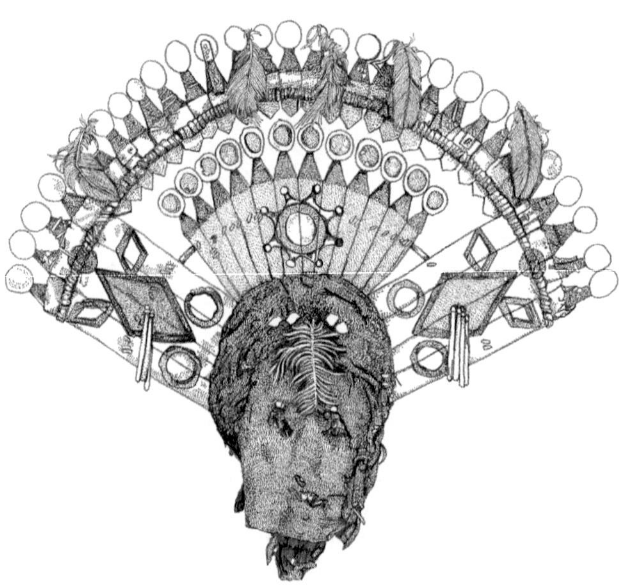

Drawing 3.8 An Apache dance mask made in southwestern United States. These masks were made of fabric (or animal skin), wood, paint, and feathers. Most of the early Apache people believed in the Mountain Spirits that represented good power. The spirits could protect people (believers) from illness. Four masked dancers selected by the group shaman were a part of the healing ceremony. The dancers circled the patient four times as a drum sounded and then waited as the shaman examined the ailing supplicant. The shaman directed the dancers to perform a series of dance steps and to "blow away" the illness.

probability of individual survival increased, the concerns for personal achievement acquired greater meaning.

The pursuit of individual advancement was included in many rituals that tested the essence of humankind. Those challenges required the individual to undergo ritual transformation and to be initiated into life phases that were often mysterious and unknown. Those rituals included the requisite abilities for surviving the symbolic "rites of passage" as well as the related social obligations.[27]

As a system of visible references for connecting the mundane and often frightening world of mortals to the liberating milieu of the spirits, masks related myths and beliefs to the rituals and symbols emanating from the distant past. The influence of masks on the supernatural inspired certain practices that had to be renewed through rituals. Masks were a primary means of transfiguration by which the relationship between the natural and supernatural worlds was achieved and maintained.

"Masks [were] meant to be worn, and it [was] only '*in situ*,' so to speak, as part of a unified performance that we can hope to understand their purpose."[28] Masks had an inner being and an outward presence. Their facades often gave the appearance of powerful, sometime horrifying, force — a nightmarish apparition designed to divert the viewer's attention and hold them in awe. In contrast, the inner being of the mask and the personal aspect of the power were devoted to more humanitarian objectives. The two parts presented the dichotomy of human existence. The dual nature of masks related to the human body that reflected the outward identity of a person while the inner element or spirit/soul was the seat of conduct.

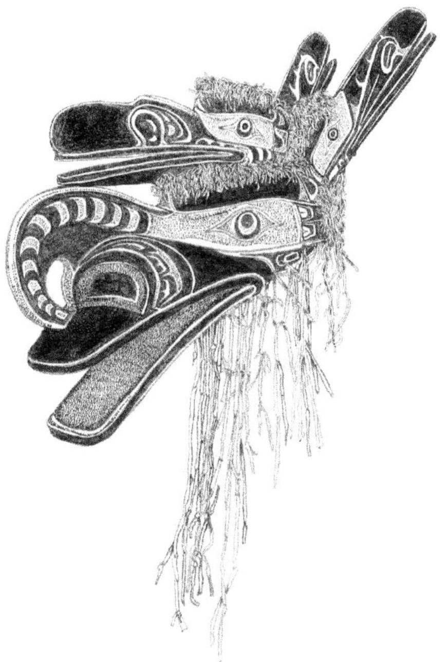

Drawing 3.9 Raven mask of the Kwakiutl made at Blunden Harbour, British Columbia. This large Hamatsa Society piece is a transformation mask with a moveable beak. The larger bottom figure relates to the Crooked Beak, a supernatural being of the sky. The other forms are ravens. Masks of this type were used in a winter season ceremony that lasted for at least four days. Initiates into the Society were "possessed by the spirit *Bakbakwalanooksiwwae* (Cannibal-at-the-North-End-of-the-World) inspired with the desire to eat human flesh."[f] George Wa'kus reportedly carved this mask in 1938.

As the belief system of early humans assigned in-dwelling spirits to animals as well as humans, it was easy to imagine that the barriers between the two were negligible.[29] That alignment allowed the joining of human and animal forms in a wholly understandable yet unique manner, producing half-human/half-animal beings complementary to accepted mythology. Masks mirroring that amalgamation were common in Mexico, New Caledonia, New Ireland, Bali, and the Northwest Coast of North America (see drawing 3.9). The associated totemic relationships and an asserted ancestral kinship further perpetuated the concept.

Although the division between the inner being (spiritual) and the outer presence (physical) was obscure, a distinction existed, and that separation extended into the social life of many cultures and served as the basis for family, clan, and group unity. Those "inside" were initiated into the secrets of the group, while those "outside" were not allowed to participate in certain activities. In ceremonial application, "Masks [were] used, recreating the division of insider from outsider, to effect a transition that [was] at once material and organizational as well as symbolic and personal."[30] The distinction between groups (insiders and outsiders) was most apparent at times relegated to ritual activities.

Masks as Mediators Between the Natural and Supernatural Worlds

The duality of masks allowed them to serve as both sacred and secular resources in the same society. They were among the most impressive forms of cultural patrimony made by the various peoples of the world.[31] Masks in their purest manifestations were concerned with organizing experience and providing information. They expressed order in ways that were appropriate to their social context and by means that could be repeated. As symbolic references to various concerns of both a social and psychological nature, their role was to portray order as a controllable and repeatable activity.

Many social activities are based on repetition. Certain acts were repeated regularly and those recurring elements were the basis for exchange. The appearance (mask), certain physical necessities, and numerous societal occurrences were repeated with extreme frequency and always with the same anticipated outcome. For most people repetition reflected familiarity, and the communal response to the supernatural was based on emotion-stimulated experience. The people in those situations observed not nature but themselves, and the truth of those observances was revealed by an emotional interplay not based on reason or logic but on social need and anticipation.

The influence of masks on their social environments (and the environments on masks) was probably greatest in those cultures that evolved slowly and where traditions were passed from generation to generation with minimal disruption. The beliefs of the grandparents were those of grandchildren. Masks, symbols, and attitudes were known, unchanged, and trusted — there was absolute cultural continuity. The social patterns of yesterday extend into the near future as each member of the society embodied the essence of the cultural past. Masks were a vivid and vital part of those societies that extended to primordial time. Beautiful or hideous, elegant or simple, sacred or profane, masks were symbols of the socio-cultural traditions in which they were produced. They spoke with and for the people as clearly discernible agents of communication. Masks and the affiliated masquerades documented the continuity and diversity of human life. Masks in their original settings were a part of the heritage that made the host culture unique, and they continued that function until forcibly changed.

It was believed in many cultures that spirits would not recognize the mask representing their earthly abode if the masks were made in other than the conventional design. Accordingly, masks were assigned to four general types according to their intended uses. There were initiation masks, secret society masks, fertility masks, and festival masks. Not all use types were found in all societies, but only a few masks fell outside these categories.

- Initiation masks were used in the ceremonies associated with preparing young people for adult life. They were also a part of the induction process for persons entering a special social order. Their purpose was to aid in the transformation, regeneration, or rebirth of the novice.
- A secret society mask concealed the identity of the person and represented a particular society or "club." They were badges of participation.
- Fertility masks were usually associated with agricultural societies. They were connected with the spirit powers that brought the rain and caused abundant crops. They were also employed to promote the renewal and regeneration of animal life.
- Festival masks were worn during special events, rituals, ceremonies, and as a part of celebrations. Generally, masks used in dramatic enactments fell into this category. However, drama masks in some cultures had a separate and unique identity that was not associated with other masking activities.

It is reasonable to believe that both the wearer and the viewer perceived the subject of a mask from the associated objects, colors, and activities rather than depending solely on the shape. "Visual form [could] be evoked by what [was] seen, but [could] not be taken over directly from it."[32]This notion does not presuppose that the mask's shape had no importance — rather that the overall effect produced a number of associated responses. Difficulty arose when the opposite occurred, and the shape was identifiable but the subject remained unperceivable. There were two possible causes in such a situation: either the crafting of the mask was deficient or the subject was beyond the viewer's adaptability range or level. The image was decontextualized. The shapes of wood or other materials, correctly constructed, were arranged into forms of visual action that gave life to the mask and ensured recognizability for the viewer.[33]

Masks representing animal forms were easily recognizable, and perhaps for that reason they were prevalent in many early cultures. The connection between animals and gods was frequent. Animal masks (see drawing 3.10) were associated with a number of activities, and many were used in rituals and ceremonies intended to multiply herd animals, assure success in the hunt, or increase the availability of the particular species. There were correlations to this practice in various world locations. As examples, the Roman goddess Diana and her Greek counterpart Artemis were allied with domestic animals as well as the wild creatures of the woods and fields. A Mexican herder wanting to increase the size of the family herd fabricated animals from wood or clay as a symbolic appeal to the spirits/deities for an animate manifestation of the inanimate models. It is also reported that in Southern India models of buffaloes made of silver were deposited in the temples for the same reason.[34] Furthermore, in West Africa animal-shaped masks were used to attract the attention of the deities for ensuring productivity and fecundity of the herd (see drawing 3.11).

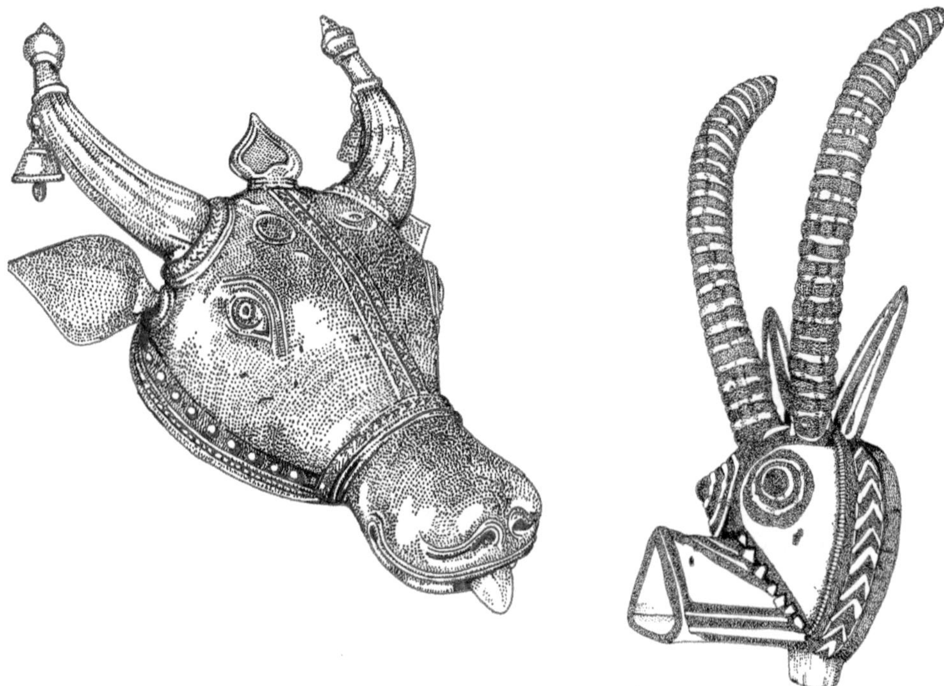

Drawing 3.10 (*left*) Buffalo head mask from coastal South Kanara, India. Rural people living in Karantaka use these masks to worship spirits called *bhutas*. The masks are made of brass and are formed in the image of tigers, boars, and buffalo. Drawing 3.11 (*right*) *Bwa Koan* mask made of carved and painted wood. This mask made in Burkina Faso has prominent concentric rings for the eyes, a triangular jaw, and long curved horns. It represented the female kob antelope called the *koan* and was associated with "bush spirits." The masquerade in which this mask was used normally occurred during the dry season. However, it might also have been used to dispel evil spirits.

To ensure communication with their spirit/deities, humans used various methods for creating similarities between themselves and the spirits. They humanized their gods and in so doing gave them human characteristics, appetites, mannerisms, attitudes, and caprices. The gods of many peoples were given food, water, alcohol, and other human staples and provided elaborate places to live. By assigning understandable and familiar qualities to the spirit/deities, their presence was more acceptable to the people. In addition, those traits helped to explain their actions. All people knew and understood hunger, anger, envy, fear, happiness, and a myriad of other human responses to daily situations.

Once the associated similarities were determined and a kindred relationship established, methods for attracting the attention of the spirit/deities were required. The contacting process included prayers, songs, music, dance, fasting, the burning of special herbs or grasses, and sometimes the consumption of food or drink. Similarly, efforts were made to reproduce elements of the deity's form or activities within the human context. As the "connectors" were identified, they were chronicled in the myths of the people and became a part of their collective history. The exact nature of those linking schemes was in the secret initiation rites of successive generations within the social group designated to interact with the appropriate spirits.

Masks were a significant part of the connecting strategy. They were elements for recreating the deity's image or representation within the recognizable context of human existence. The mask in those circumstances was or became the power symbol associated with the spirit/deity and was the link that joined the people with the universal presence.

As with all socially founded activities, there were no solid boundaries that fixed the limits of traditional or cultural influences. Societies changed. The flow of humanity across the geographic landscape during the thousands of years of human existence when viewed in a global perspective was an intellectual and emotional wonderment. The "politics" of territorial domination were among the earliest aspirations of humankind, and it was within those parameters that commonly shared objectives led to the establishment of traditions. A primary function of tradition was to safeguard customs and beliefs and thus to empower social identity and unity.[35] However, as with all practices that were transmitted from generation to generation, changes occurred. Tradition was a dynamic process that evolved to meet the needs of humanity.

The human-made object (mask) was the result of an act of genius whether it closely resembled another object or not. Despite the differences or similarities, it was in some regard a unique assemblage of materials and ideas.[36] It possessed its own identity. Culturally relevant objects were based on the traditions of the people and, although the image maker had a central role in social continuity, they were instruments of change. Masks acquired an aura of specialness simply because of their unique appearance. That special quality allowed masks used in ritualized activities to communicate attitudes and information as well as images and emotions that were otherwise incommunicable.

4

Ingenious Expression

Every work of art causes the receiver to enter a certain kind of relationship both with him who produced or is producing the art and with all those who, simultaneously, previously, or subsequently, receive the same artistic impression.[1]

Ananda K. Coomaraswamy wrote, "Art is religion, religion art, not related, but the same."[2] And while "art" as a cultural marvel is of relatively recent vintage, as an influence on human existence it has contributed to numerous ideological claims of socio-cultural development.[3] Current evidence suggests image making began 26,000 to 32,000 years ago; a fairly recent event when compared with the earliest stone tools that date from more than two million years ago. These early images were associated (in Europe) with Cro-Magnon people and related to the Upper Paleolithic Period, the last division of the Old Stone Age.[4] These early examples of artistic expression were simple outlines without structural details.[5]

Early image making was a form of social expression and in that manifestation became a part of the cultural heritage of a people. It was also an element of the magico-religious practices—a concept exemplified by masks. Although there was commonality in many aspects of masking, there was no universal characteristic of image making among early people. The one exception to this generality is that no early cultures solved the problem of perspective.[6]

The phenomenon of art as image making, in a greater or lesser form, was present in all cultures.[7] Whether masks were considered an art form or not depended on the cultural attitude and the definition of "art" as determined by those making the pronouncements. Masks in their traditional settings existed in response to social requirements, and aesthetic regard was a far less pertinent attribution. Masks were a fulfillment of a social need rather than an expression of intellectual or emotional necessity. They could be viewed as a basic product of the social system in which they were produced.

Creative Expression as a Socially Humanizing Element

Early people had a number of tools that verified a certain dexterity and inventiveness, and perhaps more important, they demonstrated an ability to make images and symbols. Along with a skill for "creative" expression, they had recognition and appreciation for music as documented by unearthed bone whistles and flutes.[8] By the time of the Upper Paleolithic Period (perhaps 25,000 years ago), these skills probably gave rise to ceremonies and rituals. Music making, although not assignable to social activities, was practiced from the Aurignacian Period (beginning ca. 34000 BCE) to the Magdalenian Period (ca. 11000 BCE). These Upper Paleolithic people as well as the San (of the Kalahari in southern Africa) and Australian Aborigines[9] left evidence of image making and musical apparatus.

The Upper Paleolithic Period in Europe

Aurignacian Period	34,000 to 30,000 years ago
Gravettian Period	30,000 to 22,000 years ago
Solutrean Period	22,000 to 18,000 years ago
Magdalenian Period	18,000 to 11,000 years ago

An interesting component of Upper Paleolithic creative expression was the presence of geometric patterns that have been attributed to shamanistic purposes. Those "signs" have been interpreted as having a variety of meanings, but none is totally acceptable or verifiable. However, contemporary with the signs and symbols are anthropomorphic figures. The images either painted or incised into the stone surfaces were often of a male figure clothed in the skin of an animal. A mask in the shape of an animal covered the face of the figure. The part-human/part-animal figures, although subject to interpretation, appear to document the use of masks for some manner of early ritualistic practices.

Sorcerer or shaman figures as incised or painted images have been found in various representations in different parts of the world including Lascaux in France (see drawings 1.12 and 2.11) and sites in Africa and Australia. Attributed to different time, cultures, and circumstances, many figures have human qualities and appear to wear masks and other articles of specialized adornment. The "shaman" figure paintings found in the rock shelters in the Lower Pecos region of West Texas are excellent examples of this application of illustrative expression. These unique figures have been described as "spirit beings" painted by persons emerging from a chemically induced trance or enraptured emotional state.[10]

Early images were rendered by various techniques. Some were in outline only, and others were shapes filled with a flat wash of color or slightly modeled with one or more colors. The pigments used for these images have been analyzed and their composition determined to be a mixture of colorants and extenders (media). Colorants included limonite (called yellow ochre), hematite known as red ochre, manganese dioxide, and iron oxide.[11] Another colorant often found in cave paintings was charcoal. These natural pigments were ground or pulverized and mixed with a medium that gave the appropriate consistency to the "paint," enhanced the color, and aided in adhering the colorants to the wall surfaces.

The people of early cultures produced numerous depictions of animals and humans, and while the exact meaning of these graphic representations is unclear, they apparently illustrate the activities and beliefs of the people. The images were symbolic of past experiences and probably delineated scenes of enjoyment or veneration.

The "figures" of the Upper Paleolithic Period, regardless of the purpose they served, demonstrated a unique technical skill and an appreciation for natural form.[12] A significant aspect of early symbolic representation was the achievement and advancement of technical skill. This accomplishment can be described as a critical threshold in cognitive evolution.[13]

Although the act of imaginative expression was an essential feature of image-making, it was seldom viewed as an aesthetic achievement. Objects had a purpose and a need to fulfill. From the most unsophisticated early society to the most sophisticated, the importance and value of creative expression were found in the group's metaphysical allusions to its survival.[14] Every object related to existence and was assigned a place in life as a referent to the supernatural world.

Image making can be viewed as a special type of human activity that evolved into a separate and distinct kind of work. It has been described as one of the most interesting and unique characteristics of the human being.[15] Over time, image making developed into a form of creative expression resulting from a consciously controlled effort. One of the extraordinary aspects of imagery was its symbolic quality because in the contemporary context and under normal circumstances, it was a human activity unlike any other. However, as a separate category of social activity, it likely had minimal meaning as creative declaration in most ancient cultures. Viewed as an effort to imitate nature, image making was a part of nearly all activities of early peoples. As the conscious arrangement of colors, shapes, and other elements in ways that affected a personal sense of composition, it was an essential part of the recognition of beliefs and practices that were central to the lives of most primordial cultures. Image making was not a separate and unique aesthetic activity.

The Parallel Nature of Science and Visual Expression

It is possible to draw a relationship between "science" and "visual arts" (image making) and to explain the imagery through the intricacies of scientific discovery. There can be no question that technology played a recognizable and substantial role in the modification of visual expression. Innovations such as processed pigments, pyrotechnology, metallic alloys, adhesives, and hundreds of other outwardly magical processes of transmutation altered the form, shape, color, and design of the imagery. It is also fair to say that the same technological wonderment transformed the creative process.

Two factors must be recognized when describing the parallel nature of science and visual expression: (1) all visual art is abstract and (2) all visual art is real. The image is abstract in that it is a representation of an idea or form; it is not the object. The image is real in that it has dimension; however, realism in image making (art) barely exists. Objects (images) can be touched, examined, and when necessary explained. The connectedness of science and art has greater credibility and reinforces the concept of masks if those factors are kept in mind.

Theories have tried to explain what ancient image making was— magic or religion but seldom simply art.[16] It has been proposed that the early imagers were limited due to intellectual or aesthetic comprehension and that the products reflected those limitations. It is equally possible (or probable) that the early image makers were extraordinarily skillful considering the technology and materials available. The quality of the object produced also may reflect the local economy, the tradition of the craft, and the producer's personal integrity and skill.[17]

Magico-religious motivation was a factor in all early image-making activities. Changes in style, design, or color often were the result of socio-cultural requirements rather than creative choice. The changing requirements might have been any of many variables that influenced the production of a particular mask or adornment. However, the meaning and use of the mask was the imager's true motive for making it. A mask, though unintelligible unless its purpose is known, had an intrinsic meaning not found in other masks. Thus, the mask exemplified the maker's objective.

Masks were an expression of humanity and nature as well as a statement of time and belief. They were a commitment to the future in that they spoke of the past in terms of the present. They were a symbol of continuation and an extrapolation of time linked to cultural survival. Human cognition had its beginning in the senses, and objects that were seen remained in the memory. Those memories could be called upon to stimulate related activities and events. Masks in that way were instrumental in maintaining the memory of society. The transfer of information was started with the perceptions (masks) that stimulated memory and subsequently generated understanding and action.

When shapes, forms, images, or icons are seen for the first time, the viewer assigns them roles within the "comfort zone of visual experience." They were absorbed into the familiar. The visual understanding of an object was limited by the intellectual or aesthetic sensitivity of the viewer. Due to the lack of normally acceptable cues, the non-African or non-Oceanic (and so on) viewer often fails to comprehend the visual elements of the objects. Their lack of understanding caused the objects to be labeled "primitive" or "uncultivated" instead of being recognized as something original and essential[18] (see drawing 4.1).

The shape of a particular object does not "...depend only on its retinal projection at a given moment. Strictly speaking, the image is determined by the

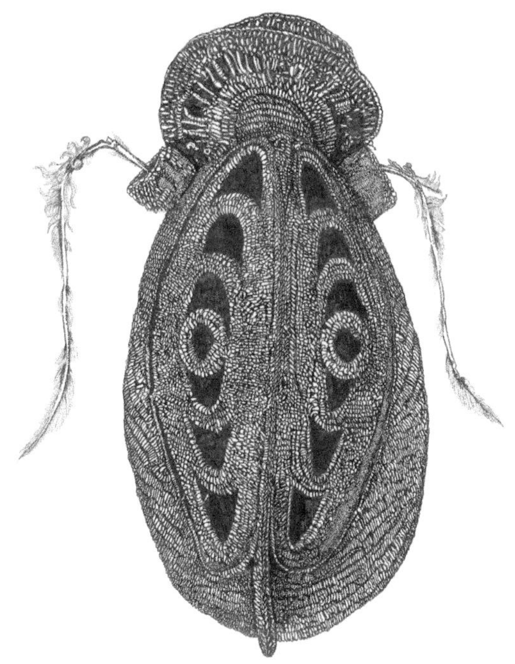

Drawing 4.1 This "*Baba*" mask of woven fiber was made in the Sepik River area, Papua, New Guinea. The plaited mask covered the head of the dancer and was remade for each use. The dancer's body was covered with a wrapping of leaf strips. The Baba masks represented a pig-like spirit being from another world that meditated between the living and the dead. These masks were to personify the intrusion of the supernatural world into the natural world.

totality of visual experiences we have had with that object, or with that kind of object, during our lifetime."[19] Therefore, the perception of an object (mask) was more than sensation; it was the impression of things. The completeness of the visual experience was not determined by the concept but the precept.[20] It was when something (the mask) was viewed against its socio-cultural background and in relation to other objects that it was seen in its entirety.

Early markings and symbols, often called "art," by contemporary viewers, had a magico-religious purpose. Masks were viewed as having a "special" value or uniqueness within the producing culture but not as works of art.[21] Many objects, though aesthetically pleasing, were not intended to represent an ideal of beauty or an expression of an emotional need. They were often attempts to connect two very different worlds—one world relating to the collective unconscious and preternatural powers and the other rooted in myths, legends, and influences of the deities that defined daily existence.[22] It was selective image making for specific ends that were installed in the collective memory of a particular culture and passed in direct transmission from generation to generation.

Perhaps the reason imagery, as aesthetic expression, was not given a priority in ancient times was because it occurred as an integrated part of most activities and therefore had no reason to stand alone. Since artistic expression was based, at least in major part, on perception and early people depended on perceptual data to understand their surrounding, there was no need to delineate between art and other forms of activity. The human mind imposed the assumptions of psychological models on physical things or events.[23] Perception in that way shaped the thought processes of early people and that reference directed the transfer of information and images. The physical and mental worlds overlapped and at times appeared to be the same.[24] It was at those times that art became real, and that reality was particularly applicable to the making and using of masks.

Masks and Secret Societies

One of the primary reasons for the importance and consequently the abundance of masks among early people was secret societies. Every male of the community had to be initiated into one or more of those organizations. The inner workings of the society were scrupulously protected, and often membership was a carefully guarded secret. Masks were worn to conceal the identity of the participants because of the community control or social regulatory functions of the society. The longer those attitudes endured, the greater the number of masks produced and the more accessible they became despite their frangible nature.

The perishable materials from which most masks were made means that despite the antiquity of many styles and cultures, only a few extant examples, such as bronze Benin masks and iron masks made in Japan date from before the nineteenth century[25] (see drawing 4.2). Some societies kept masks and refurbished them for future use. Other groups were known to destroy masks after a single ritual or masquerade.[26] Locations such as equatorial Africa and Oceania and the rain forest of Brazil were not conducive to preserving cellulosic and proteinaceous objects for an extended time. Wood rot, termites, and other natural and human-induced conditions made the preservation of fragile objects impractical if not impossible.

Often the masks of early societies were made of wood, and they were adorned with available materials including leather, skin, grass, raffia, seeds, nuts, other plant materials, shells, bark, and pigment. As trade increased, the availability of other materials such as copper, glass, beads, iron, fabric, mirrors, and other "manufactured" goods was incorporated into the images. Although the materials changed and the shapes were altered by the physical properties of those materials, the style of representation remained familiar to the cultural paradigm.

The materials from which traditional images were formed evolved from the beginning of the production process. Sharper tools allowed the carving of harder woods, and newly discovered pigments provided different colors for embellishing masks. Newly acquired skills made complex masks possible, and the arrival of outsiders offered unique objects as decorative elements. Such alterations were inevitable and necessary. Those changes influenced the appearance — both the shape and form of masks — but left undisturbed the spiritual essence. In that way, the tradition was preserved. It was only when spiritualism was replaced by materialism that the cultural traditions were forfeited.

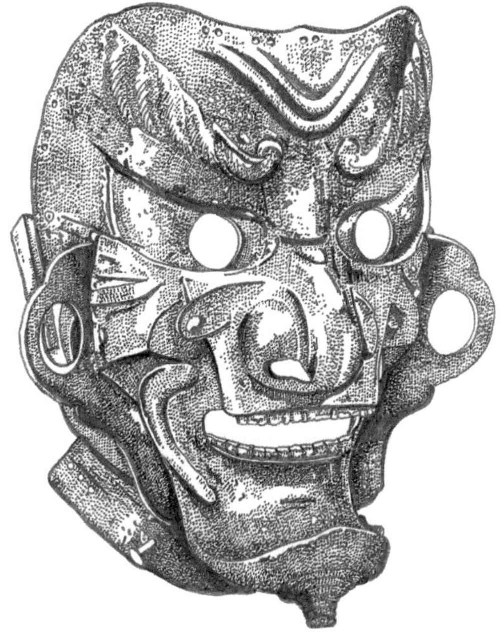

Drawing 4.2 Wrought iron battle mask made in Japan. This *men gu* ("armor for the face") from the Momoyama Period (1573–1603) was intended to frighten the enemy as well as protect the face. Full-face covers of this kind restricted the vision; therefore, they were less common, although more dramatic, than other types of "war" masks. The design and production of masks of this type required skill and training. The forging and shaping of the iron was an art form that was treasured.

Masks as "Visual Correspondence"

Perhaps the first masks were the result of spiritual inspiration because masks, in their truest forms, were often conceived and inwardly known as if seen in a dream or vision. It is possible the mask maker established an emotional self-identification with the mask whatever its peculiarities — even when the image was given supernatural characteristics. With that relationship, the maker and the mask joined in a unique commonality of purpose. The mask was the single object of the maker's attention — a transformation of vision, as a cerebral image, into a tangible object.

The quality of a mask often relied less on what the mask maker saw and more on what the person knew. In many masks, "visual correspondence" was stressed.

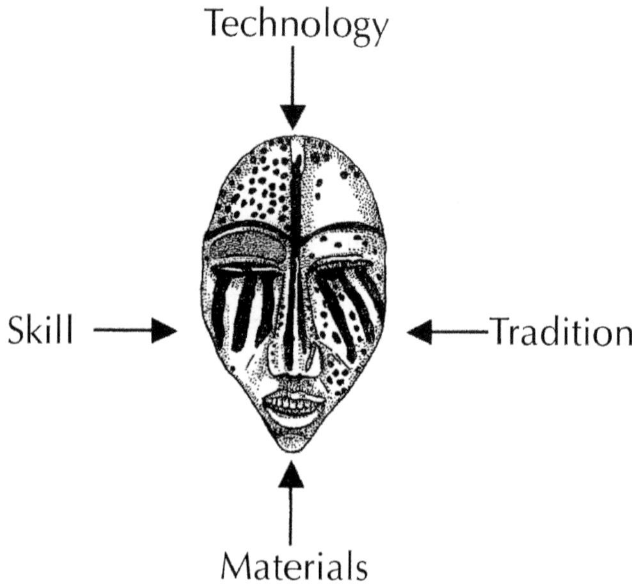

Figure 4.2 The influences on image making.

When this concern was applied to the visual similarities between the created image and nature, masks often appear deficient. However, applying the notion of visual correspondence of the sensational and emotional factors derived from appearance, masks were wholly sufficient (see drawing 4.3).

"Where the whole of life [was] conditioned by its connection with a multitude of spirits, the making of a mask [was] as much involved with ritual as its use when made."[27] The spirits were consulted at every step of the process to assure the success of the mask-making activity. The right tree was selected and cut down; the proper tools were used; and the appropriate taboos and restrictions were observed if the mask was to serve its prescribed purpose.

The concept of early image making reflected an effort to imitate, supplement, alter, or counteract the work of otherworldly force by a conscious arrangement of elements in a way that affected the viewer's

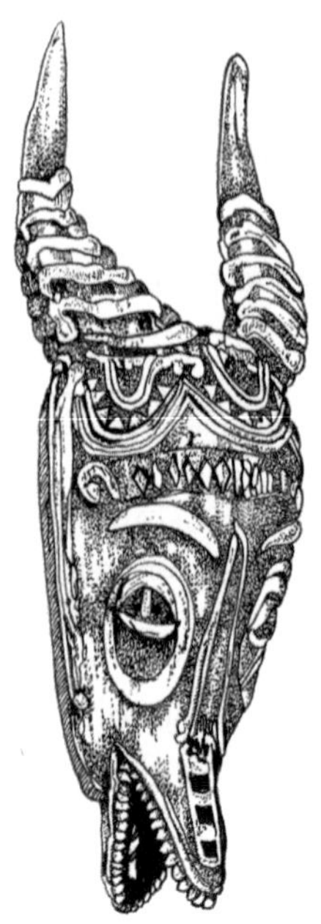

Drawing 4.3 *Guro* animal mask made of carved and painted wood from the Cote d'Ivoire. The mask has crocodilian jaws and antelope horns. The mask is of the Zamle society and was worn on top of the head. The coloration emphasized the eyes, the elongated muzzle, and the curvature of the horns. The mask was probably worn to honor ancestors.

sense of value. In other words, the activities of cultural expression were based on the information people received through their senses and that moved them to some form of meaningful response. Therefore, human adornment in its earliest revelation and in all its manifestations was not intended to be a creative process or "art." It was an act of self-expression and self-alignment with the environment in which the people lived and worked. Therefore, it had a purpose. The urge to beautify was one of the most interesting characteristics of early human beings.[28] It was a psychological element of their existence that aided in the fulfillment of an image (presence) associated with personal (self-awareness) and group identity. Unfortunately, the task of defining early forms of imagery is problematic due to the lack of first-person information. The difficulty is to distinguish between "art" as personal preferences—a subjective process—and art as the label applied by anthropologists and art historians when referencing certain kinds of object adornment that had no discernible purpose.[29]

The making of images implies a certain mastery of the form and appearance of things observed and suggests a level of knowledge or acquired information. Early humans had three ways of acquiring information and gaining that understanding. They used the word or message; they employed the senses: taste, touch, smell, and hearing; and they saw images—of the three, vision was the dominant method. Eighty percent of the information that entered the human mind was gathered through visual investigation.[30] The information amassed using one or more of those processes was acquired and assimilated easily and completely. Appealing to the other senses effectively reinforced the information gained through vision. Odors, textures, and sound were sensations associated with visual input and assisted in memory formation. The more senses involved in the gathering process, the more effectively the information was retained and used.

Once the information was acquired, it was processed within the cultural context and applied to the appropriate activity. However, despite the a priori preparation, all creative expression was imaginative. The creation of a visually discernible object was an abstraction of natural elements and a representation of images that formed in the imager's mind (see drawing 4.4). Seeking a naturalistic source for every motif occurring in masks is difficult. However, since many "special" creatures dwelled in the mythic imagery of virtually all early civilizations,[31] the mask "faces" were unlikely to be derived exclusively from

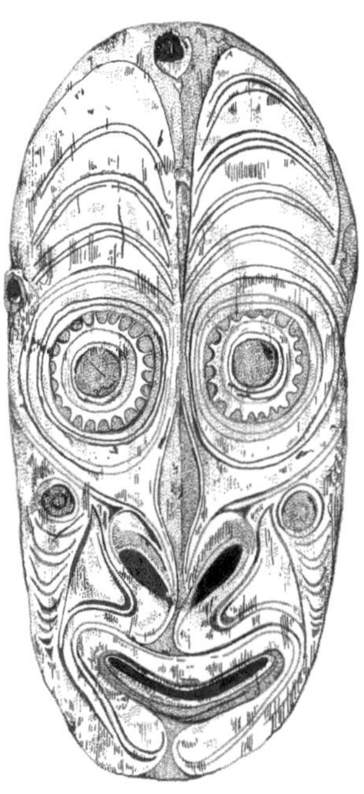

Drawing 4.4 Gable mask from the Middle Sepik River region of Papua, New Guinea. This large painted wood mask embodied female, clan-specific spirit beings (the mythical primal woman). Masks of this type were attached to the facades of the *Intmal* men's house of the middle Sepik River region. They were to protect the inhabitants of the house from various kinds of disaster. The mask has the circular eyes that were a dominant stylistic element of this region.

existing resources (see drawing 4.5). Masks were often a composite of elements derived from various animals and spirits and configured to form imaginary creatures. The imagination of early people allowed belief in a multitude of transcendental beings; therefore, it was only natural for that fantasy to give substance to images that had no equivalent in the real world of everyday things.

The image maker depended on his or her imagination to provide the specific details in making a mask to represent a popular supernatural being. When this impulse occurred and the preexisting symbol was altered, a new version of the accepted norm emerged.[32] When that variant was recognized as a standard representation of the particular being, it became a part of popular understanding. An even more interesting image formation occurred when a myth ensconced in the oral tradition of culture but with no attached imagery was represented using masks. The mythical elements were given distinctive features to establish the requisite identity. Thereafter, those images became the accepted depiction of that myth.

An image maker made a mask at a particular time, in a particular culture, and for a particular purpose. Persons of different cultures than those creating the masks did not regard them in the same manner as the creators. It was likely that the inspiration for the mask came from cultural tradition and reflected an "immaterial and timeless world."[33] Undoubtedly, the images inherent in all societies involved an enormous amount of subjectivity if, for no other reason, than as a counterbalance to the inhumanity of much of the rest of the survival process.

Of course, the presence of the mask did not confirm the presence of the spirit/deity. The purpose and image were often transferred to another service when the needs of the community changed.

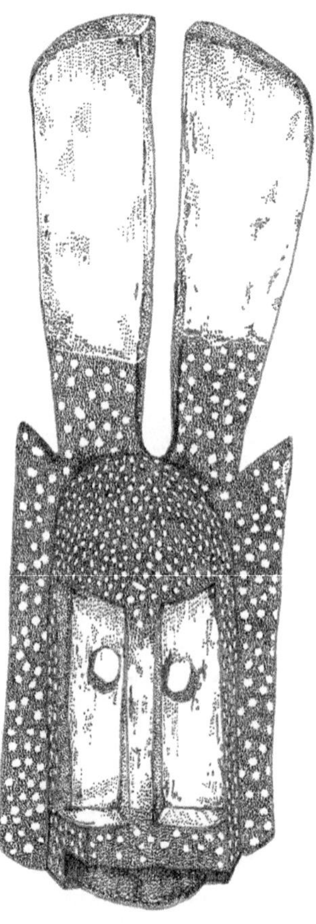

Drawing 4.5 Mask with flaring horn made by the Dogon people of Mali. This carved wood and pigment mask was used in an agriculture dance to promote the production of crops and the renewal of life. The masked dancer carried a baton (wand) and pretended to cultivate the land. The performance promoted a sympathetic response (magic) from the attendant spirits.[8]

Masks to Alter the Natural Environment

Unlike the plants and animals that shared their primal universe, early humans could alter their personal environment and give it new meaning by the images that they chose.[34] Because of their survival abilities, they interpreted their life experiences and made the vagaries of a difficult and often hostile world more "livable." The methods of shaping the environment, whether simple or complex, were an aspect of cultural adaptation. Although culture, in a rudimentary form, has existed since humans came together for food gathering and security (well within the horizon of modern humanity), it held greater significance when identified with magico-religious beliefs.

Undoubtedly, early people found stimulation for personal adornment in the natural environment. Color, shape, and form called attention to animals and birds, particularly the males of the species. While the females of the animal world were often camouflaged to blend with the available cover, males danced, sang, and performed mating rituals in the open to attract attention.[35] The male animals challenged the perils of the unknown by demonstrating their masculinity and the opulence of their appearance. It is unlikely that early hunters missed the significance of these performances, and the birds and beasts might have been the source of the idea and the materials for the first human adornments. It also is likely that the early hunters mimicked animal songs and dances.

Although most early societies probably had only rudimentary convictions about image making, people in those societies often engaged in some form of creative process.[36] Individual expression was probably an activity that explored the symbolic imagery associated with nature in all its various germane forms. This perception of the things—flora and fauna—that surrounded them formed the basis for their imagery and the symbols of spiritual recognition. Creation or imitation, as image making, was in this way an integral part of the practical life of the people. It was a humanizing factor that allowed people to express their feelings, emotions, and ideas in a way that was applicable and pleasurable.

For some groups, such as the Siouan-speaking people of North America, the concepts of art, religion, and life were interwoven and inseparable. Therefore, the study of various images is one way of understanding the universe of these early people.[37] It is reasonable to assume that early humans were so involved with the struggle for survival that they had little time to devote to the pursuit of objects for strictly aesthetic reasons. The precariousness of life caused people to undertake various methods of acquiring social and physical security. As groups were formed and individuals came to identify their personal welfare with that of the group, creative representation (image making) was used to give permanence to commonly shared practices.[38]

As soon as basic production skills were mastered, the urge to embellish objects asserted itself as superfluous modification intended to please the owner/producer or to impress others. Imaging in any form involved a very complex appeal to the mind (cerebral response) and feelings (psychological response) of both the producer and the viewer. Masks, as examples of ingenious vitality, had the magnetic power to draw people to the beliefs associated with the supernatural. The use of visual images enhanced the believability of the concept of parallel worlds—one dealing with the visible and the other occupied by the invisible. "Thus early man, the hunter, believed that in a spiritual manner, through art [as an image making activity], he could intervene in the productive processes of nature and influence them in a way favorable to himself."[39]

The significance of the mask and its importance as a socio-cultural object were the counterparts of the experiences and beliefs of the user. Masks embodied the imagination of the imagers and reflected the wholeness of their existence. The mask served as a unifying element to join the natural with the supernatural. They were symbols of tradition that bound people together into cohesive units capable of self-reliance and endurance. Masking was an established means of transformation. The mask was a world in itself, rooted in reality and expressing transmuted reality yet transcending it. Therefore, masking must be considered not by the standards that apply to reality and everyday life but by the standards that apply to the transcendental world of belief and tradition.

Early masks, although subscribing to supernatural tenets, had a decidedly practical nature; they confirmed the concept that "form follows function." This axiom was drawn from the concept that form is subordinated to function and raw material.[40] It is applicable to masks because the traditions associated with masking were founded on the purposeful practice of communication or pseudo-communication. This approach drew on cultural tradition and often included conventional external stimulants such as sound and smell as well as various forms of mind-altering exhilarates, not the least of which was adrenaline generated by belief.

Masks, in their original use, were created to meet a practical social purpose and the forms (shapes) in which they were created were appropriate to meet the assigned social need. Moreover, it was in that appropriateness that their beauty lay.[41] Since beauty in all cultures was an actualization of the symbolic and romantic relationship between content and form, masks fulfilled the requirements of that socially defined quality. They embodied a blending of the idea, shape, and purpose, and in their outward manifestations they were an abstract idea seeking expression in and through the lives of people. Masks found their origins in the natural occurrences that surrounded the people and in the human perceptions of the physical and spiritual worlds. Ultimately, masks fostered self-knowledge in a particular population by reminding people of the practices, habits, and beliefs of their culture.

Masks to Interpret Natural and Supernatural Influences

Masks interpreted the natural and supernatural influences people encountered as a form of truth that was elemental to the environment in which they lived. As all natural objects had an existence that extended beyond human knowledge, they possessed greater or universal importance no matter how small that universe might be. Perfect perception and complete understanding were not always possible. The stimulants of spiritual and visual recognition among early people were often only transcendental aspects of a natural "thing."[42] Perception had to find its way into the psyche of people through their sensibilities, and the most effective mechanism for assimilation was vision.

Seeing (vision) made it possible to recognize shapes, colors, movement, and, to some degree, space. However, as with the other physical attributes, vision was selective. It was most attracted to objects that changed in color, size, or location.[43] Therefore, it is reasonable to assume that early mask makers shaped their products based on reactions geared to fixed indicators, and those signals were most easily differentiated by pure color and simple shape.[44]

For masks to be effective, they had to transmit an immediately recognizable signal of their intended purpose. "A precept [was] classified instantaneously only if two conditions [were] met. The precept must define the object clearly and must resemble sufficiently the memory image of the appropriate category."[45] Mask recognition in the originating society required minimal concentration as visual and emotional cognizance occurred simultaneously.

"Imagery include[d] not only static representations of objects, but also dynamic representations of action sequences and relationships between objects and events."[46] When the mask or masking action adequately matched the imagined image stored in the viewer's memory, a graphic association was established and the related information was intuitively understood. The notion of "perceptional memory," that is, the recognition and interpretation of sensory stimuli based primarily on memory, was an important element of masking activities as well as a decisive factor in determining the shape and design of masks (see drawing 4.6).

Visual comprehension for most cultures was a relational process. Masks, within the societal context, were joined with a particular ritual or event and through that continued association a mask (image) prototype evolved. The relationship between the mask and its ritual purpose ensured easy

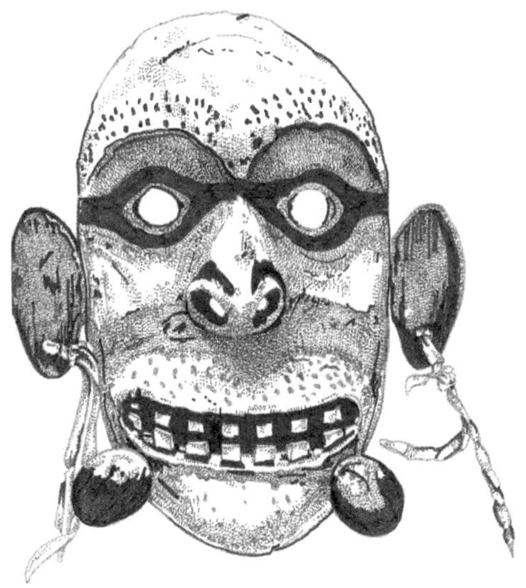

Drawing 4.6 Magemut mask made of carved wood with goggles and large labrets. Bering Sea Eskimo men wore these masks in religious and dramatic presentations. Goggles symbolically notified the viewer that the identity of the figure was concealed. The labrets extending from both sides of the lower lip gave the mask a tusk-like appearance associated with the walrus. The belief that men could change into animals and animals into men was a central element of western Eskimo religion.[h] The idea of transformational reality was pervasive among the people of that area.

recognition within the social confines. "In the perception of shape [lay] the beginnings of concept formation."[47] In the perception of a particular image the viewer discerned the structural features that gave that object identity. However, seldom did the object conform exactly to the shape by which it was perceived. When a shape corresponded to a prototypical image found in the viewer's conscious and it clearly contrasted with its environment, it was likely to be recognized and understood. Exposure and tradition within the mask-producing society reinforced both the shape and the recognition process. When the mask as a visual element was removed from its social surroundings, it became a different and disassociated object. Outside the sphere of a common set of cultural symbols, it was demystified and no longer represented a shared meaning. The more socio-magically motivated the mask, the greater the decontextualization when it was encountered outside the producing society.

The decontextualized masks often appeared unusual or unsophisticated. This conception (or misconception) reflected cultural preference such as color and shape comprehension that was complicated by visual recognition of contrasting elements. In visual information transfer, understanding was enhanced by contrasts in shape, texture, line, and color. As examples, round shapes became more round when compared with square shapes, and white colored forms were more articulated when juxtaposed to black areas. Some societies maximized contrasts while others preferred complementary colors and shapes. Those preferences in early cultures were based on past experiences that were stored in both the social and individual memory. Visual knowledge assigned an object to a place within the system of things related to a cultural view of the world.

Masks and Color

Masks were dyed, painted, colored, or stained with oil, fat, gums, and blood as well as colorants made from earth and plant materials. The natural substances created a harmonious relationship that enhanced the design and function of masks according to tradition. Although viewed differently by diverse peoples, colors such as red had a generally accepted symbolic reference to the earth, blood, or death as the counterpart of life. White, the "ghost" color, was often associated with funerals and death as the termination of life. The color black symbolized the night and those uncertain activities that took place in the darkness. Black also was used to emphasize the mask form by exaggerating the eyes, mouth, or other referential elements (see also Chapter 7).

Color and shape were important ingredients of the mask, and contrasting colors, particularly black and white, gave dimension to mask details. Extended areas painted white gave the illusion of greater extension when contrasted with black-colored recessed areas (see drawing 4.7). The arrangement of contrasting colors did not require the viewer to comprehend the color combination to see the concavity or convexity that was enhanced by the contradistinction.[48] The contrasts were strong, and the impact upon the viewer was immediate. The masks of Indonesia, by comparison, used both complementary and contrasting colors to give softness to part of the image and to balance the shape con-

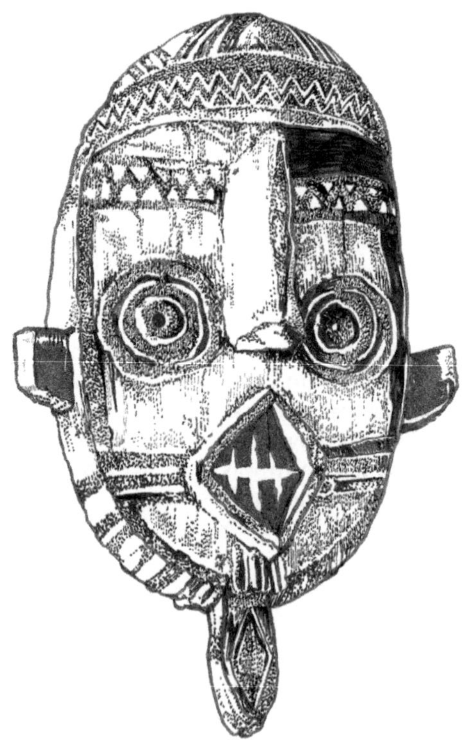

Drawing 4.7 A facemask made of carved wood by the Bakuba of Zaire. The mask has mesmeric eyes accentuated by concentric circles. The patterns on the domed forehead and face are accentuated by the use of white paint. Although of recent origin, this piece is a good example of the use of light and dark coloration to enhance the feeling of three dimensionality.

trasts of others. Complementary colors and shapes tended to assimilate or to minimize differences. The *Rangda* (Angry Widow) masks made in Bali were painted red, orange, yellow, gold, and white (see drawing 4.8). Those colors complement each other, causing the viewer to envisage the flames that extended from the top of the mask as being soft and shimmering. The technique was intended to confuse perception by creating an optical illusion.

Masks made in the Sepik River area of New Guinea were commonly painted red, yellow, black, and white. The colors of older masks often were lost to layers of soot and dust or eroded by the elements, but most were originally painted with stripes, dots, and bands of color.[49] Color often had magical qualities that communicated symbolic meanings as specific as the shape or design of masks or body decorations. In addition, although some cultures used a variety of colors, the dominant colors for all cultures are red, black, and white. Many people, such as the Asmat of Irian Jaya, only use these three colors. However, the composition and source of traditional colors differed according to custom as well as local or regional availability.

A primary source for red pigment was natural iron deposits, hematite ($Fe2O3$) also called red iron oxide, ferric oxide, or red ochre. It is a blackish-red to brick-red mineral commonly found along stream or riverbanks. The word "hematite" comes from the Latin meaning blood-like or bloodstone. The raw material from which hematite was derived is limonite, a widely occurring yellowish-

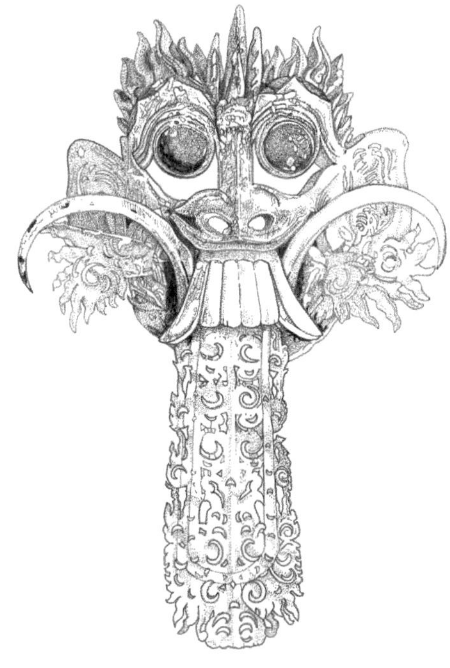

Drawing 4.8 A Rangda mask made in Bali. This mask of wood and leather represents the angry widow, a primary performer in the *Calonarang* drama.[i] This drama was first performed in the fourteenth century in Java and gained popularity in Bali during the last century. In the dramatization the Rangda represented Dewi Durga the "Queen of Witches," an expert in black magic and a symbol of evil.[j] She challenged the local witches to match her ability during the performance. Although the "temple of death" in each village was dedicated to this character, the drama also tells a story about the history of the Indonesian people.

brown to black natural iron oxide. Limonite was transformed into a red substance when treated with fire. This metamorphic process might have been viewed as magic when it was first observed by early people.[50] In a natural setting the material appeared as either red mud or ocher (yellow-brown) clods that when burned in an open fire were transformed to a rich red color.

Other colorants were generated from various natural resources depending on location, availability, and tradition. As an example, a reddish paste was produced by rubbing a wet stone on the bark of a certain kind of tree. This paste was the source of a red stain used as a paint to produce a red or red-orange coloration when applied to wood, fiber, or skin. A similar technique was used to manufacture a natural yellow pigment.[51]

The color black was made from a number of materials. One of the most common is crushed charcoal. Soot also was used. The juice or sap from certain plants produced a black stain, as did mud containing black iron oxide (FeO), manganese oxide (MnO), or manganese dioxide ($MnO2$) in combination with black cobalt oxide ($Co3O4$). In addition, masks made of wood were blackened by scorching them with a hot iron rubbed on the carved surface that was smeared with oil or fat.

Most white pigment came from two primary sources. One was calcified shell or bone that was pulverized, ground, and slaked (soaked in water to allow the larger particles to separate and settle). The resulting chalk-like powder was lime or whiting (calcium oxide, CaO, or calcium carbonate, $CaCO3$). The second source for white pigment was kaolinite clay, also called china clay or pure clay ($Al2O3 \cdot 2\ SiO2 \cdot 2\ H2O$). This material was found in natural deposits along rivers or streams. A third source, but one that was less commonly used, was talc ($3\ MgO \cdot 4\ SiO2 \cdot H2O$). In a solid form, this material was also known as steatite or soapstone. It was crushed and ground into a fine white powder.

A variety of mediums were used to adhere or fix the pigment to the mask, figure, body, or other surfaces. These binders gave the pigment bulk and density as well as adhesion. Mediums included animal fat, blood, water, and vegetable juices or a mixture of any or all these materials.[52] The colorants and mediums used for the earliest paintings continued to have a prominent position in the masks and rituals of many societies (see drawing 4.9).

For masks that were stained rather than painted, the source of colorants varied depending on local products. Different plant substances were used to produce the stains. The materials from which the masks were made had a direct bearing on the colorants and their method of use. Palm oil gave certain woods a rich reddish appearance. Masks were rubbed with oil or animal fat and smoked to cause a dark ebony-like black finish. Millet paste sometimes served as a whitening agent,

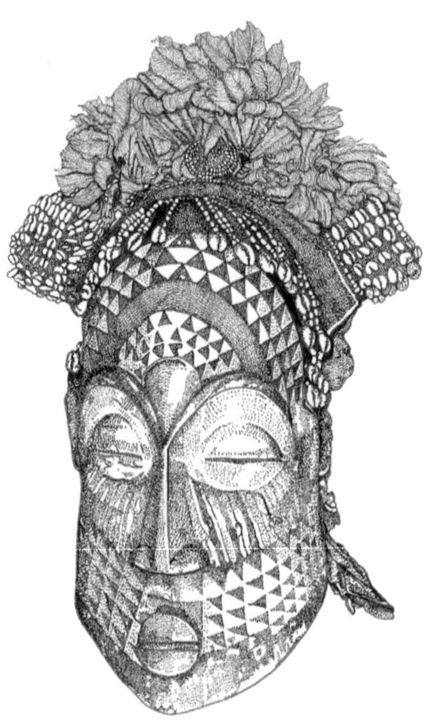

Drawing 4.9 BaKuba helmet mask used in boys' initiation rites was made with beads, cowrie shells (various tropical marine gastropods of the family *Cypraeidae*), animal skin, paint, copper, and reddish-tan feathers. This wooden mask from Zaire is very well carved to an even thickness throughout. The pubic "V" painted design illustrates the use of triangles to form an interesting repetitive pattern that was associated with regeneration — the renewal of life. The circular lobes of cowrie shells on either side of the headdress probably served as a base (receptacle) for animal horns.

and blood and soil often gave a dark crusty appearance. Masks made in Nepal acquired a black patina due to an accumulation of dust and soot from storage in the rafters of houses.[53] Need, availability, circumstance, and local custom dictated the manufacture and use of coloration.

Masks as Impressionistic Representations

Many societies in the developmental phase embraced various imaginative forms as a part of the "real" world; therefore, artful objects were an integral and profound part of the daily life of the people.[54] The symbolic presence of the powers of the world with which humans tried to keep on good terms was manifested in the imagery, music, and dance. Masks, in this employment, had emotional values that were understood by persons responding to the psychological connotations. The early masks were a cultural phenomenon designed as objects for mastery over the supernatural beings that inhabited the dominant belief systems. The creation of masks as spirit forces imparted a quality of permanence that allowed a perception of order and control. This condition led to a feeling of social confidence and security.

The image of the mask and its presence satisfied a real (practical) purpose within its societal context as masks were assigned meanings by decisions formulated on traditional practices available to the viewer. The masks were a means of alliance among people by joining them (the people) to the feelings and deeds that were necessary for their well-being.

David Pace proposed that urbanized civilizations had a tendency to create more representational imagery than preliterate cultures. The rationale for this assertion is that urbanized cultures attempted to possess the object rather than suggest it.[55] Objects made in developing societies were believed to encompass meanings that projected beyond their physical existence. The object was the nexus of magical forces that the imager attempted to express through his or her symbols.[56] This view is the opposite of the perspective of most later image makers who systematically attempted to demystify image making by both humanization and possession. This elucidation was done by assigning human references and expectations to objects and establishing imagery in a way that allowed it to be possessed.

Masking and the social activities surrounding the ritual use of masks were forms of hyper reality. Such occurrences were a part of human experience since the beginning of recorded time. Image making as a social event could not have evolved without a long developmental period.[57] Human sensitivity to beauty or visual pleasure (in its various forms) suggests a prolonged and elaborate evolutionary episode that in biological terms propounded the importance of image making to the humanization process. The quest for beauty corresponded to the simplification of form and the reduction of tension. Michael Cardew contends that image making "...as distinct from verbal discourse, [was] essentially a preliterate form of expression and belongs to 'the ages before logic.'"[58]

Masks are impressionistic in appearance and purpose, and the relationship between intellectual understanding and visual interpretation is frequently misunderstood. A mask often included features that symbolically represented or embodied humans or animals. However, the proportions were modified, the features rearranged, or elements eliminated, but the relative appearance was that of an identifiable form almost remembered. The visual impression was understood, but the factual representation appeared unclear or distorted. The reason for the "relative" likeness was seldom due to lack of manual skill or visual comprehension but to psychological and sociological decision making. Consequently, masks must be considered from two points of view. One perspective is morphological — describing the structure and form of an object, excluding its functions, and the second is cultural — defining why the mask was made and how it was used. The latter attitude most often dominated the decision-making procedure.

A well-conceived and executed mask suggested the essence of an entity (animal, human, or spiritual) rather than its appearance. The true reality of things, both natural and supernatural, was not conveyed by the way they looked but by the manner in which they were perceived. Moreover, the perceptions of all persons included the impressions suggested by the intellect and sensibility of the perceiver. People saw what they chose to see and found answers to the questions they asked themselves. Belief, for the early human, was a primary determining factor of the rationalizing process.

Extending the impressionistic aspect of masks, the shape and design often depended on the profile or silhouette of the image being represented. This approach was particularly true of West African masks that were stylized and exceptionally dramatic. Attention was not given to the detailed likeness of the subject because visual perception and the interpretation of retinal information influenced understanding. Ocular activity required the human brain to interpret the image and assign depth

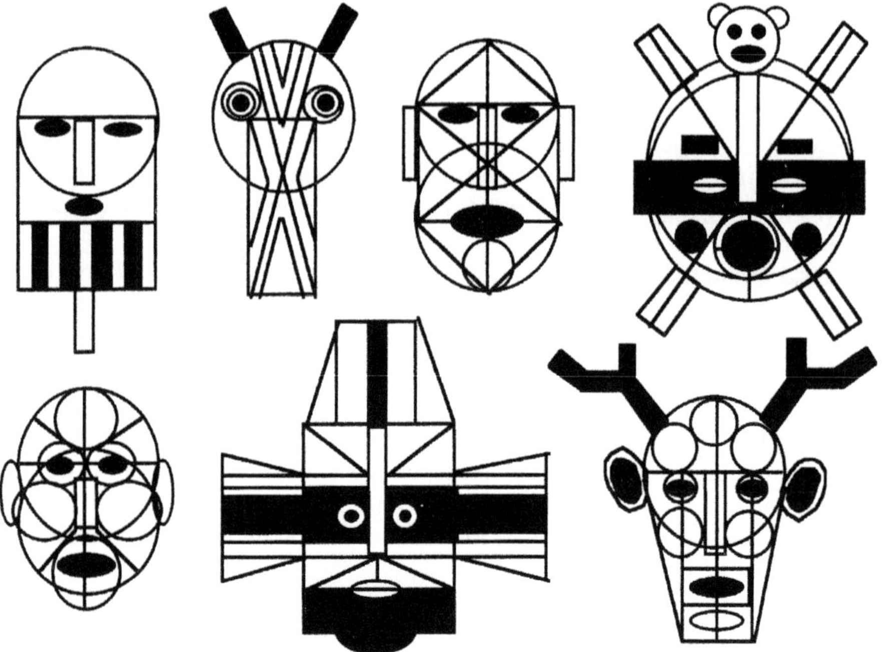

Figure 4.3 Mask shapes based on circle, square, and rectangle construction principles

and definition. The visual system interpreted a two-dimensional image so it could identify its three-dimensional correlate.[59] This facility was basic to spatial understanding that was more complicated when making a three-dimensional object. It was inevitable that greater attention was given to the profile or two-dimensional delineation of the subject.

Complementary shapes were used to convey the desired impression and to stimulate remembrance. A square next to a circle accentuates the geometric proportions of the circular form while an oval next to a circle reduces the appearance of roundness. Masks can be reduced to round, square, rectangular, or triangular shapes that interact. Shape and color were analogous with preestablished qualities understandable within the cultural context. The more recognizable the form, the easier the cognition and the more quickly and spontaneously the emotional reaction was evoked. The concepts of recognition and perception were continuing components of image making that passed from intuitive into calculated use.

As later forms of image making manifested a kind of false humanization where beauty (and purpose) was "nonobjectivized," early masks were viewed as the humanization of natural elements and deities. They were images placed within the human context. As objects with an "artistic" nature, they were both real and unreal as an impression of reality. Like all things fixed within the time

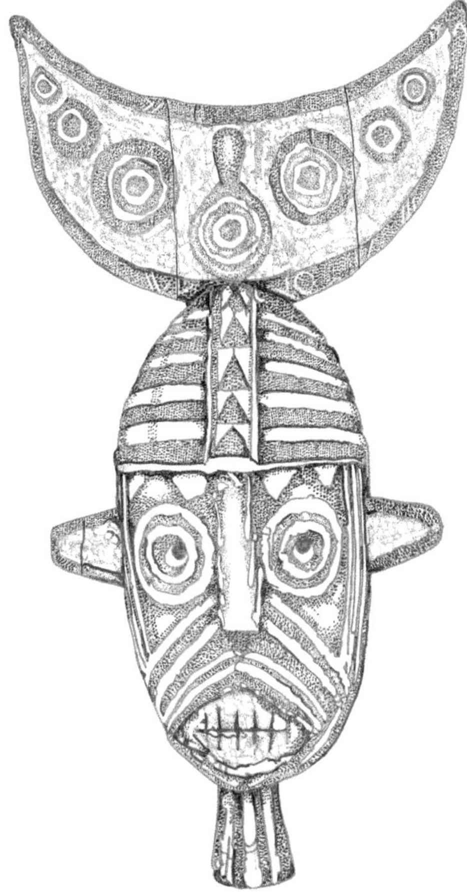

Drawing 4.10 Marka (Bwa) mask from Burkina Faso of carved wood made by the Mande-speaking Marka people. The mask reflects the stylistic characterisitics of pieces made by the Bwa, a people living near the Marka. This mask style was known as *barafu.*[k] They were worn at funerals and initiation rites and were associated with spiritual activities.

and space continuum, their reality was limited to the time and purpose of use. Simultaneously, they expressed a timeless element that related to the patrimony of the people in whose presence they existed. The visual strength (power/impression) of masks resided in the unification of their elements to express a total meaning — a time-transcending wholeness (see drawing 4.10).

The mask often included elements that the image maker knew had to be shown although they were not visible. Eyes, ears, a nose, and mouth were essential characteristics of human form; therefore, they were included whether the mask was of a plant, animal, or human. When preparing a mask, the imager made a selection of the attributes to be emphasized based on experience, imagination, and emotion as well as tradition. Because of this approach, one of the special characteristics of early masks was a disregard for the relative proportion of the essential features.

Assigning importance to visual perception is not to suggest greater or lesser optical ability in early people; rather it is to call attention to the reality of two-dimensional vision. Many masks were two-dimensional but were made in a way to suggest depth and the illusion of the third dimension (See drawing 4.11). Other masks demonstrated illusionary third dimension and were frontal by design. They gave the viewer a symbolic reference rather than a visual representation of the referenced image.

Mask Making as a Social Phenomenon

Although masks had similar functions in different cultures, distinct styles, shapes, colors, designs, and construction techniques made use of various materials and served different social objectives. The masks produced by the Aztec of Mesoamerica when compared with like objects made by the Ibo of West Africa, the Batak of Sumatra, or the Inuit of North America are very distinct. However, to understand the implications of masking, each cultural area must be considered as an inclusive whole (rather than exclusive) realizing that the total mask production is distinguishable from pieces made elsewhere. Also, the masks made in a particular area or region must be viewed as a continuum that was in constant realignment to accommodate internal and external influences. When two societies clashed, there was a tendency to destroy the old bases of morality, tradition, and social order including the cultural elements and to substitute nothing new in their place. The resulting void caused a loss of identity and direction. Eventually, a new social base was formulated drawing on characteristics of both the oppressor and the oppressed. Out of social chaos comes a "new" method of expressing "old" ideas—a pan-cultural solution.

As traditional and technical determinants influenced mask production, there were distinct periods of stylistic development that can be identified and described. Furthermore, within most cultures those influences had a degree of effect on different subgroups. To confound the stylistic

Drawing 4.11 Wagoma-Babuye shield mask made in Zaire. This interesting mask is made of wood with shallow carved areas. It has slit eyes, an exaggerated nose that continues into the forehead, and painted vertical stripes. The mask was repaired to extend its life. When "worn" this mask was held by the short handle at the bottom and positioned in front of the person's face.

identification issue further, an individual image maker might decide against adopting a new technique for the sake of tradition and continue to work in the old way. In addition, although certain imaging styles were related to a specific ethnic group, there could be a series of discernible local substyles.[60] Each of the substyles had an equal level of credibility that warranted recognition.

Masks, despite the varied influences, were seldom made to produce a pleasurable illusion. However, some had the role of presenting a culturally accepted ideal of beauty. An example of this concept was the notion of beauty associated with certain masking traditions including the Dan masks of West Africa that represented the idealized female. Also, Chinese and Japanese theatre masks were used to personify the ultimate "beautiful woman," and the Ibo's "White Maiden" masks illustrated the idea of beauty (see drawing 4.12). Those masks related to the transcendent female authority that gave attention to beauty as an element of social centrality.

The images presented by masks, although culturally significant, seldom conformed to the classical notion of sculpture when applying the "Western art" criteria. However, in many parts of the world, masks and related cultural materials have become the "standard," representative image for a particular people or culture. Rightly or wrongly, the image that comes to mind when considering the material culture of Africa or Oceania is often a mask. This association can be viewed as a positive endorsement of the developmental process for image making in that the mask, in its earliest forms, joined perception (the senses) and thought within the boundaries of environmental

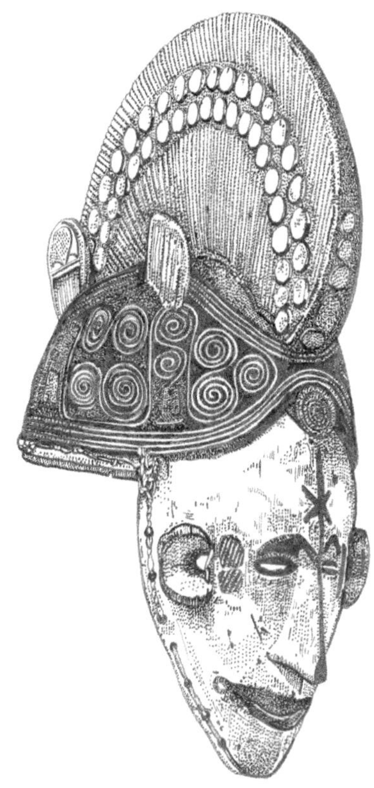

Drawing 4.12 "White Maiden" (***mmwo***) mask made by the Ibo people of Nigeria. This carved and painted wood mask depicted the ideal of Ibo beauty. Male masqueraders wore these masks in the annual "fame of maidens" festival. The masks were to represent adolescent girls and embodied the ideals of feminine beauty including a pale complexion, slender nose, and delicate mouth.

conditions. "…[T]here was much evidence that truly productive thinking in whatever area of cognition [took] place in the realm of imagery."[61]

Various persons have argued that art and beauty are directly linked, if not synonymous. However, that assumption is unlikely because there can be no dependency of one on the other, nor is it reasonable to assume that the same standards can or should be applied when determining the essence of either art or beauty. If the presumption is made that art is defined as meaning that which is aesthetically pleasing, that the notion of "pleasing" is in the eye and mind of the beholder, and that the same can be said of "beauty," then art and beauty can be joined. Obviously, these qualifying factors negate the general application of this concept. Art cannot be a manifestation of an arbitrary attribute called beauty, nor is it inevitably an expression of human emotion or pleasure, but it may include all these qualities.

Masks are a visually acknowledged image created by humans in a method requiring a certain level of skill. Therefore, they met the basic requirements to be called art.[62] Art also can be considered a practice or system of principles and methods employed in performing certain activities. However, neither of these approaches considers the complexity of producing an object of cultural significance (or art). The category of art is a concept into which some objects fit more easily than others.

It is unnecessary for all emotional expression to be deemed art. By present day standards, an object that is considered a unique assemblage of emotional tension, creative energy, and skillful use of materials will be preserved and takes its place among the paradigms of artistic achievement.[63] It is difficult, from this perspective, to understand that many masks were made to be consumed (depleted) by their use and they had no meaning once the associated purpose that precipitated their creation was completed. The role of the mask was to evoke an emotional and physical response from the viewers that reflected the message being projected by the presenter (see drawings 1.10, 2.2, and 3.9). Once that mission was accomplished, the mask had fulfilled its purpose.

The Visual Significance of Masks

The visual significance of most traditional imagery cannot be judged according to external or contemporary standards as both are relative assessments. The European artists of the late nineteenth century saw a freedom of expression in African-made objects that reflected their aesthetic values. Those image makers viewed the objects from the perspective of their European traditions and standards rather than those of the African. Undoubtedly this attitude was not limited to a particular place in time, nor can it be said to be a negative assessment; it was, however, a situation common to cross-cultural exchange.

A mask can be described as beautiful or ugly according to the subjective assessment of the viewer. However, those value judgments should be determined according to the unity and harmony of the parts of the mask rather than externally assigned measures. Unsightliness often was made a part of the "beauty" of a mask and an integral part of the impression made by the whole image (see drawing 4.13). "The interpretation of the symbols conveyed through the works of art [masks], then, can accommodate the unusual motif and form."[64] In addition, while the images incorporated in masks often were obscure or unusual, the meanings were expressively clear within the context of the intended use.

There were some persons among the makers of masks who had the imagination to create things anew; however, most were workers who repeated or elaborated an established pattern. The imagers essentialized nature and took from it what could be used as a source of inspiration. The representational aspects of image making can be defined in relation to the historico-social realities of the time and place in which the imagers lived. The concept of representationalism must take into consideration the inevitable social and intellectual transformation of the imagination. There was an implicit notion of an inherent materiality in the concept of realism that was a part of mask making since the first people covered their faces for ritual purposes.

Masks have had many different roles in cultural reality depending on the society and the particular needs, both secular and sacred, of that people. The tendency was for masks to formalize those aspects of life that transcended normal perception. Thus, they give substance to beliefs and, in some instances, desires that had no material presence. The masks allowed the users to encounter a type of reality (or actuality) that was contrived through the symbols of their culture.[65]

Unlike many traditional three-dimensional forms that included the entire figure, masks relied on the head to express an attitude that was essentially spiritual. The general attitude of the mask wearer was enhanced by the positions of the limbs, the accompanying music and dance, and the related

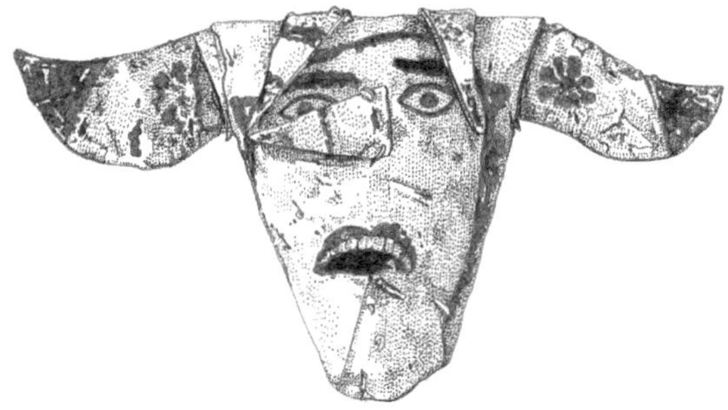

Drawing 4.13 Chapayekas mask worn during the Lenten ceremonies by the Yaqui Indians of northern Mexico. Chapayekas are the common soldiers of the Fariseos (Pharisees). They represented the people condemned for persecuting Christ.[1] The masks are called *sewa* or flowers. They were traditionally made of hide although other materials, such as cardboard and tin, were used. There are two types of masks. The older, more traditional masks have various designs that represented bulls, goats, rabbits, or bats. The newer masks are manlike but with long ears, short horns, and a pointed nose.

regalia, but the head (mask) was the prominent feature. Mask representations often included the idealized configuration associated with the particular subject. For example, the animal mask normally drew attention to the mouth as the principal organ of nourishment (see drawing 1.11). The other features of the mask related to the eyes as helpers to fulfill their particular functions in the nourishment process.[66] This concept was reflected in other identifying features depending on the subject and purpose of the mask.

The mouth, the opening through which the breath passed, was considered in many societies the most prominent feature of the human face. Other peoples viewed the upper part of the face, the forehead and brow, as the location of the spirit/soul, and for them that area was of primary significance. The eyes were believed to be of singular importance because they called attention to the ubiquitous nature of the particular deity/spirit. For some people, the nose or ears were given prominence as the physical manifestations of the associated attributes of selected spirit forms. The image assignment — the symbolic reference — aided in the recognition of the particular being and facilitated the mask-making process.

In only a few instances were attempts made to depict a specific person or beast, and in those instances the methodology was to emphasize a particular characteristic or anomaly. This approach produced masks with distinguishing features. Beasts had oversized and particularly vicious-looking teeth, exaggerated horns, or humanized characteristics. Masks with anthropomorphic attributes were given excessively delicate or grotesque features such as large eyes, big ears, and a unique hairstyle (see drawings 2.9, 2.11, and 3.7). Exaggeration was a method of focusing attention on those elements that appealed to the image maker's sense of identification.

5

Masks, Magic, and Power

Sculptured objects, including figures and masks, were often used in magical practices, with a number of other, sometimes unpleasant materials, including grasses, blood, animal skins, and viscera. Sometimes, carvings were given magical potency by the application of certain colors or painted designs; in other instances the shape of the sculptured form was in itself sufficient.[1]

It may be assumed that in the beginning, humankind was content to survive. Being weaker, slower, and less voracious than most of the carnivores that inhabited their world, the needs of daily existence were paramount. To cope with that potentially disastrous situation, early humans relied on their superior attributes including simple problem solving and the ability to shape and use tools and weapons. Once dependence was placed on external objects, a new dynamic became an integral part of human existence.

For thousands of years the primary motivating intellectual force for humans was emotion, and the most dominant emotion was fear. An external or extra-human force was needed to ameliorate that sentiment and to explain the unknown elements that influenced most aspects of human physical and emotional survival. With that transfer of emotion to the supernatural, people developed a new attitude toward existence and gave substance to basal emotion. By giving "fear" a tangible form, it could be confronted, manipulated, placated, hated, and sometimes bribed and abated.

The control of the spirits and the actions they represented caused the founding of the manipulatory activity described as "magic."[2] The relationship between magic and religion has been debated for years, and the association is one that differs from culture to culture. In general terms, magic is the belief that individuals may directly affect or impact nature or other beings, for good or bad, by their own efforts, actions, or deeds. Religion seeks to do the same thing but through prayer or sacrifice to a greater (divine) power.[3]

Magic is a generally applied term to describe that supernatural energy that is beyond the ordinary powers of humans and outside the common processes of nature.[4] Peoples in all areas of the world recognized a similar energy of occult power for which they had specific applications and unique systems of belief. According to those beliefs, both positive and negative forces were recognized, named, defined, and celebrated.

Nearly all cultural groups knew and respected the forces of the supernatural, and each developed ritual and ceremonial practices for dealing with those powerful and often unpredictable forces.

Magic, as an inclusive belief system, facilitated communication with immutable "greater beings" in contrast with the world of humans that was filled with uncertainties. As a means of dealing with routine anomalies, magic was considered an alternative to more structured belief systems. In its primary application, magic was direct and facilitated action. The results of magic were believed to be the automatic outcome of properly performed rites and correctly recited spells. Other belief systems required a spiritual intermediary to receive the request for action, and the spirit messenger may or may not choose to accommodate the request. Magic in most societies was a part of a complex belief system that sought both direct and indirect interventions on behalf of the requesting individual or group. It provided explanations that met the human need for an understandable and responsive world.[5]

In its strengths and weaknesses, magic corresponded to the social situation from which it evolved.[6] Intellectual and emotional submission was included in all aspects of belief, and absolute belief was required for it to be effective. The practitioner had to believe in the effectiveness of the technique, the patient or victim had to believe in the power of the practitioner, and the resident group had to believe in the possibility of the magical process.[7]

Masks and the Status of Magical Power

Magic for most people was a primary element of survival. It was a blend of coercion, manipulation, placation, and wishful thinking. It was the "first explanation of the interaction of the ego and the object."[8] The application of magical influence from a strictly practical perspective had primary importance in satisfying the need for food, shelter, physical well-being, and fulfilling the reproductive instinct. That same cultural prescription was apparent in the various symbols (including sexual maturity) that were inherent in masking and intended to enhance the reproductive and restorative processes.

Black and white — beneficial or malevolent — magic was installed into a socially defined practice by an unorganized mass of beliefs, practices, and superstitions. It (magic) was associated with tradition and unregulated by science or logic. Masks and masking have a long-held position as part of the magic-inducing process because magical power was often associated with prescriptive objects. Magic also had an affiliation with symbolic numbers, colors, sounds, gestures, names, times, and places. In addition, although there was nothing particularly magical in most "magic activities," the psychological influence of pseudo-scientific manifestations had a tremendous impact upon receptive participants.

The various applications of magic were recognition of the metaphysical powers capable of being controlled, directed, and used by humans. Therefore, magic as a practice was the utilization of that power for private or public purposes, and its significance varied according to the values assigned by a particular society at a particular time.[9] Magic or magic-inspired beliefs often came from the distant past, and they were bequeathed as a precious legacy from mythical ancestors to the people. No culture was exempt from that legacy.

Magic related to the special power of words (oaths, chants, and enactments) and images (masks and fetishes) and was central to the belief of most traditional peoples. The connections between magical beings and objects were created by shared properties such as color, shape, sound, and impression. These relationships were obvious to the originating society but often irrelevant or invisible to a recognition system outside the group. Once the connection between the seen and the unseen was made, it was possible to transfer qualities from one sphere to another (material to spiritual) or to influence one by actions performed on the other.[10] The power of the image (the visual material or "seen" element of the interaction) was greatly increased when it was modeled as a mask and used as an element of a ritual activity to influence the spiritual ("unseen") entities.

Undoubtedly, the belief in magic was validated by the experiences of daily life. The objectives of magical intervention in mundane activities were often attained — the lost was found, the ill recovered, a wrong was righted, and an apparently overwhelming situation was resolved. How the desired results were accomplished was an irrelevant factor after the fact. There were no inquiries into the laws of chance or probabilities, the powers of suggestion, or the natural course of events. Magical intervention was sought, and the desired results were thought achieved. In those situations when the desired results were not gained, any number of outside forces could have interfered with the magical process.

To illustrate the practicality of magic it is only necessary to consider the daily circumstances of early humans. For example, illness in all forms caused a great deal of insecurity; consequently, there were various magical cures for treating disease. Many of those curative activities included the use of masked interveners, shamans, or "medicine-men." An example of that application was the cornhusk masks of the Iroquois Husk Face Society (see drawing 5.1). These medicine society masks represented mythic figures in the curing ceremony, and they were believed to possess great power to exorcise disease.[11]

"It seems that the evolution of the human mind has only been biologically possible for so long because we continue to believe that existence has meaning and some sort of a cosmic reference."[12] Belief was a part of the biological process. People were what they believed themselves to be, and those beliefs were always relative to a people's collective intellect and range of experience. The connection between ideas and outcomes was true only for the experience

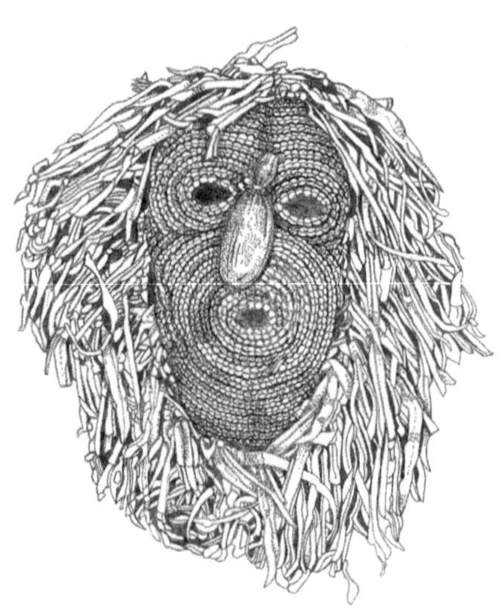

Drawing 5.1 Cornhusk mask made by the Seneca Iroquois people. This mask of the "Bushyheads" or Husk Face Society was made by the women to honor vegetation spirits — mythological "farmers" who lived on the other side of the world. Those wearing the cornhusk mask were "...messengers of the Three sisters — Corn, Beans, and Squash.... Their presence is a sign of good fortune for the next growing season."[m]

prevailing at a particular moment. Later, the connection could be replaced by new beliefs in conformity with the world of things and attitudes to which those beliefs belonged. Both the positive and negative aspects of human reality were included in extant beliefs.

Although some cultures chose to distinguish magic from ordinary daily activities, it was not entirely separated from many aspects of material life. It was a complement to the most basic survival schemes. Magic gave expression to the desires and wishes of a person or a group of people. It often provided the requisite confidence to accomplish a challenging task by reinforcing emotional resolve. The tenets of magic had universal appeal. They played upon the psychological features of all humans and fell within the accepted social patterns of group mentality. Magical activities, for that reason, must be viewed as a part of a larger cultural pattern that could not be understood if considered out of context.

From the beginning of human consciousness, people developed ideas about their environment and the conditions in which they existed. They probably had thoughts about the world and what could be done to alter their lives and to achieve greater security. They undoubtedly considered what outcomes were desirable and assessed the probability of achieving those goals. Those attitudes about the environment in which they lived became a part of their cultural tradition.[13] As an essential element of their socio-cultural adaptation, people developed methods for dealing with the unprecedented through trickery, magic, conflict, and other socially defined solutions.

All major cultural systems included magic as a way of relating to the supernatural beings that were omnipresent and influenced every activity. Magic was an accepted method for resolving problems regulated by forces that seem to have no mortally recognized or socially accepted solutions. To facilitate that act of intervention, the shaman (sometimes called a medicine man or priest) was a specialist, as was the mask maker. Often, both the shaman and mask maker took part in ameliorating the unforeseen events of daily life. Since certain types of masks were needed for each specific occasion, the task of mask making required specialized skill, knowledge, and experience. Each mask had to conform to the requirements of the group's tradition and to symbolize accepted concepts of a particular deity or spirit being.[14] The innovation of masks as a means of association with deities was a phenomenal advancement for human intellect because it transformed an abstract concept into a recognizable symbol.

Magic and the Principles of Similarity and Contrast

A people's beliefs influenced what they saw, and what they saw reinforced their beliefs. This basic concept directly influenced the two principles upon which magic was based. According to J. G. Frazer,[15] those principles were the Law of Similarity and the Law of Contact, and while recent scholarship has challenged these theories, they retain practical validity. The Law of Similarity assumed that an act or action can be recreated by imitation, and the Law of Contact inferred that whatever was done to a material object affected equally the person with whom it came into contact. Charms based on the Law of Similarity called upon the powers of homeopathic or

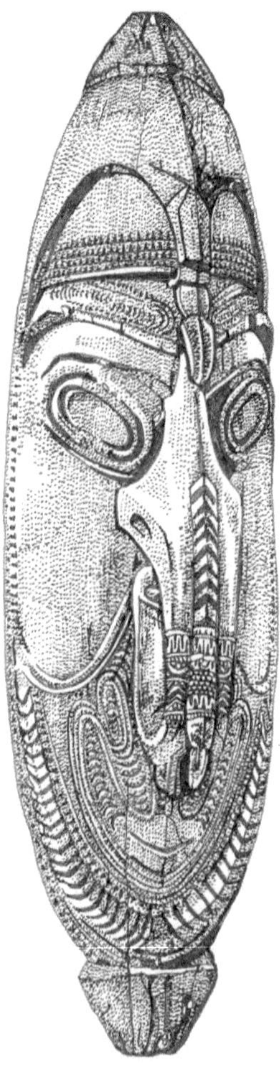

Drawing 5.2 Ancestor or spirit mask (*tumbuna*) from the village of Mindum near the mouth of the Sepik River, New Guinea. This mask was made of mangrove wood and has no paint or other decorations. The lack of adornment suggests that the mask remained in the spirit house until its power was transferred to a replacement piece. Once the spirit left the mask, it had no value to the people who created it.

imitative magic, while those associated with the Law of Contact may be called contagious magic.

The concepts of similarity and contact were considered to have universal application. Therefore, magic was viewed as a system of natural laws that ruled the events of the world, and when viewed from the prescientific viewpoint the idea appeared plausible. The level of credibility increased when early people viewed life from two fundamental perspectives— one real and one imaginary. Real life dealt with daily existence and perpetuated the real history of the people. That life was formed by tradition and custom. It was a process of imitating the past. Conversely, imaginary life found reasons for the unknown, unexplained, and unorthodox. It took the people from their menial, sometimes frightening and normally difficult lives by allowing them to imagine a better existence in the inner sanctum of the spirit world. Masks and masking found a purpose and an application in both worlds (see drawing 5.2).

It can be presumed that early magicians believed fully in the art that they practiced, for they were of the same people and time as their audience. Both forms of magic — similarity and contact — were considered "sympathetic" in nature. This idea has been explained as a process where ". . . things act[ed] on each other at a distance through a secret sympathy, the impulse being transmitted from one to the other by means of what we may conceive as a kind of invisible ether...."[16]

The power of sympathetic magic was the most commonly held belief among practitioners. Early people believed that pantomiming an act or event (often using a mask) with an adequate amount of passion and devotion would cause that event to take place. The hunter stalked an animal in a prehunt ceremony and symbolically killed the beast with arrow or spear. The successful completion of the ceremony assured the desired results in the actual hunt. Masks were used as a unifying element to align the hunter in the most sympathetic way with the animals and their spirits. Beliefs, magic, and masks were necessary and purposeful parts of the practices of survival.

Belief in similar or imitative actions had a very real application in most early cultures, and those attitudes were specifically related to the use of masks. If it was believed that destroying a figure in effigy caused harm to the individual, then it was equally conceivable that wearing an animal mask and dancing in a way that mimicked the animal's movements aided in the hunt or contributed to the abundance of the herd (see drawing 5.3).

Magic was a process of cause and effect. It was the necessary basis of all early human reasoning and experience.[17] It was also illusionary, and the first requirement for belief in illusion was desire. Masking gave substance to the illusion that proposed to fulfill the desires of the people. The notion of seeking a truth that existed outside the limits of many non-truths was difficult to accept at any time, and the difficulties were compounded when attempting to form that truth on logical and intellectual reasoning. Consequently, accepting anticipated or self-serving solutions for difficult or unexplainable problems deceived people.

However, not all magical deception was trickery to mislead the viewer. In some rituals and ceremonies, the seeming magical transfer of human suffering or pain to an inanimate object was a psychological incentive to relieve the physiological condition. Native American magicians (called jugglers) handled hot coals during curative rituals, and in so doing gave the patient confidence in their "special" pow-

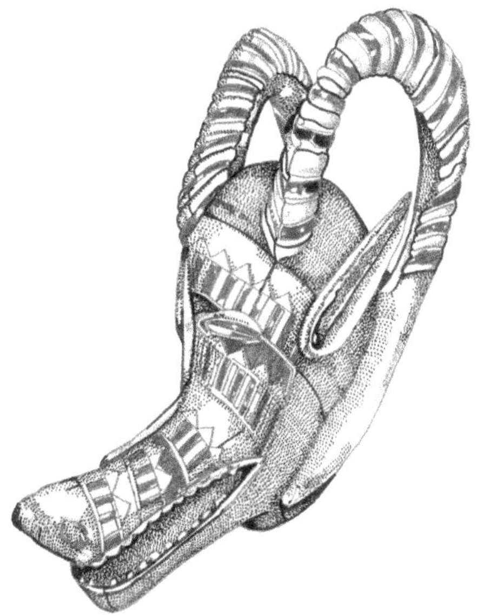

Drawing 5.3 *Bobo* antelope mask from Burkina Faso made of carved and painted wood. This mask is easily identifiable with the particular animal because of its careful carving and representative style. The horn shapes are banded in red and black.

ers. While there were spiritual usurpers in many lands and among many peoples, to assume that all ritual performances were no more than "slight-of-hand acts" is to ignore the power and purpose of the shaman and to disregard the cultural foundation that motivated them.

Magic required a visual manifestation of the magical act to be effective. In keeping with that notion, the magician or shaman caused "something" to happen as a demonstration of power. That causation was an extension of the belief that magic was a means/ends process in which certain predetermined steps were taken in a systematic progression (means) to achieve a calculated or anticipated result (end). Despite the degree of social development, the means/ends process often was applied without total understanding of either the means or the projected outcome (end). This approach reinforced the assumption that certain acts or actions could be recreated by imitation or playacting. Masks were a singularly important element in imitating spirit/deity-related activities. They aided in the symbolic transformation from the realm of the natural to the supernatural (see drawing 5.4).

The magic worked with symbols, as did almost all human action. It appeared to be a celebration of the symbolic energy, a half-exuberant, half-terrified flexing of magical powers or a discovery and exploration of its remarkable potentiality. Masks, chants, songs, and power words were a part of the act of magical initiation performed by selected persons to achieve specific results. Magic, through these activities, became a social event that involved methods recognized by society for achieving established ends, and although those ends could be negative for some persons, they were understandable by the group although the actual methods for gaining the ends were not understood by all members.

Magic in all its manifestations promoted the idea that there was more to the universe than was readily perceived and that power over all things natural and supernatural was the ultimate goal. The possibility or promise of power was perhaps the reason that magic was such a force in the life of most early people. Magic was about power, and it was successful often enough that until there was a more effective way of gaining the desired results, people continued to believe in traditional magic-inspired practices.

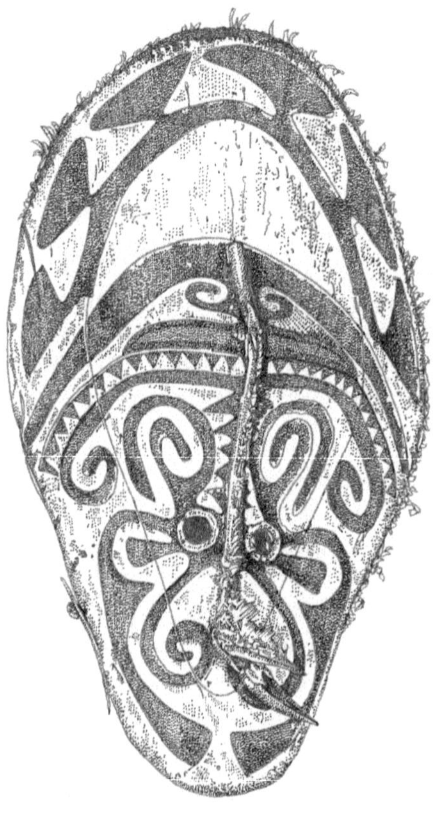

Drawing 5.4 A peace mask made by the people of New Ireland, a volcanic island of the southwest Pacific Ocean in the Bismarck Archipelago belonging to Papua, New Guinea. These painted bark cloth masks were worn on the first of May as enemies gathered for eating and dancing. One day each year they set aside active warfare to share a peaceful repast.

Magic as a Psychological Source of Power

The struggle for existence was, to a greater or lesser degree, a part of all phases of human life. This truism influenced the daily activities of people since humankind first evolved, and to address those issues, early people felt the need to construct a protection system of magical observances.[18] Magic allowed people to formulate a personalized protection system and to believe that which they desired was within reach. It also accepted self-delusion when circumstances were too distorted to achieve a desired outcome. The power of belief energized a force stronger than reality. However, it cannot be denied that the intensified self-confidence produced by genuine magical observance influenced daily existence. Any number of acts and activities, natural or human caused, were attributed to magical intervention. Inexplicable phenomena were assigned to the will of a particular deity or to sorcery, witchcraft, magic, or alchemy. Illness, drought, and famine as well as life and death were viewed as magical manifestations unexplainable in human terms.

When the primary purpose of magic was to compel the spirits or deities to comply with the wishes of the magician, then the results were easily observed. If the patient died, the magic failed; if the rains came and the crops flourished, the magic was a success. The process was self-fulfilling. People motivated by the need to vitalize economic success or ameliorate social insecurity relied on magic as a way of deliverance from their predicaments.

Masked rites associated with magical observances often were detached from the activities of daily life. They took place in an atmosphere that was paranormal, which added to their special character. They were performed in a time-honored method and often to the accompaniment of chants, songs, and dances. The overriding purpose of the magical activities was to explain, direct, or control the real and unreal worlds by ordering and validating community experience in terms of its own rationalization. Social systems and magical practices were mutually reinforcing, and it was that sense of magical release that freed masked persons from the responsibilities and reality of daily life. Magical transformation, regardless of the purpose of the mask, altered the deterministic process and facilitated emotional emancipation. Perhaps the person behind the mask inscribed in himself or herself the power related to the role portrayed and became the principle of his or her own subjugation. The experiences caused a paramnesic mental state that distorted recollection (memory) and allowed fantasy and objective experience to become confused.

Masks and masked activities were utilized to manipulate perception and emotion. They were instruments of power that attracted and focused attention. Masks incorporated numerous symbolic themes. They represented the "power beings" transported into the world of humans or served as vehicles to convey the viewer into the spirit world. The mask in many societies was the agent of action and the means and method for achieving a desired social or personal outcome. The masks, like magic, were both real and unreal — the symbolic reference and the human agent.

Often the outward appearance of masks conveyed magic and mystery as well as cultural recognition. The prevailing physiognomy depended on the perspective of the viewer. Undoubtedly, the social and ideological role of masks varies greatly from region to region and people to people because there was constant interplay among the environment, social experience, cultural contact, subsistence, and numerous other factors both natural and human caused that led to the making and using of masks. Although the relationships often were subtle, every factor that influenced the values and identity of a people altered their beliefs and affected their association with the metaphysical world.

The Sociological Significance of Masks and Magic

Many practices of archaic humans can be described as magical in orientation, and there has been much discussion about whether religion or magic came first. Some researchers have proposed that magic originated before religion because early peoples sought to compel supernatural forces to do their will by voicing specific words or phrases or by performing certain rituals. Magicians viewed the spirits as fundamentally malevolent and therefore subject to the same manipulations as humans. By contrast, most religious orders believed their deities to be gracious, compassionate, and above human frailties. There was no reverence in magic.

Early humans validated their lack of understanding of the unknown energy sources by transferring the communication process to the domain of magic for interaction with the forces of nature. Human motives and propensities were assigned by that act of transferal to those forces, and they were humanized. Early people believed there were spirits/deities that willed rain to fall, crops to grow, and the seasons to change and accounted for the unpredictability of nature. Once that supernatural assignation was made, it was possible to use the same means to deal with all phenomenological events. Therefore, in consideration of the complexities of human existence, eventually the world was populated with a pantheon of spirit forces.

To address the various roles assigned to spirit beings, magic became a social activity in which certain ritual actions were used to bring about the intervention of supernatural forces for special purposes. Magic was thought to identify the causes of human misery and offer hope for deliverance in the most desperate circumstances. It was a means for humans to deflect or redirect the forces of fate. The magical practices of early people provided the group with a scheme of social control that resulted in a sense of equanimity not found in later societies.[19] Magic was, in practice, a process or technique intended to achieve an identified purpose using mystical power.

Although magic in its earliest form was a part of the daily life of every person as intervention expectations grew and the practices became more complex, the magic-related practices generally were assigned to one member of the group. This decision corresponded to the natural evolution of social order — specialization through the division of labor or duty. The shaman or medicine man in that societal structure was recognized as the practitioner of magic, and in fulfilling that role, it is possible that the shaman was also the maker of the first mask[20] (see drawing 5.5).

Magic was not attached to a particular source and was thought conveyed by almost anything natural or human made. An unexplained force influenced anything and everything beyond the ordinary limits of mortal reasoning. Magic existed outside the common processes of nature but was ever present. It manifested itself in many ways but was most often recognized by the unexplained results that could only be ascribed to its existence. When magic is viewed from that perspective it is easy to understand why early people relegated the uncertainties of daily life to magical or mystical beings and why those practices continued for generations. Events in nature required elucidation, and the most acceptable explanation was to assign them to the supernatural.

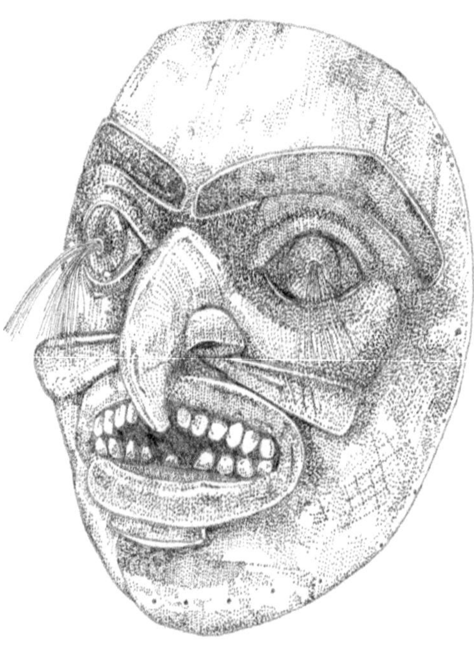

Drawing 5.5 A carved and painted Tlingit shaman mask from the Northwest Coast of North America. Most Tlingit shaman masks have closed eyes, perhaps representing death or the transitional period between life and death. This mask has two distinct features that make it unique. The exaggerated nose probably represents the female salmon spirit, but the tufts of hair emanating from the eyes have no established pupose. The hair may suggest vision or light that goes beyond earthly perception.

Magic and the Influence of Supernatural Energy

Only in recent history have people existed apart from the natural and supernatural world. Magic until that time pertained to all supernatural powers that influenced natural events and was often employed broadly in the sense that it was used to describe acts that transcend rational explanation. The shaman, as the central figure of the belief system, was the mediator between the two worlds—the natural and supernatural. His or her role was to serve the interests of a particular community. Magical practice included attitudes associated with the concepts of "white" or "good" magic. However, black magic was a practice of enchantment that corresponded to the sorcerous activities and was intended to do harm. Voodoo (vodun, vodu, or vodau) was a form of sorcery that originated in West Africa and was generally associated with fetishes. Magical practices contemporaneously described as witchcraft were associated with powers derived from evil spirits.

The symbolic realignment of magical elements in those practices was part of the expectancy of physical existence. The ability to change forms, to adopt another persona, and to control the various embodiments of human or animal anatomy were elements of magical significance. The mask was a part of this metamorphic process. It was a way of representing and regulating the spirits—the "real" face in which the spirits could reside (see drawing 5.6).

The anthropomorphization of spirits was a common and persistent practice. By assigning human characteristics to the deities, they were more approachable as well as more comprehensible. Only the body, in some circumstances, was humanoid while the head was replaced by that of an animal. The entire persona was one of a human/animal amalgamation in other representations. This transformation was not necessarily based on the belief that the spirit being had the physical appearance of an animal but that they embodied the characteristic of a particular beast or

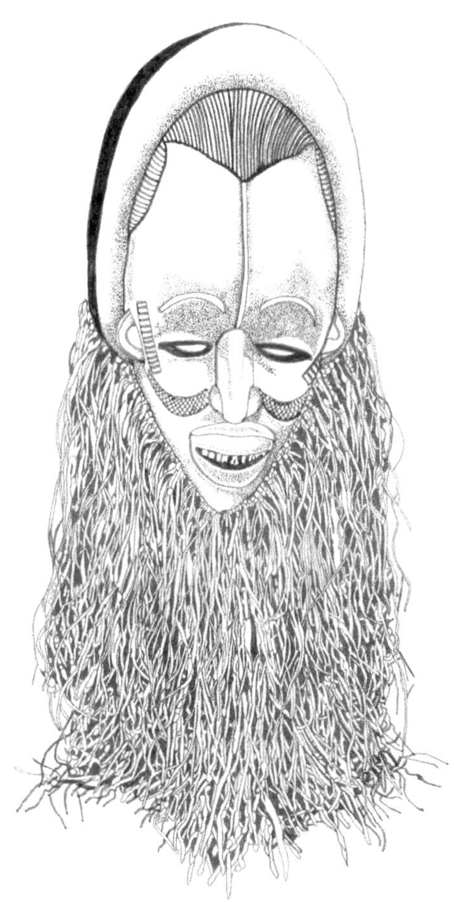

Drawing 5.6 This mask appears to be Dan from the Ivory Coast. The Dan are also known as Yacouba. Typical Dan masks have idealized human faces and smooth, polished surfaces. This piece has slit eyes and scarification marks on the cheeks—features found on Dan masks. The raised vertical line from nose to hairline, the raffia beard, and the exaggerated hairstyle suggest the influence of the Guere-Wobe group that lived in the same area as the Dan and adopted the Dan style.

fowl. From that notion to the wearing of a representative mask or costume to attract the attention of the spirit/deity was a minor step (see drawing 5.7).

The belief that magicians could transform themselves into animals was nearly as universal in "traditional" societies as the belief in magical healing.[21] Animals associated with transformation differ according to the society in which the reported act took place. In parts of Europe the animal "of choice" for transformation was the wolf; in other locations it was the eagle, raven, bat, fox, crocodile, or various snakes, reptiles, and fish. Some of the animal forms were associated with good (white) magic and some with bad (black) magic. Masks were a common form of animal identification. This masking practice was exemplified by the Ancient Egyptian jackal's mask that had a role of deception in the humanized form of Anabis that was associated with the cult of Isis.[22]

An omnipresent animal transformation belief closely associated with magic and sorcery was that of were-animals. Moreover, while superstitions and myths dealt with were-animals in different ways, from the hysterical to heroic, there were certain universal correlations. The belief that unknown forces could assume a form that played on existing fears or envy was ubiquitous. As one example of this proclivity, the belief in werewolves was most common in regions of Europe where wolves were routinely encountered. Conversely, in England, where wolves were eliminated by 1500 CE, little was recorded about lycanthropy.[23] Tales and myths of other forms of transformation that included dreadful consequences were intended as regulatory measures to control or direct social behavior.

By anthropomorphizing the spirits, they could be caused to serve society in a positive way by promises of sacrifices or threats of rejection. That approach followed the belief that an objective could be achieved by a consciously abnormal concentration of will power.[24] A small-scale imitation of the desired act or action was performed to supplement the concentrated effort. Wearing an animal mask and making the movements of the represented animal to guarantee its accessibility to hunters or sprinkling water to attract rain exemplify that kind of endeavor. It was believed there was a sympathetic or corresponding relationship between like activities in the spirit world and those in the terrestrial domain.

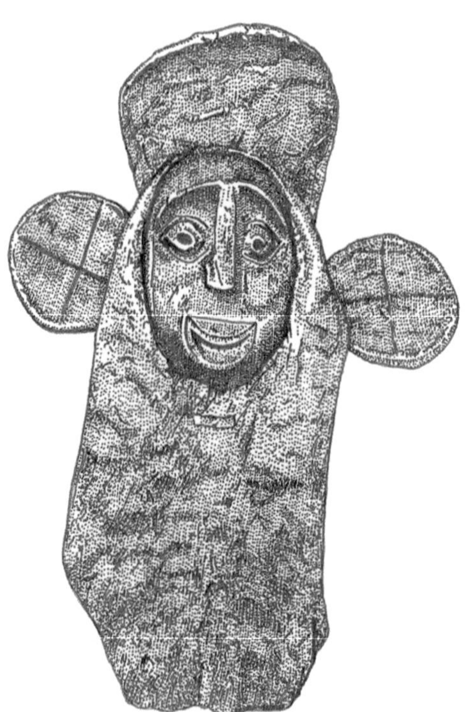

Drawing 5.7 A mask from Peru made of painted wood and bark cloth. The face is carved softwood that was attached to a bark-cloth hood. The eyes are inlaid with mica to give an "other-world" or "far-sighted" appearance. Men wore masks of this type during ceremonial performances.

Magic as an Integral Part of the Life Cycle

Magic is considered an art so ancient that there is no known source other than revelation by a power associated with magic itself — a spirit or deity. Belief in magic and the secret arts was inevitable for early people. It reinforced basic beliefs and validated the acceptance of necromancy. Magic in its various forms was an effective and accepted method for explaining, empowering, and manipulating both the material and spiritual elements of human existence.[25] To accomplish that goal, magic often used spiritual intermediaries, and masking was an integral part of the process. The intermediaries had different appearances and if they were not directly involved in magical intervention, they provided the appropriate charms, incantations, or spells to empower the magicians.

Magic in many societies was an activity carried out on behalf of an individual at times of crisis. It was a part of human history and an undeniable element in the development of social order. Spiritual beings were often credited with knowledge of magic. They were believed to have handed it down to humans and sometimes used it in their relations with the people.[26]

Humans tried to develop a practical relationship with the power that was resident in all animate and inanimate objects. In different lands, it was called by different names including "vital energy" by the Chinese, "*prama*" by the Hindus, "*mana*" by the Polynesians, and in Africa and the Americas it had many names. "Its manifestation in the universe was described by modern physical science through such concepts as the mass/energy equation and the space/time continuum. Modern psychoanalysis refers to its manifestation in the human psyche as libido."[27]

The inclusion of "magical" practices was an aspect of many social activities. Webster[28] reported that part of the training given Maori neophytes joining the "priestly" (shaman) society included various forms of magic and ventriloquism. Among the indigenous peoples of North America, the handling of potentially dangerous objects or animals was a part of the initiation process, sleight-of-hand manipulation was used to give credibility to healing and divining activities, and various forms of trickery enhanced the believability of certain rituals.

Magic offered a view of life that was reduced in complexity. It demonstrated ways of coping with everyday activities and provided the means for humans to meet and accommodate the uncertainties they confronted. All things, tangible and intangible, were potential sources of magical activity. The mingling of the physical and the supernatural, human and animal, external and internal, or life and death provided an abundant range of opportunities for magical influence.[29] Masks reflected and perpet-

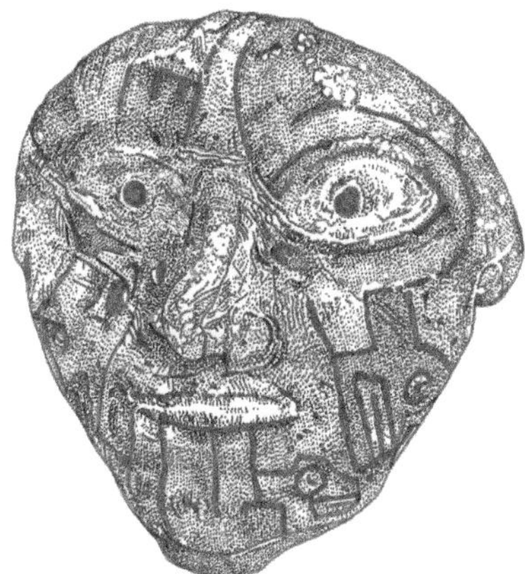

Drawing 5.8 **Peruvian mask made by the Coastal Tiahuanaco for attachment to a mummy bundle. This leather mask was originally painted red, black, and green. In addition to being attached to mummies, masks of this type were occasionally fastened to wooden idol figures.**

uated that dichotomy because they gave a view of both the secular and spiritual worlds (see drawing 5.8).

Magic, in most societies, appeared in various forms from the evil eye and soul stealing (black magic) to certain forms of folk medicine and psychic remedies (white magic). Removing a wart with a potato and kissing an injury to make it better were psychic emanation practices that were generally acceptable without the negative connotation of magical or paranormal activity. Wishing on a shooting star, carrying a rabbit's foot for good luck, and throwing a coin into a "wishing well" are examples of commonly held magical practices that are based on hope (or anticipation) and belief. The role of magic in psychological healing and physiological manipulation was extraordinary. Full knowledge of the mystical or magical nature of collective social action was understood by a limited number of people skilled in the practice of concealment and secrecy and possessing "hidden knowledge" of the principles of uncertainty.

Magic was a pseudo-action in that it was often a substitute for true action. In situations where humankind could not alter the effects of nature, magical activity provided a way for advocating an alternate action. Masked participants lent credibility to those activities. If that process changed emotional attitudes to reflect the anticipated outcome of the magical procedure, the belief was justified and an assumption of human power was maintained. The masks were the links between the earthbound petitioners and the controlling omnipresent beings.

Beneficent and maleficent magic were practice-allied activities. They were ways for adding, subtracting, or changing something because following the magical act the subject (object, practice, or activity) was altered. The alteration could be positive or negative. Normally, no "real" action occurred but because of the psychological and sociological association of the process with the anticipated outcome, the expected action was believed to follow the magical incantation. Magic was also wishful thinking. When a person wished to be physically stronger and believed they were, there was a likelihood that the desired prowess would exist for a short time. That outcome reflected subconscious manipulation. Magic rituals had remarkable effects that could be arranged on a continuum from almost-action through various degrees of defective (negative) action to almost effective (positive) action.

Faith and trust were elements of every early belief system, and when the welfare of the group depended on magical performance, the magician was elevated to a position of great importance and influence. Perhaps because early people were technologically unsophisticated, magic as spells, potions, and rituals was substituted for more systematic methods of intellectual, cultural, environmental, or physiological intervention.

Every magical activity was situation or circumstance oriented, and the correspondingly correct paraphernalia, including masks, had to be used to achieve the anticipated results (see drawing 5.9). While objective research might not have been a part of the early magician's repertoire, basic reasoning and observation-guided practical experience were components of most projections. There was an assumed link between cause and effect. The vengeance against an unknown wrongdoer could be claimed as successful with the illness or death of anyone and a plea for a good crop or successful hunt could be termed a success with minimal outcome. However, it was unlikely a magician or shaman would call for extraordinary results. They coordinated their entreaties with nature, the environment, and human conditions.

Magic was a nearly universal concept because of sociological and physiological expectations. Words for describing magical activities appeared in many languages, and those references described the same group of well-known, clearly identified, and unmistakable activities. The most recognizable magical occurrences related to "medical, ceremonial, religious, occult, paranormal, sectarian, and black magic."[30] One or more of those affiliations were synonymous with the meaning and idea of magic, and some of those same associations have continued to the present in facets of social development. Magic was a mirror that reflected society.

Magic Connection and Communication

One of the oldest and most fundamental of magical beliefs was that the name of an object embodied the basic nature of its being.[31] The distinction between the name and the object (or thing) was an intellectual decision. The charac-

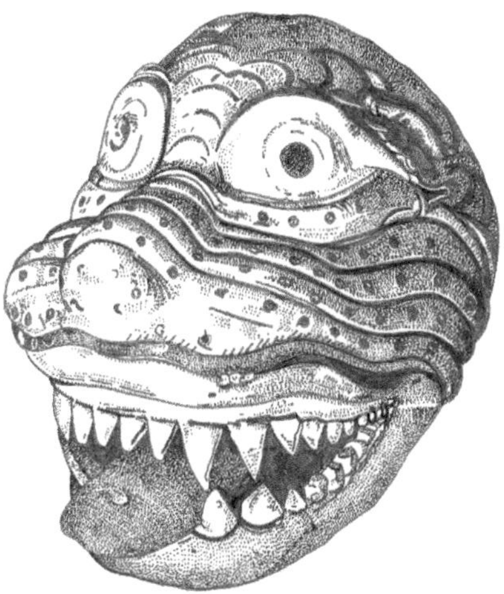

Drawing 5.9 A devil dance mask made in Ceylon. These carved and painted masks embodied evil spirits. They were used to lure the demons of fatal diseases away from their intended victims. The rounded shape of the head is repeated in the facial features, giving the "devil" a humorous quality. The masks were worn in pantomimes and plays.

teristics of the object, in magical theory, were signified in the name or its symbolic representation, including masks as a miniature version of the object. With that association in mind, it is easy to understand how the spirit being was identified with a mask carved in its society-defined image. Often, a mask was a human-size representation of a superhuman force. By name and appearance it was that force.

To associate magic with words, word sequences, symbol, or sound was a natural practice. Therefore, it is easy to assume that early people viewed the act of communication as a form of magic. The realization that spoken words conveyed the same meaning to a number of people must have had magical implications. Words and sounds connected a child to a parent even before the child knew the meaning of the words. In view of the magical significance of the spoken word, it is reasonable to believe that the same means of communication could connect humans with the inhabitants of the supernatural world.

As a socially recognized manifestation of their inherent power, words were assigned magical meanings that were believed to be sacred. Often the empowered words were restricted for use by especially authorized persons and were only used in conjunction with ritual activities. Words, in less formalized circumstances, were a part of the act of communication between humans and their deities and were available to all who wanted their personal wishes known. Those incantations, often associated with masking or special paraphernalia, were elements of daily ritual performed by those seeking assistance from their celestial benefactors. They also were a method of calling for assistance to impose negative energy or positive influences on the activities of others.

The use of certain words or phrases as part of the magical scheme was practiced in many parts of the world. The words were spoken, chanted, or sung, but if they were not voiced, the magical episode being promulgated was unlikely to be successful. The most common of this kind of verbal declaration was an oath of condemnation or an appeal for assistance. To harm an individual, an object belonging to that person was burned, pounded, or fed to animals while the person's name was spoken in a forceful and frightening manner. Only with the pronouncement of their name would harm befall that person. Masks were often used to emphasize the intent of the oath, and in early times, the emphatic connection was common.

The notion of "words of power" was so much a part of cultural traditions that great care was taken not to reveal a person's real name. This precaution stems from the belief that an evil spell could not be imposed on a person if their name were not a part of the magical oath or spell. Often, names were changed to avoid potential disaster, and women were known only by the family name or the husband's surname.[32] That practice was also associated with the naming of children, who often remained unnamed for some time after birth so they might avoid injury or death by magical intervention.

Many actions or activities required the proper accompanying blessings or curses as an appeal for assistance against the forces of the unknown. As examples of the force of words, the sinew used to sew a garment required a request for strength and durability just as a cooking pot, tool, or weapon was stronger when shaped while the appropriate words were chanted. The enemy died, crops grew, and animals were captured or slain when the right narration accompanied the magical act. The oath-making rites often required the participation of a masked practitioner to ensure their effectiveness. The connecting words and images facilitated the link between the human-originated request and the spirits capable of fulfilling the requested action.

Masks were powerful symbols that embodied the essence of magical power. They were used to gain the attention of the power source, and once the contact was made, the appropriate words focused the energy and completed the action. That practice was an integral part of many rituals and ceremonies.

Mystic Experience and Ecstatic Revelation

Magic had an impact upon that aspect of existence that fell outside the sphere of human control. Consequently, it satisfied a certain psychological need for people by giving human meanings to an indifferent and often hostile world. Early magical practice belonged to a domain where the "things" that happen appeared to be the result of chance or accident and where human activities were never certain of fulfillment. Magic offered a way of "dealing with forces and phenomena that otherwise appear incapable of control or [were] believed to contain an element of mystic danger that must be removed and nullified."[33] A model of the desired outcome was provided by magic. It was a process of encouragement rather than calculated coercion.

The division between cause and effect separated belief and outcome and attempted to control the former while depending on the latter. There was a tendency to divide the perceived world into individual and separate things that could be measured and categorized according to recognized values or outcomes. Magic was believed to influence the forces (cause) by demonstrating the desired outcomes (effects) and by connecting human activity with the environmental and ethereal forces.

Concurrent with the more holistic approach, some individuals needed to stay in communication with the spirits represented by a personal mask. That feeling was so strong that miniature masks were carried when the masker was away from the community (see drawing 5.10). Those miniatures were used when the masker was out of contact with the full-size and sacrosanct mask[34] and served as identification for contact with others belonging to the same secret society. The miniatures were described as "passport masks" among some African societies.

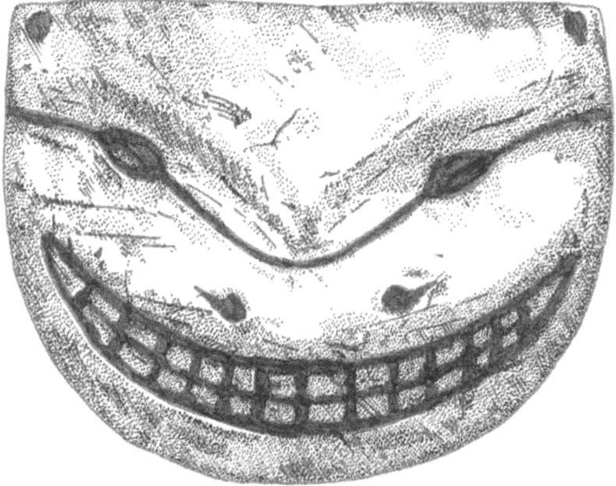

Drawing 5.10 A mask-shaped hair ornament in the form of a semi-human grimacing beast. The women of Sledge Island, Cape Vancouver, worn these carved ivory pieces. These mask forms were a part of the tradition of the people of the Bering Sea Complex (ca. 500 BCE–500 CE). The people made mask plaques and miniature masks until the middle of the second millennium of the current era. A similar creative process was practiced by the members of the Punuk Culture on the Asian side of the Bering Straits.

The mask as an object of magical importance was universally recognized. That attitude of magical identification has existed from prehistoric times. Masks as primary elements of ritual magic were made in Africa and North and South America; in Germany, Switzerland, the Balkans, and other European countries; in China, Japan, Tibet, India, Ceylon, Indonesia, and other Asian countries; and in many islands of the South Seas.[35]

The phenomenal power of nature was credited with generating magic, but it was enhanced, refined, and used by humans. The idea of magic as the source of life and all its related amenities was a simple concept. For early people, there was no science to explain why the sun rose or the rain fell. There was no evidential reasoning to determine why animals flourished and multiplied one year and died the next or why one person lived while another fell ill. The most reasonable answer to those anomalies was magic. That belief endowed many elements of nature with a superhuman presence; "the sun, the rain, the wind, the earth, each in itself, because of its magical properties, was considered to be divine."[36]

From early times, social and group needs were placed above those of the individual. Survival was a group process. Consequently, humans at all levels of societal development had disdain for uncertainty and a difficulty with noncommitment. Societies expected resident members to believe or not believe and to be either for or against a communal issue. Making a commitment was an expected social practice.

When early people found no easily explained reason for an act, condition, or circumstance, a reasonable justification was magic, black or white, malevolent or benevolent. That attitude, over time, became more refined and an organized system evolved that disavows much, but not all, magical affiliation.

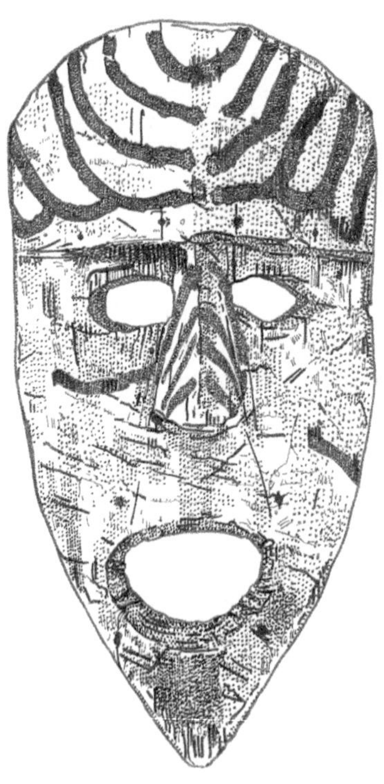

Drawing 5.11 A *Udegei* Khambabo (shaman's) mask from the Amur River region of Siberia. The simple but very powerful carved wood mask conveys a feeling of other worldness that epitomized the shaman's role within the socio-cultural community. The painted lines on the forehead have the appearance of antlers, representing either a link with animals or power rods of connection to the spirit world. This symbolic link between the material and ethereal worlds is found in many locations as both a statement of power and a quest for numinous energy.

Magic as a Counteraction to Fear and Nonhuman Forces

Early humans might have viewed themselves as frail and insignificant compared to the forces that surrounded them. They saw the energy of nature in many life-threatening forms, and they recognized their inability to change or alter that energy with the ordinary means available to them. That recognition reinforced the separation of humans and deities that held sway over their daily existence. To deal with those powers, the people turned inward to identify an energy source that they could call upon for assistance. This need evolved into an elaborate system of spirit helpers (familiars) to serve as intermediaries for conveying the wishes of humans to the all-powerful deities. Those helpers were often resident in the masks worn by the "magicians" (see drawing 5.11).

Magic in this application was a practical process to achieve desired results or to avoid unwanted outcomes. It played a special role in human existence. Consequently, it filled the voids caused by the lack of knowledge of the forces that influence life and offered a method for expressing unfulfilled desires. It took the form of positive action including the protection of a person's family and home, or it embodied a negative force intended to cause harm or loss of personal property. Magic was a part of the life of every person, and it was not viewed as a separate belief or disassociated attitude. Integrated into every aspect of survival, it was a part of the socio-religious belief system. It was used to select a building site for a new home or the burial site for a deceased family member, and it was consulted for the best day to marry and the most favorable time for making a journey. Magic was a part of all facets of life from conception to the grave.

Popular (white) magic revealed itself in many ways, but two of the most common are divination and curing. The practice of divination (prophetic) magic focused on finding lost articles, identifying favorable or unfavorable persons and situations, telling the future, and predicting generally unknowable facts or information. Curative magic healed the natural or supernatural maladies of humans and animals through special powers and incantations[37] (see drawing 5.1). Both forms of magic, divining and curing, were found in most societies and were associated with masks and masking activities.

People addressed the demands of their environment either by instinctive or learned responses. Habits were often perpetuated without conscious effort and superficially appeared to be much like instincts. The difference between those actions was that habits were learned and could be replaced by more effective or socially acceptable ones. Consequently, learned actions (habits) allow greater flexibility when people were required to adjust to environmental changes. In many societies most behavior was controlled by instinct, and in all societies, some activities were the result of instinctive response. Survival was a basic instinct, but as the population shifted from instinctive to learned response, even those actions became less automatic. In most advanced social orders, human activity modified and became more controlled and less involuntary. It is believed by contemporary assessment that the fewer instincts a species has, the greater the range of behavior that can be developed.[38]

6

Mystic Assumptions

...[T]he process of ritual masking carrie[d] with it certain fundamental mythic assumptions. Wherever and whenever the ritual mask [was] worn, it symbolize[d] not only particular gods, demons, animal companions, or spiritual states but also a particular relationship between matter and spirit, the natural and the supernatural, the visible and the invisible.[1]

Rituals were those practices associated with the realm of belief, magic, sacrifice, and transformation. Certain rituals had "religious" context, and many were closely aligned with the activities of survival. Such pursuits were a bridge between the ordinary and the extraordinary. They were objective by nature, and the outcome of a ritual was expected to be beneficial to a particular person or group.

Because the basic preoccupation of early humans was survival, it is not surprising that rituals were about the sustaining and perpetuation of life. Rituals, as psychosocial events, were intended to invest a person or object with the power to nurture human existence, including health, wealth, and fertility,[2] or to inflict the reverse conditions on others. Most socially endorsed rituals were complex events that combined personal and communal experiences and emotions. "They t[ook] their meaning from, and g[ave] meaning to, time, space, the body and its parts, human artefacts, personal experience, social identity, relations to production and social status."[3]

"Throughout the ages, from the earliest subsistence cultures up to and including our own civilization, [people have] attempted to establish order in [the] world by assigning various roles to unseen forces and divine powers."[4] To influence those forces, humans have contrived rituals and ceremonies that have been effectuated as a form of reverential belief. Those activities included the performance of dances and songs acquired from various supernatural beings and passed forward from past generations. Masks and other forms of specially prepared raiment were worn during the performance of those ceremonial displays to reinforce the message and verify the presence of the supernatural (see drawing 6.1). However, a "ritual is not solely a homeostatic mechanism for bringing society into equilibrium through affirmation of its underlying values ... but also a cathartic outlet for irrational fears and desires reflecting primordial realities of life and death from which all carefully structured institutions offer imperfect shelter."[5]

Masks were representations of the beliefs of the people as ritualistic elements.

The mask, in that context, was a link between the ritual performance and the supernatural. It was used to make "visible dream images"[6] and to fulfill the imaginary elements of the viewers' ritual expectations. Those notional elements galvanized the feelings of self-satisfaction that were drawn from the ritualistic performance.[7] Consistent with that concept, Schechner in Ingold[8] notes that the "ritual excite[d] both the right and left hemispheres of the cerebral cortex, [and released] pleasure-giving endorphins into the blood." The practical objective of the ritual and the values it represented were believed to have immediate results, thereby satisfying the immediate exigency.[9]

Once the ritual duties were fulfilled the people returned to profane life with more enthusiasm because they had aligned themselves with a higher source of energy and replenished their capacities through experiencing a life that was less tense, easier, and freer.[10]

The ritual activity was considered equivalent to, or representative of, some other symbolic action.[11] It was, in that way, both a ritual act and a symbol that established a relationship between objects and activities in the physical and metaphysical worlds. The ritual focused attention on the conditions favorable for supernatural interaction. It emphasized and perpetuated the life values of the group as determined by their traditions and beliefs. It was possible through ritual activities to interpret and manipulate the psychological counterparts of the socio-economic and cultural realities of daily life. The mask, as a representation of "another being or thing," was the perfect complement to the ritual scheme.

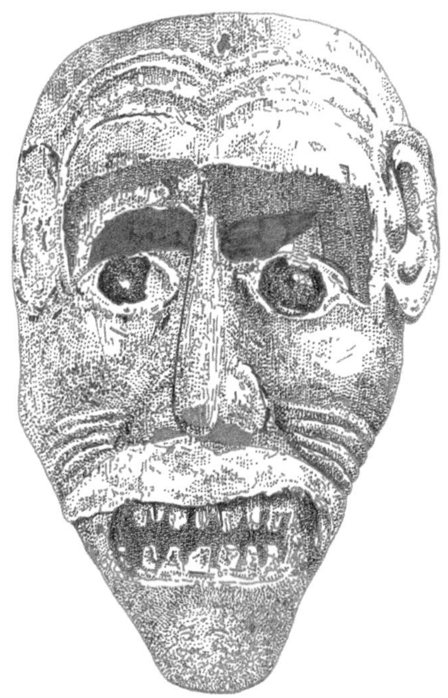

Drawing 6.1 *Los Muertos* (the dead or the corpses) **mask made of carved and painted wood. This old mask from Mexico is "a reminder of the fate awaiting all humans."[n]** *Los Muertos* **had no special dance of their own but participated in many dances. These masks often included both serious and comic elements.**

Rituals as Mystical Conduits

The ritual world created by a culture was essentially of its own making and governed by its experiences. It was a method of activating a group effort.[12] Rituals brought together group members for a predetermined purpose and to achieve an anticipated result. The mask, in this group process, lent an element of continuity that both attracted and distracted the participants. They were attracted to the mask or masked figure as the connection with the deity being addressed and, simultaneously, they were distracted from the reality of their surroundings. The masked figure vacillated between being a recognized member of the group and being a spirit in an environment of psychological uncertainty. The worshiper and the worshipped were ritually united.[13]

Rituals as affirmations of social constancy were the means for achieving and maintaining stability. They reinforced the consciousness of the participants with visual and audible stimulants. Masks, clothing, and associated accouterments provided the ocular stimulation, and chants, drums, rattles, and various other noise-making apparatus fulfilled the acoustic role. Those elements fused to become a tangible expression of belief in the ritual process and a solicitous quest for supernatural intervention.[14] Although rituals might not have been a gratuitous spiritual experience to all participants, they did influence the emotional and physical behavior of many individuals and the collective beliefs of the group as evidenced by their continued existence.

The ritual (ceremony) served as a transtemporal link that united the past to the present and the present to the future. It was a mystical vehicle for the displacement of time and place. The intended outcome of the ritual was the reinforcement of belief and a reaffirmation of the power of the spirit/deity by magnifying the omnipresence of the spirit world. In the ritual act, there was a commingling of the natural and supernatural worlds in ways that established empathy between the two spheres, and for the believers' reality and belief were joined. The mask was the embodiment of the psychic process and, as such, it was an object for focusing attention on ritual objectives.

Paul Radin noted in *Primitive Religion: Its Nature and Origin* that "ritual dramas [could] be conveniently grouped into two types: those that seem to bear a transparent relationship to tribal initiation rites and those that do not."[15] It also may be convenient to assign masks to similar general categories. In many social groups, masks were elements used by secret societies for purposes of initiation rituals (see drawing 6.2). However, rituals also gave special attention to creation, the clash between good and evil, and the requirements of socio-economic survival. Masking played an equally significant role in all those ritualistic events.

Masks also had an important role in many collateral rituals. They were a means of spanning the gap between humans and spirits while having some of the characteristics of both without being either. The horned masks worn in Yugoslavia were

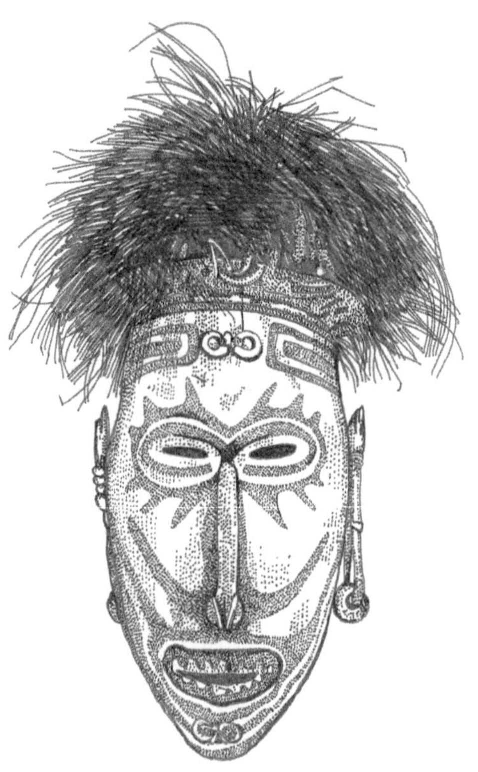

Drawing 6.2 This New Guinea, Tami-Huon area bark-cloth mask is more than life size. It is constructed of a palmwood armature over which has been stretched a piece of bark cloth. The red and black painted masks, used as spirit symbols, were placed on the roof of the men's house. These masks were a tangible representation of spirit power as controlling elements of a secret society. They represented a generally accepted authority and verified the control of that society over the spiritual life of the group.

good examples of the transformational aspects of masking. The headdress of a goat or other domestic animal was a part of the change from one profane category to another.[16] That alteration recalled the myth of the satyr (goat-men) and the legendary interaction between animals and humans. Similar masks were found in other cultures that reflect Indo-European folk traditions.

The use of masks in these activities made rituals believable. Although the observer knew the masked figures were ordinary people, perhaps neighbors or family members, the effect created influenced the imagination and caused real life attitudes to be supplanted. Believing made the ritual, in all its aspects, a paradigm of reality because imaginary existence passed beyond the control of real life measures.

There were many beliefs that reinforced the realm of daily life to promote the notion that the qualities of the whole were inherent in the parts. The teeth and bones of an animal were thought to impart the strength, speed, or cunning of the beast, an attitude that was consistent with that conviction. It was equally probable that the hair, bones, and flesh carried the strength, valor, or skills of a person.

People believing in ancestor worship were inclined to view the world as a comprehensive record of human activity. The material world, for them, was either grounded in eternity or viewed as a cyclical pattern of destruction and renewal.[17] In such a tradition-bound environment, the progenitors fixed the course of group activities, and change was limited by the anticipation of a periodical recurrence of significant events. Rituals were important components in that perception because they provided the means for reenacting historic events in a culturally acceptable setting. The ritual considered in that context had the role of maintaining stability rather than initiating change, and masks provided both mnemonic reference and visual stimulation.

Masks and Early Ritualistic Activities

Rituals influenced the lives of the earliest people. They were a recognized part of the life of Neanderthals. These early peoples flourished between 100,000 and 40,000 years ago. They had prescriptive burial practices that imply the existence of a system of complex and communally accepted beliefs. "Modern" humans either replaced or displaced the Neanderthals about 40,000 years ago, and eventually those people became the dominant creatures in most regions of the world (see drawing 6.3). With these "new" inhabitants came greater attention to the supernatural world including rituals and masks. The reliance on spiritual intervention perhaps reflected a higher level of insecurity and the unwillingness to confront the unknown. Consistent with that attitude, early mortals required a more developed method of supernatural alignment.

The ancient people apparently had complex sociological as well as physiological needs that demanded gratification. The fact that Neanderthals deliberately buried their dead suggests they were conscious of the supernatural and honored that belief with a form of ritual.[18] That attitude toward the dead probably related to the idea that the dead continued to exist and, although they had changed form, they could still influence the living in various ways. There was little distinction between the physical and spiritual worlds for many cultures, so there was a profusion of spirit beings present in every aspect of life. The phantasms manifested themselves in many ways and were responsible for fulfilling different functions. Particular spirits were involved with those privileges assigned to all members of the group, others were concerned with the activities of daily life, and some interacted with the extraordinary powers granted to shamans, sorcerers, and magicians.[19] Many of the latter type, described as "familiars," were believed to inhabit masks used for ritual events.

People at different cultural plateaus separated their social conditions into subsections and arranged those elements into an order of preference. In that differentiated state, emotion and passion were tempered by basic experience and reason, and individual reaction was moderated by group requirements. Despite the values assigned to certain aspects of survival, all people separated those things that had a direct impact upon their lives from those conditions that influenced everyone else. Human existence was a response to the interaction between the two halves of

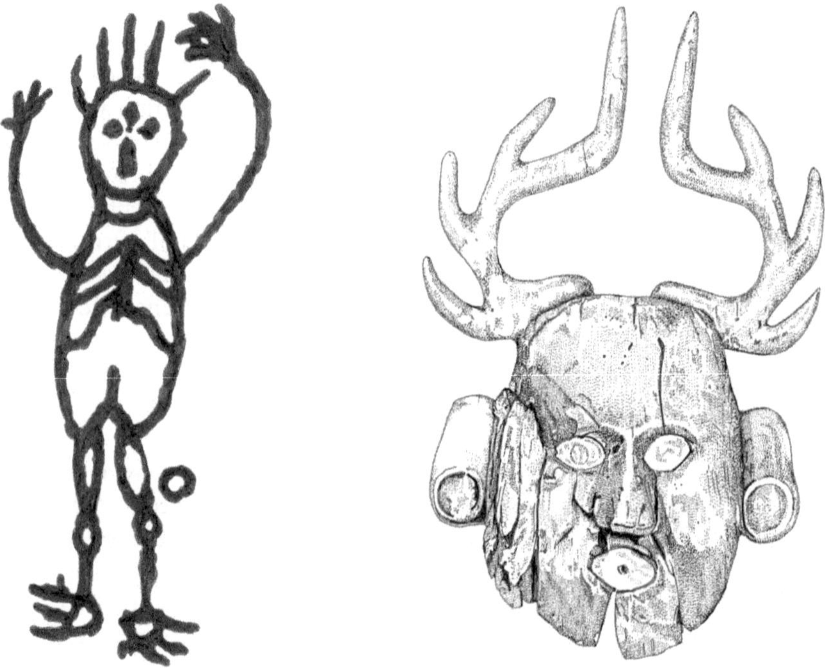

Drawing 6.3 (*left*) A skeletonized figure that referenced the shaman's journeys to the underworld. The figure has "rods" or "horns" extending from the top of its head that may signify power or a mystical connection available to certain people. Drawing 6.4 (*right*) A transformation mask with antlers uncovered at the Spiro Mound, Le Flore County, Oklahoma (1200–1450 CE). The mask was made of wood with shell inlays for eyes and mouth. It was originally painted. This mask is an example of a symbolic representation of man and animal, probably used in the deer dance to ensure good hunting. An earlier example of antlers was found in sites related to the Hopewell Period (ca. 200 BCE–400 CE). People of status were buried during that time with copper and wood replicas of deer antlers. The deer as a magical creature was found in many cultures. Indigenous peoples in the Western world prized the deer as a prototype horned god, and in the East, Buddha began teaching in a deer park.

that equation, and ritual observance guided those fundamental but complex interactions.

As the dynamic forces of the natural and supernatural worlds influenced the survival of early people, they reacted in emotional (and sometimes rational) ways to overcome or to control the related energy. The animals encountered by hunters reacted instinctively and immediately; however, human response was more calculated in deference to several possible actions (or reactions) that could be taken (see drawing 6.4). It was in that time of inaction that the forces of consciousness, reason, religion, and rituals were amassed. To address those psychological challenges, humans devised rituals to placate and appease deities and demons alike, and they made the masks to become receptacles of wandering spirits.

Rituals probably sprang from unsatisfied desires resulting from emotions that found no immediate outlet in practical action. That notion was expressed by both pleasant and unpleasant emotional circumstances. For instance, the story of a successful hunt, battle, journey, harvest, or other event required telling and retelling, and the story often included demonstration and pantomime. The same storytelling could be associated with a dead ancestor or recently departed group hero. After the story was retold a number of times, it was no longer a particular hunt, battle, journey, or significant ancestor but all hunts, battles, journeys, and ancestors (see drawing 6.5). The result was a ritualistic interpretation of an emotional event that was communicated by social action. Rituals were a response to group and not individual emotions.

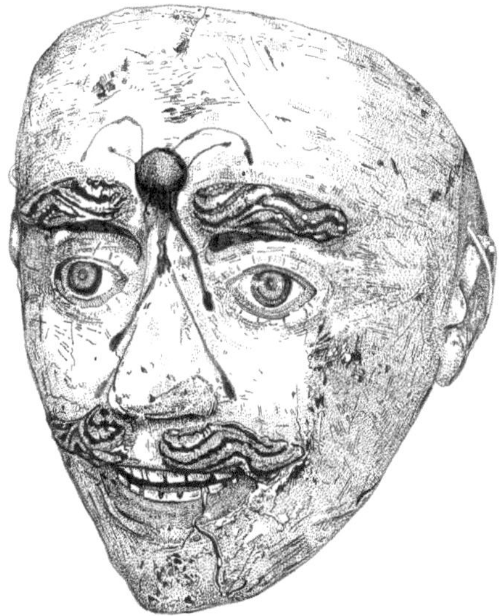

Drawing 6.5 Chunchu "proud warrior of Antisuyo" mask from Bolivia was made of painted plaster. The mask represented an important aspect of the history of the Incas and their perpetual struggle to dominate the people of the jungle or lowlands. The dancers organized themselves in two groups and engaged in mock combat. Consequently, the mask "face" displays several wounds. A tin or cardboard hat decorated with colorful designs and feathers enhanced the masks.

An early example of the ritual observance is illustrated by the anthropomorphic figures found in Les Trois Frères cave in southern France. The figure in a bison mask appears to "dance" across the rock surface. The masked head is turned to give a recognizable profile and human hands and feet extend beyond the bovine hoofs. The figure has an erect penis that might have been a symbolic reference to the continued reproduction of animals or to the human (male) dominance over bison (see drawing 6.6, see also drawings 1.12 and 2.11). The ritual event was a celebration of life and death — demise and renewal. That theme was found in many early rituals.

Eventually, ritualized activities defined the basis for cultural and societal continuation. They represented the emotions associated with particular activities and standards for acceptable practices within a specific social group. Rituals were imitations of reality that gratified, verified, or stimulated human action. They also served as instructional schemes for future generations whose character and identity were guided by the appropriate ritual acts.[20]

Although the measure by which survival was judged was defined differently by individuals as well as cultures, it was the primary motivating factor for most humans. Historical reference notes that gaining food (sustenance) and producing offspring (procreation) were the two most meaningful motivators in a person's life. Other factors acquired varying levels of significance as certain plateaus of survival were reached. Things that enriched, beautified, or otherwise gave life special meaning were added, but unless the life cycle was secure, the elaborations had little significance. It might have been from those two basic motivations (sustenance and procreation) that seasonal, constantly recurrent, ritual originated.

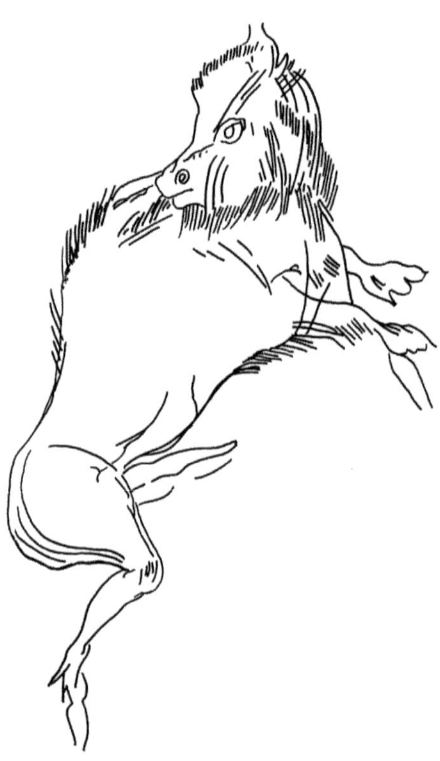

Drawing 6.6 Masked figure from Les Trois Frères, France. This bison masked figure appears to dance or to make some kind of exaggerated movement across the rock surface. This image may represent an early form of totemism or celebration of the kinship between humans and animals. The figure was perhaps imitating a respected part of human existence or acknowledging the animal life that was taken so human life might continue.

The rituals that depend on the cycle of nature — planting and harvesting, migration of animals, and ovulation — could be anticipated and formalized. The seasonal phenomenon was a cause for tension and anxiety as well as celebration. Most seasonal activities related to the vagaries of life and death. One season died and another was born; the process was anticipated and reinforced by ritual recognition. The expulsion of death in expectation of renewed life was a part of many cultures and an intrinsic element of many masked rituals (see drawing 6.7).

Rituals often included humans mimicking the exploits of nature or deities; however, the movements were seldom more than an inferior substitute because the participants were constrained by distinctive cultural characteristics. Lindsay[21] proposed that rituals were the results of the "fantasy act" that developed into unique systems and traditions. That notion suggests that early people mimed movements that they viewed as magical. Out of that impulsive mimicry there evolved a system that was a real and significant part of their lives. Humans experienced a fantasy mime state of consciousness while in a ritualized episode, and many of the difficulties of life were expunged. Therefore, most rituals, besides relieving personal trauma, fulfilled the necessary role of reaffirming and recreating the locus of humans in the accepted order of the universe.

Rituals answered the need for verification of shared beliefs, and the greater part of ritual activities was the repetition of acts attributed to mythical figures at the beginning of time, in *illo temporo* according to Mircea Eliade.[22] Those events had meaning only insofar as they repeated the tradition model; therefore, rituals, as verified by the repetitions, legitimatized belief by giving it acceptable status. The act was made "real" because it repeated the tradition-based archetype. Masks gave added continuity to rituals as they mimicked or reflected the images associated with particular beliefs. The shape, color, and form of particular masks were linked with certain rituals; thereby, the observer as well as the performer could easily recognize the intended purpose of the activity by the masks worn. Dance, stylized movements, songs, and chants were important in the ritual in much the same way because they complemented the mask and heightened the ritual atmosphere.[23]

Rituals, Masks, and Social Equilibrium

Existence for early people was unpredictable and subject to forces beyond their control. In contrast with that emotionally and physically stressful situation, rituals had the therapeutic purpose of allowing people to return to the beginning of life — to begin again.[24] The annual reenactment of significant secular events, sacred beliefs, or personal transformation was a time of regeneration. Rituals provided the proto-

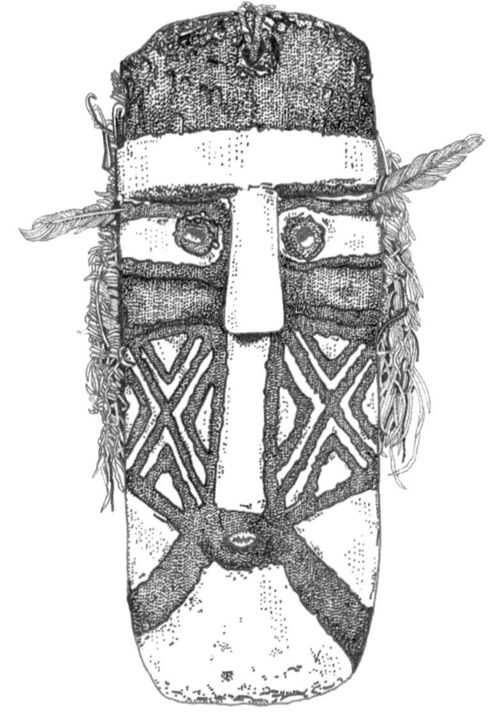

Drawing 6.7 *Meninaku* mask made of painted wood, fiber, and feathers. This mask was probably used in the curing ceremony. The Meninaku, a central–Brazilian Arawakan tribe (Upper Xinga River), believed sickness was the result of having the person's soul taken by spirits of the forests and lakes. The patient sponsored a ceremony to counteract the illness and to prevent the offending spirit from returning. This spirit mask, possibly a caiman, was used in the ceremony to dissuade the maleficent spirit from making anyone else ill.

typical models for survival and the reactualization of mystical events that occurred at the earliest of times. Similarly, traditional practices were renewed through the ceremonies and passed to the next generation. Continuity was maintained. Life and tradition were reborn, ancestors venerated, and individual requirements for personal regeneration were fulfilled. Rituals were a way of aligning individuals and groups with their universe. They were also a method of integrating the life ways of a particular people and identifying a common purpose. The communal ritual facilitated social relationships that contributed in a positive way to group survival.

The everyday activities of most peoples were supplanted by ritual events. The rituals facilitated a sociological and physiological equilibrium by balancing the emotional and economic needs (in the broadest sense) of a people. They validated traditional beliefs at the same time and made them factual. The perpetuation of popular beliefs was a necessary part of maintaining social order and structure, and rituals had a primary role in that process because they were believed to be older than the knowledge of the people who performed them.[25] That situation recognized the legacy of the ritual activities that were based on beliefs and passed from generation to generation without the benefit of accumulated knowledge.

It is likely that similar rituals were practiced over a large area and by many peoples; however, the mythological basis for a particular ritual generally differed in each community.[26] The ritual in each application was the standardized and socially approved technique for dealing with the incalculable element in life's critical situations.[27] It was an instrument for regulating the flow of emotional and spiritual energy into a socially acceptable activity, and for most cultures, rituals were central to human existence.

Rituals often enacted the events of myths, although the association was not always clearly defined. Sometimes myths were the exact script for the ritual activity, while in other circumstances the myth was only a source that stimulated a ritualistic state of awareness. It was equally probable that myths and rituals influenced each other and that interconnectedness contributed to the gradual development of both. That relationship was most apparent when both myth and ritual were altered or redirected to reflect changing social or environmental conditions.

Rituals that recognized ancestral presence and importance often involved masked performers, as did those activities that imitated the behavior of the group's spiritual avatar or totemic deity. Gradually, as the various psychic levels achieved in early cultures ceased to function, the significance of a particular ritual was lost and, although it might continue to be practiced, it was given new meaning. The ritual in those instances was perpetuated for the sake of the ritual rather than to achieve a particular outcome.

Human emotion was closely aligned with rituals and, although it was an integral part of the activity, it was not the source of the ritual. When the emotional aspects of the occurrence gained control of the participants, the ritual continuity ceased and the event became a disorganized (frenzied) emotional outpouring. As rituals were social activities, they required organization, and excessive emotion impeded organizational efficiency and allowed the participants to pursue individual responses.

It may be that rituals originated below the ultimate horizon of humanity and were a compulsive tendency generated as a response to environmental conditions and external stimulation.[28] However, it is certain that societies performed rituals to ensure the well-being of their world and to gain a desired objective. Rituals founded on tradition made use of the imagination of both those performing and those observing the activities. The mask in those circumstances was a means of giving greater expression to the imaginary (ritualized) world and aided in the transformation of the unknown into the "imaginable."

The ritual was, in many cultures, a primary element of social solidification. It was based on a desire to master the irrational forces that influenced the peoples' lives, and it confirmed their dignity as human beings and controllers of their destiny. Many ritual activities were designed to allow participants to confront and overcome the conflict between instinctual desires (or wishes) and the conduct required by society.[29] The masks worn by the performers aided in telling the ritual story (myth) and gave the mask wearer as well as the viewers a sense of inclusion in the socio-cultural history of the people. The notion of mythical recognition through ritual observance promoted an assumption of connectedness and social well-being.

Socially Endorsed Rituals of Transformation

The principal rituals that influenced the lives of most early peoples were those related to life-cycle events. For men the cycle included puberty (or circumcision), marriage, and death. Similar events had ritual significance for women — puberty (first menstruation or circumcision), marriage, childbirth, and death. Those occurrences were a part of social development and involved activities that permanently changed the participants' condition or status in the community. Each of those rituals testified to a transformation of the participants, causing them to be altered both physically or socially. In addition to these ritualized events, people placed similar emphasis on other major community-sanctioned achievements such as killing or raiding the enemy, overcoming a demonized beast, fulfilling a significant mystic mission, or enduring an agonizing sacrifice. Those activities included masks worn by both the primary participants and those coordinating the event.

The ritual was the acknowledgement of individual or group needs and the reconfirmation of the myths or traditions of a particular clan, group, or culture. Therefore, rituals were of primary importance in gaining the help of supernatural beings believed to be a necessary part of the successful transformation process. They were symbolic performances that assisted in the creation of order through mystical intervention to combat the disorder that magic precipitated. They were a form of communication that defined the status of the participants before, during, and after their spiritual and physical transformation. The ritualized displays were intended to confirm value in social actions for the participants and provide the group with a means of expressing normally inexpressible ideas and expectations.

An equally important part of the ritual was the practice of changing a social obligation into a desirable personal act.[30] This attitude was exemplified by the transformation from adolescence to adulthood or the responsibility incumbent in the change from an unmarried to a married state. Masks used in those transformational processes were symbols of tradition and mythical investment. They played important roles in facilitating an acceptable emotional response to challenging situations. The masks, along with the other elements of the ritual, helped to persuade the participants that to achieve a particular outcome the traditional acts had to be performed in a traditionally defined manner.

In all ritual activities, particularly those including masks, there was an element of make-believe. That aspect of masking was true whether the activity was sacred or secular. Mummer, actor, or shaman enacted roles the masks described, and behind the mask, they performed their parts free from the bonds of reason. Profane physical and emotional laws did not apply beyond the horizon of human experience because the presence of a system of beliefs for personal conduct that conformed to the needs of society was incumbent in the ritual practice. The features of a social system including the masks, rituals, and dramatic presentations that affected the cohesion of the society became objects of that system of beliefs.[31] Masking and ritual customs were regulated by society and served as tools to transmit the collective expression of that society from one generation to the next.

The social group defined how the ritual was to be performed and the symbolic form to be used in objectifying the transformational process. The group representative (shaman, magician, wizard, or leader) authorized the symbolic form to be used and recognized the event as significant within the group context. Thus, rituals were a part of the social and cultural continuation.

To reinforce a particular ritual activity, a masked shaman or other practitioner imitated the movements and sounds of animals. This portrayal was part of the masquerade of taking possession of a helping spirit or "friendly." The shaman, with those actions, transformed himself or herself into an animal in a similar way to putting on an animal mask.[32] The newly obtained "identity" was that of the animal spirit that allowed the practitioner to communicate in a spirit language. When the practitioner donned the mask, he or she relinquished the human condition, "died," and reemerged as a spirit force beyond the limitations of humankind. That mystical relationship between humans and animals was characteristic of the socio-cultural practices of paleo-hunters and continued through eons of traditional practices and myths.

Unusual Headgear for Ritual Practices

The ritualization of social need expressed as personal achievement was the foundation of most belief systems. When the social customs and practices within the system could no longer be justified in personal terms, that system ceased to function and was replaced because, even though early humans were concerned with ceremonial and sociological aspects of ritual practices, the mystical experience was eclipsed by the necessities of survival during daily existence.

In material and spiritual activities, time and space ordered everything, and the true origin of most rituals is clouded by tradition, leaving the intended purpose subject to interpretation. Undoubtedly, some rituals were not validated by reason but confirmed by repetition. If a particular series of tactics contributed to the success of a specific situation, then those same measures could be expected to provide the same assistance the next time they were performed. Thereafter, the strategic actions were assigned ritual status and became a required maneuver in preparing to undertake the related activity.

Many rituals placed special emphasis on the use of headgear or face covers (masks). The masks were given life by the wearer in a similar way to the assumed relationship between humans and deities that allowed communication. It was believed that deities gave life and animation to people and in return, the people gave animation to the masks representing their gods. The relationship was reciprocal. The mask protected the wearer from harmful forces emitted by hostile powers while recognizing the authority of benevolent spirits. Often, the head cover was designed to be frightening in appearance to dissuade hostile spirits and to make the wearer unrecognizable.

As a formalized process, rituals explained and sometimes validated those issues that facilitated social harmony. They celebrated the ways of the ancestors by addressing situations in a prescribed manner. Ritualized activities were the primary occasions for displaying the objects and activities described as "art" including masks, sculpture, and costumes.[33] The ability to attach special meaning to those objects because of their association with other beings or spirits was essential to the ritual process. Ceremonies (rituals), for most peoples, involved several aspects of cultural significance and were strong factors in the maintenance and continuance of cultural solidarity.[34] Those practices regularized social and cultural ambiguities and were the means for expressing and reinforcing social unity. The time-honored rites were appropriate to meet social requirements although their original meaning and purpose often were forgotten.[35]

Numerous long-standing rituals were founded on the belief in personal encounters between humans and supernatural spirits.[36] Those encounters could be divided into two segments— preparation and achievement. The human representative acted as a "joiner" or "contact" in the first part of the practice of making contact, becoming one with the desired spirit being and soliciting assistance. The second element was to direct the spirit force to achieve the desired goals.[37] The basal concept of the ritual process was to develop sympathy between the "inner being" of the person and the "outer being" or the spirit/deity. That level of attainment was not realized by all ritual participants, but once it was achieved, it altered the "receiver's" sense of reality and a state of emotion was achieved that carried the person beyond rational thought to a state of ecstasy.

Masks as the Embodiment of Ritual Power

Rituals were collective acts composed of gestures, words, and masks. They were a basic form of communication and a means of summoning supernatural entities into the visible world.[38] In some of those ritual activities, the person embodied the power. In others, it was the mask. The interaction between the elements (person/power or mask/power) was often a requisite facet of the communication process and when separated, none of the parts maintained the same levels of energy. The person in some locations was only the conduit for transmission of energy from the spirit (source) to a physical entity, and in the transformational act the joining element was the mask and associated trappings.

Although the rudiments of ritual activities included veneration of powers that existed outside the natural world, they were seldom based on abstract considerations. Instead, they tended to be pragmatic. The need was stated, the requisite tributes were presented, and the required results were expected. The concept was very straight forward. It was initiated by the people or person for the good of the presenter. When the deities failed to respond in the required manner, the fault lay with the people, a taboo broken, or offense committed. When noncompliance occurred, more complex forms of manipulation were employed. The ritualization was reinforced with purposeful and persistent expressions of supplication including sacrifice.

Rituals were a way by which a practitioner established a cosmological presence. Metaphorical and symbolic use of words and objects was essential in that process.[39] Similarly, movements and gestures common to daily behavior acquired a special ritualized purpose and significance. Face and body adornment, costumes, and masks typically added to the emotional effect of rituals (see drawing 6.8). When used for that purpose, the mask connected the performer and the spirit being as well as demonstrating the union to those participating in the ritual. The mask represented both the ethereal and material elements.

The ritual was a process of unification and communication that brought the group together to focus on a particular matter or issue. Those practices were ways for societies to confront crisis situations and, despite the nature of the crisis, rituals established principles of order recognized within the society. The symbolic actions, including masking, confirmed the relationship of those within the group and the unity of their circumstances.

Ritual Acts of Purification, Healing, and Survival

Rituals were the confirmation of life as a continuing affirmation of ancient precedents instituted by ancestors to serve as models for human actions. Each cultural group had an ordered body of meanings, symbols, and processes by which its members maintained cohesion and anticipated interaction. Masks, magic, rituals, and ceremonies were elements of a relationship that were found in numerous societies. "Sacred action, therefore, might be characterized as dramatic action in which a group of people act[ed] out things together following a script, so that the action [was] predetermined and interpreted identically by all the participants, the interpretation being part of the script"[40]

Ritual activities among early peoples were associated with particular events, and although the ritual practices were different among different peoples, there were similarities in the purposes. People performed ritual activities to achieve success in war, in the hunt, in crop renewal and abundance, in propagation, and in health. Besides these commonly held goals, there were other objectives that varied from people to people. Each group or group subset placed greater or lesser significance on particular ritual activities (see drawing 6.9).

All human life was punctuated by occurrences of special importance and the complementary rituals. Those events were passage rituals or ceremonies that signified the passing of a person from one position in life to another. Other ritualized events celebrated transitions

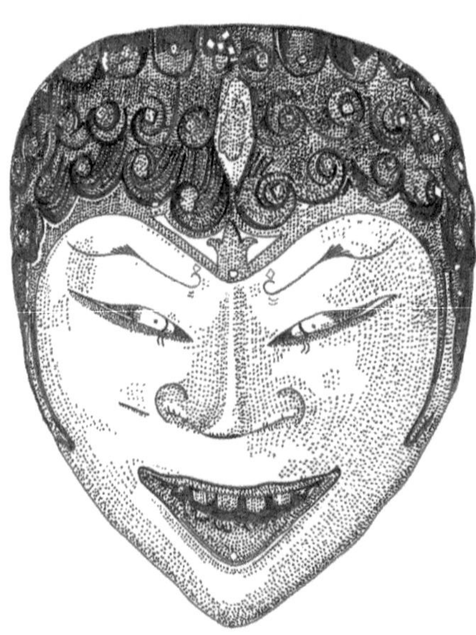

Drawing 6.8 *Topeng* (mask) Srilandi made of wood pigment, gold leaf, and leather. The West Java masked dance (*wayang topeng*) is one of the oldest of the performing arts in Indonesia. It was popular as early as the sixteenth century.° *Wayang* means "drama" and the performers used subtle head and shoulder movements in conjunction with lighting effects to change the facial expressions of the mask.

such as the completion of a particular training or initiation into a special association or group. Those rituals were a part of the method of recognizing and defining new responsibilities. They separated the person from his or her surroundings, altering their sensibilities and reintroducing them to society in the new or different role or status.

As noted, the rituals associated with puberty were examples of that practice. For example, at puberty every male Zuñi was initiated into the kachina or mask dance society.[41] This ritual sanctified the transformation from youth to adult.

Young people, male and female, were for centuries instructed in the rules and responsibilities of social life and were initiated into the secret societies that regulated the morals

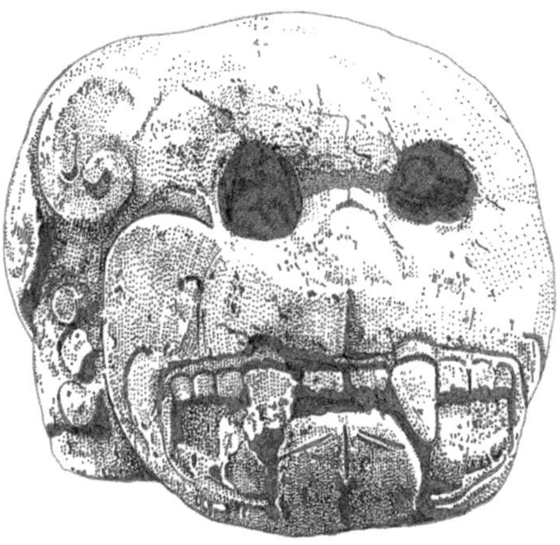

Drawing 6.9 Mask-like image of a jaguar carved in basalt. This image is from Southern Vera Cruz and is of the Middle Formative Period.

and taboos of the group. Simultaneously, they were circumcised, scarified, tattooed, or in some other way physically marked. This ritualization was associated with the supernatural to add importance to the transformation from youth to adult, and it established social boundaries for acceptable practices. The ritual was part of a regulatory system, and those who defied communal values (laws) or passed beyond the limitations established by the group were subject to demonic intervention for corrective purposes. Masking was a part of both the transformational practice and regulatory activities. The youths wore masks to mark their time of transition and community authorities used masks to actualize their social authority.

A ritualized occurrence in a particular society could fulfill numerous psychological, social, and cultural needs. However, the same activity might serve an altogether different purpose in another society.[42] Each group used rituals to transmit information important to the identity and continuity of its membership. That ritualized instructional and informational event was of particular significance to nonliterate societies (see drawing 6.10).

Rituals in communal practice placed everyday life in suspension. It was possible in ritual practice to recreate the fundamental relationship between humans and deities and to reorder that kinship. The passage from profane to sacred time brought about by a ritual also implied a transitional relationship, as the liturgical time was an extension of the period when the ritual was last performed.[43] It was a metaphorical enactment of the essential elements associated with human existence. Rituals were frequently an uncanny interaction between creation and destruction, killing and curing, comedy and tragedy, and the sacred and profane. Those parallel themes were so interwoven that it was difficult to anticipate the outcome. The most grotesque mask was capable of concealing a comedian, the most beautiful character could disguise a demon, and the granting of a life might necessitate the taking of another.

Participation in rituals was determined in many ways. Among some people, a person might be invited to participate for hereditary reasons; for others, the rules of involvement were more strictly governed. Generally, the rules fell into three classifications, and one or more applied according to social constraints. Age or level of maturity defined the first rule of participation. To qualify, a person had to reach a certain age or level of physical development to be initiated into a social group that controlled ritual activities. The second regulatory element was social evolution dictated by progress within the group. The third consideration was based on individual prowess or achievement within the society. That aspect gave attention to the skills, leadership, and personal power of individuals and often superseded the other requirements. However, as the tenets of ritual and drama merged, the conditions of participation often were set aside, allowing greater involvement by a larger portion of the community.

Masks were actual and metaphorical wonderments fixed in time and space. Their specific significance was associated with the complexities of social and personal order and the elimination of an unregulated state of existence. The psycho-social movement from disorder to order required numerous social or cultural transformations in ritual form for purification, restoration, and regulation. Those rites were often precipitated by figures identified as tricksters from beyond a community's physical universe.[44] Those "intervenes" created chaotic conditions that epitomized change and, in the disorder, they traversed the community's moral universe to formulate a new reality based on mystic order. They were the victims and the saviors, the paradoxical embodiment of good and evil. That concept was represented in multi-image masks that illustrated the duality of human nature. That notion conveys the assumption that human nature was divided against itself—again, observing the duality of all people.

In many aspects of early cultures there was only fortuitous order to life, and the creation of unity required the expenditure of energy in the ways and means available to society. Systematic cooperation that venerated supernatural beings created a common bond of belief, but in the complementary rituals, societies often lacked order. When there was no method to accommodate the inherent changes in the environment and the variations in human conditions, it was impossible to maintain an ordered society. A ritualized system integrated the feelings and emotions of the group into a collective social dynamic, thus regularizing the relationships. Through ritualized group activities such as hunting and herding, people were

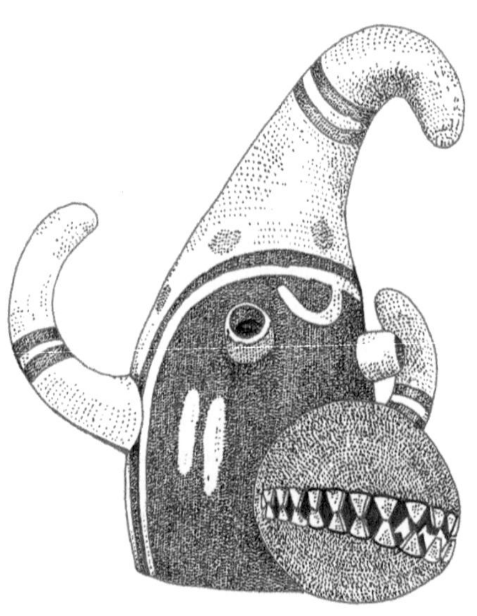

Drawing 6.10 Kachina mask made by the Zuñi and Hopi made kachina masks in many imaginative styles and shapes. This mask was made from native gourds with the curved neck used to form the headdress. Other segments of gourds were attached to form the horns and eyes. The contrasting colors, black and white, give animation to the simplified shapes. There is a certain ill-defined animal quality about the mask, particularly the exaggerated muzzle and teeth, but no direct reference to a specific beast.

guided with the help of powerful and sympathetic spirits assembled in special ceremonies.

The peoples had to develop a sympathetic understanding with the environment to survive, and to realize that goal, they ritualized almost every aspect of their existence. They ascribed supernatural meaning to many of life's activities, taking them out of common existence and giving them sacred connotations. Early peoples "recognized the cycle of propagation, birth, illness, and death as an implacable rhythm dominating physical existence. In ceremony and ritual [they] celebrated the four aspects of the rhythmic cycle; identified in the pattern of the seasons and their influence upon animal and vegetable life."[45]

Masking and the Confirmation of Life Ways

There are at least three fields of thought regarding rituals and their purpose. The first group proposed that rituals were action-oriented events because they caused something to happen. The second faction supported the notion of rituals as manifestations of belief and that they fulfilled their role by completing a part of the belief system. According to that concept, there was no need for an action to result from the ritual. The third bloc attempted to analyze each ritual according to its role in a particular social group, ignoring categorization. In practice, either or both of the first two definitions could be described as a ritual depending on how it was articulated by external assessors. As neither the forethought nor anticipated outcomes of many traditional rituals are known today, the inclusive approach as noted by the third alternative seems most germane.

However, masked ceremonies and rituals, regardless of the superimposed assumptions of purpose, had a primary relationship with spirit protection and the conditions of life and death. The recognition of death and the perpetuation of life were the two primary rituals observed by the peoples of the world. Both activities involved masked participants. The rituals symbolically communicated with supernatural powers through sacrifice, masks, chants, dances, and other means, and each activity was energized by its own spirit force.

All social groups, large or small, developed rituals to deal with calamities and afflictions. For instance, most forms of illness elicited a ritualized response, and although the ritual was not a curative in itself, it was a method of calling attention to the afflicted person and concentrating psychic energy that might have a positive influence on the well-being of the individual. The ritual focused the energy of the group on a particular issue or person of mutual interest. The common good was advocated.

The action elements of the ritual can be viewed as impractical because they often consisted of music, dance, and masquerade; however, the intent was normally quite practical. That distinction was important for understanding the ritual and the accompanying masks. Despite the outward appearance that often included a festival-like environment, the intent of the communal event was practical and of primary importance to the initiating community. No doubt there were elements of "play" or "playacting" in all ritual. Masks, garments, music, dance, or other conscious-focusing ingredients accentuated the play factor. Rituals provided a way for ordinary people to gain access to divine beings.

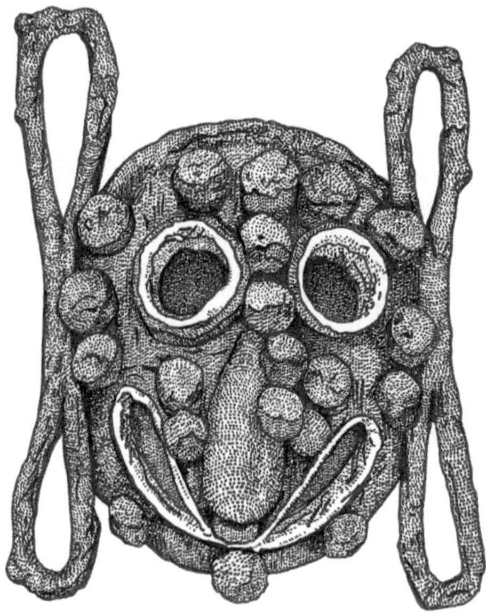

Drawing 6.11 A *Malttugi* (servant of nobleman) mask for the *Suyong Yaryu* masked play. The *Suyong Yaryu* was initiated about two hundred years ago. It was performed as a ritual for the mountain spirits the first month of the lunar year until 1937 when the Sino-Japan War erupted. The masks for the "field plays" were made from gourds.

The group-directed rituals most commonly practiced related to the continuation of life —fertility — in all its manifestations. It identified a concern for the perpetuation of the people, animals, and the land. Closely associated with fertility and renewal was resurrection as a way of renouncing the discontinuation of life due to death. Those themes were found in all locations in the world in some form and were inherent in various masks used in ritual enactments (see drawing 6.11). Symbolic death and the return to life of humans and vegetation were demonstrated in ritual form centuries ago. The basis for those rites was belief in sympathetic magic, and masked participants performed the requisite roles intended to stimulate and facilitate the tenets of life and fertility.

The most commonly practiced rituals that included masks related to individual validation — it was for making or taking of vows. This act was a personal strategy for dealing with the future and had its origin in the ancient past. Persons confronted by illness, danger, or eminent disaster sought to influence their personal spirit/deity by pledging to perform a gratuitous act of conciliation or atonement. That elementary ritualistic act was practiced by most cultures.

7

Masks as Communal Symbols

The symbol translates a human situation into cosmological terms and reciprocally, more precisely, it discloses the interdependence between the structures of human existence and cosmic structures.[1]

A symbol was a substitute for the thing, object, or commonly shared attitude for which it stood, and symbolism was an important part of all forms of social communication. Even in those societies that took pride in advancing the written word through superior literature and cultural advancement through the arts, symbols were of primary importance. However, it was not until recent times and the advent of psychoanalysis that emphasis was given to the study of symbolism and attention was drawn to the role of symbols as a basic element in the cognitive process.

The history of all people includes symbolic representation, because without symbolism there could be no culture.[2] Although early culture was not itself an amalgamation of symbols, it was the meaning behind the symbols that united the people into a common purpose. From the earliest records of human existence, symbols appeared as expressions of magico-religious activity. They were designed to convey information necessary to the people producing them and to aid in the expression of beliefs that resisted more common modes of communication. The symbols were generated from the human subconscious as a statement of a deep inner power that could not be fully formulated in other forms of expression.

Mircea Eliade[3] described a symbol as an "autonomous mode of cognition" since it aided the viewer in seeing both what was represented and what was perceived. Human sensibilities in most circumstances were inclined to "see" or recognize the objects anticipated, disallowing the overriding authority of reason.[4] In addition, although the mask was a facsimile (a symbolic representation), it was the similarity between it and the associated mental image that gave it identity and substance. Therefore, it had validity and purpose.

Selected objects, activities, or events in all societies were of special importance and identified by symbols to attract attention. The symbols denoted the kind or level of importance assigned to the individual object or activity. Similarly, the symbol aroused and nurtured an ardent commitment to those "things" determined to be important to a particular people. The mask as a magico-religious symbol might not

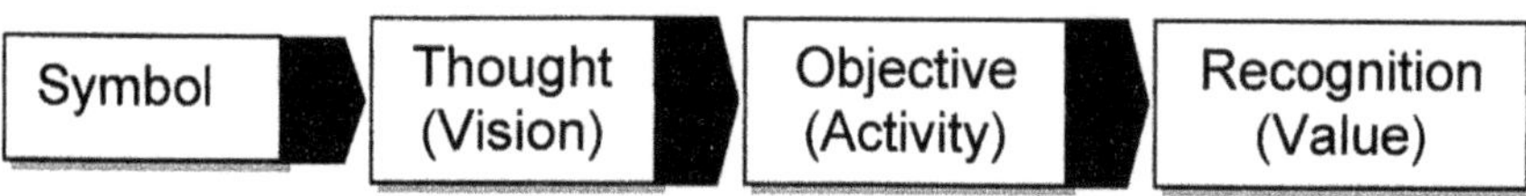

Figure 7.1 Communication using symbolic reference

have overtly communicated; however, it suggested a meaning or purpose and allowed the viewer to decipher the message. Bronislaw Malinowski[5] in *A Scientific Theory of Culture and Other Essays* stated that "symbolism, in its essential nature, [was] the modification of the original organism which allow[ed] the transformation of a physiological drive into a cultural value."

The symbol expedited an understanding of a particular condition or circumstance by providing a constant reference. The related symbolic system evolved and survived as part of a cultural pattern due to regular and repeated use. The symbols functioned well or poorly, but unless they were recognized and associated with the appropriate act, activity, or event they failed to stimulate understanding. The basic nature of most symbols facilitated transmission between individuals and generations and ensured the continuity of cultural signals. They were often uncomplicated and direct; at other times, they were complex and furtive. Symbols also became shared cultural phenomena and were the media for translating the conditions and circumstances of a human situation into cosmological terms[6] (see drawing 7.1).

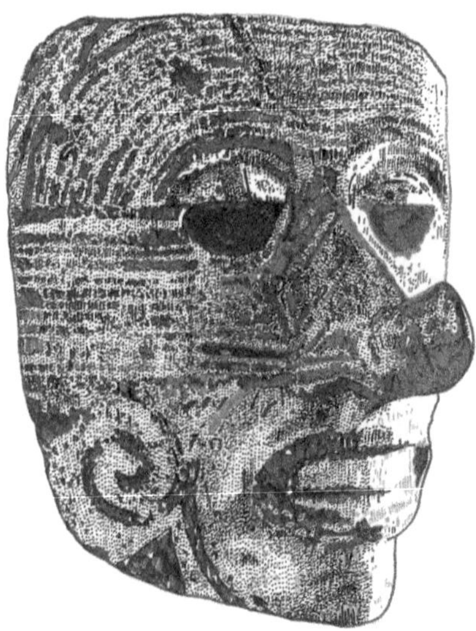

Drawing 7.1 Mask from Central Mexico that is made of clay with polychrome decoration. It is from the Late Postclassic Period. The turned-up nose is also found in the Early Postclassic Period from El Quetzal, Guatemala.

Every people, regardless of era and intellectual capability, communicated by some form of language and dealt with the symbols of the society. However, "the validity of the symbol considered as a form of knowledge [did] not depend upon any individual's degree of understanding."[7] It was likely that when the imagers made masks and other ritual objects they were not completely knowledgeable of all the symbols used, and as conditions changed, so did the symbolic meanings. Because of that variability, the exact interpretation of many mask symbols is speculative.

Traditional masks were conventional media of social expression, and for early peoples they undoubtedly were the symbols that best represented the unknown or unknowable forces that influenced daily existence. It was possible that, for them, there were no other avenues within their social order to acknowledge the existence of those forces. The masks acknowledged both the powers of the unknown that influenced the natural world and the genuine reality of the people. When the group came together to support and reinforce their beliefs, masks provided the symbolized embodiments of those beliefs and were a way for humans to project themselves toward their cerebral objectives.

Probably, symbols employed in all societies gained and retained their meanings through use. The ability of humans to invent, understand, and employ symbols at a theoretical level was one of the attributes that distinguishes *Homo sapiens* from other primates. As an element of abstract thinking, the mask was a diagram or symbol that expressed socially defined ideas. The symbolic value of a mask was identical with its psychic meaning because the mask was a materialization of the symbol. If it had no significance to the group, it could project no symbolic reference.

Symbols Made Present That Which Was Absent

Probably the first symbols were "natural signs," and the assigning of meaning to those signs constituted the beginning of symbolic understanding. An example of a natural sign was an animal track,[8] and that symbol had a direct reference. It is not difficult to assume that, following that reasoning, archaic hunters visualized the animals as they studied the tracks. That approach was "conceptual" in that the animal was an imagined beast shaped according to the intellectual comprehension of the individual. The tracks made the animal present in the mind of the hunter although it was outside the field of normal vision.

"Whether the symbol [was] a spoken word, a drawing in the sand, or a mimetic dance, the principle [was] the same, the act of symbolizing, particularly when ritualized, actually 're-present[ed]' its object, that means 'bringing it before us by calling it back from whatever place it may have reached.'"[9] Cultural symbolism revealed events and attitudes that occurred in another world and could not be compared or explained by experiences in the material world.[10] However, when the symbol was a word conveyed in a symbolic language it often was difficult to discern the reference because meanings could change according to combination, situation, and circumstance. The shaman or clan elder in most cultural groups directed the creation of symbols and often had to interpret them.[11]

For most early people, symbolism had a primary role in social life and was found, in some form, in all human societies.[12] Symbols defined certain values common to people and aided in sustaining an emotional commitment to that which was determined to be of special importance to the group. A symbol was the smallest unit of ritual activity that retained the specific properties of ritual behavior.[13] That relationship correlated with the notion of a symbol representing or causing something to be recalled due to analogous qualities or associations in fact or thought. Symbols, in that context, were an integral part of the society and socializing processes. They were aligned with human interests whether explicitly formulated as in a ritual activity or casually inferred by circumstances and practices. Masks derived their special qualities from their association with certain elements of social and cultural life and from the transference of specific ideas and qualities. In that process of shifting emotions and desires, there was a magical (symbolic) relationship between the mask and the image it depicted.

Symbolism, from the perspective of basic communication, was considered a language because it discloses dimensions that were not provided by the tangible object.

Consequently, the mask could be interpreted as a symbol of social importance or an element of local custom. Either of those views had substance because symbolism attached new value to the mask without removing or altering its perceived purpose or meaning.

Symbolic reference is a tool for analyzing cultural attitudes when they are examined in relation to fundamental beliefs and the way they were conceptualized and formulated. A part of conceptual thinking as well as the linguistic process was the ability to use symbols and to recognize the idea of one thing or image as representing another.[14] In addition, although most people communicated in words with symbolized meanings, nonliteral symbology was used. Obviously, the symbols were an element of communication only as long as they had the same value to both parties—the presenter and the receiver. However, commonly acceptable symbols such as those associated with rites and rituals communicated group-recognized messages. Therefore, because most speech was learned by imitation, it is reasonable to believe that the symbols associated with culturally specific rituals were also learned in a similar way.

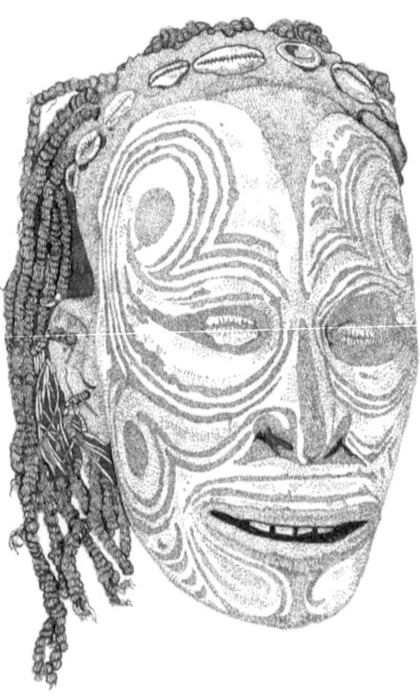

Drawing 7.2 New Guinea skull with a mask modeled of clay. The reshaped face was painted with designs in a way that gave an aesthetic quality to the remains of an ancestor. The eye sockets were embedded with cowrie shells to give "life" to the face. Distinguishing marks often represented specific reference to a deceased person.

Symbolism plays an important role in all societies because all peoples use symbols to express beliefs, desires, expectations, affiliations, and loyalties. These symbolic representations had many forms from the simplest reference to the most complex expression. Some symbols were broadly recognizable and others were known to only a few people. Figures, shapes, and colors were enhancing elements of differing importance to various peoples, as were sound symbols. However, nonverbal language was the universal referent for signifying the spiritual and emotional content of most cultures. Masks and body adornment were ubiquitous elements of nonverbal communication (see drawing 7.2).

To reinforce their symbolic purpose, early masks were embellished with abstract designs that were more than decorative. Those designs were to give visual information regarding the role of the mask in a ceremonial context and to evoke the associated myth. Regardless of the exact "message" being conveyed, the decorative elements included implicit symbolism that was familiar to at least some of the assembled viewers.[15]

Masks as Objects of Symbolic Reference

The symbols and symbolic references were derived from human convention as products of unique cultural environments. The ideas behind specific mask shapes had clearly assigned associations to validate their intentions. Natural objects—plants or animals—had an identity that existed externally (outside their physical structure) and in that reality (the natural and spiritual life) represented a universal meaning for the resident culture.[16] However, because the relationship between idea and representation was an abstract notion, the amount of information transferred often was limited. The symbol in favorable circumstances was a combination of form and content. It was a union of image and idea.

As an example of symbolic affiliation, in areas of West Africa the bird figure was associated with witches and witchcraft. Masks made by the Yoruba included the ibis, and in Senufo tradition, masks intended to ward off witchcraft had birds on the top. Conversely, the Temne (people) believed that the "witchbird" was responsible for making children ill and causing bad luck, and to protect against witchcraft they wore feathers in their hats.[17] The symbolic associations gave a physical presence to a mystic entity, thereby joining the material and spiritual domains.

Bird images were also identified with the shaman's ability to cross supernatural frontiers, and the structure of certain masks with expanded wings suggested the capacity to soar. The avian characteristics symbolically reinforced the shaman's ability to maintain an extended connection with the transcendental world (see drawings 1.10, 9.8, and 10.7). Various birds (real and metaphorical) were considered "spirit helpers" that served as messengers between the natural and supernatural worlds. Birds, like masks, were symbols of transformation that had an obvious presence in many societies and can be traced to drawings originating in the Late Paleolithic Period. Similarly, masks by their implicit rigidity were associated symbolically with the face of the dead, and in that way they created a relationship between the living and the deceased.[18]

In many societies, there was a particular affinity between shamans, magicians, and mystics and certain symbols. The wolf, jaguar, and bird were favored symbols and often served as helpers for the practitioner's spirit journeys. The bird was a meaningful symbol because of the significance of flight; therefore, feathers were a part of the shaman's regalia in many cultures. Symbolic feathers in the forms of ribbons or rods were used as connecting elements to link the practitioner with the air or space — the great beyond. Eskimo shamans wore rods and ribbons as part of their headdress, and shamans in Ecuador wore "puma" (jaguar) cloth masks with rod-like extensions (see drawing 6.3). In a like manner, the shamans of the Huichol people of Central Mexico were often portrayed with antler-like head covers or masks.

Horns of various shapes, sizes, and materials have been associated with power or energy in many cultures. The shamans in the Northwest Coastal region frequently had iron antlers attached to their head covers as representations of the wild reindeer. The antlers also served as connections with the cosmic energy that gave the shamans their power. Similarly, statuettes of Osiris, the Egyptian deity, were made with crowns that included ram horns as a representation of power. The Celtic deity, the Daghda, was shown on the Gundestrup Cauldron, found in a peat bog in Denmark, as the Lord of the Wildwood with the horns of Cernunnos on his head.[19]

Horns, rods, or antlers as energy symbols were found in many societies in all areas of the world. They were adopted by Judao-Christian symbology and were represented in some cultures as the crescent. In earlier times (Paleolithic), the horns of bison were symbolically associated with the uterus and "regenerative waters." In addition, historians have speculated that the marble statue of Moses carved by Michaelangelo (ca. 1513–15) for the tomb of Pope Julius II had cranial protrusions that were horn-like to symbolize divine connection, wisdom, and power.

Masks were symbolic vehicles designed to communicate a preestablished message or series of messages. In that interchange, they had an artificial presence interposed between the person behind the mask and the audience. The communication emanating from the masked activity often was complex and evolved on multiple levels. A special message was sent to persons in the presenting or competing social club. Viewers of the opposite gender to the performing group were given a different message, and persons of an older or younger age group received a completely different signal. All the messages were included in the masking activity, and all were calculated to have the optimum impact upon the audience — old or young, male or female, initiated or uninitiated.

Masks were symbols to the extent to which they portrayed things that were at a higher level of abstractness.[20] A mask was a symbol if it presented a deity form — a visual manifestation — to show the culturally assigned concept of the deity (see drawing 7.3). The idea or spirit determined the shape and defined the symbol, and in that way masks were objects of expression, not actual models that could be identified with a particular entity. Over emphasis on "realistic" detail could obscure rather than clarify the relevant characteristics of the mask that gave content to the superhuman powers embodied in the image. The mask replaced or represented the real object and fulfilled its role in rendering services to those seeking assistance. Through the mask, it was possible for the shaman or magician to symbolically exert magical influence upon the spirit beings.

Masks that had no symbolic reference were only disguises intended to hide the identity of the wearer. It was the idea and message behind the mask and not just the outward appearance that promoted communication. From the earliest times, "certain symbolic references, particularly those suggested by facial features, were used by mask makers to convey specific meanings."[21] Those symbolic references were found in various locations. For instance, the nose often had phallic connotations; the protruding tongue was associated with power, evil, or death; and the eyes signified the sky, water, or visionary ability. The symbolic connections were a form of communication that passed

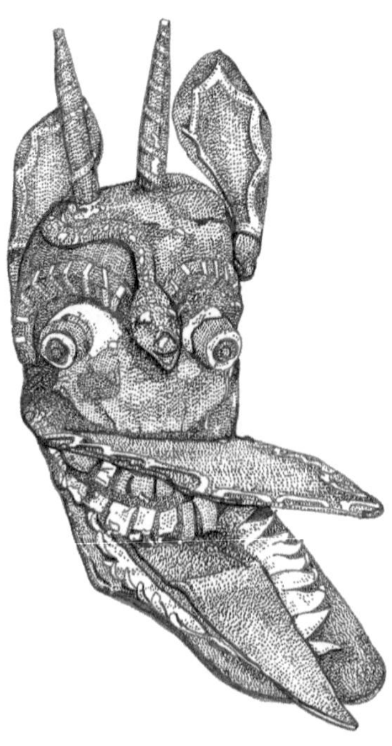

Drawing 7.3 *Tastoanes* mask made of leather, clay, and pigment. Masks of this type were worn in a variant of the Dance of the Christians and Moors, a dramatic activity that was introduced to Mexico in the early 1500s. The *Tastoanes* "dance" has religious symbology and represents the clash of good and evil. The "good" element may refer to "the intervention of Saint James on behalf of the Spanish and his death at the hands of the pagans."[p]

between the mask maker and the viewer. They were easily identified within the tradition of the masked event.

Animal Masks as Symbols of Transformation

The earliest masks were probably of animal subjects. "Given the need for man [humans] in primitive conditions to merge with the animals and natural forces of the world, the invention and use of masks as a catalyst for that transformation was not only logical but probably inevitable."[22] Masks of many cultures exemplified the ancient unity of humans and animals. The Egyptians, Aztecs, Olmecs, Eskimos, Japanese, Chinese, and Indonesians as well as various peoples in West Africa combined animal and human features in masks intended to cerebrate the inseparability of human and animal elements (see drawings 2.12, 4.13, and

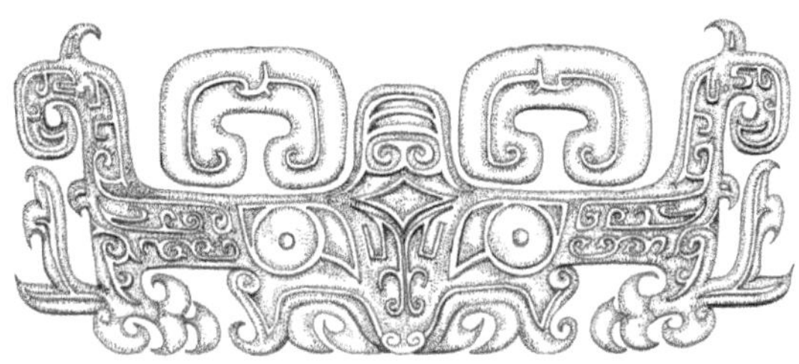

Drawing 7.4 *T'ao-t'ieh* (also *taotie*) mask called the "mask of the ogre." This stylized face is a composite formed of animal and bird elements from the Shang dynasty. The zoomorphic design could be interpreted as a tiger image.[q] It might also symbolize the generative forces to which sacrifices were made. A similar mask motif was referred to as *Kirttimukha* in the Hindi dialect and described as a jaguar in Middle America.[r] Only a part of the image was used in some representations, suggesting the figure represented an insatiable monster the gods directed to eat its own body. The design might have been placed on Shang and Zhou vessels (particularly ritual cooking vessels and food containers) to warn people against overindulging. However, the exact meaning of the image is unknown.

6.4). Such masks were used to facilitate the journey into the spirit world with the animal helper as the guide, or to illuminate myths of traditional importance.

The joining of human and animal attributes was an important aspect of masking. That practice referenced the dualistic nature of the hunter culture where humans were both the slayer and the slain. The natural and the supernatural merged in that environment, and the separation of the two worlds was neither real nor important. The mystic unity of humans and animals was a fundamental conviction and constituted an important part of the cultural life of most early peoples. The transformation of deities and humans into animals and animals into humans was accepted belief. That connection was so literal that in many cultures mystical ancestors and animals spoke the same language and that ability was thought to be restored during spirit travel.

An interesting example of a tradition-based symbolic animal mask image was the *t'ao-t'ieh*—the "mask of the ogre" (see drawing 7.4). This image first appeared in China on headgear and sacrificial vessels during the Shang dynasty (1550–1027 BCE). The exact meaning of the tiger-like monster image is unclear, but some have proposed that the image was a symbolic apparition to avert evil.[23] The *t'ao-t'ieh* was a horned dragon or tiger monster with a head and no body. Traditional folk tales related that the ogre lost its body as a punishment for eating humans. It reportedly performed the ultimate act of gluttony by consuming itself, leaving only the head to symbolize the evil of self-indulgence. This image appeared repeatedly in various stylistic forms.[24]

A second animal-aligned masking practice, also found in China, was the tiger as the beast symbolically associated with the earth. It represented the female, *yin*, principles in nature. In that relationship, the male factors, *yang*, were portrayed by the dragon. Tiger masks were commonly associated with Chinese activities in much the same manner as the jaguar mask was identified with Mesoamerica. The dragon symbol, in masks and other applications, was connected with the Chinese leadership. It originated in a way similar to the feathered serpent, Quetzalcoatl, as an element identified with the Aztec myth of creation.

One additional important animal mask was that of the lion as found among the Hindu deities. Vishnu, the cosmic dreamer, often was portrayed as the man-lion. In an ancient story (myth), Vishnu appeared in a "terrible form," part man and part lion, and during an encounter with a doubting nobleman, the man-lion ripped open the stomach of the doubter and consumed the viscera.[25] This episode was reenacted in popular plays and was narrated in the *Bhagavata Purana*.

From the seventh to the third millennium BCE, the sow mask was a part of ritual activities relating to fertility and pregnancy

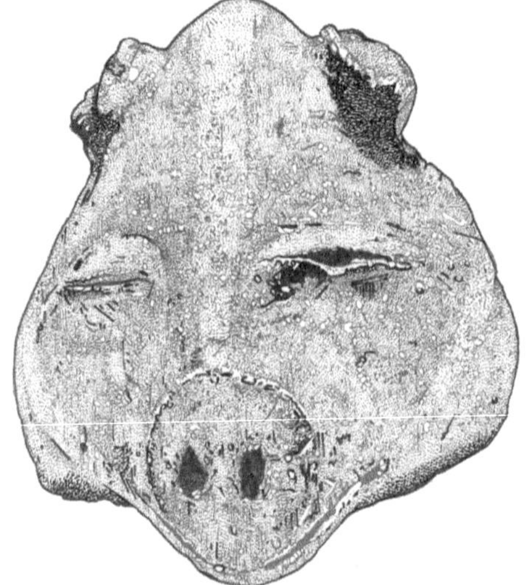

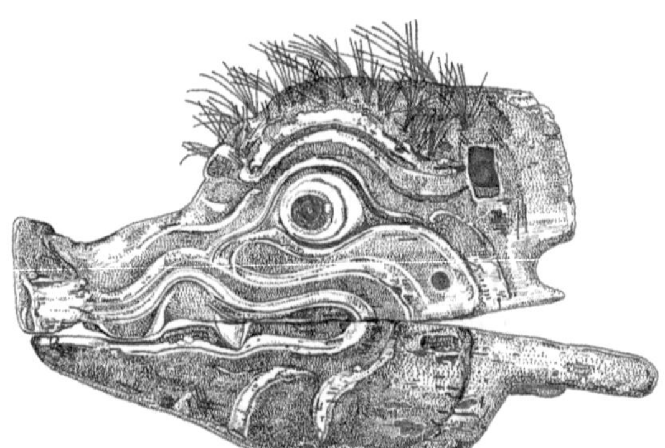

Drawing 7.5 (*left*) Sow mask associated with the Pregnant Goddess. This clay mask from the Vinca culture in Macedonia was made ca. 4500–4000 BCE. It represents the sacred animal of the Pregnant Goddess cult and was probably used in ritual activites relating to fertility. The use of the sow image continued into the third millennia BCE. "Sow-masked dancers are found in reliefs, paintings, and figurines of ancient Greek shrines."[s] A female dancer wearing a sow mask is among the dancers from the second century Shrine of Desponia at Lycosure. Among the Jarawa peoples of South Andaman (in the Bay of Bengal), the pig was associated with legends of female magic. These legends related to death and resurrection and were thought to have originated ca. 3000 BCE on the Asian mainland.[t] Drawing 7.6 (*right*) Barong Bangkal mask used in Bali. This boar mask was associated with the holidays of Galungan and Kunigan.[u] The Barong masks were among the most important masks to the people of Bali. They reflected a tradition based in ancient animism and were identified with protective spirits. The animation of these animal figures required the coordination of two dancers. One held the mask and the other was the body in costume. The mask has a movable lower jaw that allowed the dancer to operate it in a "chewing" motion. The origin of the Barong drama is unclear but is believed to precede Bali Hinduism.

(see drawing 7.5). Dancers with sow masks appeared in reliefs and paintings in ancient Greece.[26] The relationship between the round body of the sow and women during pregnancy gained prominence in parts of Europe and the Middle East, and sow-related fertility rites continued in Eastern Europe into the eighteenth century. Similarly, the boar (male swine) mask in Bali was associated with the holidays of Galungan and Kuningan[27] (see drawing 7.6).

Regardless of the "face" presented, masks were symbols of transformation, and "all transformations [were] invested with something at once of profound mystery and of the shameful, since anything that [was] so modified as to become 'something else' while remaining the thing that it was, must inevitably [have been] productive of ambiguity and equivocation."[28]

Masks as Symbolic Messengers

Images as symbols often had more than one meaning. For instance, a tiger mask (see drawing 2.9) could be viewed as simply representing the tiger as a powerful and commanding animal. It might also symbolically represent the dynamic spirit of a beast that had special meaning in the context of a ritualistic procedure for seeking assistance from the spirit world. The human mind made use of images to grasp the ultimate reality of things because reality manifested itself in contradictory ways and could not be expressed in conventional terms.

Symbols were attention-fixing factors and frequently acquired their full meanings over an extended time. Although the exact meaning of each mark, color, design, or shape might have been unclear to all observers, they were seldom meaningless. Most symbols were invested with a conscious significance and purpose. However, the level of standardization and, therefore, cognition varied according to established communal or cultural models. Many colors and designs used in mask making had multiple values.

Audience perception of a mask or masking event went beyond the limits of understanding, because not all the details about the nature of a particular mask were explained completely. The image and certain resident ideas were transmitted by the external shape, color, or material of the mask, and that information aided in the transfer of a message from the belief system to the audience. The mask in that way was the source of intrinsic information, and the ritual was the method of transmission. The message, to be successful, had to relate to the beliefs or experiences of the audience and fall within the limits of their understanding.

The mask was the source (or carrier) of the message and the audience was the receiver. The procedure of transmission required the message to be encoded in a form that was recognizable by the audience. The technique of transmission and eventual understanding (perception) depended on a number of audio and visual aids integrated into the ritual or ceremonial event. The mask in the larger view of the communication process was an element of the encoding mechanism because it gave the audience insight into the "code" by which the message was being transmitted.

To enhance the probability of reception and comprehension, the message was projected by various methods that influenced different organs. Chants, drums, rattles, and other sound–making apparatus influenced the ears; aromatic plants, smoke,

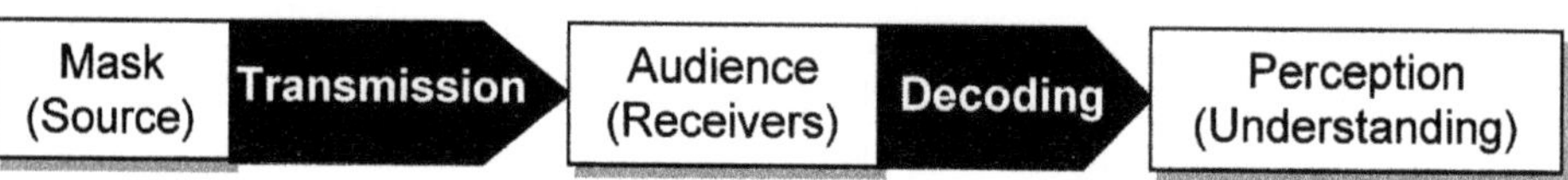

Figure 7.2 The relationship between masks as message source and the audience as receiver

and certain food stuffs sensitized the nose; the costumes, movements, and masks attracted the eyes; alcohol, tobacco, salt, or sugar caused the mouth to be stimulated; and the skin was scraped with nettles, drenched with water, scorched with fire, or exposed to hot or cold temperatures. All these activities altered the mental attitude of the person and resulted in a trance or trance-like state that afforded a greater possibility of message reception (decoding).

Masks were sign vehicles that were interposed between the performers and the audience/viewers, and that placement affected the perception of the masked performers by audience/perceivers. The mask in those activities was not the message; it was a method of communication. Much of the ritual message was directed toward the feelings (emotive response) of the audience rather than their logic (intellectual response). That was an understandable method of transmission as people usually were less perplexed by a mystery they could not explain than by an explanation they could not understand. Magic or a similar socially recognized belief system was an acceptable way of dealing with issues that were beyond normal comprehension. The mask contributed to that transposition as a visual aid for separating the physical world from the realm of spirits and emotions. It allowed the beliefs and aspirations of a person or the group to assume physical as well as cerebral control.

C.G. Jung[29] wrote in *Symbols of Transformation* that "...language, in its origin and essence, [was] simply a system of signs or symbols that denote[d] real occurrences or their echo in the human soul." Therefore, it could be assumed that visual inspiration gave three-dimensionality (or at a minimum dimensionality) to signs and symbols and verified that thinking was more than words. Furthermore, the thinking that facilitates understanding was an amalgamation of symbols (audible and visual) and emotions reinforced by recollection and imagination. Masks and other paraphernalia were the symbols of reference for time-honored rituals and ceremonies—they were the tools (stimuli) for remembering. Through the use of masks, history was allowed and often encouraged to repeat itself.

Symbolism has an inclusive relevance for understanding many human endeavors ranging from social structure and politics through rituals to language and social expression. However, not all objects, markings, and signs had or were intended to have symbolic meaning. Some marks were the imaginative gestures of one person demonstrating a personal aesthetic. Other facets of symbolism had their origins in oral traditions and dramatic performance rather than in the visual imagery.[30]

The use of symbols was one of the most distinctive of all human characteristics,[31] and masks as culturally defined symbols revealed and concealed discrete aspects of social development. Masks epitomized the psychological and emotional influence of symbols on social behavior. They projected a different order of reality and experience. Masks had a quasi-linguistic character as symbolic references to socially and culturally important events and activities. In addition, although there were associated symbolic references assigned to masks in different cultures, there was no apparent relationship between a particular mask (symbol) and the responding emotion that had universal implications with the possible exception of the skull.

Although similarities existed, symbols and their meanings were not limited by practical considerations. People learned that basic communication was necessary for mutual assistance, and like verbal transmission, symbols evolved along different lines according to the cultural context. Certain socio-cultural emblems were close to the lives of the people, and their meanings tended to remain constant or within a relatively narrow range of connotations.[32] That knowledge was used to combat the uncertainties of the universe by giving selected people control over some of the most potent symbols.[33] Those symbols were a means for regulating the external powers that influence the lives of humans. They were focal points for concentrating the forces of magic.

Symbols to Define a Different Reality

It was a relatively simple step to move from believing that all natural things, animate and inanimate, possessed innate souls to an early form of polytheism and assigning god-like power to selected objects, animals, and beings. The traditional stories (myths) were told and retold with embellishments as forms of worshipful admiration to perpetuate those beliefs. Of particular importance was the death of the chosen deities because the reasons and methods of their demise were an important part of deification. Symbols of veneration, particularly those about life and death, were assigned special meaning and became a part of reverential rituals. The ritualized rebirth of a special spirit/deity was the greatest instrument for worship. Symbolic resurrections were often facilitated by persons identified by masks and other easily recognizable objects or regalia. Those masked events frequently included the symbolic consumption of the body of the deceased — a form of ritual cannibalism (see drawing 3.9).

The early Egyptians had a fascination with the supernatural, especially those activities associated with life after death. The scarab, for them, was a symbol of the sun deity, and it was thought that by placing that indigenous beetle in the tomb, the dead would live and all that was needed to enact that magic was knowledge of the proper words of power to recite over the body. Evidently, the symbols with unlimited power were those that related to life and death. They were common to all people regardless of location, because death and the renewal of life (resurrection) were integral elements of all social patterns.

The resurrection scenario was enacted to reflect the symbolic and actual regeneration of the earth. The annual renewal or rebirth as defined by the seasons and the cycles of consumable grains and plants was reason for early humanity to believe that the related deities died and returned to life. The practices for assuring the annual rebirth evolved into rituals and the use of fetishes through which humans could initiate magical forces to influence the activities of deities. The mask was one of the fetish-like objects developed to fulfill that role. Wearing a mask was a way of impersonating the mythical being or its animal counterpart.[34]

Why a particular mask was worn in association with a particular event or activity (except for storytelling or dramatic enactments) frequently was difficult to detect. Often the choice was personal or determined by emotional intervention, because the belief systems of all peoples were complex and susceptible to the vagaries of daily existence. Historians have speculated that masking was an attempt to come to terms with the ultimate unknown in all human life — death — or that it allowed maskers to be something they could never become.[35] If that notion has validity, then masks were the definitive symbols of transformation — at least in the eschatological context. "Masks [were] the mechanism through which the past and the future, the alpha and the omega, of human existence [were] made analogous and obviated."[36]

Masks to Make the Spirits Visible

As with all magico-religious symbols, masks varied in their potency. The more potent (powerful) the mask and its relationship to its ritual role, the more control it exerts over those involved in the ritual activity. That interrelationship differed according to the demands of society and the symbolic activities (traditions) associated with the particular mask. As with an integral element of a belief system, a mask often had the role of assisting men and women to deal with the mysteries of existence. The system in which the masking took place was most times formalized as an association or "club" with specific aims and requirements sequestered within the greater social community. Compliance with the objectives of the group was guided by the desire of individual members to participate in the symbolic pursuits relating to issues that had no rational explanations or solutions outside the incumbent belief system.

The existence of a universally shared symbolism is a widely studied concept, and although there were similar images found in various cultures they do not appear to represent commonly held meanings. However, there were certain symbols such as the circle found in many locations. The circle had many meanings including the sun, the creator, paradise, a

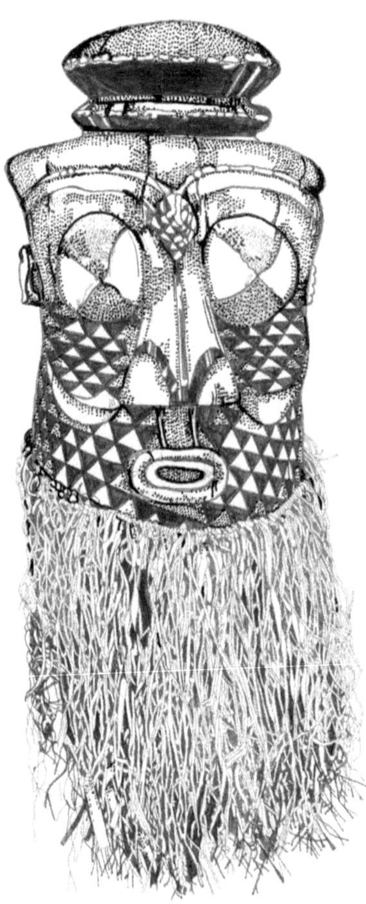

Drawing 7.7 *Mulwalwa* mask made by the Kuba people of sub–Saharan Africa. The helmet mask is made of carved wood and raffia. It has a bold "V" shaped pattern that emphasizes the roundness of the form. The bulging eyes are "chameleon-like" (a black and white "X" pattern) and the round headpiece is believed to be a reference to "stacked pots to collect plum wine."[v] The Mulwalwa may have represented the unpredictable nature of humankind as embodied in the drunkard.

well, the inner self, and female sexuality, to name only a few, and the meanings became more diverse when concentric circles were added.[37] Crossed vertical and horizontal lines forming a "cross" were a commonly used mark in "Christian" symbolism. The cross was also used by the Assyrians to represent the deity of the sky, Anu; by the Chinese to mark the earth; and it was the Toltec symbol for the deities Tlaloc and Quetzalcoatl.[38] The same easily recognized mark (+) symbolized the crossroads of the life cycle (life and death). The cross symbol appeared on masks, pottery, and basketry made in Africa and the Americas and in that application generally identified "the cosmic center."

According to Marija Gimbutas,[39] a mark that generated universal recognition was the "V" (see drawing 7.7). That symbol was the graphic representation of the pubic triangle and was associated with fertility and birth. The mark was used in many parts of the world and was incorporated into designs or design sequences as "Vs," chevrons, "Ms," "Xs," or shapes joined in a meander. The earliest examples of the pubic "V" design date to the Upper Paleolithic Period (ca. 18000 to 15000 BCE). The "X" design was associated with regeneration — new crops, springtime, and birth; it also symbolized marriage or mating. Many decorative patterns referred to the renewal of life and the related life-giving forces. Those patterns were engraved on bone and ivory pieces found in Eastern Europe. A few centuries later the same design appeared on masks and pottery. That symbolic reference appeared in different locations as an intimate connection between ornamentation and human anatomy. It was a part of the surface treatment of masks in most regions of the world.

Objects that had near universal symbolic significance were those that related to water. Of particular importance were shells — oyster, cowrie, conch, and mussel. Seashells had a symbolic association with fecundity, birth, and rebirth. The resemblance of the marine shell to the vulva elicited a connection between the shell and the magical powers of the womb. That association was affirmed by the cultural practices in most regions of the world. The myths, traditions, and ceremonies of China, Japan, India, North and South America, West and Central

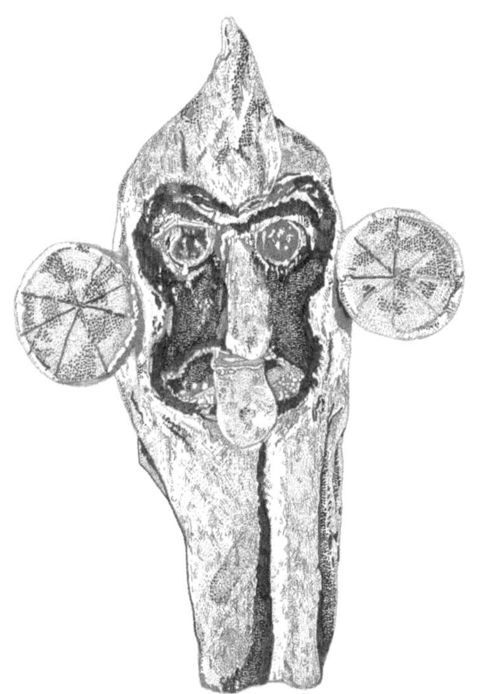

Drawing 7.8 Tukuna demon mask from western Brazil that was used in the Moca-Nova festival. This hood mask is made of a light-colored reed material with dark pigmentation around the facial features. The coloration accents the elevated eye rings, large nose, and exaggerated mouth with an extended tongue. The large round ears embellished with line drawings add to the otherworldliness of the mask. The general representation of the piece is one of aggression or unpleasantness possibly intended to frighten viewers.

Africa, the Middle East, and parts of Europe included references to the power and importance of seashells. They were a part of the belief systems and symbolic vocabulary of many peoples.

Possibly because of the vulval resemblance, shells were considered protection against the magic of others. Amulets and other forms of adornment made of shells were believed to protect women, children, and cattle against various forms of misfortune.[40] As part of the process of protection and "rebirth," cowrie shells often were used to embellish masks. Cowrie shells were used in West Africa to promote a sense of well-being, to ensure success in the hunt, and to foster renewal associated with the new-moon ceremonies.

Many decorative motifs that adorned masks had directed symbolic meaning. Often the designs that appeared to be abstract arrangement of lines and/or circles were drawn from traditional sources and were based on long-standing symbolism. Examples of this kind of reference were the "eye" and "serpent" (snake) shapes (see drawing 7.8). The eye drawn with circles and curvilinear shapes was of singular importance in many cultures, and the wavy-line serpent design had several symbolic references including water, mountains, semen, and penis.

Dots, hoops, and round shapes were symbolic eyes (cosmic eyes) to see into a world beyond the mundane, and in some societies, concentric rings represented the different levels of the universe.[41] Among the Eskimos, the wooden ring surrounding the facemask was identified with the cosmos as a heavenly symbol, and a round hole in a mask or fan was related to supernatural sight. In India, the third eye, the eye of fire, was both an inward-directed "eye" of higher perception and an outward-focused force. Known as the *urna* (or hairy mole), the eye "symbolize[d] the visual externalization of sensible experience."[42] It was the all-seeing eye of the sun and a powerful mark that was a mystic sign associated with Buddha.[43]

Another symbolic reference that attained common recognition was the twin symbols of the phallus and *pudendum muliebre* (*lingam* and *yoni*), representing the union of the male and female principles. They symbolized creative energy and the continuance of human and natural forces. These symbols were part of the basic belief systems of many cultures in both the ancient and modern worlds. This sexual reference occurred in ancient Egypt, India, Syria, Babylon, Persia, Greece, Italy, Spain, Germany, and Scandinavia. The phallus-form shape was common to masks (see drawing 7.9). In regions of Africa and New Guinea the cowrie shell represented the female symbol, and tusks of a boar were phallic.

The ability to communicate the essence of these symbolic references required a heightened level of physical and mental dexterity. Such images were at different levels of abstraction or representation depending on skill, desire, and the demands of the host society.

Often, an overt effort to produce an exact likeness of a particular image failed to provide the viewer with the essential features of the object represented. Conversely, a highly abstract mask that had little resemblance to its referent had minimal application in a self-explanatory context. To enhance the probability of recognition and transmission, the setting in which the mask was presented gave it recognizable meaning. That aspect of masking was particularly true when "part-time" symbols were used as agents for expressing specific referential factors.

A part-time symbol was one that communicated a commonly recognized message under "normal" circumstances but was used to convey another meaning in exceptional situations. That type of symbol was abundant in masking. As examples: The vulviform cowrie shell was recognized first as a shell (sometimes with assigned value in the group exchange system) and second (part-time) as a female symbol. Similarly, the skull was a commonly recognized symbol, and in some cultures, the response was negative due to association of the bone (head/skull) with death or danger. The skull at other times represented the presence of ancestors and was associated with a benevolent spirit (see drawing 7.2). The recognizable elements (shell and skull) were the same objects but the symbolic application and the associated responses were different. These were, in both instances, primary visual messages associated with the symbols. The secondary meanings—sexuality, fertility, life, or death —could be recognized but misinterpreted when decontextualized or disassociated.

Symbols and the Equilibrium of Daily Existence

Early societies had, in all probability, a limited perspective of the world in which they lived. Most peoples existed in a world in microcosm bounded by the realm of the unknown. Due partly to that isolation, the regions beyond group knowledge were believed to be inhabited by ghosts, evil spirits, and unknown creatures that sustained a state of unequivocal chaos and threatened the equilibrium of daily existence. The primary defense against those "evils" was reliance on established symbols recognized and affirmed by the society being threatened.

The belief in the microcosmic existence of a secure environment surrounded by a dangerous world was symbolically represented in many cultures. The circle defined the symbolic center of the human —the soul. It also marked the ritualistic center of social order —the safe zone. The consecrated circle has been traced to ancient

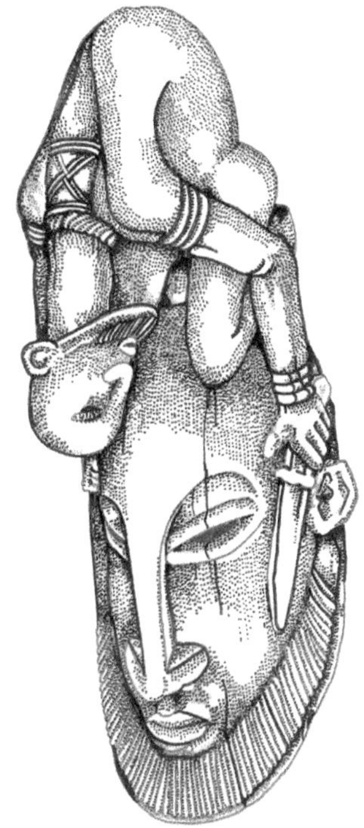

Drawing 7.9 An unpainted mask probably of Yoruba origin that is made of light-colored wood. The well-shaped face with a stylized beard is surmounted by a phallusform figure of a kneeling man. The knees of the top figure are shaped to suggest testicles and the gracefully curved back and neck represent the penis. The symbolic references in the mask draw attention to the male as progenitor without direct representation.

Assyria,[44] but it was present in many belief systems from the indigenous peoples of North America and Australia to the inhabitants of Tibet, India, China, Mexico, Egypt, the Middle East, part of Africa, and other locations. The microcosmic magic circle or "cosmic center" was exemplified in the sacred places of the Eastern and Western worlds. Those locations were commonly viewed as sacrosanct and isolated from the hazard of the secular world. The sacred grove, circle of stones, wedding band, and halo were symbols of continuity, renewal, and self-containment that were a part of many societies. Among the various indigenous peoples of the Southwestern United States, the circle was symbolically related to the universe and an opening was made in the circular design as a passageway for the human spirit to emerge, as from the womb.

Symbols in all societies were a necessary part of human interaction. They were a primary part of creating and maintaining order and maximizing communication. Symbolism and group identity were closely aligned because membership in a social order, large or small, normally included instruction in the meaning and purpose of relevant symbols. With the use of those symbols, there was a unity and distinctiveness in the social group and, in that way, the symbols had both aesthetic and inherent value. They had aesthetic value in that they were selected and arranged according to socially approved requirements and inherent value because they had greater significance than the representation of an image or recognizable design.

Masks fulfilled a role in affirming social order as symbols of authority associated with superhuman powers and, as such, they were important tools for administering control. Persons assigned the authority to adjudicate conflicts often wore masks to disguise their identity. The anonymity was for protection of the agent of justice and was a symbolic gesture of impartiality. The mask presented a face that was not of the mundane world of those in adversarial or antisocial roles. In addition, the mask was a form of authoritative continuity because it remained as the person behind it changed. Masks were the symbolic "badges" of office to which the authority associated with the position was assigned as secondary identities that were expected to exceed normal human limitations.

The symbol was an instrument of information that could be transformed into knowledge just as words served as symbols of communication and were recognized by their association with each other. "Images, symbols, and myths [were] not irresponsible creations of the psyche; they respond[ed] to a need and fulfill[ed] a function, that of bringing to light the most hidden modalities of being."[45] Symbols were messengers of social and psychological intercourse from person to person and from generation to generation.

Many masks represented ethereal beings and evoked the presence of those spirits for the purposes of the ritual or ceremony. For receptive persons, the carved, painted, or fabricated masks and figures of traditional design were symbols of antecedents and were used as evidence that the ceremony or ritual was being symbolically directed to the appropriate ancestral being. "In only a few instances were the forms used in this type of worship a realistic representation of the physical appearance of an ancestor."[46]

Symbolic Ambiguity as a Response to Reality

The phenomena of perceptive insight and intuitive transmission were integral aspects of the masking practice. Human experience demonstrated that touching a hot object burned because the heat was transferred. A similarly and equally comprehensible message was that contact with cold objects made things cold; contact with a sick person could cause illness; and children resembled their parents. As these conditions were confirmable, it was reasonable to believe that most, if not all, attributes were susceptible to transmission.[47] The mask undoubtedly was believed to imbue the wearer with special traits transmitted from the related deity.

The people saw qualities in objects (natural, animal, or human) and attempted to acquire those attributes through the processes of transmission and assimilation. By assuming the requisite appearance (wearing a mask and the appropriate costume) and acting the part, it was believed the essential characteristics were transferred. The mask of the jaguar made by the Olmec of Mesoamerica; the wolf and raven masks of the Northwest Coast; and the mythical creatures carved by the Dogon of Western Africa exemplified the materialization of this idea. The power of those objects originated in the spirit world but revealed itself to the domain occupied by humans.

All forms of visual expression depend on symbols as modes of informational transfer. Similarly, myths, legends, and traditional images were important because they perpetuate the symbolism of the peoples with whom they were associated. Ceremonies and rituals depend on symbols that were recognizable to both the participants and the deity to whom the event was dedicated. Consequently, it is reasonable to assume that early in the evolution of the human psyche there was a realization that symbols revealed certain aspects of reality.

A part of the basic premise of psychoanalysis is that it is in the human subconscious that many beliefs, ambitions, and expectations are fulfilled along with recognition of personal horrors and depravations. Any image (mask) by itself was a relative symbol with a greater meaning that had to be placed in the appropriate context to be understood and used. The human belief system gave meaning to symbols and that system reflected social customs. Therefore, it could be assumed that masks fulfilled various purposes within a single ritual. Ancestor masks referred to the recently deceased as well as to all those who came before the current generation. That concept had singular significance for a people whose entire history was entwined with the recognition and respect of progenitors.

Frequently, the symbolism of a particular mask or masked event was lost to the vagaries of time. Recollections, myths, and the imagination became intertwined, causing the symbolic references to be altered or realigned. An example of that realignment was the Batō mask of Japan. Tradition described the red face mask with corded blue hair as representing a "barbarian" wild with joy after killing the beast that devoured his father. Reinterpreted, the mask was said to depict a man stricken with grief while looking for his dead father, and another reinterpretive rendition described the mask as a representation of a white stallion killing a poisonous snake.[48] The character's hair in the latter case was said to symbolize the mane of the horse.

Symbols that encoded secrets were a part of the magical process. Objects or activities that had secret meanings in the past were drawn upon and assigned greater meaning or power in a later time. The association with the past, in either a factual or fictitious manner, gave credence and creditability to selected symbols. When a power or symbol of power was given a "secret" name, that referent gained greater importance. Secret societies were granted added potency that often exceeded their actual merit by the assignation of a special name or title. As with symbols and masks, words were recycled or redefined to give new and altered meaning to a seemingly familiar expression. The "borrowing" of words added mystification or special meaning that was beyond the understanding of those persons uninitiated to the society.

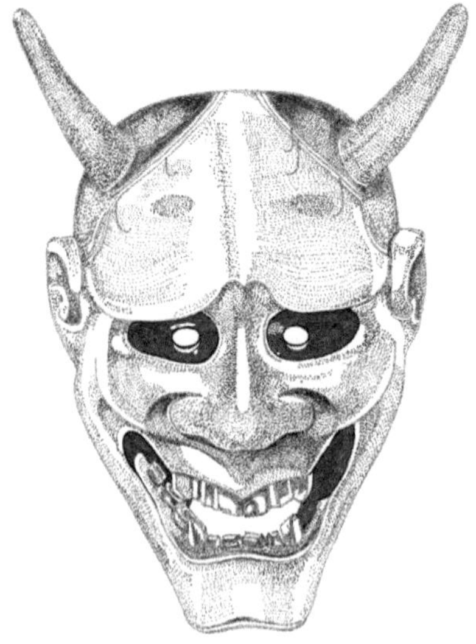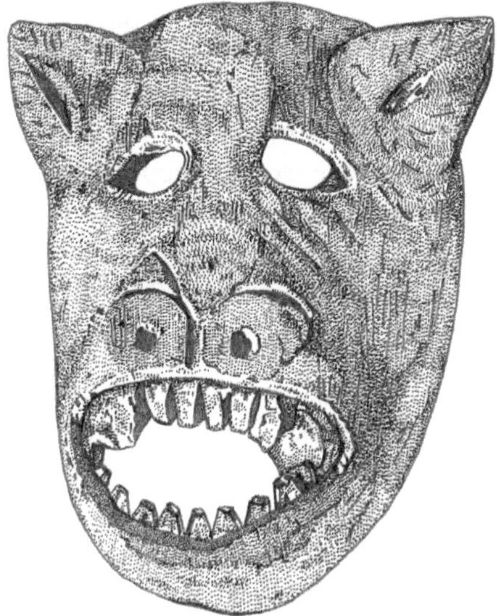

Drawing 7.10 (*left*) Noh mask "Hannya" representing the terrible nature of woman's morbid malevolence. This mask of carved and painted wood has horns, a large gaping mouth with bared fang-like teeth, and staring eyes to express the intensity of the character's expression. Masks of this type were painted white or flesh tones as required by the particular character being represented. The paler colors were to evoke a sense of female delicacy while darker colors signaled greater passion. Drawing 7.11 (*right*) This *Kamba ra'anga* mask representing a jaguar is from Paraguay. The symbolic animal form was made of carved wood for use in a *rua*— a festive event. The *Kamba ra'anga* activities included both anthropomorphic and zoomorphic characters and are popular celebrations that originated in colonial times. The masking practice, often accompanied by music and dance, brought together elements of African, Spanish, and indigenous cultures.

In a similar practice, masks were symbols of power that also were borrowed and assigned a mystical value that exceeded the originally defined purpose.

The purposes attached to symbols were numerous and inconsistent. Those ambiguities reflected both the historic associations of the symbol and the social context. The use of certain colors was an example of symbolic ambiguity based on social custom. It was common to identify black with death or bereavement in the Western world. However, white was the appropriate color for such occasions in other lands and among other peoples. White also was associated with festive events such as weddings, birthdays, and certain holidays, and in some areas of Africa, it was a war color (symbolizing death) while black was associated with fertility.

The meaning and use of some masks were equally ambiguous. Devil masks frequently were equated with demons and represented the "underworld." However, in some cultures, "devils" were jokers or clowns that harassed the public with practical jokes and socially unacceptable (but commonly recognized) activities particularly of a sexual nature. Devil masks often were disguises for persons inclined to "bedevil" the public in a humorous way (see drawing 7.10).

According to N. Ross Crumrine in *The Power of Symbols: Masks and Masquerade in the Americas*,[49] "Masking itself involve[d] the use of power-objects that [had] either transformed themselves into idols and/or produced a ritual transformation of the human actor into a being of another order." Sometimes it was the audience that provided the focus of power and they were transformed. In other events, it was the masker who was possessed by the power of the mask, and he or she was transformed. Finally, there were times when the mask itself became the locus of power, and it was transformed into an idol.[50] The transpositional processes were employed separately or, when necessary, all three were used in the same ceremony or ritual to achieve the desired outcome (see drawing 7:11).

8

Masks as Couriers of Myths

The function of myth, briefly, is to strengthen tradition and endow it with a greater value and prestige by tracing it back to a higher, better, more supernatural reality of initial events.[1]

Early humans, the hunters and planters, are thought to have occupied the temperate and tropical areas of Eurasia and Africa, and although the climate was hospitable, it may be assumed that all early people were faced with similar issues of survival. It also may be assumed that their lives were a constant challenge due to known and unknown forces. Humans, from the beginning of time, had to adjust to environmental conditions and they had to transmit that behavior accommodation to their progeny. Those adjustments were exemplified by the physical variations that evolved in response to environmental requirements.[2]

Insight into the emotional and behavioral characteristics of an individual or group is impossible without reference to the conditions that came before the most recent generation. The transmission of tradition for most cultures was facilitated by all the powers that accumulated in the history of the people. Those powers acted on one another, and the people tried to keep on good terms with all of them. One method of understanding the limits of those powers and a way for assessing cultural traditions was myths—the stories of the ancients. Through myths, people explained the world and the natural forces that influenced their lives in ways acceptable to themselves. Myths were a composite of the hopes and fears that constituted the beliefs of the people.

Archaic society had a limited number of ways for addressing important issues such as the origin of people, animals, and other elements of the physical and spiritual world and for determining the meaning and purpose of life, death, and the afterlife. Those concerns were often described in myths that were "philosophy in parables,"[3] or "narrative[s] which disclose[d] a sacred world."[4] Although myths did not explain how situations occurred, they were an acknowledgment of the occurrences. Myths and stories were created to define the group identity and to describe the importance of the social unification process. They established the foundation for common beliefs, rituals, and practices. Every culture found its origin as well as its rules and identity in the stories it told of its beginnings—the mythic time of "Once upon a time." It was the process of remembering what the ancestors and gods commanded.[5]

The term "myth" refers to the ancient stories dealing with supernatural beings as a way of explaining the natural world and defining the customs and practices of a society. A myth had a traditional association with the narration or expression of sacred history and often described activities or events that took place at the beginning of time or in the process of creation. Consequently, myths were complex elements of cultural reality that could be explained from different viewpoints depending on the predominant beliefs at the time of interpretation.

Rather than dwelling on the particulars of the chronological development of the group, myths provided the essential stories to describe the primary events that brought the people together. Myths detailed in symbolic terms the conditions and circumstances of the social and natural worlds that enabled the group to understand and endorse that affiliation. Myths of origination were an important element of the mythological sequence because they established the uniqueness of the group and defined the boundaries of personal existence.

Myths as socio-cultural narrations told about the creation of the world, humans, animals, and plants, and they described the primordial events that were the causes for the human conditions. Myths also provided an explanation of the world and defined the human role in that environment. Furthermore, and perhaps most importantly, by remembering and reenacting the myths, humans repeated what the ancestors and deities did "in the beginning." By knowing the origin of things, animals, and plants as well as people, it was possible to gain a level of control over them and to acquire the related mystical power by which they could be manipulated.

The role and range of myths throughout the ancient world were extraordinary. Early people often described themselves by their myths. In addition, it was through myths that a people knew the origin of natural-and human-made objects and practices and how they came into existence. Myths also disclosed the sacred history of the people and were a way of communicating that experiential knowledge from generation to generation. Models for social acceptability were also conveyed by myths, and they were paradigms for human activities.[6] Common values and ideals were embodied in myths; they offered insight into activities that influenced the social and sacred lives of people. Even though the myths assumed different forms and functions to fulfill their various roles depending on socio-cultural requirements, they were an external reality and the resonance of the internal vicissitudes that influenced human order.[7] An early story associated with Osiris is an example of the social-ordering role of myths. One of the earliest myths assigned to this Egyptian deity related to the abolition of cannibalism among the indigenous people of the Nile Valley. The myth-defined act altered an established custom.

An essential role of a myth was making an event or situation appear to be factual, causing it to be special, and separating it from daily activities.[8] A myth, in most societies, recounted a traditional story that explained some phenomenon, custom, or belief pertinent to the social stability of a people.[9] They were generally elaborate stories based on convictions rather than actual evidence and were associated with the extraordinary traditional activities of a particular group, society, or culture. The myths related to a sacred time that was both past and present as a reference to the existence of humankind.

Myths for most early people were a way of verifying the present by remembering the past and projecting the future. They described the sacred history of the world and its formation and the reason divine powers created the inhabitants of the earth. The people were given, in that way, an identity that delineated a "living" reality.[10] Myths were the psychotropic substance of their lives and the chronicles of their existence in forms that stimulated endorsement and reinforced cultural continuity. Mythology gave meaning to the various activities that defined a particular culture and shaped the life of that society. Although myths describe occurrences that took place "a long time ago," they reflected an attitude and message that were timeless.

Masks, as psychic and, in some cultures, physical embodiments of myths were tangible elements of cultural continuance. The mask images were associated symbolically with a known story that the viewers could recall when provided with the appropriate visual key (see drawing 8.1). However, the mnemonic value and the visual recognition were not necessarily interrelated.

All cultures included myths as part of their tradition, and many defined similar events in the historical record of the people. Often the plots expressed in myths were fanciful, but they were of sufficient psychological significance to be preserved as part of the patrimony of the culture or community. Certain mythological themes, separated by time and space, appeared in most cultures of the world. An example of a commonly subscribed myth was one dealing with creation as an explanation of the origin of humans. Other mythological concepts that had multicultural recognition were those about (1) were-animals, (2) illness or death resulting from magical means, and (3) a connection between sorcery (black magic) and incest.[11]

A range of myths from many areas of the ancient world also described geological catastrophes in detail. They characterized the turbulent environment from which they as a people emerged. Those myths often told of the earthquakes, volcanic eruptions, and other cataclysms that had a terrifying impact upon the people at the beginning of their life on earth. Those tumultuous times were enacted in masked events that gave the people a sense of group identity and a feeling of responsibility to those "who came before"—the ancient ones.

Masks were the physiological essence of myths (see drawing 8.2). In earlier times, the masked person might have represented the culture hero and attempted to gain access to the spirit world for the benefit of the community. It was through the efforts of the masked person, often a shaman, that good health, physical security, and economic prosperity were achieved and maintained. The shaman enacted a "spirit-journey" and used a mask

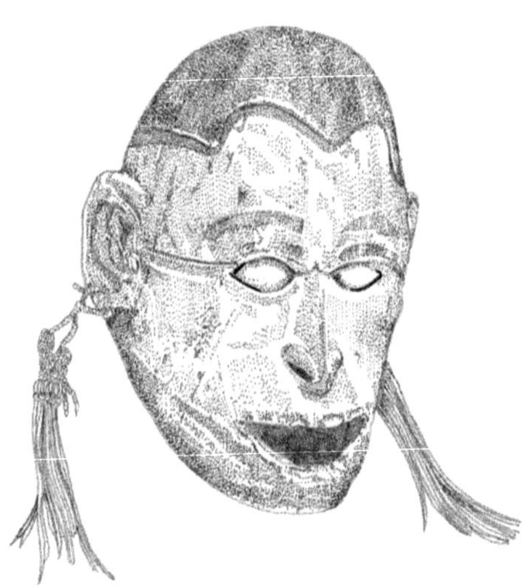

Drawing 8.1 Human head made of wood and animal hair. The Nootka people living on the Northwest Coast of the Western Hemisphere made these carved pieces to be used in ritual activities in which the dancer appeared to be beheaded.

and other ritual paraphernalia as well as ecstatic trance to facilitate the passage into the phantasmal realm.

Myths as socio-cultural parables were pervasive. They validated rather than explained, and they influenced peoples' lives both consciously and subconsciously. They were "energy-releasing, life-motivating, and directing agents"[12] that guided the actions of the populace. Myths were a part of the basic biological configuration of humans because they verified the notion that the forces of life were derived from a supreme being. In practice, myths revealed that the world, humankind, and life had a supernatural origin.[13] They also corroborated the significance of humans and their environment.

Masked events based on psychic responses to myths were enacted to assist humans to represent themselves as creatures for which the laws of reason did not apply and to confirm their divine origination. People benefited from a sense of contact with the spiritual even when it is imagined.

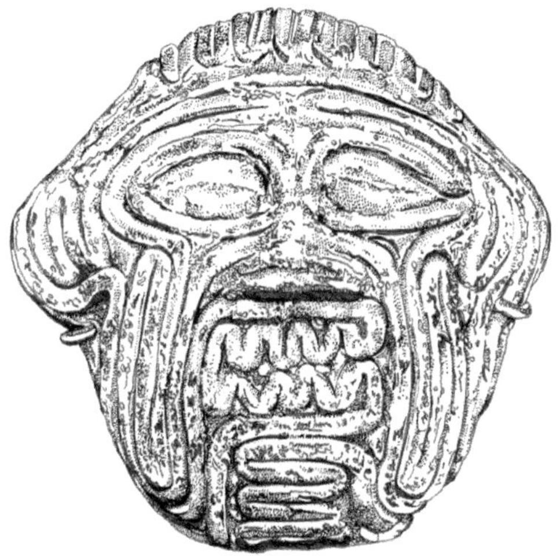

Drawing 8.2 Face of Humbaba (ca. 700–500 BCE) formed of clay and made in Babylon. The fascinating mask represented the arch foe of Gilgamesh. The face was rendered as a continuous string of viscera to relate to the practice of probing the entrails of sacrificial animals as an act of divination. The mask was also associated with the "Face of Glory" (Kirttimukha), the lion-headed demon directed by Shiva to consume itself.

Myths Defined by the Supernatural and Mysterious

Myths were the result of human fear, devotion, or curiosity. "[A] myth [was] an aesthetic device for bringing the imaginary but powerful world of supernatural forces into a manageable collaboration with the objective facts of life."[14] As a part of the oral tradition of people, a myth excited a sense of reality that was agreeable to both the rational and irrational states of human perception. In addition, myths in most societies supported the idea that humanity and the universe must improve either through the work of natural law or by divine intervention.[15] That acknowledgment was primary to individual cultural groups for use as socially delineated examples of right and wrong. Consequently, myths for those persons codified norms and illustrated proper conduct for particular situations.

Myths and masks were fundamental elements of the metamorphosis that transformed secular beings (*Homo sapiens*) into unique embodiments of spirit life (see drawings 2.2, 3.3, 3.4, 4.6, 4.8, and 6.4). In myths, early society endeavored to account for a world of wonderment by grounding it in the supernatural. Although myths referred to events that took place in the distant past, they were all embracing and shaped the activities of the present. They described events that had an emotional effect on the lives of people that were often more real or more powerful than occurrences in the corporeal world. For believers, myths facilitated the externalization of inner impulses and provided the basis for sharing inner experiences to ameliorate physical and mental confusion.

Because early cultural activities were transformed rather than transferred in their entirety and because of the variables that were a part of the daily life, myths were a paradigmatic system of ideas that passed from generation to generation as points of socio-cultural reference. Myths as complex cultural phenomena fulfilled various functions. They were an integration of social and cultural factors that achieved a symbiotic relationship. Therefore, it was reasonable to assume that myths reflected issues that were of primary concern to the originating culture and that had generally accepted applications.

Although there was a specific tradition or antecedent associated with many myths, there was also a universal quality that often went beyond the particular culture.[16] The origins and influences of myths reflected the historical and biological composition of human culture and society. A myth was an ever-changing mask that the mind of the viewer positioned over the reality they never truly saw or understood.[17] The myth and the mask, in the interchange, had different forms and functions associated with deities and ritual practices but often served the same objectives as mnemonic devices.

Myths often described apocalyptic events that took place at the dawn of time and were thought to express the absolute truth about an important part of the history of the people. Those myths gave sacred significance to the people that passed beyond the normal limitations of secular existence. Myths in many cultures were presumed to provide "a true history of what came to pass at the beginning of Time, and ... which provide[d] the pattern of human behaviour."[18] In consideration of that mythological foundation, masked rituals often included reenactments of primordial events including the transformation of humans and animals.

The human socio-cultural experience involving encounters with the natural world was a vital source of myths. Those experiences contributed to the thematic configuration of mythical events, episodes, or achievements. Certain myths, although based on and supported by psychological explanations of erroneous beliefs, were accepted as facts and transformed into group tradition. Generally, myths did not rely on truth, only the appearance of truth. Masks used as contributing elements of mythological activities were viewed in much the same way; they did not show the "face" of reality in any of its manifestations, only the necessary elements for recognition and reference. Difficulty arose when the beliefs were enshrined in parables believed to narrate actual occurrences and masks believed to portray actual beings.

The myths conveyed the great stories of the past so the people would not forget their place among the creatures of the world. The masks were a visual reference that helped the people to remember both the myth and the past.

Myth and the Cultural Fabric of a People

An early society was an organized group of people that reflected the impulses and urges of the individual on a larger scale. It was driven by the desire to dominate and survive, and a necessary part of survival was a belief system that allowed communication and emotional exchange between and among participants. People in challenging or threatening situations gravitated toward the familiar, and the more common the intellectual and emotional base, the greater the communication potential and the sense of security. The basis for a shared belief system in all societies was the unique experience of encounters with powers not of this world. The supernatural connection was a necessity because people had more wishes (wants) than resources, and early humans found the source of the unattainable to reside with the deities. To explain and justify both the "wants" and the inspirations for attainment, the myth was a viable and available instrument. The people could not maintain themselves "in the universe without belief in some arrangement of the general inheritance of myth."[19]

Primal sociological and environmental requirements caused early humans to develop a system of ceremonies and rituals including the associated paraphernalia to deal with unknown and uncontrollable forces (see drawing 8.3). That survival knowledge was transmitted to descendants and became a part of the "power" and sustainability of the people. The first ritual activities probably were performed out of fear and were a plea for help. Later, they became a part of the cultural fabric of a people and an accepted and necessary part of life. No human society has been found where such mythological motifs were not practiced in some form.[20]

Myths were indispensable elements of all cultures.[21] They explained the origin of the people and their customs as well as certain supernatural con-

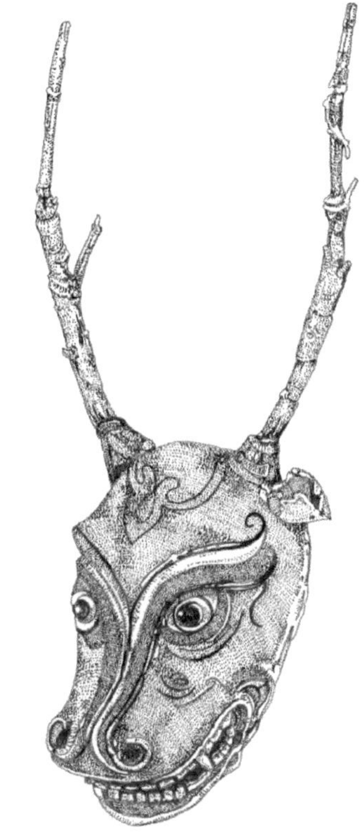

Drawing 8.3 Stag mask made of papier mâché. This mask from Tibet was painted green and blue and had bamboo horns that were wrapped with paper. Masks of this type are worn in "devil" dances. They have standardized features that represent a particular evil spirit from Tibetan mythology.

tacts and occurrences.[22] The myths gave a sense of history to a society because at the center of the myth was an element of plausibility that related to a people's existence. Mythology was a language of images, symbols, beliefs, and events drawn from the supernatural. The myths linked the supernatural with social ideology to create a circumstantial setting unlimited by everyday restrictions, and that environment reflected the imagination and desires of people. Collectively, the myths were a method of existential insight drawn from tradition and promoted by belief.

Myths, in most societal groupings, reported the activities of supernatural beings that influenced the conditions of humans. The myths often employed masks to convey the special message. It was from myths that cultures learned about the ritualistic practices of their ancestors and gained insight into the activities for attaining a desired objective. A myth was a social expression of a people that asserted the emotional and behavioral characteristics of the group. "Myth [was] a constant by-product of living faith, which [was] in need of miracles; of sociological status, which demand[ed] precedent; of moral rule, which require[d] sanction."[23]

Beliefs derived from myths that were old (emanating from the distant past) generally were held to be psychologically true[24] because they conveyed a history of social acceptance. The images associated with those beliefs were of a symbolic nature, and they were transmitted by traditional methods (see drawing 8.4). Masks as cultural markers were a primary ingredient of the transmission process, and over time the images became more stylized and less directly influenced by the originating symbols. However, they (the masks) retained a significant portion of the traditional meaning.

The relationships between myths and masks were complex in all social interactions. Because mythology shaped the thinking, imaging, and behavior of early people, the transmission of the mythic information was a dynamic fountainhead of social change. That dynamism was the energy, inspiration, and source of cultural continuity and change. Masks evolved out of mythology to acquire an earthly presence and with time gradually regained mystic status. Many masks were based on the words of myths, and the word sounds often had special powers that communicated more by their presence than their meaning.

Myths also provided the words that were recited in the performance of rituals. They called forth visions of experiences about other worlds that had group importance beyond the present and that extended into both the past and future. As vehicles of information that existed outside the mundane world of daily survival, myths projected abstract thoughts to convey symbolic meanings often encountered in masks, and through those narrative references a "consciousness of an eternal recurrence, [and] an awareness of the human continuities that span[ned] peoples and periods of human civilization"[25] was achieved. The myths united, preserved and, in some instances, created the totality of human existence.

Exemplifying that essential influence, the connection between masks and myths had a strong presence in the stories originating in Greek tradition. The satyr mask surmounted with horns announced the ancient beliefs that joined humans and beasts, whereas the masks associated with the Gorgon Medusa were founded in the myth itself. The myth related that Perseus, the hero, killed the monster and used its head (mask) to terrorize his enemies as well as the Greek people. Illustrating the gorgon myth and projecting the image of impending doom, helmet masks representing the demon were made as early as the late eighth

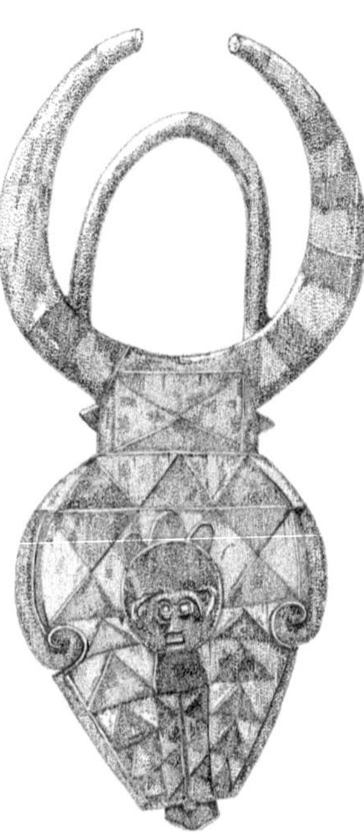

Drawing 8.4 Grunshi mask made of carved and painted wood. This mask from Burkina Faso is said by Underwood[w] to represent the divinity *Sakrobundi* and derives its shape from a local antelope with in-turned horns. The mask image is thought to be an Ashanti war fetish. The loop between the horns is not defined.

century BCE.[26] Two of the magical attributes conveyed by the gorgon head (mask) were the power to fly (transmigration) and invisibility (to mortals). Those super-human abilities were consistent with accepted shamanistic talents.

Face masks were made by the Romans in the first and second centuries of the current era as part of ceremonial helmets. The masks represented the patron deities of the specific military group. These remarkably realistic masks were made from hammered bronze and had eye and mouth openings through which the soldier could see and breathe. At that time, masks or face plates also fashioned of hammered bronze were made for war horses. The masks covered the frontal bone of the horse, had flanges in front of the eyes, and had a mask image, often the unit's patron, in the center of the forehead. Similar face plates (masks) for horses were a part of Spanish, English, and Japanese traditions.

Myths fulfilled important functions in primal society; they expressed, classified, and in many ways validated beliefs. They confirmed and enforced a concept of moral-ity, and they vouched for the effectiveness of rituals and customs.[27] Myths, in most cultural settings, provided practical rules for maintaining social order that were a vital element of civilization. The magnitude of belief in selected myths was exemplified by the male domination of the secrets of some Australian aboriginal soci-eties. According to one account, it was believed that if the women were allowed to know the secrets of the society, the entire race must be exterminated.[28] The myth predicted that at the time of disclosure the space between the earth and sky would fill with fire, and the people would go mad and slaughter each other. That attitude elucidated why only males were initiated into the secret societies and why only they were granted access to the traditions, myths, and rituals that were the means for cul-tural continuation.

This example suggests that early humans could not maintain themselves in the world without the benefit of group mythology. Those beliefs (myths) were the source of their identity, the reason for their social union, and the basis for attitudes toward food, sex, beauty, war, and many other matters associated with the fullness of life. "No human society has yet been found in which such mythological motifs have not been rehearsed in liturgies; interpreted by seers, poets, theologians, or philosophers; presented in art, magnified in song, and ecstatically experienced in life-empower-ing visions."[29] The galvanizing agents for society were the myths and beliefs. Those unsubstantiated attitudes exceeded the power of fact and technology.

Belief in the authority of the mask as a metaphysical representation was clarified and amplified by the associated myth. The story gave materialization and recogni-tion to the objects. As a embodiment of the myth, the mask became a visual sign of something invisible to the eye but clearly defined by tradition. Masks reinforced myths as fundamental units of human history that stood for or suggested something else due to their associations. An amount of what a viewer saw in a mask was trans-mitted through the senses, but an equal part was prompted by anticipation stimu-lated by the myth. The human mind was motivated by myth and traditional understanding; therefore, the viewer saw what he or she expected to see. Those con-ditioning attitudes governed visual impression.

Myths were "reasons of value" that reflected a qualified perspective of group life as well as social progress. It was myths that connected the elements of human existence and gave those activities meaning. However, when myths no longer met the needs of the culture in which they were instituted, the people sought new ways of defining and validating complicated psychic activities. New assessments of mythological traditions were initiated in the search for resolution of extant social requirements. In that transitional time, the certainty of external guidance (myths and ritual practices) was replaced by the uncertainty of internal motivation, resulting in a loss of psychic relief and sharing. Social order was corrupted. "...[M]yths form[ed] the most important part of their [a people's] traditions, not merely justifying and sanctifying all their rites and customs, but being regarded as in themselves a source of life."[30]

Whereas rituals were the enactment of cultural heritage, myths were the verbalizations of tradition. They were also clues to the spiritual potentialities of human life[31] and loci of emotional refuge. It was in times of stress or trauma that humans inevitably returned to myths, rituals, and traditions for solace rather than appealing to science and logic. There was an intuitive sense of "understanding" found in ethereal hypothesis that was wholly unattainable in intellectual reasoning. Masks were a touchstone of the reconnecting process for many cultures.

Mythology and Masks as the Foundation for Ritual Practices

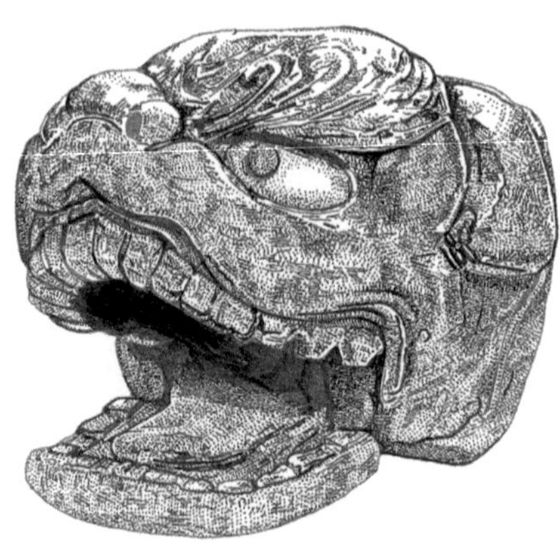

Drawing 8.5 A mythical lion mask (**shishi** or **karashishi**) made in Japan. This mask is made of carved wood and has brass eyes with iron pupils. The lion mask design probably came to China from India in the fourth or fifth centuries as an element of Buddhism. A pair of stylized lions guarded the Buddha's throne. The lion motif subsequently migrated to Japan from China by way of Korea.

The essence of ancient mythology was consigned to two categories: (1) myths that provided information about the creation of various natural elements and (2) myths that told about the origin of various objects that related to the heritage of the people. The former category explained how things came into existence, including the world, people, or animals. The latter group attested to the beginning of certain practices and identified the supernatural beings that influenced the lives of the people. Cultural continuity required both types of myths to define and pass forward the history of a people and their sacred beliefs. As stories that revealed the hopes, fears, and expectations of a people, myths were a part of the foundation of continuity.

Myths were socially motivated stories based on imagined events because they addressed issues that were beyond the horizon of human knowledge. For instance, the creation of the world and the origin of the first people myths were universal[32] and the predominate myths of most cultures. Preliterate societies emphasized ancestral affiliation in the development of their rituals of social delineation to perpetuate the creation lore. Those depictions, both visual and oral, were symbolic reminders of the cultural tradition and creative processes of a particular social group (see drawing 8.5). The act of creation (or re-creation), in all forms, was defined in myths.

It was the creation myth that fostered the masked representations of various heroes and heroines. That attitude was exemplified from the earliest times by a mythical association between the reproductive (creative) prowess of women and the fertility of the soil. For the Baga of West Africa, the Simo society mask representing Nimba, the Goddess of Increase, was one of the more important spiritual helpers. The massive mask had elongated and flattened breasts symbolizing a mother who had nurtured many children. It was the symbolic "Earth Mother." Those masks were a necessary part of ritual activities to ensure an abundant rice crop (see drawing 8.6).

Myths were an essential instrument for addressing the complexities of social adaptation. To accommodate the excesses of human nature and to give a psychological balance and order to the social structure, the concept of paradise and purgatory as opposing elements was included in the creation myth. Persons ascending into a mythologically described paradisial state were immortal, and they were thought to have a direct access to the "promised land." The significance of that state of spiritual being was reflected in the many animal masks used in ritual activities and the shamanistic practice of "talking with the animals." The power of the myth reminded people of the paradise lost (purgatory) due to human indiscretion and the importance of regaining a state of cosmic wholeness—a return to the beginning when all creatures lived in complete harmony. The human/animal kinship was a strong element in the mythical history of most cultures and a major element of masking imagery. That aspect of mythology included stories about were-animals and the ability of humans to assume the shape and characteristics of real and imaginary beasts.

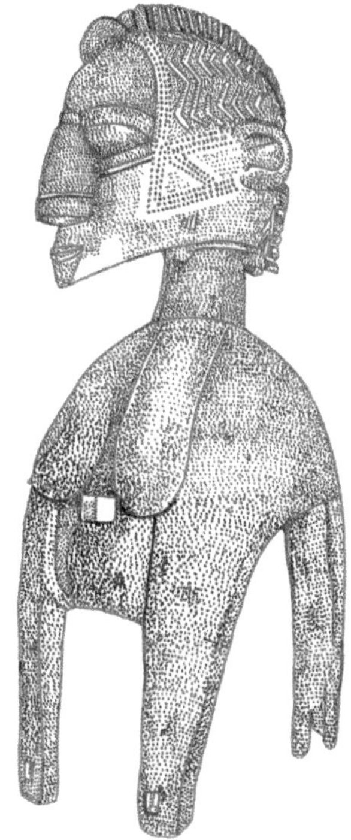

Drawing 8.6 The Nimba shoulder mask (*D'mba*) of the Baga people is associated with agriculture. The large mask has female features and breasts to emphasize the fertility of the land. These imposing masks may weigh as much as 130 pounds; they were worn at funerals, weddings, and harvest time.[x] The mask was placed on the shoulders of a dancer whose body was concealed by a fabric robe. A hole between the breasts allowed the wearer to see.

The masked practitioners (often the shaman) in enactments of myths sought to attain the paradisial state and to unite the profane and sacred worlds. The masked person became an imitator, narrator, or generator of myths and a reservoir of group tradition during the ecstatic episodes. They achieved an extraordinary state of consciousness in which they experienced phenomena beyond their mortal identity and outside their time and place. That mystical information provided a paradigmatic imprint that members of the group were expected to observe and perpetuate "in order to assure the continuity of the world, of life and society."[33] The projected model of social acceptability often was presented in mythological form with the cultural hero as the mediator.

A second element of mythological importance among early people related to animal and human procreation, including the issue of incest. There are numerous masks in all mask-making societies that were configured to promote both male and female sexual activity and fertility. An extension of the propagation obsession was the desire of men to more fully participate in the reproduction process by assigning and assuming feminine roles. Masks were an important part of that pseudo-physiological transfiguration, and the use of "female" masks worn by males was an accepted part of the masking tradition (see drawing 8.7). The cross-gender role playing was an example of a ritual event in which the males of the group ceased to be themselves so they might know themselves better. "By wearing a mask he [the inclusive male element] [became] what he [was] resolved to be: *Homo religiosus...*"[34]—the holistic being. As a further element of that role playing, the males in some cultures ceremonially lacerated their penises to symbolically represent the production of menstrual discharge.

Although numerous myths related to the issue of incest particularly as related to the creation of the world and the first people, few masks were produced to address that specific aspect of cultural praxes. The deities in myths transformed or disguised themselves before the act of copulation and in that way deceived their unwitting partners. The early people, perhaps because of that mythologically defined duplicity, developed elaborate social schemes to define appropriate consanguineous interaction. Masks were a part of the defining and regulating processes that reinforced acceptable standards of cohabitation.

A third myth type of universal proportion described the cultural "hero." Great culture heroes were associated with the invention of "all the arts and skills which are now the treasures of civilization."[35] The exploits of the cultural hero or heroine were described in myths to recount his or her triumphs. Their adventures were a necessary part of group identification and a common factor in masking events (see drawing 8.8). In myths, the hero figure assumed many roles that were of primary importance to the physical and mental well-being of the people they served. Reik in *Ritual: Psycho-analytic Studies*[36] stated that masks were an early method of identifying with the "father" as the primordial being—the

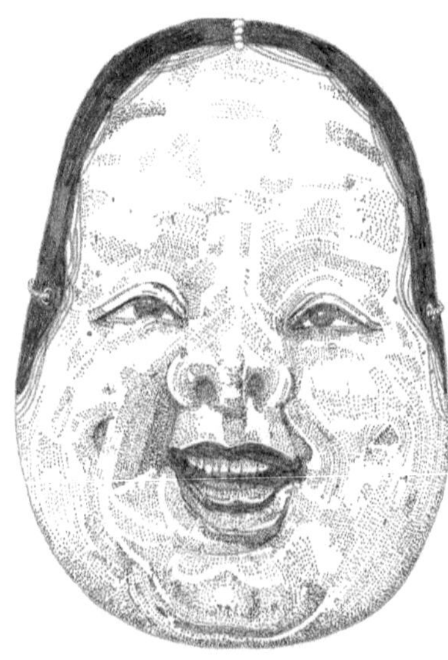

Drawing 8.7 A Japanese mask of a young woman that represents one of five categories of Noh masks—gods, men, women, the insane, and demons. Men or boys played all roles, but only the principal actor, the *shite*, and his *waki* wore masks, not the supporting actors.[y] One of the more popular and familiar characters was the "young woman." This mask symbolized the traditional Japanese notion of beauty with whitened face, straight hair, shapely eyebrows, a high forehead, and red lips.

ancestor, antecedent, or hero. That idea reflected the assumptions of Freudian psychoanalysis and associated the "father/hero" image with the creative forces of nature. The father/hero/progenitor belief was a primary element of social development. It marked the way for patrimonial continuity and was the foundation for ancestor veneration. It was also a vital link between the living and the dead.

Resident within the mythological tradition and situated outside the secular boundaries was the sacred history of the people that revealed why they followed a particular way of life in relationship with the universe and all its known elements. Therefore, myths, as a record of the connection between the people and their chosen deities, were exemplary models that society chose to emulate.

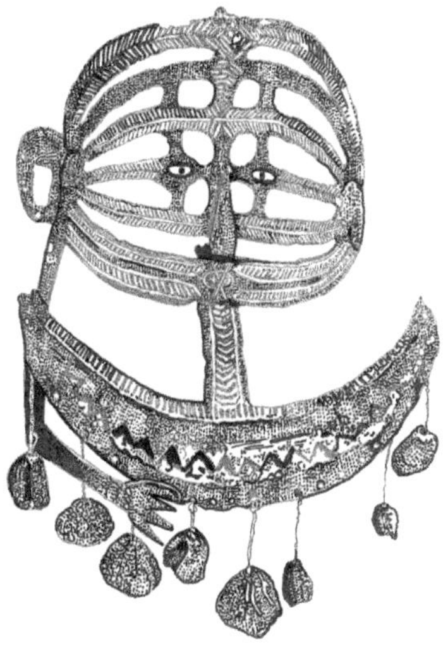

Drawing 8.8 A mask from the Torres Straits used in the *Bomai-Malu* ceremony. This turtle-shell mask represents *Bomai*, the hero who may also be called by a secret name *Malu*. This mythological entity was called on in time of illness or danger.

Myths Defined by a Special Time, Place, and Reality

Mythology, as described by E.T.C. Werner in *Myths and Legends of China*,[37] was the science of unscientific people in their attempt to explain what was termed the "Otherworld." Myths were sacred records, and although they lacked scientific validation, they were ways by which people were transported from temporal time and space to spiritual time and space. Because it was situated beyond the horizon of human authority, sacred time was indefinitely revisable and could be extended or shortened to meet the requirements of a particular situation. That flexibility allowed mystical concerns to be constantly contemporary and evolving.

Events consigned to sacred time were described as being from a time long ago or "in the beginning" when all things were created. "This mythic or sacred time [was] qualitatively different from profane time, from the continuous and irreversible time of our everyday, de-secularized existence."[38] The attitude of sacred time made transmission of the mythological history of a people a secretive process that was normally accomplished through ritual activities often involving masked participants. Sacred information was told in stages beginning with the coming of age of group members and continuing through advanced adulthood. The information was divulged in culturally defined steps that often were illustrated and reinforced by a masked event (see drawing 8.9).

Most myths included two kinds of information. The first kind was "natural information" because the details were reasonable and rational. Those data assigned the people-oriented elements of the myth and made them believable within the limits of human understanding. That aspect of mythological thinking informed people that what they were about to do had already been done, thus emphasizing continuity. The second kind of information derived from myths was "supernatural information." Those myths addressed issues that were beyond the realm of human reason or judgment. It was that part of the mythological stasis that furnished exceptional physiological and sociological details and gave insight into the beliefs of the people subscribing to the myth.

As an example of this mythical configuration, the supernatural world of the people of the Sepik region in New Guinea reflected a two-part mythological foundation. One part dealt with spirits living in specific locations such as water, land, and vegetation. Those spirits appeared in either human or animal form and were responsible for a number of "natural" phenomena such as storms, fast currents, and other environmental variables. The second part, the supernatural element, was associated with ancestors. Those myths related to the creation process of which the most recent generation is the latest example.[39] The first group of myths was recognized and revered while the second was perpetuated by social interaction and exchange. The two elements were combined to form the mythological foundation for the people that established both a historical validity and a process for continuation of traditional values. All societies depended on the two very basic concepts regardless of their status within the sociological continuum. It was when one of the elements was lost or disregarded that social order was disrupted.

Masks as elements of the mythical process had mythico-ritual roles in which they served as connective reminders between the profane and the sacred worlds. The mask put a recognizable face on mythical beings and made them identi-fiable to those who endorsed the myths (see drawing 8.10). Thus, people could disregard profane conditions and be projected into a sacred world of heroic beings, events, and proportions. Immersed in the masking activity, the people regained contact with the spiritual foundation of their beliefs. The mask and myth were unique elements of self-identification by association. Each retelling of a myth reinforced the emotional connectedness of the people with the sacred conditions that existed in a better or greater time (long ago). Similarly, the masks because of their psychogenic origin reinforced belief in those predefined conditions.

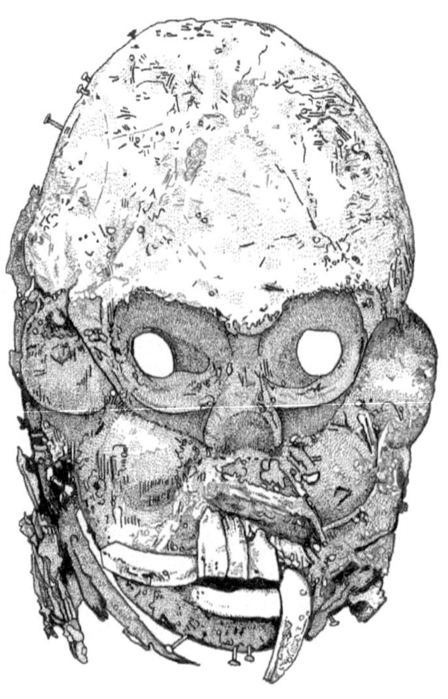

Drawing 8.9 Okoroshi Ojo mask made of wood, vegetal fiber, and pigment. The mask has a twisted, brutalized face on which features are exaggerated, rearranged, or omitted. These Igbo masks were associated with power and violence and carried the strong spiritual sanction of the *Owu* deity. They were greatly appreciated by *Mgbala Agwa* (society) members and were often passed from one generation to the next.

Myths as Indispensable Elements of Culture

The world, in the beginning, was in a state of chaos, and although there are no unequivocal data to substantiate that hypothesis, that presumption was the basis of many traditional activities. The creation myths evolved to explain the emergence of order from chaos. The mythological origination of humankind was similar in all major cultures. Rituals and masks were necessary props to reinforce that supposition and to make it real. The myths strengthened the social structure, and the society perpetuated the myths.

The formalization of myths and masks varied according to culturally determined criteria. Mythical animals functioned, in some societies, as conveyers of fundamental values while in other cultures, idealized humans were celebrated as elements of mythological importance. Early

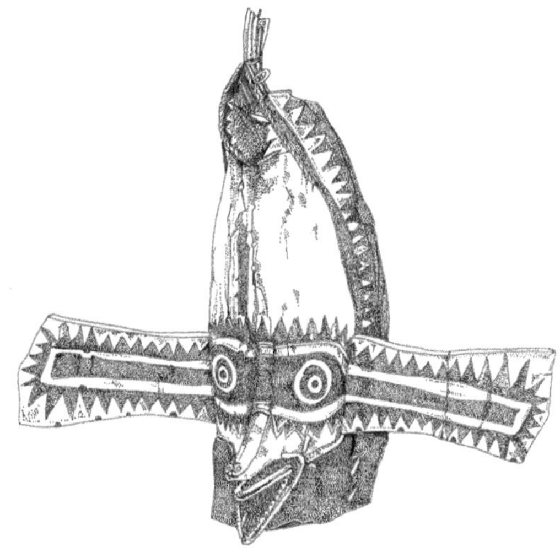

Drawing 8.10 A mask from New Guinea made of bark cloth and painted red, white, and black. This mask with the animal-like features and elaborate wings is over two and one-half feet tall. It is made of bark cloth and became more associated with dramas and dances than recognition of a spirit being.

humans believed in invisible powers that were transcendent and made approachable through myths. In many of those mythological episodes, the patterns of spiritual alignment and their relationships were consistent; the sun was masculine, and the earth was feminine. The former occupied the "regions above" and the latter represented the "regions below." The sun deity was responsible for regulating the forces of nature and maintaining their balance, while the earth deity had control of the functions of fertility and procreation as manifested in agriculture. Her (the Earth Mother's) energy was the origin of all life. Together the coexisting and codependent forces influenced every aspect of the human existence.

Just as myths described the coming into being of humankind and the relationship of the people with their environment and other humans, so did they define human interchange with the deities and provide directions for rituals.[40] Myths furnished a comprehensive view of the world, and masks were accoutrements for deciphering the myths and the worldview they embodied. As an expression of the wisdom that was assigned to the human head, the masks attested to the origin of the people as defined in the myths. The mythical progenitor of humankind in many locations was represented as a bull, serpent, or other deified creature associated with the sun. The snake often symbolized the reproductive power of the male, while the bull was symbolic of a broader idea of fecundity. The sun, above all, was the renewing energy source.

The bull, serpent, and sun have had special meaning in the myths and traditions of many peoples. Those same elements contributed to the masking traditions

of numerous early cultures. In
early European mythology the bull
was associated with regeneration
and the female reproductive
organs, while in the Indo-
European tradition it symbolizes
the Thunder God. The snake was
one of the oldest symbols of female
power. Peoples in India, Mexico,
Egypt, Turkey, and Uruguay gave
symbolic importance to snakes, as
did various cultures in West Africa
and North America.[41] The Fon people of West Africa fostered a snake
cult, and history associated the serpent with the mother of all gods,
the Earth Goddess Gaea described
in Homeric hymns.[42] The Indian
serpent goddess, Kundalini, represented the inner power of the
human body "coiled in the pelvis

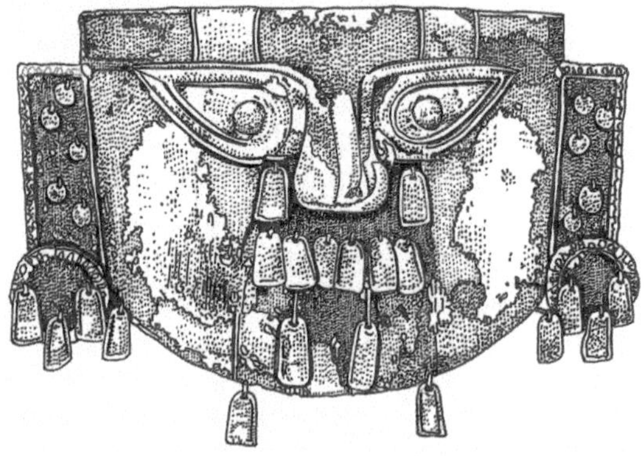

Drawing 8.11 Lambaueqie burial mask made of
embossed sheet gold. The mask has gold tears that
extend from the corners of the eyes and drip from
the chin. The danglers over the mouth conceal the
breath or spirit of the deceased. The masks covered the face of a mummy and were painted red,
the sacred funerary color. It is believed that
pre–Columbian gold work originated in Peru and
spread north to Mexico.

like a woman's organs of life-giving."[43] The serpent-mother Iusaset was one of the
oldest goddesses of predynastic Egypt. Her avatar was believed to enclose the phallus of Ra, the sun god, every night.

The sun as an energy source was venerated by many cultures and assigned human
characteristics to reinforce popular acceptance. The sun god of Peru was reputed to
weep tears of gold. A mask with teardrops represented that deity (see drawing 8.11).

It was essential for the inhabitants of archaic societies to know the myths of their
culture because they included an explanation of the world and the human role in
that world. In their ritual activities early people were connected with their ancestors
and gained insight into the mythical origins of objects, animals, and plants.[44] That
familiarity was analogous to acquiring a magical power over the environment in
which they lived. It was a form of control and a manifestation of human superiority.

Myths in all cultures appealed to the consciousness of the people by embodying cultural ideals or by giving expression to deep, commonly felt emotions.[45] When
a people (group or society) had little actual history to validate their existence, there
were numerous complex myths. However, when there was an extensive historical
record (to provide the social validation), the myths were few and seldom spectacu-
lar.

Much of what was important to early peoples was not based on fact but on beliefs
reinforced by myth and represented by masks. It was the accepted perspective of
social order and human existence that invalidated the laws of time and space. The
essential nature of a deity was consigned to a mask or a sacred place according to the
related myth. When the mask was presented or the place was visited, the deity was
revitalized. The mask was an embodiment of the mythical being it represented and

a reminder of the power it possessed because, as Lawrence Hatab noted in *Myth and Philosophy: A Contest of Truths,* "Myth does not explain the world; it is the 'world-ing' of the world, its unconcealment. Prior to myth the world, as a context of mean-ing, is 'not there' (concealment).'"[46]

9

Shape-Shifting Faces

The deeper one goes into the study of the supernatural and its devotees, the clearer it is that similar trends of thought have made men's minds work alike among communities so diverse that they might belong to different worlds.[1]

The world in the beginning was thought to be inhabited by a profusion of spirits, and their presence was reflected in every aspect of human existence. Those omnipresent spirit beings declared themselves in different ways. Some made possible a happy and productive domestic life. Others granted success in the hunt or warfare, and others concerned themselves with the power and magic assigned to special people (shamans) for the practices of communication and survival. Everything that resided in the natural world occupied by humankind possessed some form of associated power that emanated from the supernatural. The shaman was the intermediary to deal with the complex interaction between those distinct yet closely joined aspects of the natural and supernatural worlds.

Recognition of and belief in the paranormal is as old as humankind. It defined the source of those extraordinary and unpredictable occurrences that were beyond human control and complete comprehension. Although the materialistic values of an evolving society were formulated based on systematic rationale, belief in the supernatural had a far greater influence on the lives of humans. No other force was even remotely equivalent to the raw impact upon the existence of individuals and communities as that generated by endorsement of the transcendental world. The supernatural could be both wondrous and terrifying because it supported the notion that life as a transcendental concept, not material embodiment, had meaning.

Belief in the supernatural is one of the greatest of human institutions. No societies have been encountered that did not include some form of expression dedicated to belief in the supernatural. It occupied a central role in the belief systems of all peoples from the beginning of known history. How far back into time such beliefs may go is a matter of speculation, but evidence indicates that as early as ca. 10,000 BCE, ritual activities were a part of human culture.[2] Research supports the opinion that 100,000 years ago human burials were treated in a ritualistic manner, suggesting a concern for the afterlife of the dead — a conscious recognition of the supernatural.

Early people appear to have believed that confrontation between humans and the supernatural could be dangerous as well as fortuitous. Stories passed from generation to generation told of the difficulties encountered due to the unpredictable nature of supernatural power and how humans were tested by the spirit beings occupying the cosmic realm. The Apache believed the universe to be pervaded with powers that they considered cosmic in nature. Each object, thought, or person was an element of that power because it was everywhere — as pervasive as the air.[3] Supernatural power was the source of both good and evil in most belief systems. It gave life and brought death, and by its ubiquitous nature, it was incorporated into every aspect of daily life (see drawing 9.1).

The physiological and emotional needs of most early people exceeded the limits of normal understanding and required paranormal intervention to find acceptable solutions. That perspective ranged beyond commonplace experience and allowed emotional interpretation to augment an imperfect reality.[4] The acceptability of that attitude on both the physical and mental levels was continually modified by group tradition and experience. A sympathetic understanding had to exist between all elements of the transformational process to be effective.

It was likely that archaic humans lost their sense of physiological and psychological equilibrium when confronted by something unknown or unidentifiable. It was natural, in an unrelenting environment, for people to imagine that evil or danger was concealed by that which could not be seen, understood, or classified. Undoubtedly, early peoples viewed the world around them as a place immersed in peril and believed that only special persons with the appropriate prescriptive powers could alleviate the anomalies. For those persons, reliance on supernaturalism had a dual nature; it provided favorable influences or directed unfavorable ones.

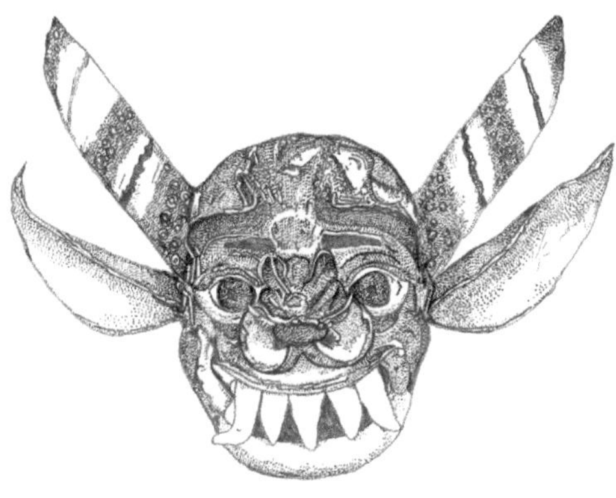

Drawing 9.1 A devil mask from Bolivia made of painted wood and with the features of a bat. Devil-masked performers first appeared in the Carnival of Oruro toward the end of the eighteenth century. The *Diablada*, Devil Dance, was a central part of the Carnival of Oruro.[2] The masks projected a fearsome appearance that often had animal traits.

Supernatural affiliation was about belief in spiritual forces that existed beyond the realm of humans. Those forces were more powerful than humans and controlled those elements in life that were important to human survival. Such beliefs were a consensual phenomenon. They were fundamental to supernatural acceptance. In most communities that acceptability was part of social tradition and was passively endorsed by both the individuals and the group.[5] Therefore, belief in the supernatural was an important way of maintaining the basic qualities of life because it preserved the values accepted by the people.

From the earliest times, humans divided the world into two realms, the sacred and the secular, and in many societies that division was clearly defined and separated. However, the two spheres were more closely aligned in other cultures. Despite the divisions or perhaps because of that separation, the supernatural played an important role in the lives of individuals as well as the community. Shamans, priests, sorcerers, and magicians were useful constituents of society for promoting an understanding of how humans related to the supernatural world. That sentiment of cosmic affiliation had both intellectual and emotional content, and in most societies, the two elements melded into one consciousness. The people accepted and endorsed the concept of the supernatural to give added meaning to life values.

Although early people may have believed themselves to be powerless to deal with the perilous and often unpredictable forces that surrounded them, certain persons had or acquired a unique ability — a power — that allowed them to overstep the boundary between the known and unknown. That ability did not denote physical strength or mental dexterity; it was of a different nature that often was acquired at the expense of physical well-being. Those powers transcended ordinary limitations and were beyond the understanding of most people. "A limited number of people were inspired by stronger spirit powers than others.... They formed an élite [group] since the numbers of men and women with shamanistic abilities were very small, and they were sometimes considered as outsiders to the community."[6]

The shaman, for traditional people, was a mediator between the inspiriting world of myth and ordinary reality. As the archetype spiritual leader, healer, and social regulator, the shaman was a creative response to the supernatural. The recognition of that unique position acknowledged the incomprehensibility of the activities of spirits, deities, and demons. It was in that environment that the vocation of the shaman developed. If humankind was to survive, the shaman, as a special person, had to enter a state of super consciousness that allowed access beyond the limitations of the natural order and into the world of spirits and ancestors (see drawing 9.2). There the shaman could gather the symbols of ritual recognition that were believed to influence the physical conditions of the people. Once the survival scheme components were assembled, the people could participate through rituals that reinforced the shaman's communicative activities.

The shaman was a person the people allowed to influence their lives. He or she

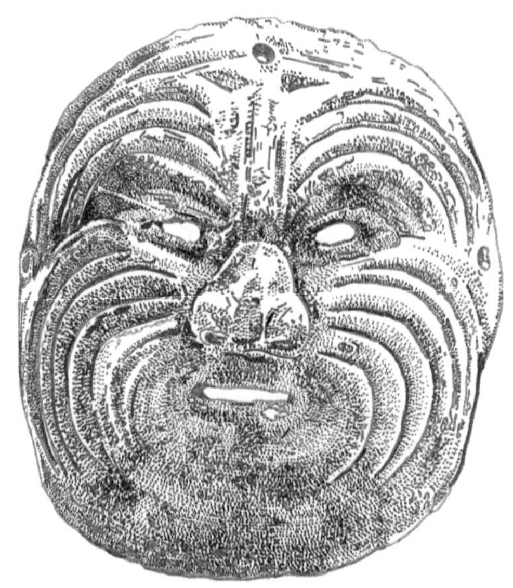

Drawing 9.2 Anthropomorphic mask (ca. 800 BCE–100 CE) depicting the face of old age. This reddish-brown clay mask with incised details is from the Calima zone, Colombia. It is an unusual example of ceramics made in the Llama-phase style.[aa] In pre–Hispanic Colombia, great emphasis was placed on the head and this mask illustrates one of the cycles of male involvement in the social system. The male's symbolic role was to "emerge and move out" and to "mature and decay," hence the mask of old age.

represented an unequaled power whether it was over objects; the way information was conveyed about objects, spirits, or activities; or the beliefs and perceptions of people. The shaman discovered or foretold what was otherwise hidden from the human eye and influenced or manipulated objects or natural phenomena to satisfy actual or assumed human needs. Perhaps most importantly the shaman also contested the various evils, real or imaginary, that afflicted humankind.[7] Those activities were wide ranging, depending on the needs of the society the shaman served. The more ideal and nonthreatening the surroundings were, the fewer demands there were for shamanistic intervention.

Belief in the supernatural acknowledged a force that explained fundamental questions regarding existence that were unanswerable in other ways. If evil spirits were the source of human problems, then the removal of negative beings should assure a better life. The shaman in that facilitating process had a primary role in attracting or exorcising spirits. The performance of duties and rituals based on traditional beliefs and myths concerned with supernatural powers were the shaman's tools.[8] Those powerful elements along with the appropriate mask and equipage were used in response to phenomenological occurrences. That approach recognized existent belief systems as well as continuing those traditions that influenced earlier generations—the ancestors.

Although precisely analogous ideas of the supernatural were not found in every culture, a distinction between the sacred and profane was almost universal.[9] The status of "supernatural" was attached to unnatural or phenomenal happenings among practically all people. Extraordinary incidents were seldom regarded with emotional detachment as they were thought to be the result of social or cultural transgressions. Accordingly, most cultures had activities or acts that were considered taboo and believed to be dangerous. Those activities evoked emphatic emotional responses that were different from those assigned to commonplace occurrences.

The traditional lifeways of many early people appear to have centered on beliefs and practices emanating from a regulatory process involving supernatural forces. A balance had to be achieved and maintained between the ethereal and material worlds for the people to survive. That equilibrium was sought through ceremonies, rituals, and various forms of self-privation or mutilation. Masks were a primary part of many of those ceremonies.

Masks often reflected "vision quests" to identify a particular bird or animal to serve as a spirit helper or "friendly." Connection with the appropriate helper

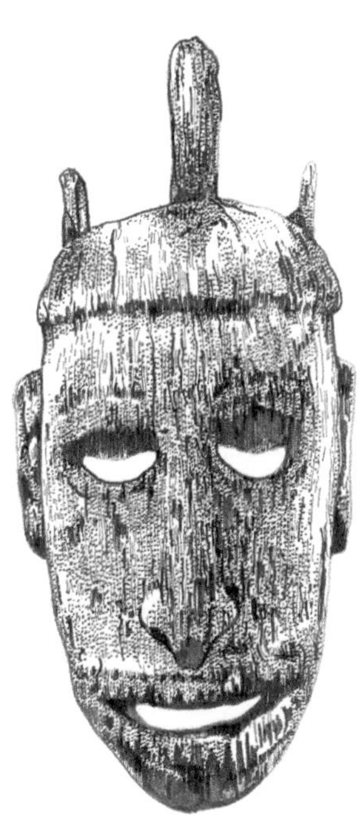

Drawing 9.3 An old mask representing an ancestral spirit from Kiari Village, Rai Coast, Astrolabe Bay area. This mask is made of wood with traces of red paint or stain. Most of the art from this area is extremely old. Many of the anthropomorphic masks and figures have intricately carved distended ear lobes and earrings.

facilitated access to powerful and important supernatural beings that were visited through dreams and visions. Those visionary images were also the principal source of inspiration for masks for numerous cultures (see drawing 9.3).

A particularly interesting example of traditional helper spirit occurred among the Akawaio Caribs of British Guyana. They believed the shaman's spirit attached itself to the swallow-tailed kite, known locally as the "clairvoyant woman." The kite helped the shaman's spirit soar aloft to commune with germane vital forces.[10]

Grim notes in *The Shaman: Patterns of Siberian and Ojibway Healing* that the "Yakut shaman's costume display[ed] a complete bird skeleton of iron amplifying this flight symbolism."[11] Flight allowed the shaman to maintain the relationships between the cosmic worlds.[12]

The Supernatural as the Center of Magico-Religious Life

Researchers have speculated that shamanism was the world's earliest form of supernatural veneration, beginning at least 50,000 years ago.[13] Most scholars have agreed that the term "shaman" as well as the practice probably originated in Siberia. Scholars also associate shamanism with the notion of "a master of spirits" because the person (man or woman) acted as an intermediary between humans and the supernatural. As the true origin of shamanism is obscure and because it probably was practiced during the Late Paleolithic Period, the location of the first ascetic is difficult to ascertain.[14] However, ideas about shamanism have influenced the philosophical foundations of reverential systems across Asia, North Africa, and areas of North and South America. "In the shamanistic world everything [was] alive, and all life [was] part of one mysterious unity by virtue of its derivation from the spiritual source of life — the life force."[15]

The shaman was the archetype healer, teacher, and redeemer as well as a magician whose power was said to come from supernatural intervention. Undoubtedly that benevolent image existed in the psyche of humankind since the beginning of time. It was inevitable that when people lost their way, they felt the need for a guide, either physical or spiritual. In shamanistic practice, there was no distinction between a shaman helping others and helping himself or herself, and it was often the case that the shamans had to protect or heal themselves before they could be of assistance to others.

Andreas Lommel, writing in *The World of the Early Hunters*,[16] contended that the shaman was a distinctly different person from the ordinary "medicine man." That conjecture was based on an assumption that the shaman was of a higher level of intellectual intensity and reflected an affiliation with the early hunting community. Regardless of the appellation by which the person was known, the shaman was an individual believed to be in communion with the spirits. That person's energies were outwardly oriented and "directed toward the community so that the trance [visionary journey] serve[d] as a medium of communication between the supernatural or non-ordinary reality and the community of men [people]."[17] The shaman and the audience were integral parts of the visionary journey, and the "ecstasy" ended if the connection was broken.

The word "shaman" came from Tungus, a family of languages spoken in central and eastern Siberia and Manchuria. The literal meaning of the word is "he who knows." The magico-religious life of the people centered on the shaman throughout that immense region of the world. However, shamanism as a magico-religious concept also was found in regions of Africa, Oceania, Australia, the Americas, and parts of Northern and Eastern Europe.[18] It was a part of every hunting-gathering culture and remained an important force for all those who maintained the ancient traditions. Although a magico-religious concept, shamanism was not a true religion but a psychological technique that could reside within the framework of any religion. It emerged primarily within early religions and predominately within the beliefs of hunting peoples.[19]

The shaman in a trance-like state was possessed by a spirit and given the powers of healing and divining. To control and direct that energy, the shaman concentrated his or her imaginative powers into an intense mental image of an anticipated outcome. A mask as a focusing device often aided that activity. The mask allowed the shaman to assume a certain appearance thought to be agreeable to spiritual powers (see drawing 9.4).

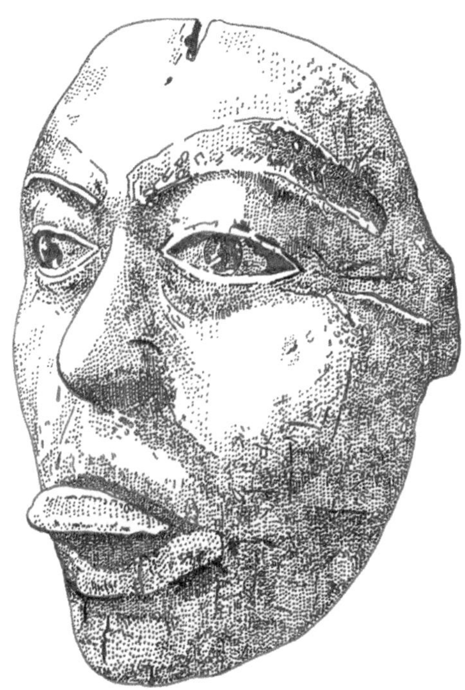

Drawing 9.4 A Tlingit (*Yakutat*) shaman's facemask made of wood with traces of pigment. "[T]he greatest concentration of a shaman's spirit power resided in his mask."[bb] When the shaman put on his mask, he became the manifestation of power. This mask, recovered from a site on the Akwe River forty miles down the coast from Yakutat Bay in the northwestern region of North America, represents the "spirit of a dead man."[cc] The finely carved mask has a very human-like appearance that is made extraordinary by the intense expression of the eyes and the protruding tongue. The exact meaning of the tongue is unclear, but it may signify the man's spirit (soul). Tlingit shaman masks generally had no eyeholes.

Omnipresent and Omnipotent Forces

Considering the expansiveness of the socio-cultural evolutionary process, humans were an intimate part of the environment—one with the other for thousands of years. The physical and spiritual planes of that relationship ran parallel, and along the lines of those concurrent projections there were points where the two came together. Those intersections occurred in different ways and for different purposes, and the outcome of the interchanges had both positive and negative results.

The intercourse between the two paths was viewed as a mirror that reflected the "real" (spiritual) world that existed beyond the spectrum of normal understanding. That concept was a common theme that inhabited both popular and secret stories and myths. Mirror-reflected images were also associated with inner life and power. That reference was found in many cultures in various locations. Examples of that association included the obsidian (smoke) mirrors of the Aztecs, mirror "eyes" of masks made in Mexico and West Africa, and the copper (bronze) mirrors of North Africa and the Middle East. Water was also associated with spirits and the spirit world because of its ability to reflect the physical world. Water-associated mask images were made in many locations, and most were connected with ritual activities pertaining to the health and physical well being of the people (see drawing 9.5).

The people in archaic times undoubtedly had apprehensions about many things both natural and supernatural. One of their primary anxieties, from a pragmatic perspective, must have related to physical debilitation. Illness was feared because of its mysterious nature and because it deprived people of the ability to participate in activities necessary to sustain life. The causes of infirmity in all probability were thought to be either the result of magical inducement or spiritual intervention. The shaman in most societies aligned maladies with cultural beliefs, in that environment of superstition and anxiety, to give meaning and reason to the patient's bewilderment and distress as well as a prescription for relief.[20] A part of the healing process often related to the mythological record of the culture. That referential reliance allowed the patient to identify with the mythical being and to discover both the cause and solution for the distress-causing conditions.

It is probable that early people were con-

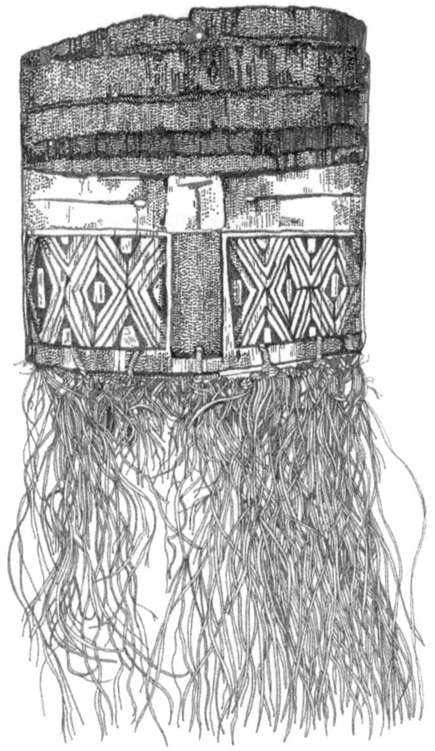

Drawing 9.5 Fish dance mask of the Kamayura from central Brazil made of wood and fiber and probably representing the fish spirit. The "T" marking on the nose "symbolizes a shape visible on a fish" and the lower part of the mask has a "net-like drawing."[dd] There is no clearly documented record of how these masks were used, but they were apparently associated with curing ceremonies.[ee] They might have been used to cure illness brought on by the loss of the patient's soul. The masking ceremony was to attract the offending spirit to the village and to convince it to return the stolen soul.

sumed by the conditions of daily existence. Judging from available evidence, many relatively mundane activities required the assistance of one or more deities. Supernatural concurrence with socio-cultural actions was required and, without that support, the activity often ceased. The power behind almost all events rested with the supernatural — a force both omnipresent and omnipotent. Therefore, it was normal to ask for assistance from the supernatural in times of physical, mental, and social distress. The shaman in a traditional belief system served as the ceremonial guide for instituting connection with the spirit world. The shaman as the leader of the ritual event dramatized a personal meeting with the spirits and announced that encounter with symbols from the natural world.[21]

The shaman had the power to heal and to make contact with the pervasive forces of the macrocosm.[22] Shamanistic powers also included interpreting dreams, divining, guiding the souls of the dead, telling the future, and directing ceremonies or rituals to appease a violated spirit. That paranormal ability came as a calling from beyond the realm of the visual world. "In this other world the shaman [was] taught certain symbolic gestures that [were] used later in ritual activities to impart a sustaining or healing energy to individuals or the community."[23]

The group members (the community) were constantly reminded of the power of the spirits because of the activities of a shaman. Moreover, the masks worn for ritual practices symbolized the spiritual presence (see drawing 9.6). Life was fragile; it could be given or taken away. The hunt was a success or a failure. The rains came or they did not. Environmental conditions changed due to unknown causes making living conditions more or less harsh and always tentative. Those transformations were evidence of the supernatural. In response to those conditions, people sought ways to communicate with the spirits as a means of regulating the natural world to which they were restricted. That attitude was a social response to interrelationships that were honored in all phases of human existence.

Some modes of communication with the spirit world were possible on an individual basis. The hunter observed the proper ritual before embarking on the hunt or an expectant mother performed the appropriate ceremony to ensure a successful and painless child delivery. Assurance of a positive response by the deities often required sacrifice, prayers, ritual, dance, or dramatization using costumes and masks. The services of a shaman were used, or group ceremonies were performed for more demanding interactions with the spirits.

Spiritual or demoniacal possessions were circumstances in which the shaman's help was also necessary. Superior supernatural power was required to dislodge the possessing

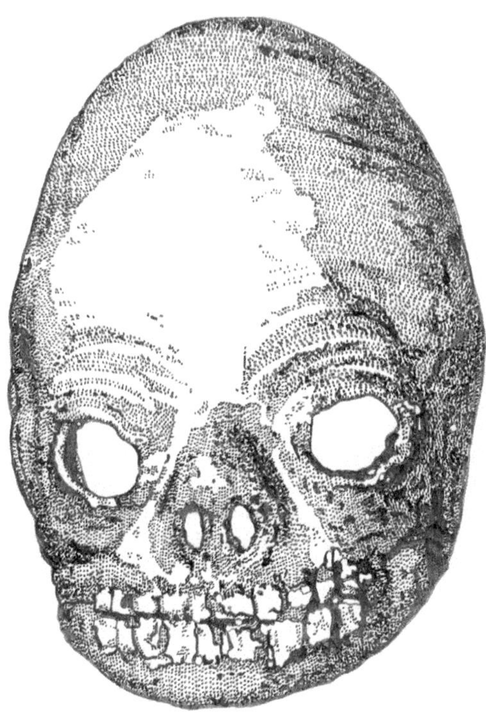

Drawing 9.6 A skull mask from Bolivia with a simple realism that was both humorous and frightening. The dead were buried with masks of gold or silver to protect them from the devil's "insidious watch,"[ff] while the living wore masks representing the bones of their ancestors. Skull masks were often viewed as sacred objects through which it was possible to communicate with the dead.[gg]

force. Shamanistic regalia including a mask, head cover, and robe as well as a rattle, drum, fan, and other types of spirit-attracting paraphernalia used to capture or exorcise the disruptive visitant. Each piece of the supporting apparatus was said to transmit a special energy that was outside the understanding of normal people. As an example of the special character of the paraphernalia, the mask separated the shaman from his or her natural associations and established a supernatural relationship with the possessive spirits (see drawing 9.7). Those masks were often frightening in appearance and had unearthly qualities.

Masks and the Extra-Human Powers of the Universe

Belief in the supernatural was a universal condition. Humans endorsed some form of spiritual reverence as a means of addressing the ethical (moral) and social issues they encountered. "[T]here is no satisfactory historical evidence that since man was man there have been peoples who did not attempt to enter into social relations with the extra-human powers of the universe."[24] Among many traditional people, the belief system found reality in practices involving the placation of spirits and diversion of their energy to benevolent purposes.

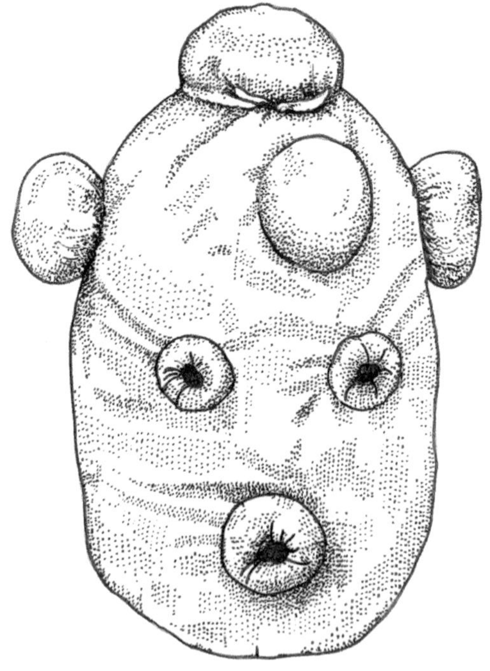

Drawing 9.7 Ball-on-head (*Koyemshi* or mud head) masks were clay-loaded bags filled with dirt scooped from the streets. Zuñi dancers wore them during ritual events. The bodies of the ten *Koyemshi* performers were coated with mud or clay that gave them an "other"-world appearance. Reportedly, the first *Koyemshis* were the result of an incestuous relationship between the son and daughter of the Sun Father. The first progeny of this union was reported to be normal and is considered the ancestor of makers or rain. The following nine siblings were believed to be insane and deformed: They "eat filth," have ritualistic intercourse, or beg for food. The Zuñi view the activities as the fruitful process of nature.

At a time when humanity was at the mercy of the extraordinary powers of nature, shamanism sought to divide the paranormal forces into matter and spirit. Thus, external threats were encountered on a psychological level rather than an intellectual one. Masks and images were an interrelated part of that process of subversion because they portrayed "spirit beings" and were not intended to represent real creatures. [25]

An important attachment to certain masks was an array of small shapes, figures, and amulets representing the shaman's spirit helpers. Other masks had strings, rods, or animal tails affixed to them. The strings and rods were connecting elements for attracting and joining with spirits, and the animal tails were another reference to the dual nature of human/animal spirituality.[26]

To address the many demands of the natural worlds, shamans were "healers, seers, and visionaries who [had] mastered death."[27] To fulfill their unique role in an increasingly complex cultural setting, the shamans often interacted with the supernatural in an animal guise, and elaborate masks often were a part of that transposition. Along the northwest coast of the United States, animal and bird masks symbolize the transformation of humans to animal forms. The masks, as symbolic references to the duality of the human subconscious, opened to reveal the human face inside — the coupling of two life forms (see drawing 9.8). Other articles of shamanistic regalia included animal-headed human figures and a variety of creatively joined animal and human elements. Many of those objects were derived from supernatural experiences as helper or totem beings and had meanings known only to their owner.

Various deities recognized by traditional cultures were endowed with the power to take different forms. Some came into the world of people as animals and they were afterwards associated with those creatures. Masks representing the particular deities often drew upon those animal images for symbolic reference. If a deity was born of a cow or took the form of a water snake, those likenesses found their way into the mask symbology for shamanistic representation or mythical reference.

The influence of animal transformation masks in the shamans' rites was significant in Oceania as well as along the northwest coast of North America. In those areas, masks expressed the dual nature of humans—part animal and part human.

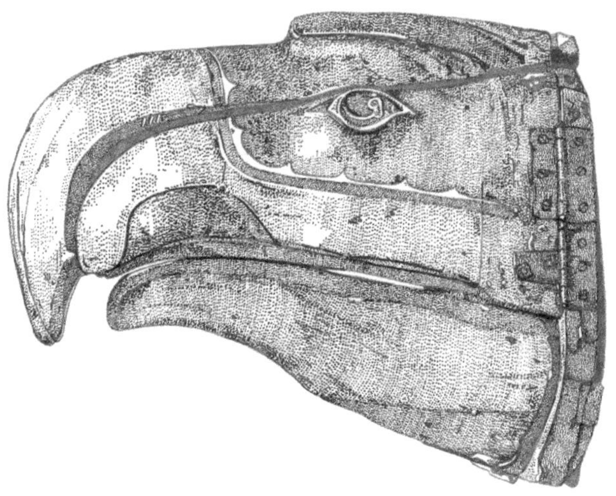

That duality was also found in areas of West Africa.[28] Those masks exposed the inner presence of the twin beings (human and animal), or they illustrated the physical union with one-half of the face showing a human likeness and the other half animal. It was believed that those masks recalled the past and referred to the time when humans could change their appearance.

Masks worn as a part of shamanistic activity frequently represented spirit beings in the "power transformation strategy." Due to the personal nature of those masks, they were placed in the shaman's grave or funeral house at the time of his or her death. The shaman's helping mask often combined anthropomorphic and zoomorphic

Drawing 9.8 Kwakiutl eagle-human mask made of painted wood from the Bella Bella culture. The mask opened to expose the human face inside. It is a transformation mask probably related to the legend that the sun flew to the earth in the shape of a bird, assumed human form, and took a Kwakiutl bride. The mythological concept of creatures changing from animal (or bird) to human form is closely related to Siberian shamanism. Among most Siberian peoples, the creature that gave power to the first shaman was the eagle from the sun. The eagle was called *Aiy* (the creator).[hh]

images. The basic shape and look were human (anthropomorphic) with superimposed animal or bird (zoomorphic) forms. These masks, common along the northwestern coastal region of North America,[29] were like the transformation masks that combined an inner and outer image. One figure contained within another referred to the life and death process that influenced the survival of all living creatures. People in all cultures were the consumer or the consumed. Shamanistic transformation called on the power of the inner image to be given to the outer or more powerful spirit image.

Masks and the Dichotomy of Reverence and Destruction

To understand the development of shamanism and shamanistic masks as elements in the traditional social structure, it is necessary to consider the survival strategies of early humans. The historic record indicates that the first peoples were primarily hunters dependent on opportunistic encounters to provide their primary food source. The hunter sought the available

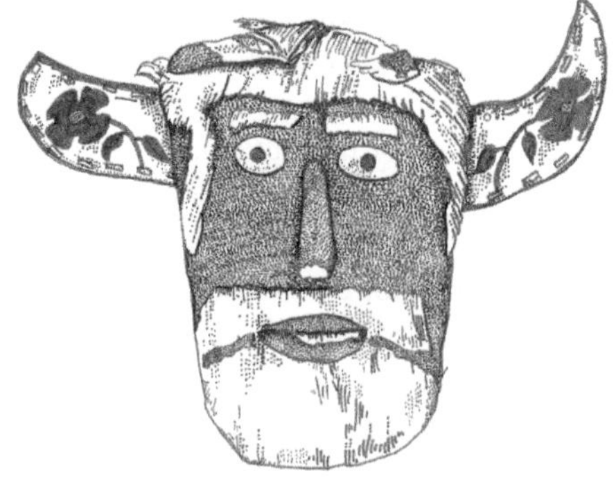

Drawing 9.9 A so-called "devil chaser" mask made by the Yaqui Indians of northwest Mexico. These masks were worn in the Fiesta de Gloria to represent the common soldiers of the Fariseos (Pharisees). The appearance is very human-like. The newer masks were made in two forms. One type was white with a smooth surface and regular features (see drawing 4.13). The second type mask had the hair side of the hide exposed and was partly "shaved." The result was a bearded face. The *tlaloache* flower design is clearly visible on the "horns" of this mask. This is a narcotic and hallucinogenic plant and is an associational reference to the blood of Christ.

products of nature and seized them to survive. Eventually, a more stable order was established and people developed a planter culture that involved planning and rudimentary technology. That calculated form of existence was the basis of modern civilization (see drawing 9.9; see also drawing 4.13).

The hunter culture adjusted its activities to find compatibility with the forces of nature and adopted an attitude of sharing rather than domination. In contrast, the planter culture endeavored to develop methods for regulating the forces of nature and the environment. Productivity was a concern as was the accumulation of tangible property. In both of those "sophisticated" activities, chance and reliance on the forces of the natural world were factors that required constant attention.

The hunter needed a harmonious relationship with the various elements of nature. To sustain that relationship and meet the communal survival requirements, a scheme had to be developed to satisfy the seemingly contradictory aspects of daily existence, the killing and consuming of creatures emanating from the natural environment. Early humans conceived the notion of immortality to address the conflicting attitudes of reverence and destruction. Therefore, living creatures were endowed with a spirit to ameliorate that contradiction, and the spirit survived when the body was destroyed. The spirits of slain animals might be appeased by proper appreciation and caused to return as a food source for future generations. Those practices of appeasement required the development of rituals and similar magico-religious acts of spirit recognition.

Because all creatures (human and animal) were composed of two parts, one physical and one spiritual, it was possible for the two to be separated. That idea accepted the death of the physical body while the spirit/soul survived. It also provided a method for humans to gain superiority over a stronger adversary through spiritual domination. It was a way for humans to gain a measure of control over the environment and especially over the animals on which their lives depended.

The shaman was an intermediary between the living and the spirit worlds and a medium for communication with animal spirits. "Shamanism seem[ed] to occur in almost every area where an early hunting economy. . . continued virtually to our own days; that is to say, in Siberia, North America, South America, various regions of Africa, and also in certain zones of Australia."[30] Once the supernatural connection was established between the material and spiritual worlds, a "pact" or contract was consummated. To initiate that contract and to further its purpose, the shaman served as the intermediary for calling the spirits and convincing them to perform his or her bidding for the good of the group.

Masking as a Channel for the Psychic Life of the Community

The image maker in the traditional community was a person who allowed the essence of the mask to realize itself through his or her activities. (As already noted, the image maker was usually a male, but in some cultures, females played an active role in this activity.) As a member of an established social order, the image maker might have had personal objectives, but as a craftsperson, he or she was a vehicle for the psychic life of the community.

The image making of early societies derived its subject matter (imagery) from the peoples' beliefs just as those beliefs depended on various forms of social expression for their fulfillment. In addition, the importance of beliefs probably had an influence on the quality of the masks produced. For instance, according to Robert Lowie in *Primitive Religion,* objects in some societies that were associated with sacred activities appeared to have been of a lesser quality than those made for secular use.[31] That assumption considered certain aspects of masks that were extraordinarily crude and ill formed. Normally, that quality reflected the design of traditional masks with the emphasis on the supernatural importance rather than the aesthetic. Certain mask types were intended to have a "rough" appearance as defined by societal beliefs and customs.

To represent the humanized appearance of particular supernatural beings, image makers often relied on personal imagination or were content to repeat the established image. If the mask were mnemonic and had a primary function of assisting the collective memory of the people, then artistic refinements were unnecessary. The mask was but one element of a particular socio-cultural expression, and it had to be in harmony with the other parts of the host environment.

To meet the various challenges of community continuance, early peoples developed regulatory societies that ranged from very secret organizations for a few individuals to those that were open to all male or female members of the group.[32] Secrecy was a complex and challenging element in all social structures, and it operated in subtle ways that were a part of both secular and ritual experience. From the earliest times masks appeared as a necessary part of secrecy because of their ability to conceal and to reveal the encoded message each contained. They were used as insignia of the particular society[33] as well as a way for concealing the identity of the participants. The mask as a social symbol was a means of communicating the secret information of the group and defining the role of that coterie within the host community. "The more secret the association, and the 'deeper' its knowledge, the more ambiguous and the less 'beautiful' its emblems, in materials, iconography and form."[34]

Secret societies were formed on the idea that people had to accumulate a certain amount of special knowledge or power during their lifetimes so they could move to the next level of being (either physical or spiritual). That concept reflected belief in the afterlife as a form of resurrection or reincarnation. The basic principle of society membership was that as a person reached a certain age or level of social status they were warranted (or earned) access to additional mystical or spiritual information. Age-grade societies used masks as visual markers for society identification. The practice of visual marking was common in many organizations where badges of rank or performance and symbols of achievement were awarded.

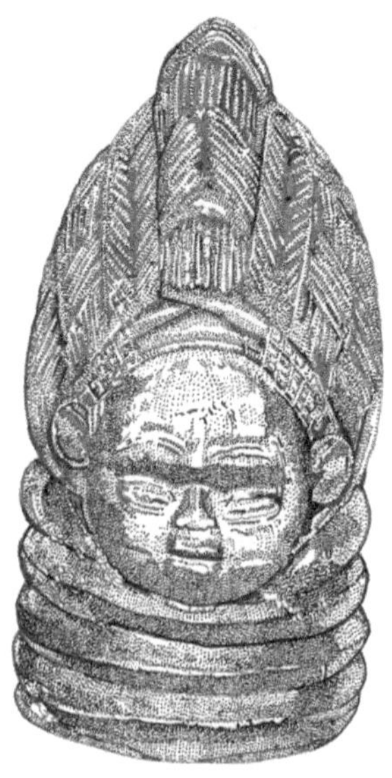

Drawing 9.10 A mask (*sowei* or *sowo-wui*) of the Sande secret society found along the Sierra Leone and Liberia border. Although the masking societies of the world were predominately for men, this African masking tradition was reserved exclusively for women. The society was concerned with initiating young women into the requirements of adulthood and taught the youth about child care, singing and dancing, sexual matters, and other home-related activities.[ii]

Secret societies served many purposes in the traditional community. Some societies had at the center of their existence a specialized knowledge that was used to benefit the interests of the community. Other groups had less honorable purposes. The secret society activities could be divided into two contrasting categories: those that served the interests of individuals and those that benefited the interests of the larger group. To function properly as a social community, people required some form of underlying structure. Beliefs and traditions were the basis for that structure. The individual was subordinate to the rules for proper conduct as defined by the secret societies. Persons in an organized community entrusted the secret society with authority greater than that of the individual members.

One of the most widely recognized secret societies was the Poro of Sierra Leone and the Ivory Coast. That association was responsible for initiating youth into the established social order by defining the responsibilities of adulthood and perpetuating ancestral customs.[35] As with many secret societies, the Poro were hierarchical in structure with the newest initiates at the bottom and the council of elders at the top. A parallel society, the Sande or Bundu, fulfilled a similar role with the initiation of girls. Besides organizing initiation rituals, the Sande society watched over the social life of the community[36] (see drawing 9.10).

Another masked group that fulfilled a special social role was the Pongsan performers in Korea. Although not a true secret society, the maskers served a covert role on behalf of the "common" people. The masked groups drew attention to the social polarities that existed in the feudal state during the Yi dynasty (CE 1392 to 1910). The performers wore masks depicting upper class stereotypes such as pockmarked monks and bearded aristocrats that substantiated their scholarly superiority by reciting sanctimonious quotations in Chinese (see drawing 9.11). The female characters in the performances were both virtuous wives and demanding concubines in deference to the woman's role in that society. Neither of the female models was well treated by the male performers. Initially, the Korean government viewed the performances as an outlet for social commentary, but eventually (in 1786) the authorities condemned the masked activities as "too volatile an expression of popular ire."[37]

A further example of a secret organization was the False Face Society of the Iroquois. That group was responsible for curing physical ailments and protecting against the evil spirits responsible for spreading disease among the people. The masked members of the society perform a "violent pantomime of action"[38] intended to disperse the demons of illness. Similarly, the red mask of fever in Ceylon offered a supernatural force to evict unwelcome spirits. Those brightly painted wooden masks were used to lure the demons of fatal diseases away from intended victims.[39]

The Komo society of the Bamana people of West Africa was a power-oriented judicial group. "Their primary purpose [was] social control and enforcing adherence to basic Bamana religious and social mores. The society also contended with powerful evil forces such as witchcraft and sorcery and with universal concerns of a cosmological and religious nature."[40] The helmet masks of the Komo society were constructed of animal horns and a variety of other animal elements. They had crocodile-like jaws and often were encrusted with sacrificial blood (see drawing 9.12). The combination of shapes and rough organic surface gave the masks a

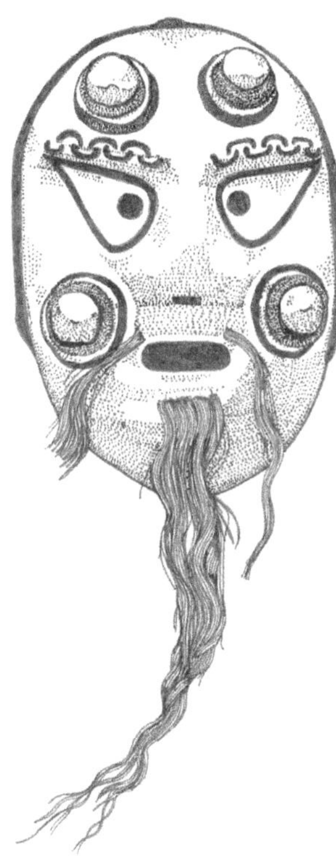

Drawing 9.11 A Ch'otchae Yangban (first nobleman) mask for the Enuyul Mask Dance. The mask was used in folk dramas originating in southwestern Korea. These masks were made of formed paper, and their tradition is said to date to the seventeenth century. The Eunyul Mask Dance was performed on Buddha's birthday and in conjuction with other events such as wrestling and swinging contests.

frightful, almost grotesque, appearance that was certain to cause social transgressors second thoughts about their actions.

Secret societies also performed assigned duties during special events hosted by the community, as exemplified by the practices of the Yaqui people of Northern Mexico. Chapayeka masks were worn by anonymous performers during the Holy Week celebration in the post-Spanish era. For the three days of the Matachines dance, the Chapayekas whipped wrongdoers with ropes as punishment and as a reminder of socially unacceptable behavior. Through the activities of the secret societies, the tensions and conflicts of the community were resolved, thereby creating a stronger feeling of communal solidarity.

The secret society masks were symbols that presented a traditional reference and pointed the way to an absolute and often mysterious reality that was either visible or invisible. That fugitive manifestation, the known and unknown, was most applicable to the secret societies that were formed to maintain the cohesion and well-being of the community. The associated masks embodied the spirit of the group and were tangible representations of the group's presence.

Masks as Shape-Shifting Faces

The supernatural was an extension of daily life, and as the central figure in ritualistic practices the shaman lost individuality and merged with the universe as a harmonious whole. Because the material and spiritual worlds were joined but different and many physical realities were the result of spiritual causes, rituals served to locate and consolidate supernatural influences. It was the shaman's role to facilitate the exchange between the two domains.

For the shaman, putting on a mask was an act of mind-altering importance. That act set aside the mundane world and provided a means for embracing the supernatural. To cross the boundaries of the two worlds, shamans were thought to be "shape-shifters,"[41] and that transformation allowed them to change their physical form and state of being. The belief that a shaman could alter his or her physical shape was commonly held throughout the world. Were-animals as transmogrified shamans walked the earth, flew in the sky, and occupied the waters. They were messengers of good and evil. Shamans used masks during ritual activities to convey the

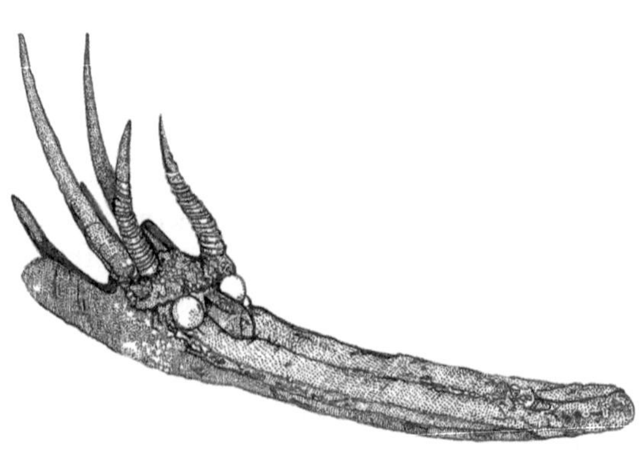

Drawing 9.12 Bambara mask made with mud, horns, porcupine quills, sacrificial blood, and various other materials. Members of the Komo, a powerful society that had the authority to enforce the law, wore this cap-like structure horizontally on top of the head.[ji] The heavily encrusted elements, often of mystical significance, were intended to frighten viewers. These masks, like similar pieces made by the neighboring Senufo people, were believed to be so powerful that contact with dancers could be fatal.

power, cunning, speed, or dexterity of certain creatures to perpetuate that popular belief. For instance, the shaman represented the dynamic and powerful nature of the beast by wearing the mask of the jaguar and a corresponding spotted robe. The people believed that as a jaguar, the shaman could more successfully convey their wishes to the appropriate deity.

The shaman's garment was at times an animal disguise that included a mask. That semblance was a reference to the past when there was commonality between humans and animals as well as a connection with the practice of shape shifting. According to legend, the Dogon people of Western Africa in primordial times did not die; they were transformed into serpents and lived eternally.[42] Consequently, the serpent form was incorporated into the "Great Mask" that was a primary element of the grand funeral feasts.

Belief in transformation was associated with the practice of journeying into the land of the spirits. That transitory act did not presume that the person became a spirit/deity but that they passed beyond the mirror (the barrier between worlds) and entered the space occupied by spirits. A number of methods were used to achieve that transformational state including group activities such as singing and dancing, ritualistic ceremonies involving fasting and sun gazing, or consuming various kinds of stimulants or hallucinogens. The only way of passing beyond the mirror for some cultures was death. The corpse, in that finale, stayed behind while the spirit journeyed to where it was transformed and remained or where it was rejected and returned to reunite with its material body.

Ego, Power, Shamanism, and Masks

Shamanism evolved from the group's beliefs and understanding of the relationship between the living and life-giving worlds. The material and spiritual realms were viewed as interrelational rather than distinct from one another.[43] However, it was power that was central to shamanism wherever it was found. The concept of power as a protraction of existence was essential to all animate and inanimate objects.[44] The powers of shamanism were the result of an intensification of the "ego potency" at a time when early people were at the mercy of the forces of nature.[45]

The shamans' role in many societies was essentially the presentation of the mythological images of the group in a believable manner and employment of those images to strengthen the collective spirit of the group. To fulfill that responsibility and to install the mythical imagery into the conscious of the group, the shaman relied on acting, singing, dancing, and the use of masks. Shamans used the mask to go beyond the limits of daily life. They relinquished their ego with the assistance of the mask and allowed the spirits of animals and gods to enter their psyches. Through that spiritual metamorphosis, they achieved a desired goal.[46]

The power-aligned role of the shaman varied in different cultures or ethnic groups. "[W]itchcraft [black magic] may [have been] as important a part of shamanism as the curing of disease or the charming of game." Among the Jivaro of South America (Ecuador), shamanistic activities for good or evil were separated and were arranged by different persons.[47] The "black" and "white" aspects of shamanism in other cultures were assigned to one person. However, in most places, shamans were involved with the activities of daily life, and their authority (power) reflected their personal experience (ego potency).

Shamanism was subject to historical development and change, as are all social phenomenon. The supernatural alignment differed at times since some shamanistic practices required the spirit of the shaman to ascend to the ethereal plateau, and in other applications the greater being (spirit) descended to interact with the earthbound shaman. Both transactions demonstrated the assumed power associated with shamanism. Whether that aspect of spiritual interaction was a manifestation of psychic power or ego potency was unclear; however, the shaman's role was primary in each encounter with the spirits.

The quest for spiritual power was inherent in most early cultures, and one way to gain that power was to kill other human beings.[48] Members of headhunting societies took heads as trophies to mark their prowess and to assure a measure of mystical power because the head was believed to be the spirit home.

A less dramatic form of supernatural empowerment occurred during the puberty ceremonies among the Cibecue Apache. The qualities of the Changing Woman entered the bodies of the young women at that time for four days. That "power" brought "longevity and usefulness," and for the time of empowerment the girls were "able to heal the afflicted and to bring rain."[49]

It was during conditions of change that limited forms of supernatural power were granted to ordinary people. The initiation ceremony was one example of that "special" time, as was the killing of an enemy or the birth of a child. Times of life and death were universally accepted occasions of special empowerment. That idea extended to rituals that include symbolic cannibalism, the eating of particular parts of the human body, or the consuming of plants or animals that represented ancestors or spirit beings. Masks were instruments for gaining paranormal powers as were medicine bundles and the use of special words, chants, songs, or symbols. The supernatural forces were derived from beliefs and concepts of a personal nature that took forms emanating from the mythology of the people. They expressed traditional ideas and a system of beliefs belonging to the most basic levels of human existence.[50]

10

Somatic Metamorphosis

Death masks command our utmost reverence, for the face is symbolic and perpetuates the final impression of a human spirit whom we once knew, or who had made his mark on all men's minds.[1]

Natural death was a concept that exceeded the understanding of many traditional cultures. Consequently, both sickness and death were phenomena that were frightening. That assumption was substantiated by the separation of the sick and dying from the rest of the community in deference to the forces that caused the physical conditions. The segregation was to prevent the causal forces from migrating and attaching themselves to healthy persons. It was, for that reason, often considered taboo to be in the presence of a sick person or to touch the dead.

Other early peoples rejected the attitude of segregation and celebrated the dead by placing them at the center of their belief system and preserving their heads, bones, or names as symbolic representations of their time among the living. When a departed ancestor was transformed into a supernatural being, there was a greater personification of the ethereal world and the probability of earthly contact with a benevolent spirit.

Illness as a physiological manifestation of mental or physical disorder was an obvious threat to human survival. However, the ill sometimes survived and other times died. That contradiction could only be explained as supernatural intervention. In response to that unfathomable situation, life after death was one of the earliest mystical conjectures. Moreover, that thesis was the basis for numerous masking activities. The socially recognized fear of death was the disclosure of a subconscious instinct common to humans because they did not want to believe their existence would end. They undoubtedly found it difficult to accept the concept of the complete cessation of being.

It was from that perspective that the idea of the spirit and spiritual existence — immortality — probably evolved as people reached for the comforting belief in life after death. However, with the sense of personal salvation came the discomforting hazard of the malevolent spirits of enemies and ancestors. If the good survived, so might the evil. The hopes and fears associated with life after death were fertile materials for ritual activities involving the wearing of masks representing ancestors and revered deities as group and individual intermediaries.

All deaths were attributed to supernatural forces, and even the most obvious mishap was believed to be the work of malicious spirits. Both mental and physical illnesses, though usually caused by recognized psychobiological factors, were in their manifestations highly influenced by cultural example.[2] When a person conceded to an ailment of the mind or body, it was usually in a culturally defined manner. Personality traits, social and cultural expectations, and family unity combined to induce and to relieve the symptoms of illness.[3] Belief in the supernatural flourished across socio-cultural boundaries because the conditions of insecurity necessitated the reaffirmation of traditional rituals and ceremonies.

Early humans apparently did not wish to abrogate death by their activities; rather they attempted to place death within a cyclical process of demise and rebirth. Life and death in all cultures were an inseparable cycle that imposed a temporal state of existence on all creatures. Death was a transformation of life that included the translocation of energy from one source to another. As a permanent metamorphosis, death was a complete separation from the world of the living.

"The spirit went out of the body when it died, but it could go into some strange-shaped stone or a piece of carving. Such a thing had power."[4] A lingering spirit had a potency that was mobile and illusive. It could change and take another form, and it was capable of injuring a person even when they were alert. To guard against the attack of a living enemy was possible, but the malingering spirit of the dead was another matter. Special means had to be developed to regulate the activities of the dead and to prevent unwanted interaction with malevolent spirits. By using the proper charms, actions, substances, and mask, people could restrict the actions of spirits.[5]

An example of a ceremony relating to belief in life after death was the Medicine Dance of the Winnebago.[6] That ceremony was a complex representation of death and rebirth that gave special consideration to reincarnation. The participants in that social-biological enactment experienced symbolic death and were reborn on a higher level. Those ritualistic activities affirmed group faith in the existing social order, evoked a community of shared experiences, and helped to formulate responses to questions about the ultimate destiny of the group.

The grave, for traditional cultures, was the great destroyer and the eater of flesh.[7] It was the womb of the Earth Mother who brought forth new life and devoured the bodies of the dead. The doctrine of "passing the soul" at the time of death was a favored notion of many cultures. To provide for the passage of the soul from the physical confines of the human (or animal) body, ritualized activities were contrived. The dead of the late Paleolithic Era (Cro-Magnon) were buried with ornaments and sprinkled with red ochre,[8] and later people made similar special preparations for the deceased.

Societies endorsed the belief of rebirth in which the soul was transferred to another being. The migrating soul, in some belief systems, sought a higher manifestation that did not require a corporeal presence. The people sanctioned a spiritual reality for the dead that relinquished earthly presence for a sustained existence in paradise. The concept of paradise for others was viewed as simply an intermediate resting place for righteous souls awaiting resurrection. Death for all people was an imperfect state of being, and those attitudes found a symbolic presence in masks and masking activities.

Masks, Rebirth, and Ancestor Worship

Although death was the ultimate transformation of a person from a life of activity to one of inactivity, it was also a process of physical change that correlated with other elements of the life cycle. The symbolic enactment of death and the corresponding act of rebirth were significant aspects of the physiological metamorphosis of a person (see drawing 10.1). It was the time when life could be discarded in exchange for a metaphysical state. While not all persons could achieve the desired transpersonalization, the use of masks and the related ritualized activities reinforced the concept and sustained the belief. It was human nature to desire physiological and intellectual fulfillment. However, symbolic attainment through masked rituals was acceptable when total actualization of divine status was not possible.

A lack of knowledge about death and the physical limitations of the human body undoubtedly influenced early beliefs about the metaphysical realm that ultimately resulted in the adoration of ancestors. "The critical feature of the live world [was] the horizon of death which present[ed] the ultimate limit."[9] The primary symbolic references in the mystical practices of archaic people related to death and rebirth. In almost all cultures when a person passed from one level of existence to another—from birth to death—the transmigration of the inner being followed a culturally defined process. Grounded in that belief, it was reasonable to assume that the spirits associated with the dead served as the incentives for ancestor worship in its earliest form.

Some peoples professed no notion of an afterlife while others believed in a paradise for departed souls. The precedence for belief in rebirth could be found in natural cycles that challenged early human understanding. Seasonal change; perennial crops; the repetitious movements of the sun; some forms of illness, especially when the patient lost consciousness; and the complex process of childbearing for humans and animals were phenomena most easily explained by the notion of death and rebirth. Examples of natural transformation were abundant in the lives of all people as some organisms were consumed so others could live. The dynamic paradox of death and life was not easy to understand or explain.

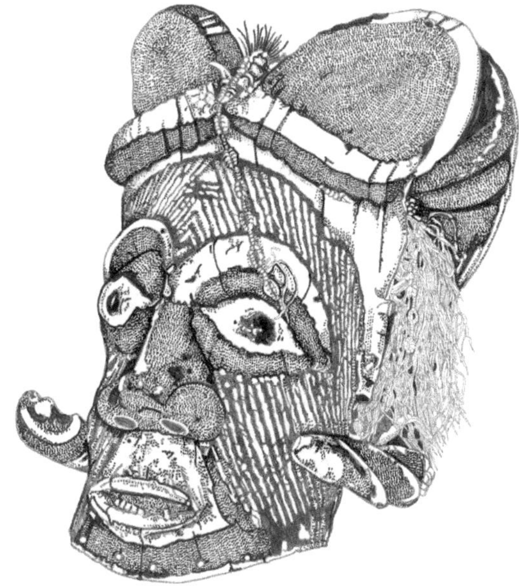

Drawing 10.1 Helmet mask probably used in the initiation ceremonies of the Northern BaKeta who lived among the BaKuba in Central Africa. This well-carved wood mask with paint, fiber, and shells has Kuba characteristics including the parallel stripes on the cheeks and forehead. The mask has ram horns and is surmounted with a cluster of fibers and a strand of cowrie shells.

The concept of rebirth was fundamental to many socially proscribed events in the life of an individual. The act of renewal or reemergence was a necessary part of perpetuating the social order of a particular people and a form of individual "spirit quest." It was a future-oriented belief that marked the physical and psychological transformation of the participants. In contrast, veneration of the dead—ancestor worship—focused on the past as an immutable force that was central to group cohesion.[10] The future was, for ancestor-revering societies, but an imperfect repetition of the past from which no person should stray. Pursuing that attitude, ancestor-associated masks held a special synergistic role in society. The masks were a tradition-defined reference that verified the belief and defined the relationship.

Ancestor worship was an important element of the belief system endorsed by many traditional peoples. It was commonly believed that the spirit of a deceased person was in a position to aid or harm descendants. Therefore, various ceremonies were inaugurated to solicit the assistance of departed family members and to avoid the wrath of hostile progenitors. People made an effort to induce the spirit of an illustrious ancestor to reside in an appropriately shaped mask or spirit figure. Once the act of transposition was believed to have occurred (spirit to mask or figure), the living had a tangible object whereto devotion and sacrifice could be directed. "Such permanent or temporary containers of ancestral spirit power were believed by those people to denote, tangibly, the actual presence of the ancestor."[11] Spirit containers held a special place of sacred significance in the households and devotional activities of many early cultures.

The Chinese made a cult of ancestor worship,[12] and among the Zuñi people, reverence was expressed for "the ancestors" as the inclusive predecessors of most recent generations. Recognition of the primogenitors was a part of upholding traditional customs and demonstrating respect for the past. Ancestors in Japan were venerated but not all were assigned *kami* designation. That identification did not denote a deity; instead, it recognized those forces in humans that exceed the ordinary.[13] Japanese ancestor belief was a part of a well-defined religious system, and masked "ancestor figures" were often included in historical dramatizations. Ruth Benedict wrote in *The Chrysanthemum and the Sword*[14] that the ritual recognition of ancestors as practiced by the Japanese was a remembrance of "the indebtedness to all that had gone before." That practice differed with the Chinese, who worshipped all deceased members of the family.

The ancestor-oriented society professed a long past and an inconsequential future.[15] Life was a backward-looking series of events with little or no anticipation of change. That attitude often relied on an elaborate tradition of representative masks and masking activities for guidance. The past of the ancestors dominated the people's thinking, leaving little time to consider the future. Ancestor veneration confirmed the correctness of the past activities and signified the continuity of the established social and natural order. Rituals and festivals in such societies were held to demonstrate respect for ancestors. Those events often included music and dance and were attended by masked performers impersonating ancestral figures of particular importance.[16]

Masks as Manifestations of the Dead

Death was regarded as an occurrence of great significance in most early societies; therefore, death cults were among the most common ritual-related activities (see drawing 10.2). However, because the boundary between life and death lacked clear delineation for many early peoples, some cultures viewed death as a condition of "nonlife." Death began with illness and was a progressive condition resulting in inactivity. The lack of productivity (activity) had a natural and understandable outcome. Among cultures that recognized death as a conclusive physical condition, the cessation of life was seen as a release from the current cycle of existence and the beginning of another. Death for other peoples was an opportunity for renewed life through the transferal (to others) of guilt, sin, and other social transgressions, a concept reflecting the mingling of the material and spiritual worlds.[17]

Death was the ultimate transitional state of being. It was, for some people, one element of the cyclical continuum that allowed individuals to alter their status among the living. For others, it provided the opportunity to become one with their deities. Therefore, the anticipated dividend of death was the possibility of knowledge and wisdom (enlightenment). That ideology was found among many people as life expectations passed from generation to generation while awaiting "special" liberating achievements to occur. The mask, as a part of the human life cycle, was a connecting appliance that joined the living with the spiritual beyond. In addition, at the time of death, the mask was used to give the corpse a favorable and dignified "face" for the journey to an empyrean place (see drawing 5.8).

The notion of new life and salvation existed among virtually all people in all times, and masks were used to represent that regenerative concept. Life and death in many cultures were the same; only the state of physical being changed. The Tibetan Buddhists believed there was a short interval between the time the spirit left the body of the deceased and the beginning of a new cycle of life. The spirit, during that interlude, was thought to dwell in the intermediate world and experienced many strange and unusual encounters. Buddhist monasteries held familiarizing devil dances in which the dancing monks wore grotesque masks made of painted wood or *papier mâché* to prepare the spirits of the living for the after-death episode[18] (see drawing 10.3).

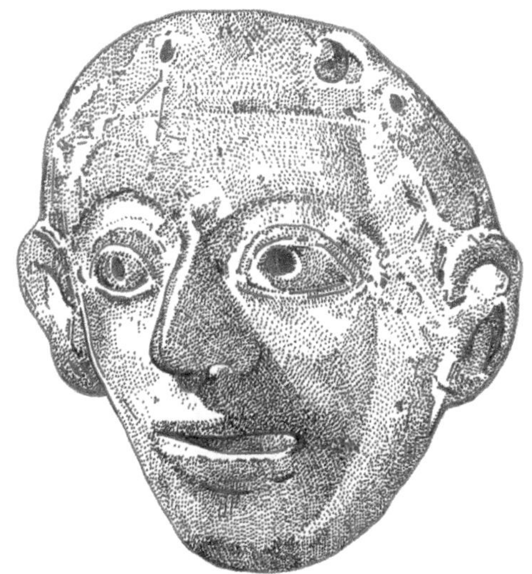

Drawing 10.2 A clay mask discovered in the coastal region of Ecuador. These masks were too small to be worn on the face and the holes around the upper edge suggest they might have been fastened to mummy bundles, attached to wooden figures, or used as ornaments on ceremonial regalia. The mask was modeled of coarse clay and was probably made by pressing the moist clay into a mold. That production technique was common in many areas of Central and South America.

The belief in survival of the spirit was an important factor in most societies. Humans believed that the inner being — the spirit — did not end at death but continued for an indefinite time long after the body ceased to exist. Concern for the dead and the subsequent disposition of the spirit were of primary importance. The Neanderthal and probably earlier peoples interred their dead in prepared "graves,"[19] and the peoples of the late ice age buried their dead in dwelling caves. They placed the corpses in layers of ocher, an oxide of iron that had a reddish tint reminiscent of blood.[20] The early people, by those acts, addressed the need to provide a "resting place" for the spirits of the deceased and validated their belief in an afterlife existence.

The masks used in fulfilling socio-cultural responsibilities were powerful instruments for interaction with the spirits of the dead. They established human contact with the forces of the supernatural world and strengthened the bond with the spirits. The successful early hunter believed the spirit of a slain animal was released to roam the world and to exact retribution from the slayer. Therefore, the hunter sought to capture, control, or appease the spirit before harm was done. That situation was resolved by fabricating an animal mask to attract the spirit of the dead beast. The hunter wore the mask and the correct ceremonial trappings to be safe from the vengeance of the dispossessed animal spirit (see drawing 10.4).

Masks used in activities pertaining to the dead, ghosts, and ancestors were associated with rituals of placation. They were intended to attract, reject, humor, or appease the restive spirits. "The universality of man's faith in the survival of the soul after death [was] attested partly by the universality of the belief in ghosts, and the uniform practice of placing food in the tombs of the departed."[21] The indigenous peoples living along the northwest coast of North America used Spirit-of-a-Dead-Man masks, and skull masks were made by the people of New Britain in the South Pacific and other locations.[22] Masks in preconquest Mexico and Ecuador were placed on the dead to emphasize the continuing importance of the human spirit. The cults of the dead generally involved the use of masks, and those masks were "thought of as essential to the conquest of the difficult trials that beset the road of the dead."[23]

Masking in Oceania very probably originated as an act of remembrance using the remodeled skull of an ancestor, and from that beginning numerous vari-

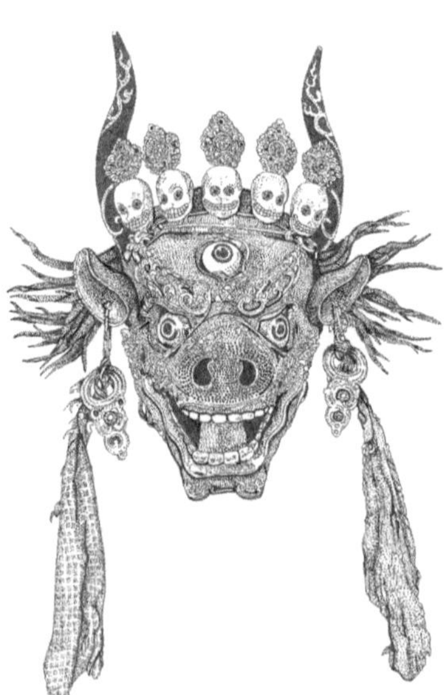

Drawing 10.3 Papier mâché mask of Yama (*gShin rje*), the bull-headed Lord of Death and ruler of the nether world. This masked figure is central to most sacred dances of the Gelugpa and appears in both the Tibetan and Mongolian pantheon. Yama is comparable with Erleg Khan, a shamanistic lord of the underworld,[kk] and it is he or one of "his stag-headed messengers who ceremonially kills the *lingka*, a figure that embodies demonic force."[ll] In some dances four minor Yamas appear to denote the cardinal points.[mm] The Yama also appears as an ancient Hindu god of death who is generally portrayed as a placid figure riding a buffalo.[nn]

ations evolved.[24] Skulls overlaid with clay or gypsum and fitted with stone or shell eyes and human or animal hair were visual reminders of deceased relatives. The modeling practice reinforced the concept of the dead as the primary source of life and the dwelling place of spirits. That attitude allowed the transfer of human characteristics, spiritual energy, and essential qualities to masks, thereby giving them a worshipful presence.

Fear of as well as respect for the dead was an important aspect of the human psyche. The corpses of early people were bound in a fetal-like position in accordance with special rituals that were designed to restrict the movements of the dead. Other corpses were buried face down, a practice used in many cultures of the world. It was believed that the "front side down" position confused the dead and denied them easy return to the world of the living. From prehistoric time cadavers were fettered, disjointed, burned, and buried under earth and stones or put in clay jars for a variety of reasons. However, all those practices

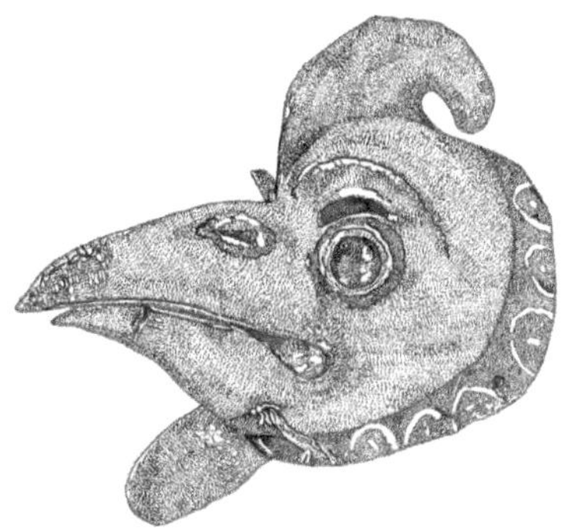

Drawing 10.4 A rooster mask from Bolivia made of carved and painted wood. Masks often represented animals that symbolized a deity or a spirit from which the people, or a segment of the people, were descended. Such masks and the related ritual activities summoned the deity for needed assistance or to imbue the participants with the qualities of that animal.

had one factor in common; they impaired the movement of the body after death. That the spirit moved was accepted, but the body could become a frightening tool of evil if it were allowed to wander among the living after death. Commonly held superstitions alleged that the body had "…an intense desire to live again, like the Mesopotamian vampire-corpses that would suck people's blood to recover life…."[25]

Belief in the ritual consumption of human flesh or blood, in all applications, was related to spirit or power transferal. In that practice, the soul or spirit — the center of power — of one being was transferred by a culturally defined process to another being (the dead to the living). Belief in vampires as sinister manifestations of the "non-living" related to the concept of shape shifting and power transfer. The form of a bat (vampire) was found in the mask-making traditions of diverse cultures. Use of the bat image for masks and forms of adornment was particularly prevalent in the Americas (see drawing 10.5).

The dead in many early societies were considered a primary threat whether they were an ancestor, enemy, or animal. Therefore, the ethereal world was occupied by a variety of potentially harmful spirits that had to be pacified. The spirits of the dead were feared because of the secretive powers they possessed. Their dynamic force could provoke any number of calamities from sickness and infertility to bad luck and privation. To circumvent the powers of the dead required a combination of activities and spirit-evoking devices including ceremonies, sacrifices, rituals, masks, and fetishes.

Death as an Antecedent to the Celebration of Life

Perhaps because death was a concern for most early peoples, death's counterpart—the regeneration of life—was a primary focus for celebration. For many cultures that practice reflected a concept of time that was a qualifying factor in the endorsement of life and the recognition of death. Time, in traditional thinking, was cyclical; it ended and began anew.[26] Consistent with that concept, death was followed by rebirth as demonstrated by the cyclic renewal of nature. That perspective was unlike the concept of time as a linear configuration in which the present was preceded by the past that extended backwards from generation to generation and was followed by a future that was infinite. The linear configuration offered no promise of renewal.

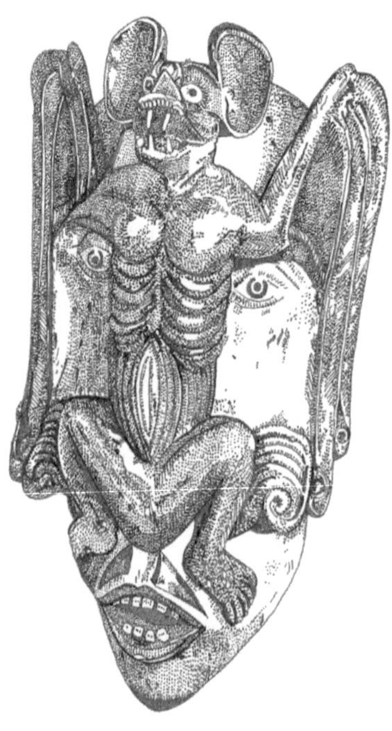

Drawing 10.5 A bat mask from Mexico used in the bat dance (December 23). This dance is attributed to pre–Hispanic origins, but there is limited evidence to support that claim. However, there is a strong relationship between the bat and the human face in Mexican masking practices. The bat is often associated with devil and skull masks and may be superimposed on almost any anthropomorphic face. This mask was reportedly made in the state of Guerrero, the center of bat dance activities.

Death and resurrection were recurring themes in myth and superstition—the theme of transformation. Heroes or villains overcame the powers of death to return to the world of the living. Masks were shaped to celebrate those events in recognition of their achievements.

The doctrine of return and renewal was inherent in most initiation rites in which neophytes were subjected to mental and physical manipulation to a point where rational thinking was replaced by an instinct for survival. When the stress was relieved and the initiates were returned to their familiar surroundings, they were figuratively (and sometimes physically) reborn into a new life. The symbolic affirmation of an enhanced social order granted the initiate new life disassociated from the old. A new name, new language, and new privileges were inherent accompaniments to that transformation.[27]

The socio-cultural concept of rebirth included many symbols. Cave, pits, or closed structures were symbolic wombs from which the reborn emerged. The emergence from darkness into the light signaled a new day as did the passing of night. The covering and uncovering of the initiates' eyes or head symbolized a similar transformation. The double mask, one within the other, was an adaptation of the metaphor of death and rebirth.

Masks with half of the face as a fully fleshed image and the other half showing only the skull represented a similar attitude (see drawing 2.1). When the life and death mask was worn in a ritual, the viewers experienced the realization that death was a necessary part of life.

One of the essential mystical concepts about the forces of the universe was the doctrine of opposites, as exemplified by the significance of death and rebirth in all major belief systems. Symbolic death and rebirth were aspects of the recognition process for many mythical heroes and heroines as well as other lesser beings. Walter Burkert wrote in *Ancient Mystery Cults* "...[T]here [was] a dynamic paradox of death and life in all the mysteries associated with the opposites of night and day, darkness and light, above and below...."[28] Mystics sought physical and mental balance through reconciliation to accommodate the connections between opposites. These opposing forces were given an equitable measure of importance in establishing and maintaining stability.

The concept of equity and balance was also represented in some masks. Examples of that configuration are the double mask representing the inner and outer being or the spirit force and the human form. The dual energy was portrayed in the Janus (two-faced) masks (see drawing 3.1) recalling the Roman mythological figure with forward-and backward-looking faces. There were also masks with male and female features demonstrating a balance between the sexes. The reconciliation of the male and female nature was bisexuality in the mystical theory of opposites. The Japanese believed in the dual sexuality of spirit beings; the *mitama* was male and female simultaneously. In many traditional belief systems, spirits and deities had both male and female manifestations that reflected the dual forces of procreation.

The power in humans to generate life was a shield against death. For that reason, the act of procreation was a natural foundation for early belief systems, and the symbols of regeneration were found in most cultures. Of particular significance were the primordial couples of Africa; the phallic monuments and emblems of China, India, Japan, Korea, and many other parts of the world; and the fertility dramas of ancient Europe, North Africa, and the Middle East. Honored deities embodying male and female capacities were found among many peoples. They were the dual elements — the two halves of the whole — necessary to create life. There were Osiris and Isis in Egyptian mythology; the Greeks had a pantheon of mythical pairs including Dionysus and Demeter, Zeus and Hera, and Uranus and Gaia; and in Tibet, the dual nature of regeneration was embodied in Yab and Yum.[29]

There was an equal concern for the equity between the constructive and destructive forces in many traditional activities. The opposing elements coexisted in balance with neither gaining nor retaining excessive power. The concern for equality was also reflected in the male/female principles of the *lingam* and *yoni* as well as the primordial couple considered the source of all human existence. The male and female attributes were equal elements of the creative process.

The concept of spiritual "oneness" and the inclusion of both aspects of gender in one superhuman being correspond with Hermetic teaching.[30] The same concept was included in numerous myths that featured a hero/heroine capable of exchanging identity (and gender) according to the circumstances. Masking activities often accommodated transvestitism with male dancers or actors portraying women. That sexual transformation was particularly prevalent in cultures of West Africa, South America, China, and Japan where tradition defined a clear separation of gender-related activities.

Masks themselves were a factor of the life emanation from death cycle. Old or "used" masks often were destroyed or allowed to decay. Replacements were made not as copies but as "re-creations." They were brought into the world to replace their degraded predecessors. As replacements, they inherited the spiritual roles previously occupied by the masks they replaced. When that cycle of renewal and rebirth was broken, the masking tradition was lost.

As with a mask's mystical essence, a person's "life" was considered indestructible because the dead did not actually die according to the beliefs of many cultures. Fear of and respect for death were real considerations, and for most people the possibility of dying, whether real or imagined, caused concern about issues that might have otherwise gone unattended. Human sacrifice is an example of cyclical thinking that was an essential part of the death rituals practiced by the Aztecs. In other societies, the threat of death, humiliation, and pain was fundamental to the initiation or "purification" ceremony. Those intimidating experiences had the effect of unsettling the basic nature of a person and making them vulnerable to new identities.[31] Masked initiation ceremonies were transformational activities (see drawing 10.6).

Death embodied in the sacrifice of animals or birds was a part of many rituals. Such activities were intended to honor the dead by returning to them the benefits they left for their heirs. The animals, in a ritual sense, were offered as nourishment for the spirits of deceased ancestors.[32] The sacrifice was often accompanied by requests for aid to overcome family difficulties such as infertility, sickness, or general misfortune. The sacrifice was, in that way, a part of a healing ritual, and frequently it was the blood from the offering that had the most sacred (restorative) significance. Masks were anointed, and the ill or infertile was washed with the blood to allow the energy to pass from the sacrificed beast or fowl to the living.

An example of animal sacrifice that influenced a masking practice was the Greek association of the bull with Zeus. In recognition of their "fertilizing force," bulls were sacrificed to increase virility and to enhance the deity's potency and bliss.[33] As a way of paying tribute to those symbols of fertility, the ancient Greeks wore masks with horns to represent both the beast and the deity.

Elsewhere, human sacrifice was required to satisfy the ritual event. "The Pawnee and the Sioux in North America, the Bagados of Min-

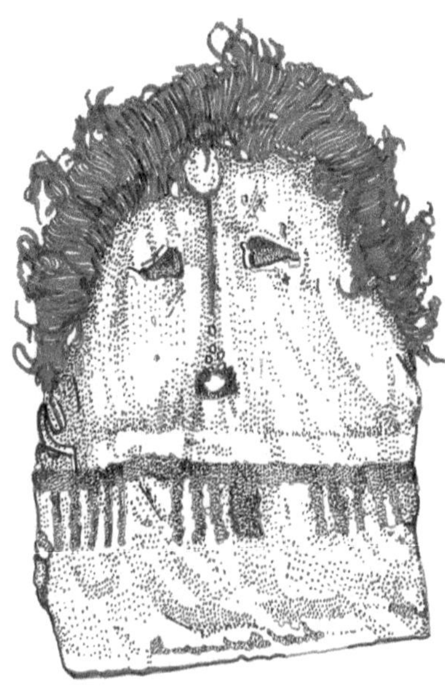

Drawing 10.6 Yei mask of painted hide, hair, and shells made by the Navajo. These masks represent spiritual beings that held a position of great importance among the Navajo people. Humans depended on the benign intentions of the supernatural beings (Yeis) that determined whether crops grew or life continued uncomplicated by disease or conflict. Equally, the Yeis depended on humans because they had an overwhelming need to be praised and worshipped.[oo] In a universe where all beings — human and supernatural — were mutually dependent for survival, humans placated the spirits through prayers and rituals.

danao in the Philippine Islands, the Gonds of Dravidian India, and the Incas of Peru, among others, all practiced human sacrifice to ensure the fertility of crops."[34] The belief that the fertility of the earth was linked to blood, particularly, the blood from human sacrifice, can be traced to creation myths. The "creators" of the world often were killed and dismembered. The elements for sustaining life emerged from their cadavers.

The ritual response to sacrificial activity included wearing an animal or human skin (a body mask), and by that masquerade the priest or performer assumed the identity and power of the skin — the identifiable persona of the animal or human. For instance, in the Yaqui deer dance the desiccated head of an animal was mounted above the head of the performer (see drawing 2.2). Similarly, the Japanese *yanabushi* (shaman of the Shugendo Sect) wore an animal skin during the purification ceremony that led to symbolic reincarnation.[35]

In Aztec mythology "There is no better single example of the fundamental idea that life [came] from death, that sacrifice release[ed] the life force, than the flayed god ... Xipe Totec.... By donning the skin of a sacrificial victim who had been flayed, the priest became the god."[36]

Masking and the Concept of Life Emerging from Death

Many cultural groups supported the notion that sacrifice and creation were two parts of one whole — the alpha and omega of bodily existence. That attitude was undoubtedly inspired by the sacrifice of the sun to make possible the birth of the moon. The moon, in turn, was sacrificed to facilitate the rebirth of the sun. That cycle was an endless one of immolation and creation. The goal of life after death as a positive experience and the absorption into a changeless and timeless state of being were integral parts of many mystic doctrines. The need for reassurance and the anticipation of a "better life" were resident in the psychological composition of all people.

It was common for men in ancient Rome to masquerade as spirits to display belief in the afterlife. Individuals specifically chosen for that task impersonated the dead at funerals. The impersonators wore masks made in the likeness of the deceased, and they dressed in the appropriate robes of office.[37] That was the cult of the *imago*.[38] The masks used in that society were made using a wax mold taken from the corpse at the time of death. A person with the same physique as the deceased and who was trained to imitate his mannerisms wore the mask. (The dead honored in that way were most often males being recognized for social service.) The masked "actor" participated in the funeral as a living incarnation of the dead person.[39] Reportedly, the reason for the activity was to demonstrate to young men the immortality to be gained by serving the public.

The "life from death" belief also extended to the notion of rebirth by regurgitation. Devouring spirits swallowed or ate evildoers and vomited them alive and purposefully. That myth existed among the Bushmen of South Africa, the Greeks, the Hindus of India, and others. The bird-like Garuda was a filth eater and the vehicle of Shiva. Zeus was swallowed and disgorged (see drawing 10.7). Indra once entered the body of a cow and a deity of the African Bushman, Cagn, entered the body of an elephant before emerging to assist the people.[40] Reemergence was a part of the transformation of life for humans, plants, and animals. Those life-altering mythological experiences were the source of images used in mask making and the perpetuation of cultural traditions.

The practice of placing food, clothing, tools, money, and even horses and servants with the body of the dead supported the concept of resurrection or life after death. To further the acceptability of the deceased for rebirth, elaborate funeral rites were performed to prepare the corpse. Out of that belief came the skills of embalming and mummifying to preserve the body as a place for the soul/spirit to reside. The Chinese placed rice (or gold) in the mouth of the deceased to feed the soul and to facilitate the journey of renewal, while the early Egyptians opened the mouth to allow the soul to escape.

The Transference of Physical and Spiritual Properties

Some of the reasons death had such a prominent role in so many activities of early societies were that life expectancy was short, the child mortality rate was high, and life was generally difficult. To reduce the negative impact of daily hardship, death in ceremonies and rituals was made to play the role of a trickster or clown that caused havoc but was hardly a dreaded or feared specter. Death masks complemented that perception by presenting images that appeared to be foolish or half-witted and easily deceived.

Masks fulfilled many purposes in recognizing and defining the socio-cultural role of death. Some of these masks represented the forces of the supernatural, and others symbolized deceased ancestors or enemies killed in battle. Animal masks used in ceremonies often depicted animals killed during hunting expeditions. Death, whether human or animal, was a circumstance of adequate importance in most societies to require some form of ritualized acknowledgment.[41] For instance, people living on the upper west coast of North America hunted whales to survive. In that activity the fishermen were aware of the spirit activity associated with whale hunting, but hunting was intended to gain a practical end — the taking of a whale. However, in the ritualistic enactment of whale hunting, the fishermen wore masks, a seemingly impractical act, and danced to induce "the whale," an abstract concept, to return as a future food supply (see drawing 10.8).

Another death-related ritual was the anointing of the symbolic reference (the

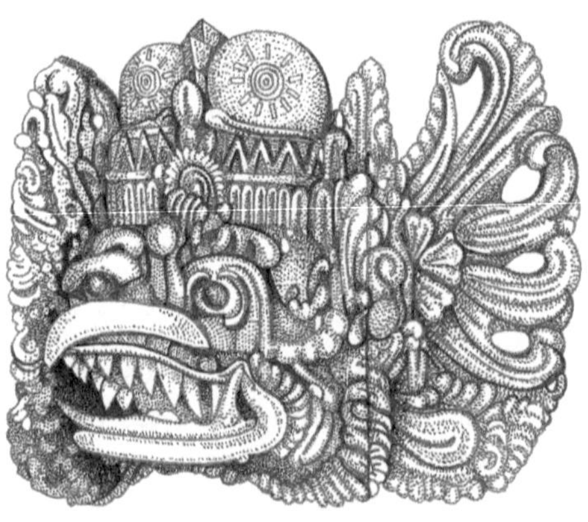

Drawing 10.7 Garuda mask made of painted and gilded wood. The Garuda or "sun bird" of the upper world is one of two traditional vehicles of Vishnu. The transport of the lower world is the serpent Ananta. The Garuda as a manifestation of Hindu mythology is found in many cultures. As a representative of Vishnu, especially in one of his favored incarnations — Krishna — the Garuda is described as the "filth eater." In this persona, the Garuda rids the world of foul words and deeds. This mask is from Bali.

mask or fetish) with the blood of the victim or a surrogate. In regions of Africa where the application of color was not an integral part of mask making, masks were often encrusted with a thick layer of dried blood mixed with a variety of other consecrated matter. The power of the dead was transferred to the living in that way. It was a transformation of one being or object by infusing the dynamic energy of another, and the transforming element was the mask. The wearer, by donning a mask, became both visually and figuratively another or separate reality. As part of communication between the people and the power being, the masked person often alternated between wearing and removing the mask to perform the roles of both the requester and the granter of power and assistance.

The practice of transformational release served many objectives, including the purging of sins and maladies that were conveyed to either animate or inanimate objects. The weaknesses of the body could be transferred to a stone, stick, plant, or effigy, and casting the object away eliminated fatigue or pain. Alternatively, social misconduct, misfortune, illness, and "sin" could be transferred to other humans or animals. To actuate the exculpation process, a masked dancer performed in the presence of the errant person and accepted the malady or sin. Immediately following the transposition, the masked dancer adjourned to a traditional burial place and reclined on a bier or the ground as though dead. The act of dying exorcised the negative spirits, leaving both the patient and the dancer free from the malady.[42]

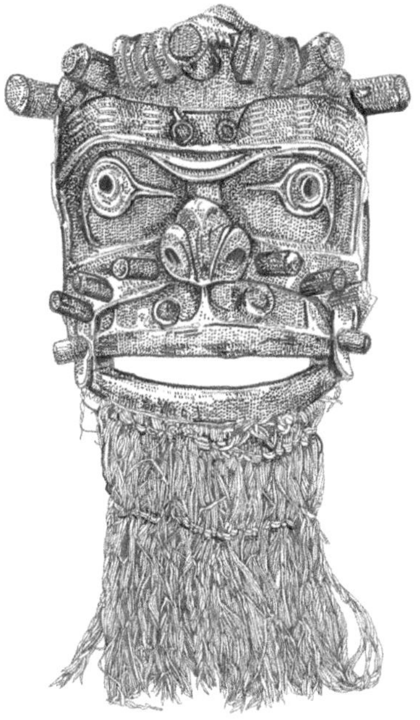

Drawing 10.8 A sea monster (Yagim) mask made of wood, cedar bark, and cotton thread. This painted mask was made by the Kwakiutl to represent the shark-like creature that prowls behind canoes or creates catastrophic storms. The seafaring people of the Northwestern Coast of the Americas often included monsters and bringers of bad situations in their myths and stories. The Yagim was a destroying monster that symbolized the evil of the world. This mask has an articulated jaw that could open and close, causing the cedar bark beard to move.

Similarly, a person was allowed to confess to an unacceptable deed (taboo) while placing his or her hand on the head of a beast. After responsibility for the malfeasance was transferred, the animal was set free in a remote area, carrying with it the offense. An example of that cleansing activity occurred in China during the Chou period (1027–221 BCE). In an act of social absolution, the emperor of that dynasty prayed that the sins of the people might be transferred to him. Thereafter his hair was cut, and the clippings were attached to the forehead of a black bull that was sacrificed in place of the magnanimous ruler.[43] In Mesoamerica the goddess Tlazoltéotl gave absolution to errant Aztecs. Absolution by confession was an extension of the practice of transferal, and the rituals associated with that activity included masks and special raiment.

Masks used in those ritual activities were receivers of authority, power, and respect. As an example of that unique role, the death mask had special meaning for members of the Poro society in the Côte d'Ivoire. Decisions affecting the community were made by the secret society that only males were eligible to join. The more important the decision, the more select the decision makers. An elite contingency of society members made the most consequential determinations. At the death of one of the society leaders, a special mask was carved. "Thus the death masks came to be worshipped in and of themselves, representing as they did individuals who were of the very highest importance during their lives and who, after their deaths, were believed to be free spirits capable of interceding between earthly men and the town of the dead."[44]

The Karo Batak shamans of Sumatra wore large anthropomorphic funeral masks. Those helmet masks had piercing eyes, darkened faces, and grinning mouths with carved teeth.[45] A similar practice existed among other societies in Polynesia. The principal participants wore "mortuary costumes" including large masks during funeral ceremonies. When people saw those masks, it was a signal for the uninitiated to vacate the area.[46] The masks transmitted a symbolic message to the living as well as the dead.

Masks had a special role in the bereavement activities of the Gelede Society among the Yoruba of West Africa. Forty days after the death of a Gelede member, a masquerade performance was held to acknowledge the dead.[47] The main function of that society, according to Yoruba Gelede tradition, was the placation of witches and their spirit helpers and the neutralization of the negative influence of the supernatural upon the community. The essence of their activities was a medicine called *ife*,[48] a concoction made of bark mixed with rum, blood, and sundry other materials. It was thought that the elixir gave women power over men.

Gelede masks were often fastened to the top of the head with a cloth extended over the wearer's face (see drawing 10.9). Other society masks were helmet-like and rested on the shoulders of the masker. Another important mask of the Yoruba was that of the *Engungun* secret society. Those elaborate masks had anthropomorphic faces and were often surmounted by animal figures. The *Engungun* celebrate the importance of ancestors.

Shaman among the Aleutian Eskimos

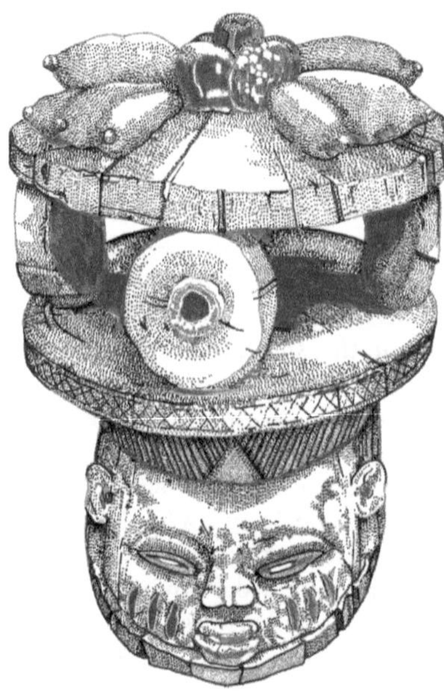

Drawing 10.9 Gelede masks are helmet- or cap-mask types, that is, they either completely cover the head of the wearer or rest on the top of the head with the mask extending to cover the upper part of the face. The masks are carved in identical pairs so two dancers can perform together. Most Gelede masks represent females, some are very elaborately carved, and most are painted. Members of the Gelede society wore these masks to promote fertility, to honor the god of the earth, and to placate the witches.[PP]

wore death masks made of wood to transform themselves into spirits.[49] For some northern peoples there
was a contradiction of attitudes about death and the
dead — a further manifestation of the dichotomy of
opposites. Although a corpse was an object of aver-
sion and thought "poisoned" by the powers of death,
there was the Cannibal Dance performed by the
Kwakiutl in which the initiates ate or pretended to
eat a dead body (see drawing 3.9), whereas on the
western coast of Vancouver Island, British Columbia,
and Cape Flattery, the call by Nootka people for dead
whales to drift ashore involved the building of a
shrine with human corpses arranged in poses to imitate the harpooning of a whale.[50] The bodies for those
assemblages were reportedly stolen from their graves.
The dead in that usage benefited the living by fulfilling
a dual role as both sacred and profane objects.

Masks as Representations of Externalized Spirits

The symbol most closely associated with death
was bone because a dead person's bones were thought
to retain elements of the soul.[51] The bones were
considered the seeds of renewed life, and although
there are more than two hundred bones in the human
body, the skull was of primary importance. The fascination with the head as the center of life was found
in most cultures and it manifested itself in various
ways. Representative skull masks and masks made of
skulls with the flesh partly removed were illustrative
of the folklore and mythology associated with the
head.

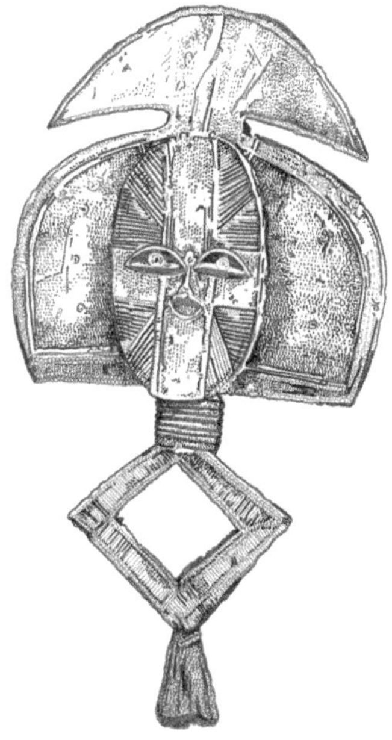

Drawing 10.10 *Mbulu Ngulu* ("image of the spirit of the dead")[qq] reliquary mask made of wood, red brass, and copper. These Kota guardian figures were placed in wicker or bark baskets containing the bones of ancestral leaders in the belief that their extraordinary pow-ers survived mortal death.[rr] The objective of the practice was to beseech the ancestors to protect the family. The figures also served to memorialize the deceased.

The skull fulfilled a fundamental role in many
societies as the reference source for many masks associated with death and funeral
rites (see chapters 1 and 2). The "skull cult" as the socialized indication of skull veneration was closely connected with ancestor worship. Skulls, as symbols of recognition or power, were arranged on poles over graves in ancient times to emphasize the
unity of the material and spiritual worlds. Eventually, the skulls were carved or shaped
to meet the needs of the particular culture.

Substitute ancestor imagery was exemplified by the reliquary figures (masks) of
the Gabon of Africa (see drawing 10.10). The objective of these masks and the associated rituals was to maintain contact between the living and the spirit world. That
relationship recognized that life was only a temporary state of being and an imperfect peculiarity of a cosmic whole. The other elements of that equation, the spirit
world and death, were equally real and worthy of recognition. The reliquary figures

(masks) were symbolic representation of ancestors. They portrayed the dead and conferred symbolic life.

Ancient peoples in the Middle East modeled portraits over family skulls filling the empty eye sockets with shells or obsidian to serve as materializations of the externalized spirits.[52] Skulls modeled over with clay and gypsum have been found in numerous locations including near Jericho. Although those early pieces (ca. 7000 BCE) were not masks in the traditional sense, they represented an early form of face covers relating to the dead.

Head worship among traditional peoples was a very strong and prominent part of the cultural belief system. The people of New Britain used the anterior part of the skull modeled with clay as masks, and the Mayans in Mesoamerica had a similar practice.

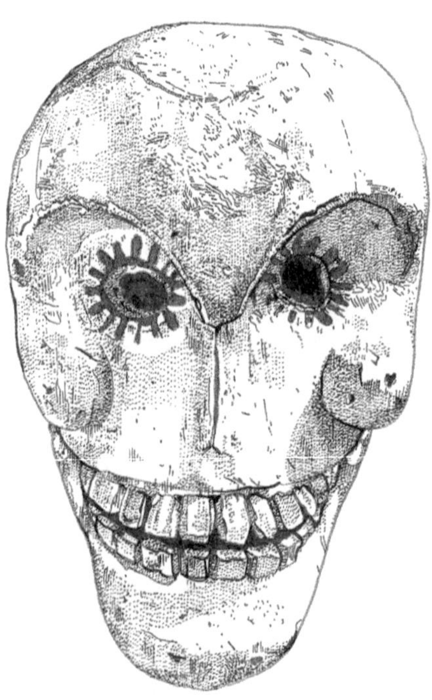

The skull was transformed into a mask such as one reported used by a shaman at the Hopewell site (300 BCE–550 CE) in Ohio.[53] The posterior portion of the cranium and the lower jaw were removed along with part of the nose cavity to form the mask. The remaining segment of the skull covered the eyes and forehead of the wearer. Altered in that way and adorned with hair and animal skin, the skull was a very effective death mask.[54] A fearsome image of that kind was reflected in the carved and painted wooden skull masks worn in Mexico (see drawing 10.11).

The burial masks found among the people of the Old Bering Sea culture (ca. 500 BCE–500 CE) fulfilled a special purpose.[55] Those extraordinary masks were placed on the faces of shamans at the time of their deaths, and the eye openings were covered or plugged with ivory "eyes" to prevent the spirit of the deceased from returning. The burial masks were removed from the face of the corpse and placed between the knees at the time of burial.

Drawing 10.11 Mask worn in the Danza del Dia de Todos Santos (All Saints' Day). This painted wood mask was reportedly made in Oaxaca, Mexico. Humorous masks representing the dead, which appeared as skulls, were worn in numerous festivals in Mexico. Los Muertos (the dead) were a motif with strong pre–Columbian tradition. The significance of the death symbol was enhanced by the allegorical morality plays that were brought by the Spanish to instruct the indigenous peoples.

The death mask in various forms was a ubiquitous feature of early cultures. Burial masks used by the Ipiutak people of the Bering Sea Complex were stylistically related to the burial masks used by the Eastern Chou dynasty of China.[56] The Incas made face covers (masks) of gold for the dead, and in other areas of the Americas, burial masks of fiber, stone, clay, ivory, and wood have been found. The Egyptians used precious metal and painted wood to shape masks for their dead, and in West Africa burial masks of bronze were used. The masks in Central Europe were made of clay, bone, and stone, and in Asia, the Chinese covered the faces of the dead with masks of wood and ivory.

The qualities of a death mask were associated with the inner presence (the spirit) that left the body at death and, in Kwakiutl mythology, the spirits themselves wore masks to fool, frighten, or coerce disagreeable spirits encountered in the "afterlife."[57]

11

Dramatic Apparitions

... [W]e defined masking as the ritual transformation of a human actor into a being of another order. This broad conceptualization permitted the inclusion of ritual drama, carnival, clowns, face painting, and various kinds of transforming costume elements in a general domain of symbolic transformation.[1]

The cultural core of early humans included many elements, but two of the more significant were memory and symbols. Memory, as the foundation for tradition, directed thinking and aided in maintaining continuity. Symbols consolidate ideas into recognizable images to reinforce memory. The mask, in the orig-inating culture, assisted in identifying, organizing, and preserving social memory. As a visual representation, it called to mind a significant deity, person, animal, plant, or event related to the history of the particular group. Masks in preliterate societies fulfilled an important role in communication in much the same way as petroglyphs, pictographs, or other culturally acknowledged marks. Both knowledge and memory were resident in the mask as a cultural symbol. The theatre (dramatization) probably began as a masked ritual.[2] It provided a perspective of the universe as envisioned by the actors and affixed in the collective memory of the people.

The use of masks in dramatic activities, in all probability, had its foundation in the fraternal societies of early people. Those associations were often secret, and the dramatic elements of their founding motives were part myth, part imagination, and part social. Their activities were, at times, elements of an indoctrination procedure for neophytes and a calculated occasion to demonstrate the power and importance of the group. Those dramatizations frequently centered on the myth describing the founding of the society or the beginning (creation) of the people or clan. Masks had an integral role in those enactments as they were the visual reminders of the relevant spirit beings as well as disguises for the performers.

Dramatic activities used imitative movements and dances to placate the supernatural powers that were thought to control activities and events critical to human survival. A social leader (shaman or priest) performed ritual dances or dramas as a means of appeasement and to pursue supernatural beings to fulfill the people's wishes or grant them success in various adventures. Masks were a primary element of those activities. The masks represented the spirit beings evoked or the animal or plant intermediaries of those entities.

Groups or clans in early societies included secret organizations, and each of those fraternities (as most were male oriented) had a privy order and traditional method of spiritual association. The initial secret societies that developed in Africa, Melanesia, and elsewhere were puberty related, and all men could be members following initiation that often included circumcision. However, due to a number of reasons including changing initiation requirements and limitations for membership especially at the upper ranks, other secret societies were formed. Many of those organizations included instructional activities in the requirements of community life as one of their purposes. Other groups assumed political and judicial duties that helped to control and regulate community affairs. Gradually the social authority was transferred to a centralized governing body that proved to be more effective, and secret societies were transformed into social clubs. The social club, in many cultures, performed the mythical dramas and maintained the traditional masks and costumes.

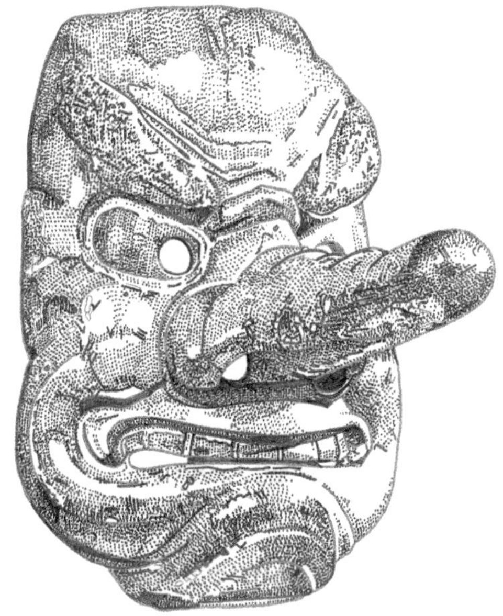

Drawing 11.1 Konoha Tengu mask made in Japan and worn in open-air folk dances-dramas. The Tengu were mythical beings that lived in remote regions of Japan. These eighteenth century masks were made of carved and painted wood. The long phallic noses had both an erotic and a comic appearance. Konoha means "the leaves of trees" because in the mountains, this type of Tengu were said to wear only leaves.[ss]

Masking in its earliest practices manifested specific socio-cultural values. Later, masks were identified with "role playing." It is possible that preliterate humans realized that wearing a mask changed only a person's appearance and not their physical presence and, with that realization, dramatic performances replaced rituals.

Masks in Greek and Japanese dramatizations enhanced the individual qualities of the characters and allowed the audience to identify more closely with them.[3] The sense of identification was an element of socially understood activity because the notion of role playing or play acting was considered an acceptable form of behavioral practice for most mammals. It was equally normal, in most cultures, for people to assume roles and to act out fears and psychological concerns (see drawing 11.1).

The mask aided in the illusion of transporting the wearer into that special being the mask portrayed. It gave the wearer the power to baffle the viewers' senses and to make them believe in the persona represented by the mask.[4] The visual transformation influenced the wearer as well as the viewer. Those who wore masks often altered their behavior "to act like the being the mask typifie[d]."[5] The information conveyed by the drama mask fascinated, amused, or frightened viewers; it also had the power to confuse and disturb. The ability to mystify and to inculcate a certain paranormal presence gave masks a singular importance in both dramas and rituals.

The drama mask had at least two prominent roles: One was helping in the transformation of the actor into the character, and the second was establishing the identity, history, and physiognomy of the character without extensive introduction. Those attributes were especially apparent in the dramatic presentations of Japan, Korea, China, and other areas of the East Asia. Masks played a similar role in most parts of the world where dramatic performances were a common part of the cultural life of the people (see drawing 11.2).

Masking to Appease the Natural and Supernatural Assemblage

The world of drama masks embraced realities that existed beyond perceptual or intellectual comprehension because those attributes are central to normal discernment and directly accessible to subjective experience. Masks, as dramatic accoutrements, were formed of belief and imagination and constructed of raw materials that were transformed to a point of being unrecognizable. Undoubtedly, as the cultural horizon expanded, some masks were made for the pleasure of creation while others represented a dedication and reverence that could only be found in true believers. The vitalities inherent in both image-making methods were instilled with the energy to influence the emotions and attitudes of those who came into contact with these materializations of the paranormal.

The history of a culture was a form of contextual memory that included a selection of events, objects, and situations organized in a manner to configure a narrative explanation of the physiological, sociological, and emotional inheritance of the group. Within that arrangement of semi-tangible elements lay the methods and means for locating and explaining the past. Masks, as elements of the narrative process, were central to the historical perspective of many cultures and represented an extraordinary record of the skills, beliefs, and attitudes of diverse peoples. The mask had two faces: one that represented a contemporary experience to validate the present and a second that conveyed a record of the past to verify all time before the present.

The history of masking includes the reality that some cultures reproduced or repli-

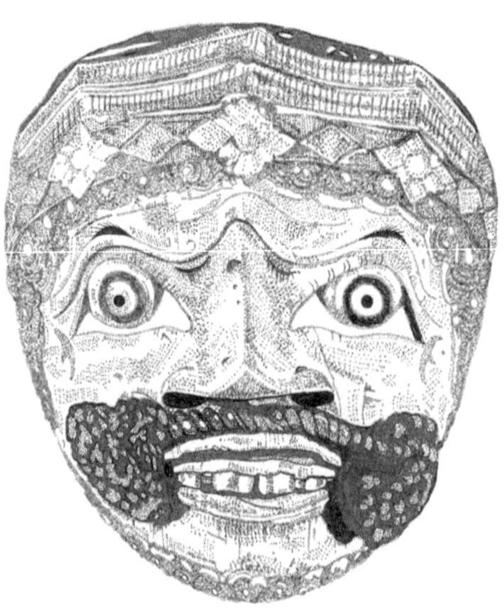

Drawing 11.2 Javanese Topeng (mask) of carved wood, pigment, rope, gold leaf, and other materials. The mask was used in traditional dramas probably to represent Klono, a foreign king who threatened Kediri because he wanted to capture Candra Kirana.[11] There was no mouth opening in masks used for the dramatic enactments because the lines were not spoken by the actors but by puppeteers.

cated ceremonial objects. Scores of masks were made to depict the same deity or mythological entity. Each of those depictions was "original" although it was a "replica" of a traditional design. That practice was most common for masks used in dramatizations, as they were the essence of social communication embodying the stereotypes, beliefs, and attitudes of a particular community.

Ritual dramas, for most of the world's peoples, were a method of cultural transmission evolving from imitation and mimicry. Masks facilitated the imitative practice by allowing the actors to resemble other persons or beings, and it was by that interchange that the act of transformation was achieved. "[T]he human face [was] transformed by the mask into a symbol...."[6] That transformation was the first requirement of dramatic practice.[7]

One of the earliest uses of the mask was magical,[8] and the magic-religious dramatizations were among the first organized applications of masking. "The dynamic rendering of myths, accompanied by dances, antiphonal singing, and recitation, contain[ed] the seeds of theatrical art. The transition to the drama [was] imperceptible."[9] In association with the source myth, legend, or ceremony, drama masks functioned properly only when used by performers in the culturally validated dramatizations. To comprehend the true significance of drama masks, they had to be viewed within the dynamic context of their dramatic purpose.

Masks as Dramatic Raconteur

Dramatic enactment probably had its origins in the cultures of archaic societies that used imitative dances to placate the supernatural forces controlling the events critical to their survival.[10] Shamans often directed the activities of ritual dramas designed to persuade the deities to regulate the critical forces in a way that allowed the people success in procreating, cultivating, hunting, or waging war. Special dramas also were enacted to expel malevolent spirits that caused disease and to direct the souls of the recently dead from the world of the living. As part of those dramatic activities, the shaman wore a mask that corresponded with the deities being petitioned.

Pursuing the concept of dramatic performance to its earliest and most rudimentary form, mimicry was "an instinctive mammalian tendency."[11] As early people "acted out" their thoughts, a generalized method of communication evolved that allowed group interaction. When a person put on a drama mask, it was not necessarily to become something or someone else. Wearing a mask expanded the individual's persona and that transformation was closely connected with sympathetic magic. In a state of ecstasy-supplanted physical awareness there was no essential qualitative difference between humans and other forms of life, or for that matter, humans and deities. Direct connection was possible — human to deity.

"The drama in non-literate societies affirm[ed] some of the deepest sanctions of living."[12] Dramatic presentations addressed a variety of cultural needs and concerns according to the societal structure in which they were enacted. However, despite the culture and the purpose served, all forms of dramatic expression appeared to have one element in common. They had a starting point and a conclusion; therefore, they had a rudimentary structure. That factor was significant in that the dramas told stories, and those stories verified the accepted history of the people. Thereby, the dramas were unifying factors that drew the past and the present together and gave the people a protracted view of their existence.

As knowledge of the environment and natural phenomena increased, dramas gradually ceased being primarily ritualistic and became increasingly educational. They conveyed culturally approved information.[13] That role was particularly important in acquainting the youth of the group with traditions and cultural identity. The dramatic instruction included enactments of legends and myths that revealed the lives and activities of deities and heroes.

Impersonation, like mimicry, was a natural part of communication. That which a person could find no other means of expressing was acted out by impersonating undefined characters. The stamping or swaying movements of animals or the strutting of a hero when characterized in a ritual or ceremony exemplified that routine. A mask enhanced the act or impersonation and was an element that gave credence to the dramatic reenactment of the mystic past. That approach corresponded with the shamanistic practice of visual manipulation to establish a personal pathway to the supernatural.

The Egyptian *Coffin Texts* (third millennium BCE) demonstrated the sophisticated nature some enactments achieved. In those documents were mythical narratives arranged as dramas with speaking parts and connected dialogue.[14] Passages in the *Texts* described how the world would end when the creating deity became weary. The *Texts* presented the notion that the universe was subject to the same frailties as humans including "a cycle of decay, death, and renewal."[15] The Jackal god of Upper Egypt whose name, *Wepwawet*, meant "opener of ways" was believed to guide the deceased into the underworld.[16] That important Egyptian deity was associated with ritual drama and was depicted in human form with a jackal head or mask.

The drama in its various manifestations offered a unique view of life, and the various episodic presentations were of primary importance to the host community. The performances were repeated as needed and generally remained the same, but in time, the intent of the activity changed. Eventually, the human element of the drama became less personal and more abstract, and the enabling people were transformed into spectators. When that shift occurred, the drama deemphasized its ritualistic connections.[17] It moved from real-life representation to the "emotional contemplation of life,"[18] without the practical responsibility or implications of reality. With that shift of emphasis, entertainment became a qualifying measure for dramatic performance.

As the line between ritual and traditional drama blurred, the two activities often referenced similar events. Dramatic performances were held as a part of festivals honoring local deities and participation in those proceedings was a form of worship or divine recognition.[19] The actors often wore ritual vestments and masks for those activities to impersonate legendary heroes and heroines, thereby adding to the mnemonic significance of the performance.

The motivation behind traditional drama was aligned with the desire to recreate an emotion-charged event, a stereotyped action to which the viewers (audience) could relate. In contrast to traditional rituals that had an objective purpose, the drama, as it evolved, was an end unto itself. Eventually, the actor detached himself or herself from the action that was a part of the ritual and became a demonstrator of life or a messenger of death, and with that separation, the nature of the drama changed.

The mask, while concealing the face of the wearer, exposed his or her spiritual or emotional condition. Masks were thereby vehicles of expression that gave credibility to dramatic activities. They "radically transform[ed] that part of the human body, the face, which the audience relie[d] most upon for understanding."[20] The drama mask defined the character portrayed and identified the type of person represented. The persons wearing the masks were not individuals but prototypes. They were established personae, and their characters were immediately recognizable to the audience. The masks also reinforced the essence of human emotion by elaborating expressions of fear, hope, pleasure, and belief. The masks were emotional metaphors that had their origins in the psyche of all people.

According to Ananda K. Coomaraswamy, dramatic themes were demonstrated by four components: "...[1] gestures, [2] speech, [3] costume, and [4] natural adaptation of the actor for the part."[21] The fourth element, the actor, was adapted (or modified) for the part by theatrical makeup or a mask that defined his or her role in the production. It was important in traditional dramatic activities that the actor did not overreact to the emotions of the part but performed the role dictated by the mask. The idea, not the image, was the essence of the character, and the mask revealed that attribute (see drawing 11.3).

Another function of masks used in dramas was to make real ideas and beliefs that were inaccessible in the realm of reality. They (masks) combined elements of the spiritual and material worlds that both clarified and distorted the hopes and fears of spectators. Masks, as integral parts of dramatic presentations, were powerfully descriptive and synonymous with pretense. They portrayed the distorted nature of humankind or nourished a sense of supremacy that validated human accomplishment. Masks stimulated the metaphysical proclivities of people that were expressed in culturally reinforced myths and beliefs.

The use of evocative masks in dramatic performances had a dual purpose. They allowed the masked performers to transmit myths and stories in ways that separated the human element from the

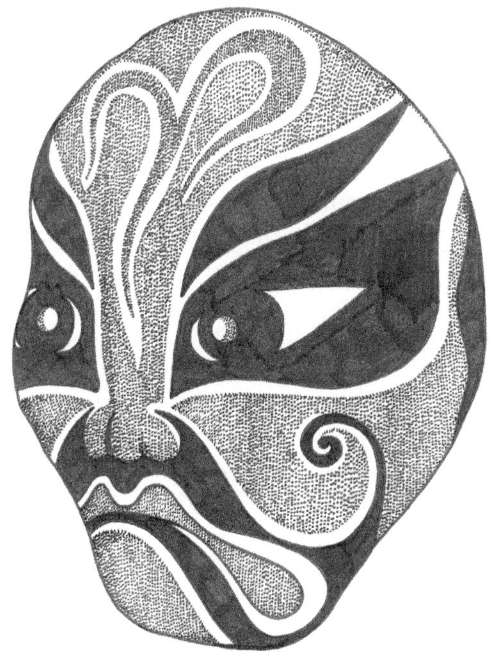

Drawing 11.3 A Chinese theatrical mask painted with an arabesque design that resembles traditional patterns found in rock engravings.[uu] The actor (usually a male) painted his face to portray a particular character type that was recognizable by the audience. The painted mask-like face gave a supernatural quality to the actor's appearance.

message, and they gained recognition with each performance as representing the encoded message told in the drama. The performances were often of a very practical nature because they conveyed messages to the viewers that were of special social significance. An essential aspect of dramatization was to make the past current in the people's minds by maintaining the vitality of group beliefs and preventing them from being forgotten.[22] The drama presented in that way impressed the historical significance of the group more deeply upon the minds of the viewers.

The presence of a mask as a recognizable symbol signaled to the audience that it was attending a dramatic performance and that the natural world had been temporarily made static and formalized.[23] When the masked person (actor) appeared on stage, he or she was transformed and claimed the identity of the represented character. Attention was focused on the mask, and the mask spoke with and for the audience in ways that fulfilled the ethereal needs of the group. When the masked performer attained a level of spiritual rapture so did the audience. The effects of the mask as a symbol separated the presenter from the audience physically while linking them emotionally.

Masked Dramatizations as the Essence of Social Beliefs

A traditional drama was an act, performance, or contest that might have or have not required a stage as a formalized setting. It also might have been "…an imaginative actualization of a vicarious nature" or "…a sacred performance, which represent[ed] the change of seasons, the rising and setting of the constellations, the growth and ripening of crops, birth, life, and death in man and beast."[24] Dramas were enactments such as the ancient Greek tragedy, miracle plays, and the Japanese Noh performances. Early people used the presentations to represent cosmic events as examples of what they expected or wished to occur. Many dramatizations required the performers to portray mythical beings, legendary heroes, revered ancestors, or powerful spirits, and they used culturally acknowledged masks to verify those portrayals (see drawing 11.4).

Masks as elements of conventional dramatizations were introduced into the Greek and Roman theatre during the fifth century bce and were used from that time. Tragic actors in Greek dramas before the fourth century bce wore helmet-like masks with attached wigs. Those masks had elevated foreheads proportional to the social status of the character. In contrast, actors in Old Comedy (a comedy form that was prolific in the fifth century BCE) wore grotesque masks and stuffed phalluses[25] to give an appearance that was the antithesis of the dialogue. Old Comedy was not permitted after the defeat of Athens by Sparta in 404 BCE because of its caustic satire and lack of moral restraint.

Dramatic activities in Rome included pantomimic

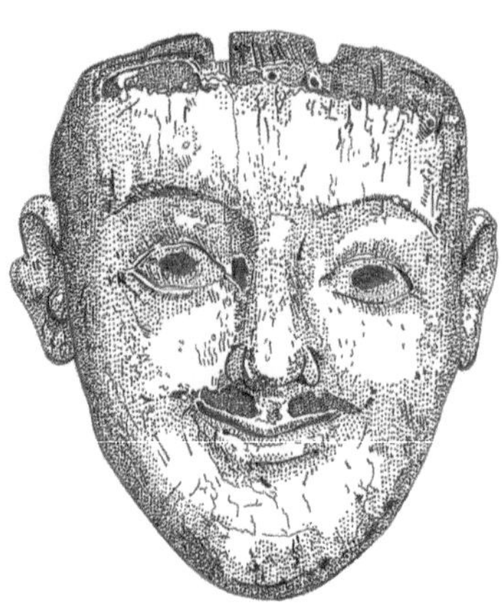

Drawing 11.4 A carved and painted dance mask from Mexico made of wood. This well-formed and very realistic mask from the state of Jalisco was worn for the Danza del Chayacate.

acts in which a single actor performed several roles. To give the performance greater credibility, the actor changed masks for each character. Those dramatic productions ceased with the rise of Christianity when the theatre was viewed less favorably than during Greek and Roman times. However, the church was responsible for the revival of dramatic acting with the inception of mystery plays. Priests and clergy performed the various roles in those dramas. In Europe during that time and into the sixteenth century, the actors were all men and they wore masks to aid in distinguishing the meaning and nature of the characters they portrayed. The mystery plays introduced into the Americas by European settlers and missionaries were transformed and given a distinctive indigenous character due, partly, to the use of highly stylized masks.

The drama masks as they were originally conceived and used did not endure in European theatre. With few exceptions, masks were gradually discontinued as part of dramatizations. They also lost favor in the performances that celebrated the prowess of a hero and benevolent deity. However, the presence of the masquerade continued to influence the epistemology of the theatre as the word "person" came from the Etruscan word for "mask," *phersu*. In addition, the Latin word *personare* meaning "sounding through" was used in reference to the voice of actors passing through the mask. Early theatre masks were built to project and direct the actor's voice.

The earliest dramatic theaters in Asia were believed to have been in India, although other countries developed sophisticated theatrical traditions that included masking. Japan, China, Korea, and many other countries had well-developed and uniquely original dramatic practices. Many dramatizations in East Asia were highly symbolic and made extensive use of masks or makeup that gave a mask-like appearance. The Asian theatre drew its origins from ritual performances in which music and dance were of importance.

Horrific masks were used in Balinese dramas to frighten and captivate the audience, and in Korea, Pongsan dramas (named for the city in North Korea from which they originated) used unusual masks made of *papier mâché*, pigment, fabric, and wood. The Korean masks were designed to impersonate stereotypical humans (including a sorceress) and animals in traditional Korean dramas. In Japan, Gi-gaku, a ritual drama, was performed from 672 CE. The performers of that highly stylized court dance wore expertly carved and skillfully painted masks. Gyodo masks, another important element of the Japanese masking tradition,

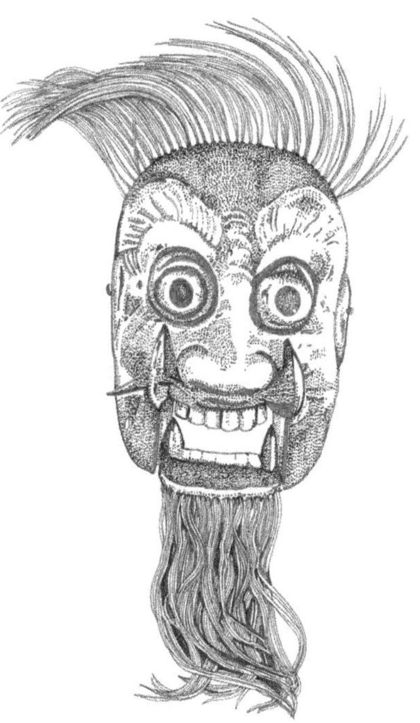

Drawing 11.5 Bugaku mask made of carved and painted wood. This mask made during the Kamakura Period in Japan was used in a form of ritual dance associated with Buddhist ritual. The dance that originated in Tang dynasty China was popular with the Japanese aristocracy. As Bugaku declined in popularity, Gigaku and Bungaku performances developed in the folk tradition.

represented Buddhist deities. They were used in drama-laden activities such as memorial services and temple processions. In those magico-religious events, the masked participants resembled statues that came to life. Those masking activities recalled a similar use of masked players in Greek dramas.

As with many traditional practices, the beginning of Gi-gaku performance was shrouded in myth and nostalgia. The dance drama was probably imported from Korea or China and with it came a significant masking practice to sustain the "dance from Korea."[26] The dance was reportedly introduced in Japan by a Peakche (an early Korean kingdom, 57–668 CE) man named Mi Ma-ji.[27] The Gi-gaku performances were associated with temple activities, and participants wore realistic masks reflecting non-Japanese influences. Gi-gaku masks appeared to have a foreign aesthetic quality, and some scholars have suggested the influential resource might have been ancient Greek.[28] The characters represented were often fantastic beings with unusual expressions, and the masks they wore covered the entire head instead of just the face[29] (see drawing 11.5).

The more recent classic dance drama, Noh, first made its appearance in Japan during the Muromachi Period (1392–1573 CE). This Buddhist-inspired art form used small masks that covered only the front of the actor's face, and many performers were without masks. The masks used for the dramatic dances combined abstract symbols with realistic portrayals of different character types. Masks were carved in a way to allow different moods to be expressed by the actors.[30] The ingenious face coverings represented all categories of women (young and old) and men (young, old, warriors, nobles, and priests). The Noh repertoire of character masks included supernatural beings such as ghosts and demons as well as an array of humans. Performers in the Noh theatre wore masks of purely Japanese origin rendered in a fantastic manner. The Noh mask types were recurrent and carved in the same way for centuries (see drawing 11.6).

In nineteenth century Japan, "ghosts, spirits, demons, ogres, and animal transformations crowded into the world of art, in part reflecting the disturbed social conditions of the times."[31] Those supernatural characters found their way into the Kabuki theater. The theatrical representations of "unearthly" beings were so popular among the public that they were illuminated in the art of *ukiyo-e* (the so-called "floating world" wood block prints) as well as the literature of the day. Demonic figures had especially severe and mask-like facial features created by makeup. Those "masks" were applied according to governmental regulations.

Masks allowed performers to present characterizations of persons or groups of persons that exercised social, religious, or political control. That type of masked event was exemplified in the dance plays of ancient Korea called "*Sandae-dogam*" dramas. Those performances included a set of twenty four grotesque masks painted in colors assigned to the points on the compass and five guardian gods represented the nature of the person type being portrayed.[32] The color black represented the north (direction) and communicated a dark nature; white was in the center and represented virtue or purity; the color red associated with virility was to the south; blue was to the east; and yellow was to the west. The *Sandae-dogam* dramas were in ten acts and thirteen scenes, and the actors followed a script that depended on pantomime with a few spoken words.

Korean masked dramas had five major socially relevant themes:

1. repulsion of evil spirits and prayer for the repose of the dead
2. satirization of apostate monks
3. ridicule of the ruling class
4. confrontation and friction between the two sexes
5. reality of the life of the ruled.[33]

Performances of the unique dramas were staged in villages on holiday occasions. The performances started after sunset and continued late into the night, allowing the darkness to add to the surreal qualities of the dramatizations.

There were also traditional dramas in Tibet that involved masked performers. Of particular importance were the New Year dances of the *dGe-lugs-pa* and the "Murder of the Evil King *Glang-dar-ma.*"[34] The performers wore masks of carved wood and *papier mâché* and acted the parts of demons and priests in mystery dramas that involved the acquisition of supernatural powers to overcome evil. The awe and fear inspired by the demon masks were dramatically represented in performances that depicted the victory of good over evil. The plays were performed on two levels: One catered to the lay audience, and the other was directed to initiates of Buddhism.

Masks worn on the island of Bali have been a part of dramatic performances for over a thousand years.[35] Three types of masks were used in those traditional dramatizations: human, animal, and demon. The human masks often had movable jaws and were either "full-faced," covering the entire face of the masker, or "half-faced," covering only the upper part of the face. As with other eastern drama masks, the anthropomorphic masks of Bali represented character types, heroes and villains, the young and the old. They were stereotypes of humanity with fine or coarse features that were exaggerated or refined to emphasize appropriate characteristics.

Balinese animal masks referenced mythological creatures associated with protective spirits acknowledged and respected by various social groups. The animals had the general appearance of tigers, lions, monkeys, bulls, birds, boars, and frogs but with protruding fangs and stringy hair. The masks often had dark bulging eyes and wild expressions to emphasize the differences between humans and animals.

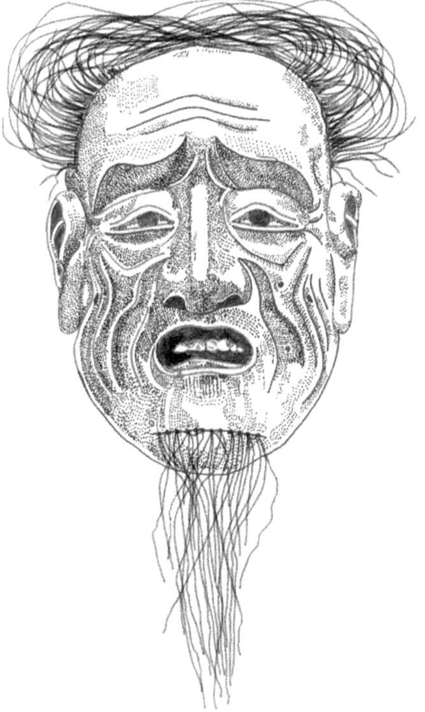

Drawing 11.6 This mask of an old man, Sanko, is one of the three hundred masks employed in the various Noh plays. Two hundred forty Noh plays, divided into five groups, are still performed. The Noh stage is bare of scenery, and production is simple. Prose passages are chanted. The actors and a seated chorus sing verse sections in a style based on the chanting of Buddhist prayers. Noh movements are extremely slow in tempo.

Those societies identified with the animals and conjoined that alliance to an ancestral connection.

These dramatic animal masks were not worn by performers but were held in front of their faces and a drape or costume concealed their head and shoulders. That masking position was exemplified by the Barong Macan and Barong Ket masks that resemble feline characters and was associated with the Chinese lion and Japanese dragon masks.

Masks and the Implicit Dramatic Purpose

Out of the mythical history of the "group" often came a social system for keeping the world in balance, and the recitation of myths was a reminder of the continuity of life and the necessity for equilibrium. Elements of play acting were active throughout much of the cultural process, and that practice produced many rudimentary forms of social life.[36] The historical record was fertile with people "playing" at being heroes, victims, and gods. Some manifestations were incorporated into superstitions, magico-religious beliefs, ritual formulae, legends, and social ideals while others retreated into parochial tales or anecdotes. The images associated with those "play actors" often reflected a mask-like appearance drawn from the popular mythology of the people (see drawing 11.7).

The use of masks in dramatic presentations depended on rules of performance established and recognized by the relevant society. Masks identified the unique characteristics of a particular character or character type and fulfilled the dramatic role by asserting parity with a social category. The mask used in dramatic performance had "reflective identity" that mirrored the established beliefs of the society in which the drama was presented. The mask without an established affiliation had no power to transform and was viewed as a disguise. The mask was, at times, simply intended to change the appearance of the performer in a comic or playful manner. The mask in those enactments altered the image of the wearer but had no significant social or spiritual implications. That form of transformation was a mere inversion of social hierarchy.

Most masking activities had an implied dramatic purpose whether the wearer mimed the role of a mythological hero, represented a persistent demon, or projected a desired objective. Recognition of the actor as the dramatic

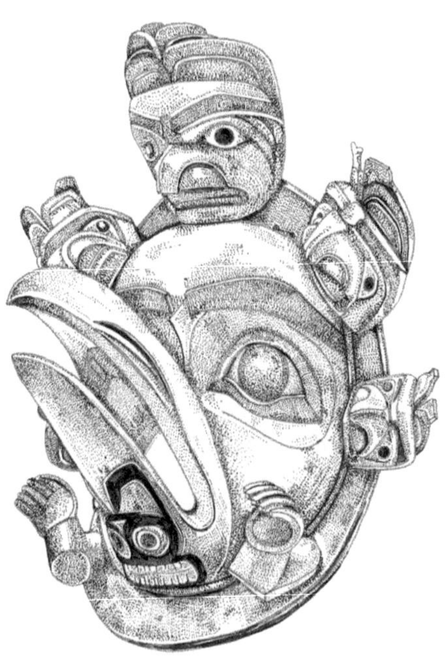

Drawing 11.7 Northwest Coast mask made of carved wood and pigment. This piece is an example of the human/animal transformation role assigned to masks. The human face has a raven's beak and is surrounded by head shapes that may represent other manifestations of the human/raven relationship.

character was of primary importance, and that identity was accomplished by using masks of various types including makeup and other face-altering methods as well as rigid face covers.

Early dramatizations with mythical foundations generally related to the daily needs of the people. One example was the annual enactment of the "...dancing of the bull-dance, a magical practice, ... [by] which a supply of buffalo would be secured for the coming season."[37] In those dramatic performances the participants were covered with the skins of animals; the heads of the animals were used as masks. That activity, performed by Mandans of North America, was characteristic of the hybrid nature of many dramas. They recalled the mythical traditions of the ancestors while addressing the sociological and physiological needs of the current generation.

However, some dramas had no mythical or ritual basis and were only dramatizations of social activities that had popular acceptance. Those dramas varied with each enactment (or location) while the basics of the story remained the same. Dramas of that type often included a statement of acceptable practice (morals) or were intended to unite or validate a social or cultural deed or custom. Good examples of that type of dramatization were those to confirm the healing process, recognize the birth of a "special" child, or acknowledge the departure for a journey. For each of those occurrences, the shaman or group leader organized a dramatic enactment that portrayed the event from beginning to end (see drawing 11.8). Such dramas served as guides for the people. They described the difficulties of the activity and showed the "way" to the conclusion. They predicted happiness or sadness, fortune or misfortune, good or evil, or life and death.

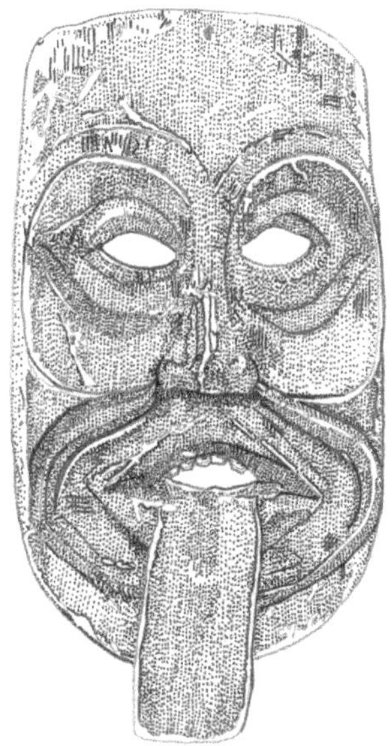

Drawing 11.8 Carved wood mask from southern Colombia with embellishing cuts around the eye openings has a striking resemblance to masks made along the Northwest Coast of North America. The exaggerated expression, sunken eyes, extended tongue, and open-mouthed expression might have offered a warning, but the exact use of this mask is undocumented.

Many European masks originally used in performances represented ancestors, spirits, and deities associated with cosmic events.[38] Eventually that practice was lost, but the tradition, in an evolved form, continued in the festival events that celebrated the various social and cultural customs of a particular community. Old practices survived as masks fulfilled necessary social functions, but the presentations (and the masks) had new justifications. Old symbols were carried forward and assigned new meaning and, as in the past, the masks as well as the dramas could be experienced on different levels. Subliminally, the mask continued to portray a cosmic connection and at times cosmic law.

The masked drama in much of the Western World lost much of its importance as the "powers of the subconscious were no longer encouraged to flower."[39] Many traditional dramatizations were viewed as demonic and determined to be antisocial due to the intellectual realignment of society and theology. One dreadful example of the corruption of masking was the "mask of shame" (see drawing 11.9). Those deceptively comic masks were forced on women accused of being witches at the time of their trial and, wearing those contraptions, they appeared to personify the evil of which they were accused.[40]

Masks and the Presentation of Supernatural Beings

One of the first requirements of any successful drama was for the actor to be transformed from himself or herself into the assigned character, whether hero or rogue. When the audience viewed the actor as only acting the part, then the character lacked validity and remained only the performer pretending to be someone else. In early theatre the features of the actor were disguised by a mask to facilitate that transformation.

Persons participating in social dramas often were selected and trained carefully. They underwent long periods of probation while they learned the songs and dances associated with specific dramatic performances. Because the words and actions were not written, they had to be memorized through an arduous process of transferal prompted by senior members of the group. Use of masks, costumes, and the related paraphernalia was allowed only after the aspirants achieved a certain level of proficiency. Those joining a particular society, as in Tahiti[41] and areas of Western Africa, often lived apart from the rest of the people and devoted the major part of their daily activities to the interests of the fraternal organization.

The masks fulfilled several roles in the dramatization of socially or culturally specific events. The mask, when used in that manner, separated the character being portrayed from the person inside the mask. The intention was not to disguise the wearer or to trick the viewer; instead it was to establish a separate persona. There was to be a clear distinction between the actor and the character being portrayed. That approach was different from the one projected in magico-religious ceremonies where the mask was often the manifestation of power. The drama mask was a separator that divided the fanciful from reality.

As an example of fanciful and traditional masks, the supernatural beings of the

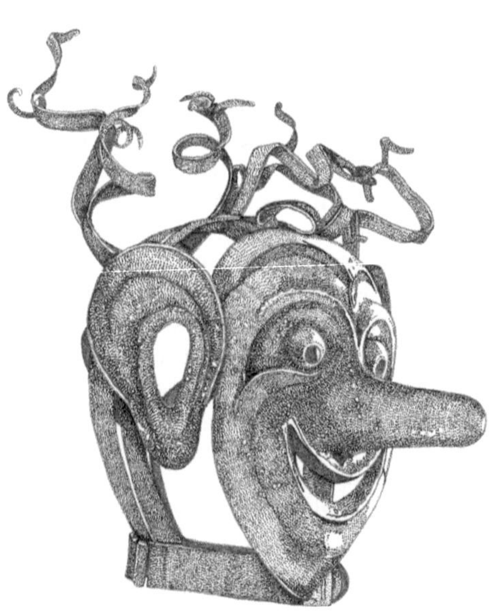

Drawing 11.9 Mask of Shame made in areas of Western Europe. These metal masks were intended as "symbols of shame" forced upon women accused of witchcraft. The women went to trial wearing these masks designed to personify the evil of which they were indicted. The masks imposed an image intended to vilify the women in the eyes of the public and to marginalize their credibility.

Balinese drama were the most fascinating and grotesque. They gave "life" and energy to supernatural characters that represented both benevolent and malevolent attributes. The masks were endowed with powers or forces that reflected their roles in society. Those masks often had elaborate hairpieces of fiber or horsehair that emphasized the head of the wearer. Tongue-like protrusions dangled from their mouths, and wild bulging eyes were circumscribed with concentric rings of color. Their gaping mouths displayed evil-looking fangs. They were frightening in appearance and graphically conveyed to the spectator the need to guard against psychological trauma. Those masks were made of painted wood and had a cap-like arrangement of cloth or fiber that fit on the wearer's head to hold them in place.

Artisans making masks for theatrical performances seldom had opportunity for creativity. The "look" of the mask (as with rituals) was defined by the role in the performance and by tradition. Image makers were expected to reproduce older masks carefully and deliberately to perpetuate established practices. Those controls were necessary because the style and expression of the mask had a direct influence on the meaning of the story being presented. For instance, in Bali where the same characters had many roles, different masks were carved to express different emotions, but with the general characteristic remaining the same. For Noh performances, one mask was used for several characters, and the identity of the player was recognizable by the costume. Each Gi-gaku dance character had a particular and specific appearance that required a unique mask.[42]

Unlike most of the masks used in theatrical activities in other cultures of the world, drama masks in Japan often were capable of changing expression and appearance to accommodate the movements of the performers. Jaw and tongue movements were common to many areas of Africa and South America, and Northwestern Coastal peoples made masks with moving parts. However, Japanese carvers produced masks with movable jaws, eyes, eyebrows, teeth, cheeks, noses, and ears. The separately carved parts are attached with string, allowing them to move to the rhythm of the dance.

Often the masks used in dramatizations expressed the extremes of human qualities: good/bad, happy/sad, beautiful/ugly, kind/cruel, and responsible/delinquent. Drama masks were divided into two categories: the refined and the grotesque. The more refined or dignified masks were carefully made with elegant features and

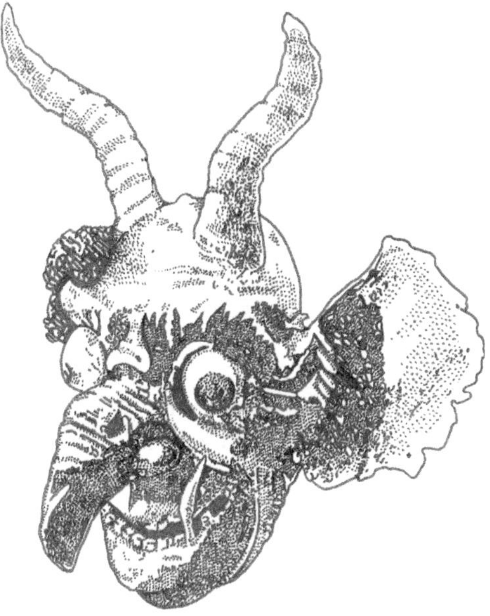

Drawing 11.10 Tyrolean demon mask worn in the Alps of western Austria and northern Italy during seasonal festivals of planting and harvesting. The church frowned on the use of masks but eventually allowed masked activities by assigning festival status to the events. This mask-type was associated with the Feast of Fools.

deliberately painted surfaces. They were usually of carved wood while the grotesque masks were made of a variety of discarded materials. Grotesque masks often were a combination of natural matter such as fur, cloth, and plant fiber.[43] The two categories were in strong contrast one with the other (see drawing 11.10).

A secondary role of masks in dramatization was to reinforce ambiguity or anonymity. Not only was the identity of the performer obscured but frequently the gender was as well. Men often were assigned the roles of women in the drama. The origin of that practice probably extended to the social and sometimes secret organizations that first assumed the responsibility for performing traditional dramatizations. Regardless of the motive or reasoning, men traditionally played the role of the "beautiful lady," "tragic heroine," "temptress," "shrew," and "hag" in Chinese, Japanese, and Mexican dramas. Men were especially trained for those roles in many locations.

In some societies, male performers masquerading as women had a purpose that went beyond the dramas in which they participated. "By disguising as women, men [were] able to instruct women of the community in correct behavior and present the consequences of deviance to them in dramatic form."[44] The mask used in that way served as a mechanism for social regulation. Traditional dramatizations were also used to sensitize the public to social or political issues that influenced the people of the community.

Other societies appear not to have been so restrictive and allowed women and men to participate equally in dramatic activities. However, that attitude was more common in dances and dramatizations where the participants painted their faces rather than wore masks. In the South American Andean region where face painting was common, that was the practice. "The original custom of face painting was to smear sacrificial blood around the eyes and extending it as a line or band from ear to ear."[45] The practice of painting the foreheads and chins of women with red iron oxide was customary in the Andean region of South America.

The activities of traditional people described as "dramas" were associated with veneration of deities, burial of the dead, and celebrations of the other events of the life cycle. They were often infused with ritual themes. The performances were a unifying element of community life that made drama

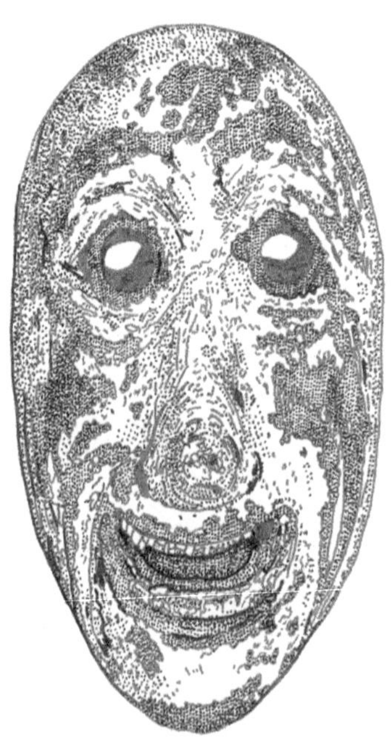

Drawing 11.11 White-faced clown mask made in Ecuador and intended for use in a carnival. These festive celebrations combined parades, pageantry, folk drama, and feasting, and often include clowns, jesters, or fools. Professional jesters were employed by the wealthy and powerful from ancient Egyptian times until the 18th century. Probably originating in pagan spring fertility rites, carnivals celebrated the death of winter and the rebirth of nature. Sociologically, they recommitted the individual to the group codes of the culture.

an integral part of the social environment (see drawing 11.11). Cultures and subcultures were known by the dramas performed and the masks produced. A few mask makers were often responsible for making all the masks used in a particular community and they, with the dramatists, were recognized for giving "life" and importance to annual or seasonal dramatizations.

12

Masking the Other Face

Doubtless the use of masks has some influence on the emphatic gestures and ornate presentation of every scene, which make ancient art seem like a stage performance enacted in pertetuum. Asia, too (where art was ritual), was obsessed by the mask. Till the great age of Christian art the mask reigned supreme; even in Roman portraits, where every face seems either unconscious of its feelings, or affirms its mastery of them.[1]

Masking as a tradition-directed metaphor could be viewed through the cultural prism. Each facet projects a different symbolic reference that can be extrapolated beyond the sociological horizon. Many secrets of the mask are outside the realm of interpretation even for those persons ensconced in the producing culture. "It was as if men mask themselves in immortality only to recover their own mortality."[2]

No assessment of the history of masking is absolute. Each view, no matter the perspective or predilection, assigns a personal value to each element of the historical process. Many aspects of cultural patrimony are aligned with the "consensus" view of historical events that tend to focus on commonly recognized heroes, battles, and institutions (transformational activities). Most of the assignations are subjective and based on perspectives that are far removed from the actual event.

Early peoples were oriented to the world as they understood it rather than in accordance with objective theory, and masks were indicative of that understanding. The masking practice evolved from the most basic survival instincts. Therefore, it is possible to draw upon the Jungian[3] prescription of the "psychological" and "visionary" creation processes, as noted in *The Spirit in Man, Art, and Literature,* to predict the original reasons for masks and the images they represented. The psychological element was an extension of the image maker's conscious life while the visionary stimulant was derived from the supernatural world that challenged the observer's understanding. To assume that the visionary scope reflected a primordial experience recognized the enormity, value, and potential influence of masking. Both concepts (psychological and visionary) undoubtedly motivated the mask-making process at different times and in different circumstances.

Recognizing the psychological and physiological needs of the human element was fundamental to developing masking practices. The amount and kind of information to be transferred by each mask or event were critical to successful communication. However, all interactions were in one of two modes: one that considered a material need and the other that met an emotional (or spiritual) requirement.

The conception of the mask was determined outwardly by the use in which it was to be applied and inwardly by the purpose behind that use. Masks for early people were representations of the spirits they (the masks) concealed and symbols that expressed in visual terms community beliefs. Masking emphasized the importance of the connections between the fundamental activities of life and the attitudes around which a particular people assembled. That response acknowledged that the people in every society reacted according to the examples provided by their history and the characteristics of their social order. Those patterns of behavior had a measurable impact upon the different levels of human existence including their social, political, and cultural lives.

The fundamental qualities of the masking were realized at the psychogenic level because the techniques and technology related to mask making were applied when a defined need existed and when it was ideologically appropriate. Masking, acknowledged in that way, stimulated confidence in the beneficial nature of the supernatural and enhanced the ability of humans to solve practical problems.

Because masking activities in most cultures took place in the service of needs, the defining of those needs was the provenance of the community. Therefore, it was impossible to stipulate the precise mechanism to achieve the desired results in each situation. However, the traditional world in all its domains operated in accordance with a number of fundamental laws. Decisions were made by societies, and those determinations were often shaped by the conditions of the physical and spiritual worlds and reflected in the masking practice.

Masking was a primary manifestation of the cultural life of early people and an essential part of human development in response to environmental and societal demands. The ambient factors of communal life often required complex ritualized events because the socio-cultural setting in which the people existed was circumstantially ambiguous. The behavioral patterns changed as well as the conditions in which the people existed because the masks, once created, altered their surrounding by their presence. The masks gave substance to abstract ideas and perpetuated previously undefined beliefs.

The masking concept dealt with the mask itself, the accumulation of related ritual events, and other activities within that context. A mask was not only the source of cultural information but an emitter or conveyer of tradition (the message) within a communication process. The mask was an element that contributed to the enrichment of human society and performed a role in verifying various beneficial entities. The praxes of masking widened the possibilities of mystical veneration and contributed to a greater appreciation of traditional attitudes, thereby influencing the lives (and the laws) of people. Masking activities developed from practice and were confirmed by use. Consequently, mask making was an inseparable part of sociocultural survival.

Each mask provided a glimpse into the diversity of life and insight into the complexity of the human mind. Masks conveyed belief, and the essence of that belief could not be considered from the perspective of true or false, right or wrong, or real or unreal. Basal beliefs were immune from verification because they existed in an attitude that was beyond sociological challenge. However, despite patrimonial endorsement, social and cultural attitudes evolved causing masking practices to change in different ways in different lands. Where there were patterns of increased sophistication and variation in the imagery of masks, those models were the results of increased specialization, material availability, and technical skill.

The core of the masking tradition in all sanctioning societies emanated from that part of the human mind where the boundaries between the real and the metaphorical, the signifier and the signified, were shifting and uncertain. Cultural attitudes declared by masking defined the ordinate qualities of a people as well as their ephemeral nature, and those sensations were untranslatable to other than symbolic terms. The mask as a cultural symbol was the messenger, and the message could not be restated in the popular vernacular.

The mask as a messenger held a unique place in preliterate society as a symbolic reference that lost much of its referential significance in literate communities. Masks bonded people into cohesive units (groups or societies) capable of self-reliance and endurance — they articulated a socio-cultural totality. The language of the mask was complete. It was two halves of the whole — the material and the spiritual. Masking was perhaps early humanity's most essential, universal, and meaningful language.

In language and meaning, the role of a mask was greatly influenced by the viewer's attitude and the setting. Visual indicators such as size, shape, and color assigned certain characteristics. However, it was the attitude and ambience that contributed to the full impact of the accumulated elements.

Each mask was a blend of the place in which it was made, the history of the producing people (tradition), the available materials, the skills of the maker, and the embedded symbols. The context in which the mask was presented often blinded the viewer to the realities (content) of their existence and superimposed an alternative world more compatible with the beliefs and needs of the time. The interconnectedness of people, place, time, and belief allowed a socio-cultural identity to be sustained without declining into chaos.

Masking had many special qualities, and the greatest single attribute was communication. Inherent in all aspects of masking was the process of interchange including the transmission of thoughts, messages, and information. Masking as communication was a systematic procedure of using symbols to impart ideas. Masks conveyed stories and provided information about people, places, and things. They facilitated an encounter between the viewer and the cosmos.

Belief and the expression of that belief were so concordant that they were intuitively joined. The masked event theatricalized communal beliefs and provided a public arena for the empowering language of symbols and emotions. The mask in those dramatizations was the essential link among belief, spiritual realization, and societal fulfillment. It connected the material and the ethereal domains into an inaudible but persuasive form of communication.

Masking was a multifaceted, multipurposed, and multidimensional activity. It was a method for transferring information and there were three ways of transfer that applied to all audiences. The first was direct interaction. The mask, at that level, influenced the viewer's immediate world in a predetermined manner. The second method was for the mask to stimulate emotions by interacting in a direct way with the viewer, thereby stimulating their involvement in the mystical activity. The viewer could experience both the mask and the process of gaining information through observation. The third technique was to connect the masks with the environment (natural and cultural) in which the viewer existed. Consequently, the mask related in a very direct way to the daily lives of the individual or group. The intent of that relationship was to verify the very real and understandable correlation between the viewer and the mask.

When compared with other methods of communication, the mask had specific features derived from its status as an object of cultural heritage. Because the mask was often a embodiment of an acknowledged spiritual entity, it was necessary to understand the unique language it conveyed. Comprehending the specific information of a mask was often complex. It required knowledge of the shapes, forms, colors, and materials to decode the message. However, the mask as a general symbolic reference was an element of information that was central to human understanding. It encompassed a language that was direct, complete, and meaningful. The informational exchange achieved using the language of the mask validated human understanding by formalizing the symbolic reference.

The intuitive characteristics of the people in early societies patterned the collective congruity of the group and gave substance to their identity. The way a people viewed the world in which they live was tradition bound, and that view was communally conceived. The cultural community rather than the individual was restricted by the time and space in which it existed. Space for the individual was relative and time was linear; therefore, different times did not exist simultaneously. People created artificial barriers to define the spaces they claimed and established traditions and practices to transcend the limitations of secular time.

The mask was a cultural phenomenon that evolved within the time and place of its origination. Whether "time" was a definitive factor in the actualization of the masking tradition or a precondition associated with a "place" of creation is impossible to determine. However, masking was a socially defined activity in the service of humankind and cultural evolution. The masks stimulated people to accomplish culturally approved activities.

Masks as Expressions of Time and Place

Much of the understanding process for ancient peoples undoubtedly was based on a belief in the similarity of things. Therefore, many scholars have assumed that traditional knowledge was based on placing things in an order where the visible features of the objects were related. That attitude ignores the possibility that early people respected the relationships between objects that were both visible and invisible and that those relationships included beliefs and perceptions as well as the discernible elements.

It is common practice for persons (anthropologists, historians, and scholars) dealing with various forms of imagery to arrange objects into stylistic categories and cultural divisions. That process apparently gives the organizer (or chronicler) a structure into which an object can be placed with a reasonable amount of confidence. In certain cultures and for some objects that methodology works well and, fortunately, many image makers intentionally situated themselves within an easily definable group. Unfortunately, the "cataloging" process is inefficient when applied to most traditional imagery. The difficulty arises when clearly defined cultural boundaries are obscured or the stylistic differentiation is arbitrarily applied.

An accepted method for identifying "art" objects from the scholastic perspective is the same as that used in many other comparative (systematic rather than synoptic) processes. Certain objects are identified as "types" and subsequently used as models against which other objects are compared. That methodology is used in scientific disciplines as an organizational technique for arranging like objects. Although it is a systematic process, the obvious problem with the scheme for most imagery is finding a "typical" example to use as a reference point.

To compensate for the absence of typical examples of artistic expression, individual objects often are placed within the context of era or style to describe the images and image-making processes. To identify a work as being from the Renaissance immediately places it into a chronological frame of reference. Or, to define an object as pre–Columbian or Late Shunga Period transmits an idea of the style and places it within an intellectual and emotional structure. Objects made by early people often lack true stylistic benchmarks and for want of a descriptive category, too often the style has been defined as "primitive." That designation was used in various parts of the world for a vast collection of objects made during an undefined span of preliterate time.

Masks are an expression of the human spirit regardless of the stylistic designation. They are products made to represent both the simplicity and complexity of human beliefs. They are inextricably associated with the beliefs and practices inherent in the major aspects of the culture in which they were made. However, in all areas of the world, there were numerous underlying aspects of culture as well as stylistic devices used in image making, and that was particularly true of masks.

Discrete human activities in most cultures proceeded according to different temporal cycles. Physical time was an arrangement of external events while ethereal time facilitated responses to the supernatural that were culturally defined. The physical environment was marked by the cycles of nature and the changes in human physiology. Those recognizable aspects of objective reality were often assigned predominant places in masking events. They were markers that could be anticipated, shaped in the human conscious, and shared within the community. There was also another time — the ethereal — that was associated with the transcendental nature of the individual or group.[4] That time had a different reality unrelated to mundane events.

Time in all societies was divided into separate realities, and humans were a minor part of both temporal spheres but had greater prominence in the physical realm. People identified with the present (time), but socio-culturally they recognized the past and anticipated the future. In contrast, ethereal time was continuous and unlimited by concepts of past, present, and future. Ceremonies, rituals, and masks linked the two temporalities and gave continuity (identity) to the people. Masks, as symbolic representations of the union, were a "living force" in the expression of human consciousness. They connected time and place. Masks conveyed the images people believed they knew from a time that occurred before their physical existence — in the beginning.

Ideally configured masks reminded the viewer "of nothing in everyday life, but rather in dreams, night-time fears, and the dark, uncanny recesses of the human mind."[5] Nevertheless, the shaman (or carver) often described the visionary event that was the source of the mask as the true representation of a particular supernatural encounter. The power of the mask in that manifestation laid not only in the cultural tradition but also in the visionary experiences it expressed. That symbolic expression eventually established a physical presence upon which the psychological process could draw.

The people interacted socially and culturally with the perceptions and memories stimulated by the mask image. The memories of life on earth and the story of human skills were included in masked ceremonies and rituals. Those adventures were imparted by masks as reminders of past events.

Masks and Social Interconnectedness

The history of mask making is the history of humankind. The motivations for mask making were fundamental ingredients for determining the concept and development of social order and cultural identity. Masking reinforced perspectives of spirituality and expanded societal reality beyond human limitations.

The person and the cultural life in which the individual existed were identical. They were constrained by time and place. Bound by the range of forms (activities) available, early cultural life was only capable of mirroring the history from which it emerged. As the world became more complex and the cultural construct and the boundaries between cultures became more fluid, societies lost their cohesion and confidence.

All early cultures were composed of separate but unifying parts. Some social structures were very complex with hundreds or even thousands of separate but associated components that joined to give identity to a particular people. The identifying elements were in a continual process of interaction and evolution as new influences were incorporated into the cultural agenda. The adaptability of new socio-cultural stimulants depended on the ability of the group to integrate the change into the existing cultural context.

The impetus for masks was requisite to the socio-cultural mix because their inspirations were sequestered deep within the traditions of the people. The resulting objects (masks) were not derivations, copies, or reproductions; they were true symbols of social reference. They were manifestations of something that was real but often previously unknown. The primordial experience was the fountainhead of cultural expression that "require[d] the related mythological imagery to give it form."[6] Masks conveyed the essence of their origins; they were quintessential elements of the belief systems from which they were derived and they were a part of the continuing cycle of renewal.

Almost all objects, including masks, despite the intended use or construct, might have been assigned a measure of aesthetic value. However, it was the perception of the object (mask) that was valued rather than the object itself. People viewed masks in two principal ways. One perspective was literal. The mask was what it appeared to be. The appearance was the identity. The second way of considering a mask was cerebral. It was what the viewer believed it to be. The appearance was the reference. Ultimately, the purpose of masks in most locations was to enhance self-knowledge in a particular population by reminding people of the practices, habits, and beliefs of their culture. The role of the mask evolved out of tradition and was perpetuated by the collective need for identity verification.

The issue of identity was an important and basic concern that was significant in the lives of individuals, the existence of the group, and the survival of cultural traditions. Identity was a psychological, cultural, or a political phenomenon that evolved on three levels:

1. Psychologically, it involved self-perception and projection and it provided self-esteem for the group.
2. Culturally, it provided a sense of distinctiveness for the group.
3. Politically, it created a sense of pride that empowered the group.

Masks in many cultures facilitated all three elements of group identification and promoted self-realization.

Globally the functions of masks were so diverse and so intermingled that they resisted a precise definition. Cultural diffusion as the process of adopting and borrowing by one culture from another was a real and recognized practice.[7] The role of masks as well as their shape, color, and design evolved over hundreds and perhaps thousands of years due to environmental, geographical, and political influences. Adding to that mixture, there were other changes resulting from evolutional, technological, sociological, and spiritual factors. Masks in an infinite variety enriched the lives of people and gave identity to their beliefs. Cultures in all regions of the world developed an understanding of masks and a masking system that promoted spiritual and physical well-being. Masking was a socio-cultural activity where cultural and ethnic pride found a release and where respect and community relationships were established and reinforced.

Masking was a living tradition. The mask as a symbol of human perseverance was a continuing cultural phenomenon that both confirmed and defied time and space. It mirrored the earliest forms of human belief and expressed the socio-cultural nature of humanity. Masks were a reflection of the past and a prediction of the future. They delineated the essence of human survival by recognizing that each succeeding generation was what their ancestors had been — products of their beliefs.

Masks as socially defined objects connected fragments of belief into the collective memory of humankind, and distinct cultures were formed around those fragments. The masking tradition was a part of the story of human existence. Social structures were derived from a collection of parts, and those irreducible ingredients, such as masks and masking practices, distinguished one people from another.

The mask did not exist outside the realm of what is human. The viewer and the masker in the masked event had two psychogenic options. One option was to individualize the mask and the second was to be absorbed by the emotion and spiritual energy represented by it. When the mask was individualized, the viewer and the masker visualized (imagined) a circumstance involving the mask and they watched the event unfold. When they were absorbed by the emotion and spiritual energy, they became one with the mask and the spiritual element it represented. The mask as an object of human initiation was equally emotive as the mystical reference it conveyed in that they both provided directions on what to do and how to respond to social activities. The mask gave humans a means of revealing their beliefs, fears, and aspirations.

Because certain mystical ideals stirred emotions and dictated group activities, it was natural that the symbolic references to those idealizations should have similar property. When a people follow certain ideals and give special attention to the representative symbols, they often do so because their ancestors did. However, at times the ideal is so deeply rooted in the cultural group that it exceeds the limits of its original purpose.

Masks have gained transhistorical significance while other objects of sociocultural reference have been forgotten. There are fundamental differences between the way anthropologists, psychologists, art historians, and aestheticians view masks. That was true whether aesthetics were defined as a branch of philosophy that provides a theory of the beautiful and of the fine arts, the psychological response to beauty and artistic experiences, or the branch of metaphysics concerned with the laws of perception.[8] The values particular to each area of investigation may be irrelevant for the others. Yet each discipline views masks and masking as a means for assessing certain, though different, aspects of various cultures.

Many assumptions are made about the practices of the past including the premise of ignorance. Often, the actual beliefs were not so different from those practiced today; only the perspective differed. In this age of telecommunication and global exchange people continue to rely on symbols as points of cultural reference. Recognizable markers are used to trigger memories, connect ideas, and stimulate responses. In some instances, these cultural expressions serve as generators of introspection and reflection — the infusion of recollections. Most often, the mnemonic elements are defined by the collective history of the people. They are symbols of the past that have continuing connotations.

People were the reason for the masking practice to exist. Although that is an obvious point, it is frequently overlooked in the assessment of masking activities. Masking was not an end in itself. It fulfilled the needs and expectations in the host community.

> The only thing that is different from one time to another is what is seen and what is seen depends upon how everyone is doing everything. This makes the thing we are looking at very different and this makes what those who describe it make of it, it makes a composition, it confuses, it shows, it is, it looks, it likes it as it is, and this makes what is seen as it is seen.[9]

Notes to the Captions

a. Lee, D. *Masks of Korea* (Seoul: Korean Overseas Information Service, 1981), p. 13.

b. Jacobson, L., and D. Fritz, *Changing Faces: Mexican Masks in Transition* (McAllen, TX: McAllen International Museum, 1985), p. 20.

c. Napier, A. D. *Masks, Transformation, and Paradox* (Berkeley and London: University of California Press, 1986), p. 122.

d. Jacobson, and D. Fritz, *Changing Faces*, p. 20.

e. *Ibid.*, p. 17.

f. Teuten, T. *The Letts Guide to Collecting Masks* (London: Studio Editions Ltd., 1991), p. 66.

g. National Museum of American Art. *Celebration: A World of Art and Ritual* (Washington, DC: Smithsonian Institution Press, 1982), p. 62.

h. Fitzhugh, W. W., and S. Kaplan, *Inua: Spirit World of the Bering Sea Eskimo* (Washington, DC and London: Smithsonian Institution Press, 1982), p. 187.

i. Mair, L. *Witchcraft* (New York and Toronto: McGraw-Hill Book Co., 1969), p. 72.

j. Slattum, J. *Masks of Bali: Spirits of an Ancient Drama* (San Francisco: Chronicle Books, 1992), p. 80.

k. Hahner-Herzog, I., M. Kecskési, and L. Vajda. *African Masks from the Barbier-Mueller Collection* (Geneva and New York: Prestel-Verlag,1998), p. 243.

l. Painter, M. T. *A Yaqui Easter* (Tucson: University of Arizona Press, 1971), p. 13.

m. National Museum of American Art, *Celebration*, p. 62.

n. Cordry, D. *Mexican Masks* (Austin and London: University of Texas Press, 1980), p. 248.

o. Jessup, H. *Court Arts of Indonesia* (New York: Asia Society Galleries in association with Harry N. Abrams, 1990), p.164.

p. Kerstetter, J. *Colorado Springs Fine Arts Center: A History and Selections from the Permanent Collection* (Colorado Springs: Colorado Springs Fine Arts Center, 1986), p.108.

q. Campbell, J. *The Mystic Image* (Princeton, NJ: Princeton University Press, 1974), p. 121.

r. *Ibid.*, p. 118.

s. Gimbutas, M. *The Language of the Goddess* (San Francisco: HarperCollins, 1991), p. 146.

t. Campbell, J. *Historical Atlas of World Mythology*, vol. 1 (London: Summerfield Press, 1983).

u. Slattum, *Masks of Bali*, p. 106.

v. Sasser, B. *The World of Spirits and Ancestors in the Art of Western Sub-Saharan Africa* (Lubbock, TX: Texas Tech University Press, 1995), p. 98.

w. Underwood, L. *Masks of West Africa* (London: Alec Tiranti Ltd., 1952), p. 45.

x. Hahner-Herzog, Kecskési, and Vajda, *Masks*, p. 22.

y. Smith, S.V.H. *Masks in Modern Drama* (Berkeley and London: University of California Press, 1984), p. 54.

z. McFarren, P. ed. *Mascaras de los Andes Bolivianos* (La Paz, Bolivia: Editorial Quipas/ banco Mercantil, S.A., 1993).

aa. Labbé, A. J. *Colombia Before Columbus* (New York: Rizzoli International Publications, 1986), pp. 44–45.

bb. Holm, J., and J. Bowker, eds. *Myth and History* (London and New York: Pinter Publishers, 1989), p. 232.

cc. Campbell, *Historical Atlas of World Mythology*, vol.1, p. 202.

dd. Hartmann, G. *Masken südamerikanischer Naturvölker* (Berlin: Veröffentlichunger des Museums für Völkerkundt, 1967), p. 42.

ee. Urban, G., and J. W. Hendricks. "Signal Functions of Masking in Amerindian Brazil In *Semiotics* 47-1/4 (Austin, TX: University of Texas at Austin, 1983), pp. 181–218.

ff. McFarren, *Mascaras*, p. 36.

gg. Maksic, S., and P. Meskil. *Primitive Art of New Gunea Sepik River Basin* (Worcester, MA: Davis Publications, 1973).

hh. Waite. In Fraser, D. ed. *The Many Faces of Primitive Art* (Englewood Cliffs, NJ: Prentice-Hall, 1966).

ii. Morphy, H. "The Anthropology of Art." In Ingold, T. ed. *Companion Encyclopedia of Anthropology* (London and New York: Routledge, 1994), pp. 648–679.

jj. Segy, L. *Masks of Black Africa* (New York: Dover Publications, 1976), p. 22.

kk. Berger, P. "Buddhist Festivals in Mongolia" In Berger, P. and T. T. Bartholomew, eds. *Mongolia: The Legacy of Chinggis Khan* (London: Thames and Hudson, Ltd., 1995), p. 150.

ll. *Ibid.*, p. 168.

mm. Nebesky-Wojkowitz, R. *Tibetan Religious Dances* (The Hague: Mouton, 1976), p. 77.

nn. Pal, P. *Art of Tibet* (Berkeley and London: University of California Press, 1983), p. 171.

oo. Wade, E. L. "Straddling the Cultural Fence: The Conflict for Ethnic Artists within Pueblo Society." In Wade, E. L. ed. *The Arts of the North American Indian* (New York: Hudson Hills Press, 1986), p. 243.

pp. Segy, *Masks of Black Africa,* caption 152.

qq. Segy, L. *African Sculpture Speaks* (New York: A. A. Wyn, 1952), p. 186.

rr. National Museum of African Art. *Selected Works*, vol. 1. (Washington, DC: National Museum of African Art, 1999), p. 103.

ss. Moes, R. *Mingei: Japanese Folk Art* (New York: Universe Books, 1985), p. 45.

tt. Jessup, *Court Art of Indonesia*, pp. 164–166.

uu. Lommel, A. *Masks: Their Meaning and Function* (New York and Toronto: McGraw-Hill Book Company, 1972).

Chapter Notes

Introduction

1. Huizinga, J. *Homo Ludens: A Study of the Play-Element in Culture* (London, Boston, and Henley: Routledge & Kegan Paul, 1949), p. 26.

2. Conrad, J. *Heart of Darkness* (New York and Toronto: Alfred A. Knopf, 1967), p. 50.

3. AHED. *American Heritage Electronic Dictionary* (Houghton Mifflin Company. U.S. Pat. No. 4,724,523. ©1992, Word Star International Inc., (©1991).

4. Shalleck, J. *Masks* (New York: the Viking Press, 1973), p. 10.

5. Burne, C. S. *The Handbook of Folklore: Traditional Beliefs, Practices, Customs, Stories and Sayings* (London: Random House, 1995), pp. 23–39.

6. Bettelheim, B. *Symbolic Wounds: Puberty Rites and the Envious Male* (Glencoe, IL: Free Press, 1954).

7. Eliade, M. *Symbolism, the Sacred, and the Arts*, edited by D. Apostolos-Cappadona (New York: Continuum, 1992), p. 64.

8. Murray, H. A., ed. *Myth and Mythmaking* (New York: George Braziller, 1960), p. 33.

9. Huizinga. *Homo Ludens*, p. 15; see also J. Campbell, in Murray, *Myth and Mythmaking*, pp. 41–43.

10. Teuten, T. *The Letts Guide to Collecting Masks* (London: Studio Editions Ltd., 1991), p. 59.

11. Grolier Electronic Publishing, ©1993.

Chapter 1

1. Oettinger, M., Jr., and S. Kenagy. "The Many Faces of Mexico: Masks in Cultural Context," in *Masterkey* (Los Angeles: Southwest Museum, vol. 62, Nos. 2 and 3, Summer/Fall 1988), p. 9.

2. Webster, H. *Primitive Secret Societies: A Study of Early Politics and Religion.* 2d ed. (New York: Macmillan Company, 1932), p. 205.

3. Birket-Smith, K. *The Paths of Culture.* (Madison and Milwaukee: University of Wisconsin Press, 1965), p. 195.

4. *Ibid.*

5. Lindsay, J. *A Short History of Culture* (New York: Citadel Press, 1963), p. 51.

6. Young, D. *Origins of the Sacred* (New York: St. Martin's Press, 1991), p. 223.

7. Bourke, J. G. *Apache Medicine-men* (New York: Dover Publications,1993), p. 35.

8. *Ibid.*, p. 36.

9. Grolier Electronic Publishing, ©1993.

10. Boas, F. *Primitive Art* (New York: Dover Publications, 1955), p. 348.

11. Thomas, K. *Religion and the Decline of Magic* (Oxford and New York: Oxford University Press, 1997), p. 446.

12. Monter, E. W. *Witchcraft in France and Switzerland* (Ithaca and London: Cornell University Press, 1976), pp. 25, 157–166.

13. Pace, D. *Claude Lévi-Strauss: The Bearer of Ashes* (London: ARK Paperbacks, 1986), pp. 52–53.

14. Boas, F. *The Mind of Primitive Man* (New York: Macmillan Company, 1938), pp. 159–174.

15. Carmichael, D., J. Hubert, B. Reeves, and A. Schanche, eds. *Sacred Sites, Sacred Places* (London and New York: Routledge, 1994), p. 91.

16. Lévy-Bruhl, L. *How Natives Think* (Princeton, NJ: Princeton University Press, 1985), pp. 228–262.

17. Walker, B. G. *The Woman's Dictionary of Symbols and Sacred Objects* (Edison, NJ: Castle Books, 1988), p. 316.

18. Maringer, J. *The Gods of Prehistoric Man* (New York: Alfred A. Knopf, 1960), p. 279.

19. *Encyclopedia of Magic and Superstition* (London: Octopus Books Limited, 1974), p. 188.

20. Lindsay, *A Short History*, p. 111.

21. Strathern, A., and M. Strathern. *Self-deco-*

ration in Mount Hagen (Toronto and Buffalo: University of Toronto Press, 1971), p. 171.

22. Lindsay, *A Short History*, p. 111.

23. Napier, A. D. *Masks, Transformation, and Paradox* (Berkeley and London: University of California Press, 1986), p. 210.

24. Weitz, M. *Problems in Aesthetics* (New York: Macmillan Company, 1964), p. 50.

25. Eliade, M. *Symbolism, the Sacred, and the Arts*, edited by D. Apostolos-Cappadona (New York: Continuum, 1992), p. 64.

26. Lommel, A. *Masks: Their Meaning and Function* (New York and Toronto: McGraw-Hill Book Company, 1972), pp. 57–59.

27. Lewin, R. *The Origin of Modern Humans* (New York: Scientific American Library, a division of HPHLP, 1993), p. 140.

28. Napier, *Masks*, p. 199.

29. Lee, D. H. *Masks of Korea* (Seoul: Korean Overseas Information Service, Ministry of Culture and Information, 1981), p. 7.

30. Fitzhugh, W. W., and S. A. Kaplan. *Inua: Spirit World of the Bering Sea Eskimo* (Washington, DC: Smithsonian Institution Press, 1982), p. 180.

31. Lommel, *Masks*, p. 15.

32. Monti, F. *African Masks.* (London, New York, Sydney, Toronto: Hamlyn Publishing Group Limited, 1968), p. 25.

33. Wingert, P. S. *Primitive Art: Its Traditions and Styles* (New York: Oxford University Press, 1962), p. 15.

34. *Ibid.*, p. 16.

35. Doty, W. G. *Mythography: The Study of Myths and Rituals* (Tuscaloosa: University of Alabama Press, 1986), p. 118.

36. Wingert, *Primitive Art*, p. 17.

37. Jung, C. G. *The Spirit in Man, Art, and Literature*, vol 15 (Bollingen Series XX, New York: Pantheon Books, a Division of Random House, 1966), p. 96.

38. Palmer, J. "Need and Function: The Terms of a Debate" In Palmer, J. and M. Dodson, eds. *Design and Aesthetics* (London and New York: Routledge, 1996), pp. 110–122.

39. *Ibid.*

40. Walens, S. "Analogic Causality and the Power of Masks." In: Crumrine, N. R., and M. Halpin, eds. *The Power of Symbols: Masks and Masquerade in the Americas* (Vancouver: University of British Columbia Press, 1983), pp. 70–78.

41. Markman, R. H., and P. T. Markman. *The Flayed God: The Mesoamerican Mythological Tradition* (New York: HarperCollins, 1992), pp. 35–36.

42. Riley, Olive L. *Masks and Magic* (New York: Studio Publications and Thomas Y. Crowell Co., 1955), p. 1.

43. Lewin, Roger. *The Origin of Modern Humans* (New York: Scientific American Library, a division of HPHLP, 1993), p. 154; see also Eliade, M. *Symbolism, the Sacred, and the Arts*, (New York:

Continuum, 1992), p. 65; Halifax, J. *Shaman: The Wounded Healer* (London: Thames and Hudson Ltd., 1982); Marshack, A. *The Roots of Civilization* (New York and Dusseldorf: McGraw-Hill Book Company, 1972), pp. 272–273; Herskovits, Melville J. *Man and His Works: the Science of Cultural Anthropology* (New York: Alfred A. Knopf, 1948). pp. 14–16.

44. AHED. *American Heritage Electronic Dictionary* (Houghton Mifflin Company. U.S. Pat. No. 4,724,523. © 1991, Word Star International Inc., ©1992).

45. Christian, P. *The History and Practice of Magic*, 2 Vols (Secaucus, NJ: Citadel Press, 1972), p. 19.

Chapter 2

1. Cordry, D. *Mexican Masks* (Austin and London: University of Texas Press, 1980), p. 3.

2. Vlahos, O. *Body, The Ultimate Symbol* (New York: J. B. Lippincott Company, 1979), p. 74.

3. Gimbutas, M. "The Mask in Old Europe: 6500–3500 B.C." In *Archaeology*, October 1974, 27 (4), pp. 263–269.

4. *Ibid.*

5. Segy, L. *Masks of Black Africa* (New York: Dover Publications, 1976), p. 4.

6. Underwood, L. *Masks of West Africa* (London: Alec Tiranti Ltd., 1952), p. 2.

7. Birket-Smith, K. *The Paths of Culture* (Madison and Milwaukee: University of Wisconsin Press, 1965), p. 193.

8. Paulme, D. *African Sculpture* (New York: Viking Press, 1962), p. 16.

9. Napier, A. D. *Masks, Transformation, and Paradox* (Berkeley, Los Angeles, and London: University of California Press, 1986), p. xvi.

10. Lommel, A. *The World of the Early Hunters* (London: Adams and Mackay Ltd., 1967), pp. 11 and 107.

11. Reik, T. *Ritual: Psycho-analytic Studies* (New York: International Universities Press, 1958), p. 256.

12. *Ibid.*

13. Cordry, D. *Mexican Masks*, p. 245.

14. Grolier Electronic Publishing, ©1993.

15. Lissner, I. *Man, God and Magic* (New York: G. P. Putnam's Sons, 1961), p. 244.

16. *Ibid.*, p. 245.

17. Capra, F. *The Tao of Physics*, 3d ed. (Boston: Shambhala Publications, 1991), p. 138.

18. Haile, B. *Head and Face Masks in Navaho Ceremonialism* (New York: AMS Press, 1978), p. 39.

19. Cirlot, J. E. *A Dictionary of Symbols* (London: Routledge & Kegan Paul, 1962), p. 196.

20. Ernest, C. "Spatial-Imagery Ability, Sex Differences, and Hemispheric Functioning." In: Yuille, J, C., ed. *Imagery, Memory and Cognition*

(Hillsdale, NJ and London: Lawrence Erlbaum Associates, 1983), p. 1.

21. Küchler, S., and W. Melion, eds. *Images of Memory: On Remembering and Representation* (Washington and London: Smithsonian Institution Press, 1991), p. 3.

22. Yates, F. A. *The Art of Memory* (Chicago: University of Chicago Press, 1966), pp. 1–26.

23. Küchler and Melion, *Images of Memory,* p. 3.

24. Yates, *Art of Memory,* pp. 1–26.

25. Slattum, J. *Masks of Bali: Spirits of an Ancient Drama* (San Francisco: Chronicle Books, 1992), p. 22.

26. *Ibid.,* p. 22.

27. Burland, C. A. *The Magical Arts: A Short History* (London: Arthur Barker Limited, 1966), p. 1.

28. Arnheim, R. *Art and Visual Perception: A Psychology of the Creative Eye* (Berkeley and London: University of California Press, 1974), pp. 136–137.

29. Gerbrands, A. A. *Art as an Element of Culture, Especially in Negro-Africa* (Mededelingen Van Het Rijksmuseum Voor Volkenkunde, No. 12, Leiden: E. E. Brill, 1957), p. 111.

30. Leenhardt, M. *Folk Art of Oceania* (New York: Tudor Publishing Company, 1950), p. 42.

31. Wingert, P. S. *Primitive Art: Its Traditions and Styles* (New York: Oxford University Press, 1962), p. 46.

32. Chiari, J. *Art and Knowledge* (New York: Gordian Press, 1977), p. 31.

33. Merriam-Webster, eds. *Webster's Dictionary of Word Origins* (New York: Smithmark, 1995), p. 353.

34. Morphy, H. "The Anthropology of Art." In: Ingold, T., ed. *Companion Encyclopedia of Anthropology: Humanity, Culture and Social Life* (New York and London: Routledge, 1994), p. 663.

35. Vlahos, *Body, The Ultimate Symbol* p. 83.

36. *Ibid.,* p. 82.

37. Child, A. B., and I. L. Child. *Religion and Magic in the Life of Traditional Peoples* (Englewood Cliffs, NJ: Prentice Hall, 1993), p. 168.

38. Markman, R. H., and P. T. Markman. *The Flayed God: The Mesoamerican Mythological Tradition* (New York: HarperCollins, 1992), p. 42.

39. Werbner, R. P. *Ritual Passage, Sacred Journey: The Form, Process and Organization of Religious Movement* (Washington, DC: Smithsonian Institution Press, 1989), pp. 151–52.

40. Hiler, H. *From Nudity to Raiment* (London: Simpkin Marshall Ltd., 1929), p. 124.

Chapter 3

1. Doty, W. G. *Mythography: The Study of Myths and Rituals* (Tuscaloosa: University of Alabama Press, 1986), p. 111.

2. *Ibid.,* p. 5.

3. Malinowski, B. *A Scientific Theory of Culture and Other Essays* (Chapel Hill: University of North Carolina Press, 1944), p. 36.

4. Hanson, F. A. *Meaning in Culture* (London and Boston: Routledge & Kegan Paul Ltd, 1975), p. 4.

5. AHED. *American Heritage Electronic Dictionary* (Houghton Mifflin Company. U.S. Pat. No. 4,724,523. ©1992, Word Star International ©1991)

6. Malinowski, *Scientific Theory,* p. 37.

7. Wilson, F. A. *Art as Revelation* (Fontwell, Sussex: Centaur Press Ltd., 1981), p. 17.

8. "Culture" Grolier Electronic Publishing, ©1993; see also Schusky, E., and P. Culbert *Introducing Culture,* 3d ed. (Englewood Cliffs, NJ: Prentice-Hall, 1978), p. 5.

9. Jensen, A. E. *Myth and Cult Among Primitive Peoples* (Chicago and London: University of Chicago Press, 1963), pp. 92–96.

10. Leakey, R. *The Origin of Humankind* (New York: Basic Books, A Division of HarperCollins, 1994), p. 139.

11. Segy, L. *Masks of Black Africa* (New York: Dover Publications, 1976), p. 9.

12. Kuper, A. *The Invention of Primitive Society* (London: Routledge, 1988), p. 105.

13. Grolier Electronic Publishing.

14. Lévi-Strauss, C. *The Savage Mind* (Chicago: University of Chicago Press, 1966), pp. 205–208.

15. Benedict, R. F. *Patterns of Culture,* 2d ed. (Boston: Houghton-Mifflin Company, 1989).

16. Underwood, L. *Masks of West Africa* (London: Alec Tiranti Ltd., 1952), p.1.

17. *Ibid.,* p. v.

18. Bascom, W. "Creativity and Style in African Art." In Biebuyck, D. P., ed. *Tradition and Creativity in Tribal Art* (Berkeley and Los Angeles: University of California Press, 1969), p. 119.

19. Anderson, R. L. *Art in Primitive Societies* (Englewood Cliffs, NJ: Prentice-Hall, 1979), pp. 90–91; see also Sieber, R., and A. Rubin. *Sculpture of Black Africa: The Paul Tishman Collection* (Washington, DC: International Exhibitions Foundation, 1970), p. 14; and Gerbrands, A. A. *Art as an Element of Culture, Especially in Negro-Africa* (Mededelingen Van Het Rijksmuseum Voor Volkenkunde, No. 12, Leiden: E. E. Brill, 1957), p. 81.

20. Beals, A. R. *Culture in Process* (New York, Chicago, and San Francisco: Holt, Rinehart and Winston, 1967), p. 172.

21. Boas, F. *The Mind of Primitive Man* (New York: Macmillan Company, 1938), p. 159.

22. Breasted, J. H. *The Dawn of Conscience* (New York: Charles Scribner's Sons, 1933), p. xxv.

23. Wingert, P. S. *Primitive Art: Its Traditions and Styles* (New York: Oxford University Press, 1962), p. 28.

24. Malinowski, *Scientific Theory,* p. 117.

25. Cayne, B. S. ed. dtr. *New Webster's Dictionary and Thesaurus of the English Language,*

Revised (Danbury, CT: Lexicon Publications, 1992), p. 36.

26. Riley, O. L. *Masks and Magic* (New York: Studio Publications and Thomas Y. Crowell Co., 1955), p. 24.

27. Norman, D. *The Hero: Myth/Image/Symbol* (New York and Cleveland: World Publishing Co., 1969), pp. 4–5.

28. Walens, S. "Analogic Causality and the Power of Masks." In Crumrine, N. R., and M. Halpin, eds. *The Power of Symbols: Masks and Masquerade in the Americas* (Vancouver: University of British Columbia Press, 1983), pg. 70.

29. Riley, *Masks and Magic*, p. 6.

30. Werbner, R. P. *Ritual Passage, Sacred Journey: The Form, Process and Organization of Religious Movement* (Washington, DC: Smithsonian Institution Press, 1989), p. 156.

31. Bascom, W. *African Art in Cultural Perspective* (New York: W. W. Norton, 1973), p. 11.

32. Arnheim, R. *Art and Visual Perception: A Psychology of the Creative Eye* (Berkeley and London: University of California Press, 1974), p. 139.

33. *Ibid.*, p. 136.

34. Frazer, J. G. *The Fear of the Dead in Primitive Religion*, vol. III (London: Macmillan and Company, Ltd., 1936).

35. Dugan, E. A. *Tradition in Transition* (Montréal: Galerie Amrad African Arts, 1989), p. 13.

36. Anderson, *Art in Primitive Societies*, pp. 133–134.

Chapter 4

1. Bayley, J. *The Portable Tolstoy* (New York, London, Victoria, Toronto: Penguin Books, 1978), p. 835.

2. Coomaraswamy, A. K. *Why Exhibit Works of Art?* (New York: Dover Press, 1956), p. 62.

3. Lewin, R. *The Origin of Modern Humans* (New York: Scientific American Library, a Division of HPHLP, 1993), p. 138; see also Davis, W. "The Origins of Image Making" In *Current Anthropology*, vol. 27, No. 3:1986, pp. 193–215; Wilson, F. A. *Art as Revelation* (Fontwell, Sussex: Centaur Press Ltd., 1981); Anderson, R. L. *Art in Primitive Societies* (Englewood Cliffs, NJ: Prentice-Hall, 1979); Greenhalgh, M., and V. Megaw, eds. *Art in Society: Studies in Style, Culture, and Aesthetics* (London: Gerald Ducksworth and Company, Ltd., 1978); Fraser, D. ed. *The Many Faces of Primitive Art: A Critical Anthology* (Englewood Cliffs, NJ: Prentice-Hall, 1966); and Read, H. *The Origins of Form in Art* (New York: Horizon Press, 1965).

4. "Paleolithic Art" Grolier Electronic Publishing, ©1993; see also Lewin, *The Origin of Modern Humans*, pp. 143–145.

5. Davis, W. "The Origins of Image Making." In *Current Anthropology*, vol. 27, No. 3, 1986, pp. 193–215

6. Hoebel, E. A. *Man in the Primitive World*, 2d ed. (New York, Toronto, London: McGraw-Hill Book Company, 1958), p. 254.

7. Dark, P.J.C. "What is Art for Anthropologists?" In Greenhalgh and Megaw, eds. *Art in Society*, pp. 31–38.

8. Lewin, *Origin of Modern Humans*, p. 146; see also Marshack, A. *The Roots of Civilization* (New York and Dusseldorf: McGraw-Hill Book Company, 1972).

9. Lewin, *Origin of Modern Humans*, p. 146.

10. Furst, P. T. In Shafer, H. *Ancient Texans* (Austin, TX: Texas Monthly Press 1986), p. 211.

11. Mithen, S. "The Origin of Art: Natural Signs, Mental Modularity, and Visual Symbolism." In: Maschner, H.D.G., ed. *Darwinian Archaeologies* (New York: Plenum Press, 1996), p. 198; see also Lewin, *Origin of Modern Humans*, pp. 148–150; Wreschner, E. E. "Red Ochre and Human Evolution: A Case for Discussion." In: *Current Anthropology*, vol. 21, No. 5,1980, pp. 631–633; Shafer, H., *Ancient Texans*, p. 138.

12. Schusky, E., and P. Culbert. *Introducing Culture*, 3d ed. (Englewood Cliffs, NJ: Prentice-Hall, 1978), p. 79.

13. Mithen, S. "The Origin of Art: Natural Signs, Mental Modularity, and Visual Symbolism." In Maschner, *Darwinian Archaeologies*, p. 197.

14. Wilson, *Art as Revelation*), p. 4.

15. Hoebel, *Man in the Primitive World*, p. 252.

16. Biebuyck, D. P., ed. *Tradition and Creativity in Tribal Art* (Berkeley and Los Angeles: University of California Press, 1969), p. 27.

17. *Ibid.*, p. 6.

18. Hatab, L. J. *Myth and Philosophy: A Contest of Truths* (La Salle, IL: Open Court, 1990).

19. Arnheim, R. *Art and Visual Perception: A Psychology of the Creative Eye* (Berkeley and London: University of California Press, 1974), p. 47.

20. Read, *The Origins of Form in Art*, pp. 30–32.

21. Clifford, J. "Four Northwest Coast Museums." In Karp, I., and S. D. Levine, eds. *Exhibiting Culture: the Poetics and Politics of Museum Display* (Washington and London: Smithsonian Institution Press, 1991), p. 241.

22. Ambesi, A. C. *Oceanic Art* (London, New York, Sydney, Toronto: Hamlyn Publishing Group Limited, 1970), p. 7.

23. Arnheim, R. *Toward A Psychology of Art* (Berkeley and Los Angeles: University of California Press, 1966), pp. 31–33.

24. *Ibid.*, p. 40.

25. Teuten, T. *The Letts Guide to Collecting Masks* (London: Studio Editions Ltd., 1991).

26. Sasser, E. S. *The World of Spirits and Ancestors in the Art of Western Sub-Saharan Africa* (Lubbock, TX: Texas Tech University Press, 1995), p. 5.

27. Underwood, L. *Masks of West Africa* (London: Alec Tiranti Ltd., 1952), p. 18.

28. Wilson, *Art as Revelation*, p. 115.

29. Anderson, *Art in Primitive Societies*, p. 23.

30. Edson, G., and D. Dean. *The Handbook for Museums* (New York and London: Routledge, 1994), p.178.

31. Munsterberg, H. *Symbolism in Ancient Chinese Art* (New York: Hacker Art Books, 1986), p. 40.

32. Lowie, R. H. *Primitive Religion* (New York: Liveright Publishing Corp., 1970).

33. Wilson, *Art as Revelation*, p. 5.

34. Dissanayake, E. *What is Art For?* (Seattle and London: University of Washington Press, 1988), p. 113.

35. Saarinen, E. *Search for Form* (New York: Reinhold Publishing Corporation, 1948), p. 29.

36. Dissanayake, *What is Art For?* p. 108.

37. Guiart, J. "The Concept of Norm in the Art of Some Oceanian Societies." In Biebuyck ed. *Tradition and Creativity in Tribal Art* pp. 84–97.

38. Meier, N. C. *Art in Human Affairs* (New York and London: McGraw-Hill Book Company, 1942).

39. Lommel, A. *The World of the Early Hunters* (London: Evelyn, Adams and Mackay Ltd., 1967), p.16.

40. Palmer, J. "Need and Function: The Terms of a Debate." In Palmer, J., and M. Dodson, eds. *Design and Aesthetics* (London and New York: Routledge, 1996), pp. 110–122.

41. *Ibid.*

42. Paolucci, H. *Hegel: On The Arts* (New York: Frederick Unger Publishing Co., 1979), pp. 11–12.

43. Arnheim, R. *Visual Thinking* (Berkeley and Los Angeles: University of California Press, 1970), p. 24.

44. *Ibid.*, p. 28.

45. *Ibid.*, p. 91.

46. Yuille, J. C., ed. *Imagery, Memory and Cognition* (Hillsdale, NJ and London: Lawrence Erlbaum Associates, 1983), p. 184.

47. Arnheim, *Visual Thinking*, p. 27.

48. Hyman, J. *The Imitation of Nature* (New York and Oxford: Basil Blackwell Ltd., 1989).

49. Newton, D. *Crocodile and Cassowary* (New York: Museum of Primitive Art, 1971), pp. 19–20.

50. Wreschner. "Red Ochre and Human Evolution: A Case for Discussion," *Current Anthropology*, 1980, 21:631–644.

51. Ottenburg, S. cited in Anderson, R.L. *Art in Primitive Societies* (Englewood Cliffs, NJ: Prentice-Hall, 1979), p. 101.

52. "Prehistoric Art — Techniques." Grolier Electronic Publishing, ©1993; see also Lewin, *Origin of Modern Humans*, pp. 148–150.

53. Teuten, *Letts Guide to Collecting Masks*, pp. 61–62.

54. Wilson, *Art as Revelation*, pp. 13–14.

55. Pace, D. *Claude Lévi-Strauss: The Bearer of Ashes* (London: ARK Paperbacks, 1986), p. 51.

56. *Ibid.*, p. 51.

57. Wilson, *Art as Revelation*, p. 2.

58. Cardew, M. In Greenhalgh and Megaw, eds. *Art in Society* p. 15.

59. Hyman, *Imitation of Nature*, p. 73.

60. Bascom, W. *African Art in Cultural Perspective* (New York: W. W. Norton, 1973), pp. 6–7.

61. Arnheim, *Visual Thinking*, p. v.

62. *Webster's New Twentieth Century Dictionary*, 2d. ed. (William Collins+World Publishing Co., © 1975), p. 105.

63. Riley, O. L. *Masks and Magic* (New York: Studio Publications and Thomas Y. Crowell Co., 1955), p. 16.

64. Biebuyck, *Tradition and Creativity in Tribal Art*, p. 12.

65. Urban, G., and J. W. Hendricks. "Signal Functions of Masking in Amerindian Brazil." In *Semiotica* 47-1/4 (Mouton Publishers, Amsterdam. Reprinted: Offprint Series No. 255, Institute of Latin American Studies, University of Texas at Austin, 1983), pp. 181–218.

66. Paolucci, *Hegel: On The Arts*, p. 88.

Chapter 5

1. Wingert, P. S. *Primitive Art: Its Traditions and Styles* (New York: Oxford University Press, 1962), p. 24

2. Macgowan K., and H. Rosse. *Masks and Demons* (London: Martin Hopkinson and Company, Ltd., 1924), p. viii.

3. Middleton, J., ed. *Gods and Rituals* (American Museum Sourcebooks in Anthropology published for the American Museum of Natural History, Garden City, NY: Natural History Press, 1967), pp. ix–x.

4. Webster, H. *Magic: A Sociological Study* (Stanford, CA: Stanford University Press, 1948).

5. "Magic" Grolier Electronic Publishing, © 1993.

6. Lindsay, J. *A Short History of Culture* (New York: Citadel Press, 1963), p. 23.

7. Lévi-Strauss, C. *Structural Anthropology* (New York: Basic Books, A Division of Harper-Collins, 1963), p. 168.

8. Radin, P. *Primitive Religion: Its Nature and Origin*, 2d ed. (New York: Dover Publications, 1957), p. 60.

9. Webster, *Magic* p. 38.

10. Pinch, G. *Magic in Ancient Egypt* (Avon: Bath Press, 1994).

11. Wade, E. L., ed. *The Arts of the North American Indian: Native Traditions in Evolution* (New York: Hudson Hills Press in association with Philbrook Art Center, 1986). p. 164.

12. Wilson, F. A. *Art as Revelation* (Fontwell, Sussex: Centaur Press Ltd., 1981), p. 16.

13. Beals, A. R. *Culture in Process* (New York, Chicago, and San Francisco: Holt, Rinehart and Winston, 1967), p. 38.

14. Riley, O. L. *Masks and Magic* (New York: Studio Publications and Thomas Y. Crowell Co., 1955), p. 2.

15. Frazer, J. G. *The Fear of the Dead in Primitive Religion*, vol. III (London: Macmillan and Company, Ltd., 1936).

16. *Ibid.,* p. 54.

17. Clodd, E. *Magic in Names and Other Things* (Detroit, MI: Singing Tree Press, 1968) pp. 1–2.

18. Shah, S. I. *Oriental Magic* (New York: Philosophical Library, 1957).

19. Meier, N. C. *Art in Human Affairs* (New York and London: McGraw-Hill Book Company, 1942), pp. 28–29.

20. Macgowan K., and H. Rosse. *Masks and Demons* (London: Martin Hopkinson and Company, Ltd., 1923), p. ix.

21. Monter, E. W. *Witchcraft in France and Switzerland* (Ithaca and London: Cornell University Press, 1976), p. 145.

22. Burkert, W. *Ancient Mystery Cults* (Cambridge and London: Harvard University Press, 1987), p. 107.

23. Monter, *Witchcraft*, p. 149.

24. Gleadow, R. *Magic and Divination* (Totowa, NJ: Rowman and Littlefield, 1976).

25. Marshall, R. *Witchcraft: The History and Mythology* (New York and Avenel, NJ: Crescent Books, 1995), p. 99.

26. Webster, *Magic*, p. 39.

27. Sharon, D. *Wizard of the Four Winds* (New York: Free Press, 1978), p. 49.

28. Webster, H. *Primitive Secret Societies: A Study of Early Politics and Religion*, 2d ed. (New York: Macmillan Company, 1932), p. 170.

29. Clodd, *Magic in Names and Other Things*.

30. O'Keefe, D. L. *Stolen Lightning: The Social Theory of Magic* (New York: Continuum, 1982), p. 1.

31. Cavendish, R. *The Black Arts* (New York: Capricorn Books, 1968), p. 43.

32. Shah, *Oriental Magic*.

33. Webster, *Magic*, p. 407.

34. Teuten, T. *The Letts Guide to Collecting Masks* (London: Studio Editions Ltd., 1991), p. 20.

35. Segy, L. *African Sculpture Speaks*, 4th ed. (New York: Da Capo Press, 1975), p. 82.

36. Czaja, Michael. *Gods of Myth and Stone* (New York and Tokyo: Weatherhill, 1974), p. 147.

37. Monter, *Witchcraft*, p. 167.

38. Linton, *The Tree of Culture* (New York: Alfred A. Knopf, 1957), p. 8.

Chapter 6

1. Markman, R. H., and P. T. Markman. *The Flayed God: The Mesoamerican Mythological Tradition* (New York: HarperCollins, 1992). p. 41.

2. Hocart, A. M. *The Life-giving Myth* (New York: Grove Press, 1952).

3. Seeger, A. In Ingold, T., ed. *Companion Encyclopedia of Anthropology: Humanity, Culture and Social Life.* (New York and London: Routledge, 1994), p. 686.

4. Bancroft-Hunt, N. *People of the Totem* (New York: G. P. Putnam's Sons, 1979), p. 103.

5. Torrance, R. M. *The Spiritual Quest: Transcendence in Myth, Religion, and Science* (Berkeley, Los Angeles, and London: University of California Press, 1994), p. 72.

6. Smith, S.V.H. *Masks in Modern Drama* (Berkeley, Los Angeles, and London: University of California Press, 1984), p. 10.

7. Durkheim, É. *The Elementary Forms of Religious Life.* Translated by K. E. Fields (New York: Free Press, 1995), pp. 340–342.

8. Ingold, T., ed. *Companion Encyclopedia of Anthropology,* pg. 632.

9. Harrison, J. E. *Ancient Art and Ritual* (New York: H. Holt 1913), p. 138.

10. Durkheim, *The Elementary Forms*, pp. 349–350.

11. Needham, R. *Symbolic Classification* (Santa Monica, CA: Goodyear Publishing Company, 1979), pp. 27–29.

12. d'Aquill, E., C. Laughlin, and J. McManus. *The Spectrum of Ritual: A Biogenetic Structural Analysis* (New York: Columbia University Press, 1979), p. 253.

13. Durkheim, *The Elementary Forms*, p. 337.

14. Smith, W. J. "Ritual and the Ethology of Communicating." In: d'Aquill, Laughlin, and McManus, *The Spectrum of Ritual*, p. 74.

15. Radin, P. *Primitive Religion: Its Nature and Origin*, 2d ed. (New York: Dover Publications, 1957), p. 290.

16. Napier, A. D. *Masks, Transformation, and Paradox* (Berkeley and London: University of California Press, 1986), pp. 63–70.

17. Kahler, E. "Culture and Evolution." In Montagu, M.F.A., ed. *Culture: Man's Adaptive Dimension* (New York: Oxford University Press, 1968), p. 6.

18. Schusky, E., and P. Culbert. *Introducing Culture*, 3d ed. (Englewood Cliffs, NJ: Prentice-Hall 1978), pp. 74–75.

19. Bancroft-Hunt, N. *People of the Totem* (New York: G. P. Putnam's Sons, 1979), p. 76.

20. Napier, A. D. *Masks, Transformation, and Paradox* (Berkeley, Los Angeles, and London: University of California Press, 1986), pp. 21–22.

21. Lindsay, J. *A Short History of Culture* (New York: Citadel Press, 1963), p. 15.

22. Beane, W. C., and W. G. Doty, eds. *Myth, Rites, Symbols: A Mircea Eliade Reader*, vol. I (New York and London: Harper Colophon Books, Harper and Row, 1976), p. 5.

23. Smith, S. V. H. *Masks in Modern Drama* (Berkeley and London: University of California Press, 1984). p. 51.

24. Beane and Doty, eds. *Myth, Rites, Symbols,* p. 33.

25. Bettelheim, B. *Symbolic Wounds: Puberty Rites and the Envious Male* (Glencoe, IL: Free Press, 1954), pp. 11–14.

26. Fontenrose, J. "The Ritual Theory of Myth." In *Folklore Studies*, vol. 18 (Berkeley and Los Angeles: University of California Press, 1966), p. 50.

27. Wallis, W. D. *Religion in Primitive Society* (New York: F. S. Crofts, 1939), p. 147.

28. Campbell, J. In Murray, H, A., ed. *Myth and Mythmaking* (New York: George Braziller, 1960), p. 23.

29. Bettelheim. *Symbolic Wounds*, p. 229.

30. Cohen, A. In Lewis, I., ed. *Symbols and Sentiments: Cross-cultural Studies in Symbolism* (London and San Francisco: Academic Press, a subsidiary of Harcourt Brace Jovanovich, 1977), p. 121.

31. Radcliffe-Brown, A. R. *The Andaman Islanders* (London: Cambridge University Press, 1933), p. 264.

32. Eliade, M. *Shamanism: Archaic Techniques of Ecstasy* (Princeton, NJ: Princeton University Press, 1964), p. 93.

33. Dissanayake, E. *What is Art For?* (Seattle and London: University of Washington Press, 1988), p. 80.

34. Wingert, P. S. *Primitive Art: Its Traditions and Styles* (New York: Oxford University Press, 1962), pp. 49–50.

35. Jensen, A. E. *Myth and Cult Among Primitive Peoples* (Chicago and London: The University of Chicago Press, 1963), pp. 76–79.

36. De Laguna, F. "Potlatch Ceremonialism on the Northwest Coast." In: Fitzhugh, W. W., and A. Crowell. *Crossroads of Continents: Cultures of Siberia and Alaska* (Washington, DC and London: Smithsonian Institution Press, 1988), p. 271.

37. Walens, S. "Analogic Causality and the Power of Masks." In Crumrine N. R., and M. Halpin, eds. *The Power of Symbols: Masks and Masquerade in the Americas* (Vancouver: University of British Columbia Press, 1983), pp. 70–78.

38. Segy, L. *Masks of Black Africa* (New York: Dover Publications, 1976), p. 9.

39. Dissanayake, *What is Art For?*, p. 84.

40. O'Keefe, D. L. *Stolen Lightning: The Social Theory of Magic* (New York: Continuum, 1982), p. 66.

41. Goode, W. J. *Religion Among the Primitives* (Glencoe IL: Free Press, 1951), p. 74.

42. Anderson, R. L. *Art in Primitive Societies* (Englewood Cliffs, NJ: Prentice-Hall, 1979).

43. Eliade, M. *Images and Symbols: Studies in Religious Symbolism* (New York: Sneed and Ward, 1961), pp. 57–59.

44. Werbner, R. P. *Ritual Passage, Sacred Journey: The Form, Process and Organization of Religious Movement* (Washington, DC: Smithsonian Institution Press, 1989), p. 3.

45. Underwood, Leon. *Masks of West Africa* (London: Alec Tiranti Ltd., 1952), p. 5.

Chapter 7

1. Eliade, M. *Symbolism, the Sacred, and the Arts* (New York: Continuum, 1992), p. 18.

2. Foster, M. L. "Symbolism: The Foundation of Culture." In: Ingold, T., ed. *Companion Encyclopedia of Anthropology: Humanity, Culture and Social Life* (New York and London: Routledge, 1994), p. 366.

3. Eliade, M. *Images and Symbols: Studies in Religious Symbolism* (New York: Sneed and Ward, 1961), p. 9.

4. Hyman, J. *The Imitation of Nature* (New York and Oxford: Basil Blackwell Ltd., 1989), pp. 66–67.

5. Malinowski, B. *A Scientific Theory of Culture and Other Essays* (Chapel Hill: University of North Carolina Press, 1944), p. 132.

6. Eliade, *Symbolism*, p. 13.

7. Eliade, *Images and Symbols*, p. 25.

8. Mithen, S. In Maschner, H., ed. *Darwinian Archaeologies* (New York and London: Plenum Press, 1996), p. 204.

9. Young, D. *Origins of the Sacred* (New York: St. Martin's Press, 1991), p. 169.

10. Wilson, F. A. *Art as Revelation* (Fontwell, Sussex: Centaur Press Ltd., 1961), p. 4.

11. Wingert, P. S. *Primitive Art: Its Traditions and Styles* (New York: Oxford University Press, 1962), p. 66.

12. Needham, R. *Symbolic Classification* (Santa Monica, CA: Goodyear Publishing Company, 1979), p. 5.

13. Turner, V. *The Forest of Symbols: Aspects of Ndembu Ritual* (Ithaca and London: Cornell University Press, 1967), p. 48.

14. Dissanayake, E. *What is Art For?* (Seattle and London: University of Washington Press, 1988), p. 118.

15. Meyer, L. *Black Africa: Masks, Sculpture, Jewelry* (Paris: Pierre Terrail, 1992), p. 74.

16. Paolucci, H. *Hegel: On The Arts* (New York: Frederick Unger Publishing Co., 1979), p. 11.

17. Nunley, J. W. *Moving with the Face of the Devil* (Urbana and Chicago: University of Illinois Press, 1987), p. 108

18. Kerérnyi, C. "Man and Mask." In Campbell, J., ed. *Spiritual Disciplines* (Papers from the Eranos Yearbook, Bollingen Series XXX, Vol. 4, Princeton: Princeton University Press, 1960), p. 154.

19. Burland, C. A. *The Magical Arts: A Short History* (London: Arthur Barker Limited, 1966), p. 58.

20. Arnheim, R. *Toward A Psychology of Art* (Berkeley and Los Angeles: University of California Press, 1966), pp. 28–30.

21. Cordry, D. *Mexican Masks* (Austin and London: University of Texas Press, 1980), p. 212.

22. *Ibid.*, p. 147.

23. Campbell, J. *The Mystic Image* (Princeton, NJ: Bollingen Series C, Princeton University Press, 1974), p. 121.

24. Christie, A. *Chinese Mythology* (New York: Barnes & Noble Books, 1996), pp. 16–17.

25. Campbell, *Mystic Image*, p. 117.

26. Gimbutas, M. *The Language of the Goddess* (San Francisco: HarperCollins, 1991), p. 146.

27. Slattum, J. *Masks of Bali: Spirits of an Ancient Drama* (San Francisco: Chronicle Books, 1992), p. 106.

28. Cirlot, J. E. *A Dictionary of Symbols* (London: Routledge & Kegan Paul, 1962), p. 196.

29. Jung, C. G. *Symbols of Transformation*, vol 5 (Bollingen Series XX, New York: Pantheon Books, a Division of Random House, 1956), p. 12.

30. Biebuyck, D. P., ed. *Tradition and Creativity in Tribal Art* (Berkeley and Los Angeles: University of California Press, 1969), pp. 190–191.

31. Cohen, A. "Symbolic Action and Structure of the Self." In Lewis, I., ed. *Symbols and Sentiments: Cross-cultural Studies in Symbolism* (London, New York, and San Francisco: Academic Press, a subsidiary of Harcourt Brace Jovanovich, 1977), p. 117.

32. Fontana, D. *The Secret Language of Symbols* (San Francisco: Chronicle Books, 1993), p. 21.

33. OKeefe, D. L. *Stolen Lightning: The Social Theory of Magic* (New York: Continuum, 1982), p. 39.

34. Wissler, C. "Masks." In *Guide Leaflet Series* of the American Museum of Natural History No. 96 (New York: Reprinted from *Natural History* vol. XXVIII, No. 4, 1938), pp. 339–352.

35. Zuidema, R. T. "Masks in the Incan Solstice and Equinoctial Ritual." In Crumrine and M. Halpin, eds. *The Power of Symbols, Masks and Masquerade in the Americas* (Vancouver: University of British Columbia Press, 1983), pp. 149–156.

36. Walens, S. "Analogic Causality and the Power of Masks." In Crumrine, and Halpin, eds. *The Power of Symbols*, pp. 70–78.

37. Faïk-Nzuji, C. M. *Tracing Memory: A Glossary of Graphic Signs and Symbols in African Art and Culture* (Quebec: Canadian Museum of Civilization, 1996), pp. 29–32.

38. Fontana, *The Secret Language of Symbols*, p. 51.

39. Gimbutas, *The Language of the Goddess*, pp. 15–23.

40. Eliade, M. *Images and Symbols*, pp. 128–129.

41. Fitzhugh, W. W., and A. Crowell. *Crossroads of Continents: Cultures of Siberia and Alaska* (Washington, DC and London: Smithsonian Institution Press, 1988), p. 266.

42. Napier, A. D. *Masks, Transformation, and Paradox* (Berkeley and London: University of California Press, 1986), p. 141.

43. *Ibid.*, pp. 139–140.

44. Shah, S. I. *Oriental Magic* (New York: Philosophical Library, 1957), p. 96.

45. Eliade, *Symbolism*, p. 12.

46. Wingert, P. S. *Primitive Art: Its Traditions and Styles* (New York: Oxford University Press, 1962), p. 21.

47. Webster, H. *Magic: A Sociological Study* (Stanford, CA: Stanford University Press, 1948), pp. 60–86.

48. Nishikawa, K. *Bugaku Masks* (Tokyo and New York: Kodansha International Ltd., 1978), p. 104.

49. Crumrine and Halpin, eds. *The Power of Symbols*, p. 2.

50. *Ibid.*

Chapter 8

1. Malinowski, B. *Magic, Science and Religion* (Glencoe, IL: Free Press, 1948), p. 122.

2. Linton, R. *The Tree of Culture* (New York: Alfred A. Knopf, 1967).

3. Parrinder, G. *African Mythology* (London: Hamlyn Publishing Group Ltd., 1967), p. 15.

4. Hatab, L. J. *Myth and Philosophy: A Contest of Truths* (La Salle, IL: Open Court, 1990), p. 19.

5. Young, D. *Origins of the Sacred* (New York: St. Martin's Press, 1991), p. 164.

6. Beane, W. C., and W. G. Doty, eds. *Myth, Rites, Symbols: A Mircea Eliade Reader*, vol. I (New York, Evanston, San Francisco, and London: Harper Colophon Books, Harper and Row, 1976), p. 3.

7. Brumer, J. S. "Myth and Identity." In Murray, H. A., ed. *Myth and Mythmaking* (New York: George Braziller, 1960), p. 276.

8. Dundes, A., ed. *Sacred Narrative: Readings in the Theory of Myth* (Berkeley and London: University of California Press, 1984), p. 9; see also Segy, L. *African Sculpture Speaks*, 4th ed. (New York: Da Capo Press, 1975), pp. 37–38.

9. McKechnie, J. L., ed. *Webster's New Twentieth Century Dictionary of the English Language*, 2d. ed. (New York: William Collins+World Publishing Co., 1977), p. 1190.

10. Hatab, *Myth and Philosophy*, pp. 19–20.

11. Kluckhohn, C. "Recurrent Themes in Myths and Mythmaking" In Murray, ed. *Myth and Mythmaking*, p. 49.

12. Campbell, J. "The Historical Development of Mythology." In Murray, ed. *Myth and Mythmaking*, p. 20.

13. Beane, and Doty, eds. *Myth, Rites, Symbols*, pp. 3–4.

14. Chase, R. *Quest for Myth* (Baton Rouge: Louisiana State University Press, 1949), p. 97.

15. Stafford, B. M. *Symbol and Myth* (Cranbury, NJ and London: Associated University Presses, 1979), p. 23.

16. Doty, W. G. *Mythography: The Study of Myths and Rituals* (Tuscaloosa: University of Alabama Press, 1986), p. 12.

17. Larsen, S. *The Shaman's Doorway* (Barrytown, NY: Station Hill Press, 1976), p. 16.

18. Eliade, M. *Myths, Dreams and Mysteries: the Encounter between Contemporary Faiths and Archaic Realities* (New York: Harper and Brothers, 1960), p. 13.

19. Campbell, J. "The Historical Development of Mythology." In Murray, ed. *Myth and Mythmaking*, p. 20.

20. *Ibid.*, p. 19.

21. Malinowski, B. *Magic, Science and Religion and Other Essays* (Glencoe, IL: Free Press, 1948), p. 122.

22. Bancroft-Hunt, N. *People of the Totem* (New York: G. P. Putnam's Sons, 1979), p. 89.

23. Malinowski, *Magic*, p. 122.

24. Jung, C. G. *Symbols of Transformation*, vol 5 (Bollingen Series XX, New York: Pantheon Books, a Division of Random House, 1956), p. 231; see also Campbell, J. "The Historical Development of Mythology." In Murray, ed. *Myth and Mythmaking*, pp. 22–23.

25. Doty, W. G. *Mythography*, pp. 18–19.

26. Napier, A. D. *Masks, Transformation, and Paradox* (Berkeley and London: University of California Press, 1986), p. 92.

27. Malinowski, B. *Myth in Primitive Psychology* (Westport, CT: Negro Universities Press, 1971).

28. Lang, A. *Myth, Ritual and Religion*, vol. II (London and Calcutta: Longmans, Green, 1913), p. 16.

29. Campbell, J. *The Masks of God: Primitive Mythology* (New York: Penguin, 1976), p. 3.

30. Hocart, A. M. *The Life-giving Myth* (New York: Grove Press, 1952), p. 6.

31. Campbell, J. *Historical Atlas of World Mythology*, Vol. I, The Way of the Animal Powers, Part 2: Mythologies of the Great Hunt (New York: Harper & Row Inc., 1988), p. xii.

32. Kluckhohn, C. "Recurrent Themes in Myths and Mythmaking." In Murray, ed. *Myth and Mythmaking*, p. 47.

33. Beane and Doty, eds. *Myth, Rites, Symbols*, p. 9.

34. Eliade, M. *Symbolism, the Sacred, and the Arts*, (New York: Continuum, 1992), p. 64.

35. Huizinga, J. *Homo Ludens: A Study of the Play-Element in Culture* (London, Boston, and Henley: Routledge & Kegan Paul, 1949), p. 170.

36. Reik, T. *Ritual: Psycho-analytic Studies* (Westport, CT: Greenwood Press, 1975), pp. 144–148.

37. Werner, E.T.C. *Myths and Legends of China* (London and Sydney: George G. Harrap and Company, Ltd., 1958), p. 60.

38. Eliade, M. *Images and Symbols: Studies in Religious Symbolism* (New York: Sneed and Ward, 1961), p. 57.

39. Newton, D. *Crocodile and Cassowary* (New York: Museum of Primitive Art, 1971), p. 10.

40. Rivers, W.H.R. "The Sociological Significance of Myth." In George, R. A., ed. *Studies on Mythology* (Homewood, IL: Dorsey Press, 1968), pp. 27–45.

41. Shah, S. I. *Oriental Magic* (New York: Philosophical Library, 1957), p. 4.

42. Walker, B. G. *The Woman's Dictionary of Symbols and Sacred Objects* (Edison, NJ: Castle Books, 1988), p.72.

43. *Ibid.,* p. 387.

44. Beane and Doty, eds. *Myth, Rites, Symbols,* pp. 8–9.

45. AHED. *American Heritage Electronic Dictionary* (Houghton Mifflin Company. U.S. Pat. No. 4,724,523. ©1991, Word Star International Inc., ©1992).

46. Hatab, L. J. *Myth and Philosophy: A Contest of Truths* (La Salle, IL: Open Court, 1990), p. 40.

Chapter 9

1. Shah, S. I. *Oriental Magic* (New York: Philosophical Library, 1957), p. 1.

2. Collins, J. J. *Primitive Religion* (New York: Rowman and Littlefield, 1978), p. 7.

3. Melody, M. E. *The Apache* (New York and Philadelphia: Chelsea House Publications, 1989), p. 33.

4. Lévi-Strauss, C. *Structural Anthropology* (New York: Basic Books, A Division of HarperCollins, (1963), p. 168.

5. Radin, P. *Primitive Religion: Its Nature and Origin*, 2d ed. (New York: Dover Publications, 1957), pp. 3–4.

6. Bancroft-Hunt, N. *People of the Totem* (New York: G. P. Putnam's Sons, 1979), p. 76.

7. Webster, H. *Magic: A Sociological Study* (Stanford, CA: Stanford University Press, 1948), p. 213.

8. Fontenrose, J. "The Ritual Theory of Myth," In *Folklore Studies* vol. 18, (Berkeley and Los Angeles: University of California Press, 1966), pp. 50–60.

9. Wallis, W. D. *Religion in Primitive Society* (New York: F. S. Crofts, 1939).

10. Lewis, I. M. *Ecstatic Religion: An Anthropological Study of Spirit Possession and Shamanism*, 2d ed. (London: Routledge, 1989).

11. Grim, J. A. *The Shaman: Patterns of Siberian and Ojibway Healing* (Norman: University of Oklahoma Press, 1983), p. 39.

12. *Ibid.*

13. Lommel, A. *The World of the Early Hunters* (London: Evelyn, Adams and Mackay Ltd., 1967), p. 149; see also Peters, L. *Ecstasy and Healing in Nepal* Malibu, CA: Undena Publications, 1981), p. 7.

14. Torrance, R. M. *The Spiritual Quest: Transcendence in Myth, Religion, and Science* (Berkeley, Los Angeles, and London: University of California Press, 1994), pp. 39–40.

15. Markman, R. H., and P. T. Markman. *The Flayed God: The Mesoamerican Mythological Tradition* (New York: HarperCollins, 1992), p. 6.

16. Lommel, *Early Hunters*, pp. 8–11.

17. Peters, *Ecstasy and Healing*, p. 13.

18. Halifax, J. *Shamanic Voices* (New York: E. P. Dutton, 1979), p. 3.

19. Lommel, *Early Hunters*, p. 25.

20. Peters, *Ecstasy and Healing*, p. 18.

21. Grim, *The Shaman*, p. 12.

22. *Ibid.*, pp. 8–9.

23. *Ibid.*, p. 10.

24. Barton, G. A. *The Religions of the World*, 4th ed. (Chicago: University of Chicago Press, 1937), pp. 3–4.

25. Lommel, *Early Hunters*, p 111.

26. *Ibid,,* p 110.

27. Halifax, J. *Shamanic Voices*, p. 3.

28. Lommel, *Early Hunters*, p.110.

29. Corbin, G. A. *Native Arts of North America, Africa, and the South Pacific: An Introduction* (New York: Harper and Row, 1988), p. 59.

30. Lommel, *Early Hunters*, p. 10.

31. Lowie, R. H. *Primitive Religion* (New York: Liveright Publishing Corporation, 1970), p. 264.

32. Riley, O. L. *Masks and Magic* (New York: Studio Publications and Thomas Y. Crowell Co., 1955), pp. 19–21.

33. Segy, L. *Masks of Black Africa* (New York: Dover Publications, 1976), p. 25.

34. Nooter, M. "Secrecy: African Art that Conceals and Reveals." In *African Arts*, 1993 Vol XXVI—No. 1), p. 59.

35. Parrinder, G. *African Mythology* (London: Hamlyn Publishing Group Ltd., 1967), pp. 96–99.

36. Meyer, L. *Black Africa: Masks, Sculpture, Jewelry* (Paris: Pierre Terrail, 1992), p. 90.

37. Cunningham, A. M. "Masked Messages." In: *Natural History* March 1977, 86 (3), p. 47.

38. Riley, *Masks and Magic*, p. 20.

39. *Ibid.*, p.21.

40. Corbin, *Native Arts*, p. 133.

41. Lang, A. *Myth, Ritual and Religion*, vol. II (London, New York, Bombay, and Calcutta: Longmans, Green, 1913), p. 90.

42. Corbin, *Native Arts*, p. 125.

43. Grim, *The Shaman*, p 120.

44. Sharon, D. *Wizard of the Four Winds* (New York: Free Press, 1978), p. 50.

45. Lommel, *Early Hunters*, p. 70.

46. Fontana, D. *The Secret Language of Symbols* (San Francisco: Chronicle Books, 1993), p. 130.

47. Peters, *Ecstasy and Healing*, p. 8.

48. Child, A. B., and I. L. Child. *Religion and Magic in the Life of Traditional Peoples* (Englewood Cliffs, NJ: Prentice Hall, 1993), p. 17.

49. *Ibid.*, p. 16.

50. Lommel, *Early Hunters*, p.11.

Chapter 10

1. Benkard, E. *Undying Faces: A Collection of Death Masks* (New York: W. W. Norton, 1927), p. 17.

2. Fox, J. R. "Witchcraft and Clanship in Cochiti Therapy." In Middleton, J., ed. *Magic, Witchcraft, and Curing* (American Museum Sourcebooks in Anthropology published for the American Museum of Natural History, Garden City, NY: Natural History Press, 1967), p. 255.

3. *Ibid.*

4. Macgowan K., and H. Rosse. *Masks and Demons* (London: Martin Hopkinson and Company, Ltd., 1923), p. viii.

5. *Ibid.*

6. Radin, P. *Primitive Religion: Its Nature and Origin,* 2d ed. (New York: Dover Publications, 1957), p. 214.

7. Burland, C. A. *The Magical Arts: A Short History* (London: Arthur Barker Limited, 1966), p. 27.

8. Lindsay, J. *A Short History of Culture* (New York: Citadel Press, 1963), p. 23.

9. Hatab, L. J. *Myth and Philosophy: A Contest of Truths* (La Salle, IL: Open Court, 1990), pg. 51.

10. Torrance, R. M. *The Spiritual Quest: Transcendence in Myth, Religion, and Science* (Berkeley, Los Angeles, and London: University of California Press, 1994), p. 65.

11. Wingert, P. S. *Primitive Art: Its Traditions and Styles* (New York: Oxford University Press, 1962), p. 21.

12. Czaja, M. *Gods of Myth and Stone* (New York and Tokyo: Weatherhill, 1974), p. 154.

13. *Ibid.*

14. Benedict, R. F. *The Chrysanthemum and the Sword* (Boston: Houghton Mifflin Company, 1974), p. 98.

15. Torrance, *The Spiritual Quest*, p. 65

16. *Ibid.*, pp. 66–68.

17. Frazer, J. G. *The Golden Bough: A Study of Magic and Religion*, vol. I. (New York: Macmillan and Company, 1958), p. 624.

18. Pott, P. H., "Tibet." In Griswold, A. B., C. Kim, and P. H. Pott. *The Art of Burma, Korea, Tibet* (New York, Toronto, London: Greystone Press, 1968), p. 185.

19. Maringer, J. *The Gods of Prehistoric Man* (New York: Alfred A. Knopf, 1960), p. 23.

20. *Ibid.*, p. 75.

21. Barton, G. A. *The Religions of the World*, 4th ed. (Chicago: University of Chicago Press, 1937), p. 5.

22. Riley, O. L. *Masks and Magic* (New York: Studio Publications and Thomas Y. Crowell Co., 1955), p. 40.

23. *Ibid.*, p. 108.

24. Lommel, A. *Masks: Their Meaning and Function* (New York and Toronto: McGraw-Hill Book Company, 1972), p. 56.

25. Cavendish, R. *The Black Arts* (New York: Capricorn Books, 1968), p. 10.

26. Grolier Electronic Publishing, ©1993.

27. Webster, H. *Primitive Secret Societies: A Study of Early Politics and Religion*, 2d ed. (New York: Macmillan Company, 1932), pp. 40–41.

28. Burkert, W. *Ancient Mystery Cults* (Cambridge and London: Harvard University Press, 1987), p. 101.

29. Czaja, *Gods of Myth and Stone*, p. 163.

30. Three Initiates. *The Kybalion: A Study of the Hermetic Philosophy of Ancient Egypt and Greece* (Chicago: Yogi Publication Society, 1908).

31. Burkert, *Ancient Mystery Cults*, p. 96.

32. Werbner, R. P. *Ritual Passage, Sacred Journey: The Form, Process and Organization of Religious Movement* (Washington, DC: Smithsonian Institution Press, 1989), pp. 157–160.

33. Norman, D. *The Hero: Myth/Image/Symbol* (New York and Cleveland: World Publishing Co., 1969), p. 59.

34. Frazer. In Czaja, *Gods of Myth and Stone*, p. 216.

35. Czaja, *Gods of Myth and Stone*, p. 159.

36. Markman, R. H., and P. T. Markman. *The Flayed God: The Mesoamerican Mythological Tradition* (New York: HarperCollins, 1992), p. 4

37. Frazer, J. G. *The Magic Art*, 3d ed. vols I and II (London: Macmillan and Company, Ltd., 1922), p. 178.

38. Wiles, D. *The Masks of Menander* (Cambridge, New York, Melbourne: Cambridge University Press, 1991), p. 130.

39. *Ibid.*

40. Lang, A. *Myth, Ritual and Religion*, vol. II (London and New York: Longmans, Green, 1913), p. 38.

41. Teuten, T. *The Letts Guide to Collecting Masks* (London: Studio Editions Ltd., 1991), p. 12.

42. Frazer, *Study of Magic and Religion*, p. 628.

43. Linton, R. *The Tree of Culture* (New York: Alfred A. Knopf, 1957), p. 529.

44. Anderson, R. L. *Art in Primitive Societies* (Englewood Cliffs, NJ: Prentice-Hall, 1979), p. 38.

45. Teuten, *Letts Guide*, p. 58.

46. Webster, *Primitive Secret Societies*, p. 168.

47. Nunley, J. W. *Moving with the Face of the Devil* (Urbana and Chicago: University of Illinois Press, 1987), p.108.

48. *Ibid.*

49. Haberland, W. *The Art of North America* (New York, Toronto, and London: Greystone Press, 1968), p. 48.

50. Fitzhugh, W. W., and A. Crowell. *Crossroads of Continents: Cultures of Siberia and Alaska* (Washington, DC and London: Smithsonian Institution Press, 1988), p. 279.

51. Gimbutas, M. *The Language of the Goddess* (San Francisco: HarperCollins, 1991), p. 211.

52. Vlahos, O. *Body, The Ultimate Symbol* (New York: J. B. Lippincott Company, 1979), pp. 112–113.

53. Snow, D. *The Archaeology of North America* (New York: A Studio Book, Viking Press, 1976), pp. 54–55.

54. *Ibid.*

55. Fitzhugh and Crowell, *Crossroads*, p.126.

56. *Ibid.*, p. 127.

57. Walens, S. "Analogic Causality and the Power of Masks." In Crumrine, N. R., and M. Halpin, eds. *The Power of Symbols: Masks and Masquerade in the Americas* (Vancouver: University of British Columbia Press, 1983), p. 72.

Chapter 11

1. Crumrine, N. R., and M. Halpin, eds. *The Power of Symbols, Masks and Masquerade in the Americas* (Vancouver: University of British Columbia Press, 1983), p. 1.

2. Smith, S.V.H. *Masks in Modern Drama* (Berkeley, Los Angeles, and London: University of California Press, 1984), p. 50.

3. Fontana, D. *The Secret Language of Symbols* (San Francisco: Chronicle Books, 1993), p. 131.

4. Benda, W. T. *Masks* (New York: Watson-Guptill, 1944), p. 1.

5. *Ibid.*

6. Smith, *Masks in Modern Drama*, p. 50.

7. Napier, A. D. *Masks, Transformation, and Paradox* (Berkeley and London: University of California Press, 1986), pp. 63–65.

8. Lee, D. H. *Masks of Korea* (Seoul: Korean Overseas Information Service, Ministry of Culture and Information, 1981), p. 5.

9. Birket-Smith, K. *The Paths of Culture* (Madison and Milwaukee: University of Wisconsin Press, 1965), p. 386.

10. Grolier Electronic Publishing, ©1993.

11. Foster, M. In Ingold, T. ed. *Companion Encyclopedia of Anthropology: Humanity, Culture and Social Life* (New York and London: Routledge, 1994), p. 368.

12. Herskovits, M. J. *Man and His Works* (New York: Alfred A. Knopf, 1948), p. 427.

13. Grolier Electronic Publishing, ©1993.

14. Pinch, G. *Magic in Ancient Egypt* (Avon: Bath Press, 1994), p. 23.

15. *Ibid.*, p. 22.

16. Hart, G. *A Dictionary of Egyptian Gods and Goddesses* (London and New York: Routledge, 1996), pp. 222–223.

17. Harrison, J. E. *Ancient Art and Ritual* (New York: H. Holt, 1913), p. 127.

18. *Ibid.*, p. 136.

19. Harrison, *Ancient Art and Ritual.*

20. Smith, *Masks in Modern Drama*, p. 9.

21. Coomeraswamy, A. K. *The Transformation of Nature in Art* (Cambridge MA: Harvard University Press, 1934), p. 14.

22. Durkheim, É. *The Elementary Forms of Religious Life* (New York: The Free Press, 1995), p. 349.

23. Smith, *Masks in Modern Drama*, p. 51.

24. Huizinga, J. *Homo Ludens: A Study of the Play-Element in Culture* (London, Boston, and Henley: Routledge & Kegan Paul, 1949), p. 15.

25. Grolier Electronic Publishing ©1993.

26. Nishikawa, K. *Bugaku Masks* (Tokyo, New York, and San Francisco: Kodansha International Ltd., 1978), p. 20.

27. Lee, *Masks of Korea*, p. 7.

28. Nishikawa, *Bugaku Masks*, p. 21.

29. Munsterberg, H. *The Arts of Japan: An Illustrated History* (Rutland, VT and Tokyo: Charles E. Tuttle Company, 1957), p. 54.

30. *Ibid.*, p. 118.

31. Secor, J. L., and S. Addiss. "The Male Ghost in Kabuki and Ukiyo-e." In Addiss, S., ed. *Japanese Ghosts and Demons* (New York: George Braziller in association with the Spencer Museum of Art, University of Kansas, 1985), p. 49.

32. Cunningham, A. M. "Masked Messages." In *Natural History*, March 1977, 86 (3), pp. 42–47.

33. Lee, *Masks of Korea*, pg. 7.

34. Ott, P. H., "Tibet." In Griswold, A. B., C. Kim, and P. H. Pott. *The Art of Burma, Korea, Tibet*, (New York, Toronto, London: Greystone Press, 1968), p.185.

35. Slattum, J. *Masks of Bali: Spirits of an Ancient Drama* (San Francisco: Chronicle Books, 1992), p.10.

36. Huizinga, *Homo Ludens* p. 13.

37. Webster, H. *Primitive Secret Societies: A Study of Early Politics and Religion*, 2d ed (New York: Macmillan Company, 1932), p. 183.

38. Lommel, A. *Masks: Their Meaning and Function* (New York and Toronto: McGraw-Hill Book Company, 1972), p.198.

39. *Ibid.*, p. 200.

40. *Ibid.*

41. Webster, *Primitive Secret Societies*, p. 165.

42. Nishikawa. *Bugaku Masks,* pp. 19–21.

43. Esser, F. B. "Tarascan Masks of Women as Agents of Social Control." In Crumrine and Halpin, eds. *The Power of Symbols*, pp. 126–27.

44. *Ibid.*, p. 122.

45. Zuidema, R. T. "Masks in the Incan Solstice and Equinoctial Ritual." In Crumrine and Halpin, eds. *The Power of Symbols,* p. 149.

Chapter 12

1. Malraux, A. *The Psychology of Art: The Creative Act* (Bollingen Series XXIV, New York: Pantheon Books, 1949), p. 69.

2. Werbner, R. P. *Ritual Passage, Sacred Journey: The Form, Process and Organization of Religious Movement* (Washington, DC: Smithsonian Institution Press, 1989), p. 183.

3. Jung, C. G. *The Spirit in Man, Art, and Literature*, Vol 15 (Bollingen Series XX, New York: Pantheon Books, a Division of Random House, 1966) p. 89.

4. Thomas, J. *Time, Culture and Identity: An Interpretive Archaeology* (London and New York: Routledge, 1999), p. 33.

5. Jung, *The Spirit in Man*, p. 91.

6. *Ibid.*, p. 96.

7. Malinowski, B. *A Scientific Theory of Culture and Other Essays* (Chapel Hill: University of North Carolina Press, 1944), p. 17.

8. AHED. *American Heritage Electronic Dictionary* (Houghton Mifflin Company. U.S. Pat. No. 4,724,523. ©1992, Word Star International Inc., ©1991).

9. Stein, G. *Selected Writings of Gertrude Stein* (New York: Modern Library published by Random House, 1962), p. 513.

Bibliography

Abrahams, Roger D. *African Folktales: Traditional Stories of the Black World*. New York: Pantheon Books, 1983.

Abrahamsson, Hans. *The Origin of Death*. New York: Arno Press, 1977.

Addiss, Stephen, ed. *Japanese Ghosts and Demons*. New York: George Braziller in association with the Spencer Museum of Art, University of Kansas, 1985.

AHED. ©1991. *American Heritage Electronic Dictionary*. Houghton Mifflin Company. U.S. Pat. No. 4,724,523. ©1992 Word Star International.

Ahern, Emily. *The Cult of the Dead in a Chinese Village*. Stanford, CA: Stanford University Press, 1973.

Ahmed, Rollo. *The Black Art*. London: Studio Editions 1994.

Ambesi, Alberto Cesare. *Oceanic Art*. Translated by R. Montgomery. London, New York, Sydney, Toronto: Hamlyn Publishing Group 1970.

Anderson, Richard L. *Art in Primitive Societies*. Englewood Cliffs, NJ: Prentice-Hall, 1979.

Arnheim, Rudolf. *Toward A Psychology of Art*. Berkeley and Los Angeles: University of California Press, 1966.

______. *Visual Thinking*. Berkeley and Los Angeles: University of California Press, 1970.

______. *Art and Visual Perception: A Psychology of the Creative Eye*. Berkeley and London: University of California Press, 1974.

Attenborough, David. *The Tribal Eye*. New York: W. W. Norton, 1976.

Bakan, David. *The Duality of Human Existence: An Essay on Psychology and Religion*. Chicago: Rand McNally, 1966.

Baltimore Museum of Art. *The Alan Wurtzburger Collection of Oceanic Art*. Baltimore: Museum of Art, 1956.

Balzar, Marjorie M., ed. *Shamanism: Soviet Studies of Traditional Religion in Siberia and Central Asia*. Armonk, NY, and London: M. E. Sharpe, 1990.

Bancroft-Hunt, Norman. *People of the Totem*. New York: G. P. Putnam's Sons, 1979.

Barton, George A. *The Religions of the World*. 4th ed. Chicago: University of Chicago Press, 1937.

Bascom, William. "Creativity and Style in African Art." In *Tradition and Creativity in Tribal Art*, Daniel P. Biebuyck, ed., pp. 98–119. Berkeley and Los Angeles: University of California Press, 1969.

______. *African Art in Cultural Perspective*. New York: W. W. Norton, 1973.

Basso, Keith H. "Western Apache Witchcraft." In *Anthropological Papers of the University of Arizona*, No. 15. Tucson: University of Arizona Press, 1969.

Bayley, John. *The Portable Tolstoy*. New York, London, Victoria, Toronto: Penguin, 1978.

Beals, Alan R. *Culture in Process*. New York and San Francisco: Holt, Rinehart and Winston, 1967.

Beane, Wendell C., and William G. Doty, eds. *Myth, Rites, Symbols: A Mircea Eliade Reader*. Vol. 1. New York, Evenston and London: Harper Colophon Books, Harper and Row, 1976.

Bell, Catherine. *Ritual Theory, Ritual Practice*. New York and Oxford: Oxford University Press, 1992.

Belo, Jane. *Bali: Barong and Rangda*. Seattle: University of Washington Press, 1953.

Benda, Wladyslaw Theodore. *Masks*. New York: Watson-Guptill, 1944.

Bendix, Deanna Marohn. *Diabolical Designs: Paintings, Interiors, and Exhibitions of James McNeill Whistler*. Washington, D.C. and London: Smithsonian Institution Press, 1995.

Benedict, Ruth Fulton. *The Chrysanthemum and the Sword*. Boston: Houghton Mifflin, 1974.

_____. *Patterns of Culture*. 2d ed. Boston: Houghton-Mifflin, 1989.

Benthall, Jonathan, and Ted Polhemus, eds. *The Body as a Medium of Expression*. London: Allen Lane, 1975.

Berger, P., and T. T. Bartholomew, eds. *Mongolia: The Legacy of Chinggis Khan*. London: Thames and Hudson 1995.

Bettelheim, Bruno. *Symbolic Wounds: Puberty Rites and the Envious Male*. Glencoe, IL: Free Press, 1954.

Biebuyck, Daniel P., ed. *Tradition and Creativity in Tribal Art*. Berkeley and Los Angeles: University of California Press, 1969.

Bihalji-Merin, Otto. *Masks of the World*. Translated by Herma Plummer. London: Thames and Hudson, 1971.

Birket-Smith, Kaj. *The Paths of Culture*. Translated by Karin Fennow. Madison and Milwaukee: University of Wisconsin Press, 1965.

Blacker, Carman. *The Catalpa Bow: A Study of Shamanistic Practices in Japan*. London: George Allan and Unwin, 1975.

Bloch, Maurice, and Jonathan Parry, eds. *Death and the Regeneration of Life*. Cambridge and New York: Cambridge University Press, 1982.

Boas, Franz. *The Mind of Primitive Man*. New York: Macmillan Company, 1938.

_____. *Primitive Art*. New York: Dover, 1955.

Bodrogi, Tibor. *Oceanian Art*. Budapest: Athenaeum Printing House, 1959.

Bouisson, Maurice. *Magic: Its History and Principal Rites*. Translated by G. Almayrac. New York: Dutton, 1961.

Bourke, John G. *Apache Medicine-men*. Re-publication of "The Medicine-Men of the Apache," in the Ninth Annual Report of the Bureau of Ethnology to the Secretary of the Smithsonian Institution, 1887–88, pp. 443–603. New York: Dover, 1993.

Breasted, James Henry. *The Development of Religion and Thought in Ancient Egypt*. New York: C. Scribner's Sons, 1912.

_____. *The Dawn of Conscience*. New York: Charles Scribner's Sons, 1933.

Brown, Joseph, ed. *The Sacred Pipe: Black Elk's Account of The Seven Rites of the Oglalla Sioux*. Norman: University of Oklahoma Press, 1953.

Brundage, Burr Cartwright. *The Phoenix of the Western World: Quetzalcoatl and the Sky Religion*. Norman: University of Oklahoma Press, 1982.

Budge, E. A. Wallis. *Egyptian Magic*. New York: Dover, 1971.

Burkert, Walter. *Structure and History in Greek Mythology and Ritual*. Berkeley: University of California Press, 1979.

_____. *Ancient Mystery Cults*. Cambridge and London: Harvard University Press, 1987.

Burland, C. A. *Magic Books From Mexico*. Harmondsworth, Middlesex: Penguin, 1953.

_____. *The Magical Arts: A Short History*. London: Arthur Barker, 1966.

_____. *North American Indian Mythology*, London, New York, Sydney, Toronto: Hamlyn Publishing Group, 1968.

Burne, Charlotte S. *The Handbook of Folklore: Traditional Beliefs, Practices, Customs, Stories, and Sayings*. London: Random House, 1995.

Burns, Michael. "Figures from Chisel and Adze." *Orientation*. Vol. 11, No. 6, June 1980.

Bushnell, G.H.S. *Ancient Arts of the Americas*. New York and Washington: Frederick A. Praeger, 1965.

Butler, Eliza Marian. *The Myth of the Magus*. Cambridge and New York: Cambridge University Press, 1948.

Campbell, Joseph, ed. *Spiritual Disciplines*. Papers from the Eranos Yearbook, Bollingen Series XXX, vol. 4. Translated by Ralph Manheim. Princeton: Princeton University Press, 1960.

_____. *The Masks of God: Occidental Mythology*. New York: Viking Press, 1964.

_____, ed. *The Mystic Vision*. Papers from the Eranos Yearbook, Bollingen Series XXX, vol. 6. Translated by Ralph Manheim. Princeton: Princeton University Press, 1968.

_____. *The Mystic Image*. Princeton, NJ: Bollingen Series C, Princeton University Press, 1974.

_____. *The Masks of God: Primitive Mythology*. New York: Penguin, 1976.

_____. *Historical Atlas of World Mythology*. Vol 1, The Way of the Animal Power. London: Summerfield Press, 1983.

_____. *The Power of Myth*. New York, London, Toronto, Sydney, and Auckland: Doubleday, 1988a.

_____. *Historical Atlas of World Mythology*. Vol. I, The Way of the Animal Powers, Part 2: Mythologies of the Great Hunt. New York: Harper & Row, 1988b.

_____. *Historical Atlas of World Mythology*. Vol. II, The Way of the Seeded Earth, Part 2: Mythologies of the Primitive Planters: The North Americans. New York: Harper & Row, 1989.

Capra, Fritjof. *The Tao of Physics* 3d ed. Boston: Shambhala Publications, 1991.

Carmichael, David, Jane Hubert, Brian Reeves, and Audhild Schanche, eds. *Sacred Sites, Sacred Places*. London and New York: Routledge, 1994.

Carritt, Edgar Frederick, ed. *Philosophies of Beauty*. Westport, CT: Greenwood Press, 1976.

Cassier, Earnest. *The Philosophy of Symbolic Forms*. 3 vols. New Haven: Yale University Press, 1955.

Castaneda, Carlos. *The Teachings of Don Juan: A Yaqui Way of Knowledge*. New York: Ballantine Books, 1969.

_____. *A Separate Reality: Further Conversations with Don Juan*. New York: Pocket Books, 1972.

_____. *The Eagle's Gift*. New York: Simon and Schuster, 1981.

Cavendish, Richard. *The Black Arts*. New York: Capricorn Books, 1968.

Cawte, Edwin C. *Ritual Animal Disguise: A Historical and Geographical Study of Animal Disguise in the British Isles*. Totowa, NJ: Rowman and Littlefield, 1978.

Cayne, B. S., ed. director. *New Webster's Dictionary and Thesaurus of the English Language*, revised edition. Danbury, CT: Lexicon Publications, 1992.

Chase, Richard. *Quest for Myth*. Baton Rouge: Louisiana State University Press, 1949.

Chiari, Joseph. *Art and Knowledge*. New York: Gordian Press, 1977.

Child, Alice B., and Irvin L. Child. *Religion and Magic in the Life of Traditional Peoples*. Englewood Cliffs, NJ: Prentice Hall, 1993.

Christensen, Erwin. *Primitive Art*. New York: Thomas Y. Crowell, 1955.

Christian, Paul. *The History and Practice of Magic*. Edited and revised by R. Nichols. 2 vols. Secaucus, NJ: Citadel Press, 1972.

Christie, Anthony. *Chinese Mythology*. New York: Barnes & Noble Books, 1996.

Cirlot, Juan Edwardo. *A Dictionary of Symbols*. Translated by J. Sage. London: Routledge & Kegan Paul, 1962.

Clifford, James. "Four Northwest Coast Museums." In I. Karp and S. D. Levine, eds. *Exhibiting Culture: The Poetics and Politics of Museum Display*. Washington, D.C., and London: Smithsonian Institution Press, 1991.

Clodd, Edward. *Magic in Names and Other Things*. Detroit: Singing Tree Press, 1968.

Coe, Michael D. *The Jaguar's Children: Pre-Classic Central Mexico*. New York: Museum of Primitive Art, 1965.

Cohn, Norman. *Europe's Inner Demons*. London: Sussex University Press in association with Heinemann Educational Books, 1975.

Cole, Herbert M., and Chike Aniakor. *Igbo Arts: Community and Cosmos*. Los Angeles: Museum of Cultural History, University of California, 1984.

_____, ed. *I am not Myself: The Art of African Masquerade*. Los Angeles: Museum of Cultural History, University of California, Monography Series, No. 26, 1985.

_____. *Icons: Ideals, and Power in the Art of Africa*. Washington, DC: Smithsonian Institution Press, 1990.

Collins, John J. *Primitive Religion*. New York: Rowman and Littlefield, 1978.

Colton, Harold S. *Hopi Kachina Dolls*. Albuquerque: University of New Mexico, 1949.

Conrad, Joseph. *Heart of Darkness*. New York and Toronto: Everyman's Library, Alfred A. Knopf, 1967.

Coomeraswamy, Ananda K. *The Transformation of Nature in Art*. Cambridge: Harvard University Press, 1934.

_____. *Why Exhibit Works of Art?* New York, Dover Publications, 1943.

_____. *Time and Eternity*. 2nd rev. ed. Bangalore: Select Books, 1989.

Corbin, George A. *Native Arts of North America, Africa, and the South Pacific: An Introduction*. New York: Harper and Row, 1988.

Cordry, Donald. *Mexican Masks*. Austin and London: University of Texas Press, 1980.

Courlander, Harold. *A Treasury of African Folklore*. New York: Crown Publishers, 1975.

Covarrubias, Miguel. *The Eagle, the Jaguar and the Serpent: Indian Art of the Americas*. New York: Knopf, 1954.

Craine, Eugene R., and Reginald C. Reindrop, eds. *The Chronicles of Michoacan*. Norman: University of Oklahoma Press, 1970.

Crapanzano, Vincent, and Vivian Garrison. *Case Studies of Spirit Possession*. New York, London, Sydney, and Toronto: John Wiley and Sons, 1977.

Crocker, J. Christopher. "Being an Essence: Totemic Representation Among the Earnern Bororo." In N. Ross Crumrine and Majorie Halpin, eds. *The Power of Symbols, Masks and Masquerade in the Americas*. Vancouver: University of British Columbia Press, p. 157–76, 1983.

Crumrine, N. Ross, and Majorie Halpin, eds. *The Power of Symbols, Masks and Masquerade in the Americas*. Vancouver: University of British Columbia Press, 1983.

Cunningham, Ann Marie. "Masked Messages."

In *Natural History* 86 (3), pp. 42–47, March 1977.

Czaja, Michael. *Gods of Myth and Stone*. New York and Tokyo: Weatherhill, 1974.

Dagan, Esther A. *Man and His Vision: The Traditional Wood Sculpture of Burkina Faso*. Westmount, Canada: Galerie Amrad African Arts, 1987.

Dall, William Healey. "On Masks, Labrets, and Certain Aboriginal Customs, with an Inquiry into the Bearing of their Geographical Distribution." In *Bureau of American Ethnology Annual Report* 3:73–151. Washington, D.C.: U.S. Government Printing Office, 1884.

Daniel, Ana. *Bali Behind the Mask*. New York: Alfred A. Knopf, 1981.

d'Aquill, Eugene, Charles Laughlin, and John McManus. *The Spectrum of Ritual: A Biogenetic Structural Analysis*. New York: Columbia University Press, 1979.

Dark, Philip J. C. "What is Art for Anthropologists?" In Michael Greenhalgh and Vincent Megaw, eds. *Art in Society*. London: Gerald Ducksworth and Company, Ltd., 1978.

Darwin, Charles. *The Expression of Emotions in Man and Animal*. New York: Philosophical Library, 1955.

David-Neel, Alexandra. *With Mystics and Magicians in Tibet*. London: John Lane, 1931.

Davis, Whitney. "The Origins of Image Making." *Current Anthropology*. Vol. 27, No. 3: 193–215, 1986.

d'Azevedo, Warren L., ed. *The Traditional Artist in African Societies*. Bloomington: Indiana University Press, 1973.

de Barradas, José Perez. *Orfebreria Prehispanica de Colombia*. Bogota: Museo del Ord del Madrid Banco de la República, 1954.

de Coppet, Daniel, ed. *Understanding Rituals*. New York: Routledge, 1992.

DeMott, Barbara. *Dogon Masks: A Structural Study of Form and Meaning*. Ann Arbor, MI: UMI Research Press, 1982.

de Nebesky-Wojkowitz, René. *Oracles and Demons of Tibet*. Graz, Austria: Akademische Druck-u.Verlagsanstalt, 1975.

______. *Tibetan Religious Dances*. Edited by Christoph von Fürer-Haimendorf. The Hague: Mouton, 1976.

de Rios, Marlene Dodbin. *Amazon Healer: The Life and Times of an Urban Shaman*. Lindfield, Australia: Unity Press, 1992.

de Zoete, Beryl, and Walter Spies. *Dance and Drama in Bali*. New York: Oxford University Press, 1973.

Dissanayake, Ellen. *What is Art For?* Seattle and London: University of Washington Press, 1988.

Dockstader, Frederick J. *Indian Art in Middle America*. Greenwich, CT: New York Graphic Society Publishers, Ltd., 1964.

Doore, Gary. *Shaman's Path: Healing, Personal Growth and Empowerment*. Boston and London: Shambhala Publications, 1988.

Doty, William G. *Mythography: The Study of Myths and Rituals*. Tuscaloosa: University of Alabama Press, 1986.

Douglas, Mary. *Natural Symbols: Explorations in Cosmology*. New York: Pantheon Books, 1982.

Douglas, Mary, ed. *Witchcraft: Confessions and Accusations*. London: Tavistock Publications, 1970.

Doyle, Arthur C. *The History of Spiritualism*. New York: George H. Doran, 1926.

Dugan, Esther A. *Tradition in Transition*. Montréal: Galerie Amrad African Arts, 1989.

Duncan, Carol. *Civilizing Rituals*. London and New York: Routledge, 1995.

Dundes, Alan, ed. *Sacred Narrative: Readings in the Theory of Myth*. Berkeley, Los Angeles, and London: University of California Press, 1984.

Duran, Diago. *Book of the Gods and Rites and the Ancient Calendar*. Edited and translated by Fernando Horcasitas and Doris Heyen. Norman: University of Oklahoma Press, 1971.

Durkheim, Émile. *The Elementary Forms of Religious Life*. Translated by Karen Fields. New York: Free Press, 1995.

Dwyer, Daisy Hilse. *Images and Self-Images*. New York: Columbia University Press, 1978.

Dwyer, Jane P., and Edward B. Dwyer, *Traditional Art of Africa, Oceania, and the Americas*. San Francisco: Fine Arts Museums of San Francisco, 1973.

Edson, Gary, and David Dean. *The Handbook for Museums*, New York and London: Routledge, 1994.

Eliade, Mircea. *Birth and Rebirth: The Religious Meanings of Initiation in Human Culture*. Translated by Willard R. Trask. New York: Harper, 1958.

______. *Myths, Dreams and Mysteries: The Encounter between Contemporary Faiths and Archaic Realities*. Translated by P. Mairet. New York: Harper and Brothers, 1960.

______. *Images and Symbols: Studies in Religious Symbolism*. Translated by P. Mairet. New York: Sneed and Ward, 1961.

______. *Shamanism: Archaic Techniques of Ecstasy*. Translated by Willard R. Trask. Princeton, NJ: Princeton University Press, 1964.

______. *Symbolism, the Sacred, and the Arts*. Edited by D. Apostolos-Cappadona. New York: Continuum, 1992.

Encyclopedia of Magic and Superstition. London: Octopus Books Limited, 1974.

Esser, Frances B. "Tarascan Masks of Women as Agents of Social Control." In N. Ross Crumrine, and Majorie Halpin, eds. *The Power of Symbols, Masks and Masquerade in the Americas.* Vancouver: University of British Columbia Press, p. 126–27, 1983.

Evans-Wentz, Walter Y., ed. *The Tibetan Book of the Dead [Bardo Thödol].* New York: Oxford University Press, 1960.

_____, ed. *Tibetan Yoga and Secret Doctrines; or, Seven Books of Wisdom of the Great Path.* London, New York, and Oxford: Oxford University Press, 1968.

Fagg, William. *African Tribal Images.* Cleveland: Cleveland Museum of Art, 1968.

Faïk-Nzuji, Clémentine M. *Tracing Memory: A Glossary of Graphic Signs and Symbols in African Art and Culture.* Quebec: Canadian Museum of Civilization, 1996.

Farb, Peter. *Man's Rise to Civilization as Shown by the Indians of North America from Primeval Times to the Coming of the Industrial State.* New York: E. P. Dutton, 1968.

Fergusson, J. *Tree and Serpent Worship,* 2d ed. London: W. H. Allen, 1873.

Finch, Margaret. *Style in Art History.* Metuchen, NJ: Scarecrow Press, 1974.

Firth, Raymond. *Symbols: Public and Private.* London: George Allen and Unwin, 1973.

Fitzhugh, William W., and Susan A. Kaplan. *Inua: Spirit World of the Bering Sea Eskimo.* Washington, D.C.: Smithsonian Institution Press, 1982.

_____, and Crowell, Aron. *Crossroads of Continents: Cultures of Siberia and Alaska.* Washington, D.C.: Smithsonian Institution Press, 1988.

Fontana, David. *The Secret Language of Symbols.* San Francisco: Chronicle Books, 1993.

Fontenrose, Joseph. "The Ritual Theory of Myth." *Folklore Studies.* Vol. 18. Berkeley and Los Angeles: University of California Press, 1966.

Fox, J. Robin. "Witchcraft and Clanship in Cochiti Therapy." In John Middleton, ed. *Magic, Witchcraft, and Curing.* American Museum Sourcebooks in Anthropology published for the American Museum of Natural History. Garden City, NY: Natural History Press, 1967.

Franklyn, Julian, ed. *A Survey of the Occult.* London: Arthur Barker Limited, 1935.

Fraser, Douglas, ed. *The Many Faces of Primitive Art: A Critical Anthology.* Englewood Cliffs, NJ: Prentice-Hall, 1966.

Frazer, James George. *The Belief in Immortality and Worship of the Dead.* 3 vols. London: Macmillan, Ltd., 1913–24.

_____. *The Magic Art.* 3d ed. Vols. I and II. London: Macmillan, 1922.

_____. *The Fear of the Dead in Primitive Religion.* Vol. III. London: Macmillan, 1936.

_____. *The Golden Bough: A Study of Magic and Religion.* Vol. I. New York: Macmillan, 1958.

Freud, Sigmund. *Beyond the Pleasure Principle.* Translated by James Strachey. New York: Liveright, 1970.

_____. *Totem and Taboo.* Translated and edited by J. Strachey. New York and London: W. W. Norton, 1989.

Frost, Gordon. *Guatemalan Mask Imagery.* Los Angeles: Southwest Museum, 1976.

Fry, Roger. *The Artist and Psycho-analysis.* London: L. and V. Woolf, 1924.

Furst, Peter T., ed. *Flesh of the Gods: The Ritual Use of Hallucinogens.* New York: Praeger, 1972.

Gablik, Suzi. *Progress in Art.* London: Thames and Hudson, 1976.

Gardner, Howard. *The Arts and Human Development.* New York: John Wiley and Sons, 1973.

Gardner, Joseph, ed. *Mysteries of the Ancient Americas.* Pleasantville, NY, and Montreal: Reader's Digest Association, 1986.

Geertz, Clifford. *The Interpretation of Cultures.* New York: Basic Books, 1973.

Gelber, Carol. *Masks Tell Stories.* Brookfield, CT: Millbrook Press, 1993.

George, Robert A., ed. *Studies on Mythology.* Homewood, IL: Dorsey Press, 1968.

Gerbrands, Adrianus A. *Art as an Element of Culture, Especially in Negro-Africa.* Translated by G. E. van Baaren-Pape. Mededelingen Van Het Rijksmuseum Voor Volkenkunde, No. 12. Leiden: E. E. Brill, 1957.

Gibson, James, L. *The Perception of the Visual World.* Boston: Houghton Mifflin, 1950.

Gillon, Werner. *Collecting African Art.* New York: Rizzoli International Publications, 1979.

Gimbutas, Marija. "The Mask in Old Europe: 6500–3500 B.C." In *Archaeology,* October 1974, 27 (4), pp. 263–69.

_____. *The Language of the Goddess.* San Francisco: HarperCollins, 1991.

Glaze, Anita J. *Art and Death in a Senufo Village.* Bloomington: University of Indiana Press, 1981.

Gleadow, Rupert. *Magic and Divination.* Totowa, NJ: Rowman and Littlefield, 1976.

Gluckman, Max. *Politics, Ritual, and Law in Tribal Society.* Oxford: Blackwell, 1965.

Gombrich, Ernst H. *Art and Illusion.* New York: Pantheon Books, 1960.

Goode, William J. *Religion Among the Primitives.* Glencoe, IL: Free Press, 1951.

Goodman, Felicitas D. *Ecstasy, Ritual, and Alternate Reality: Religion in a Pluralistic World.* Bloomington: Indiana University Press, 1988.

Goodman, Mary E. *The Individual and Culture.* Homewood, IL: Dorsey, 1967.

Goodman, Nelson. *Languages of Art.* Indianapolis: Bobbs-Merrill, 1968.

Goonatilleka, M. H. *Masks and Mask Systems of Sri Lanka.* Colombo: Tamarind Books, 1978.

Greenhalgh, Michael, and Vincent Megaw, eds. *Art in Society: Studies in Style, Culture, and Aesthetics.* London: Gerald Ducksworth and Company, Ltd., 1978.

Gregor, Joseph. *Masks of the World: An Historical and Pictorial Survey of Many Types and Times.* New York: B. Blom, 1968.

Greub, Suzanne, ed. *Art of the Sepik River: Papua New Guinea.* Basel: Tribal Art Centre, 1985.

Grim, John A. *The Shaman: Patterns of Siberian and Ojibway Healing.* Norman: University of Oklahoma, 1983.

Grimes, Ronald L. *Research in Ritual Studies: A Programmatic Essay and Bibliography.* ATLA Bibliography Series, No. 14. Metuchen, NJ, and London: American Theological Library Association and Scarecrow Press, 1985.

Griswold, Alexander B., Chewon Kim, and Peter H. Pott, *The Art of Burma, Korea, Tibet.* New York, Toronto, London: Greystone Press, 1968.

Grof, Stanislav, and Joan Halifax. *The Human Encounter with Death.* New York: E. P. Dutton, 1978.

Grolier Electronic Publishing, ©1993.

Groose, E. *The Beginnings of Art.* New York: Appleton, 1897.

Gryaznov, Mikhail. *The Ancient Civilization of Southern Siberia.* Translated by J. Hogarth. New York: Cowles Book Company, 1969.

Guiart, Jean. "The Concept of Norm in the Art of Some Oceanian Societies." In Daniel P. Biebuyck, ed. *Tradition and Creativity in Tribal Art.* pp. 84–97, Berkeley and Los Angeles: University of California Press, 1969.

Guralnik, D. B., ed. *Webster's New World Dictionary of the American Language.* New York, Simon and Schuster, 1979.

Haberland, Wolfgang. *The Art of North America.* Translated by Wayne Dynes. New York, Toronto, and London: Greystone Press, 1968.

Hahner-Herzog, Iris, Maria Kecskési, and László Vajda. *African Masks from the Barbier-Mueller Collection.* Geneva, Munich, and New York: Prestel-Verlag, 1998.

Haile, Berard. *Head and Face Masks in Navaho Ceremonialism.* New York: AMS Press, 1978.

Halifax, Joan. *Shamanic Voices.* New York: E. P. Dutton, 1979.

_____. *Shaman: The Wounded Healer.* London: Thames and Hudson Ltd., 1988.

Hallpike, Christopher R. *The Foundations of Primitive Thought.* Oxford: Clarendon Press, 1979.

Hanson, F. Allan. *Meaning in Culture.* London and Boston: Routledge & Kegan Paul Ltd., 1975.

Harner, Michael J. *The Jivero.* Berkeley, Los Angeles, and London: University of California Press, 1972.

_____, ed. *Hallucinogens and Shamanism.* London: Oxford University Press, 1973.

_____. *The Way of the Shaman.* Toronto, New York, London, Sydney, Auckland: Bantam Books, 1980.

Harris, Marvin. *Culture, People, Nature.* 2d ed. New York: Thomas Y. Crowell, 1975.

Harrison, Jane E. *Ancient Art and Ritual.* New York: H. Holt, 1913.

Hart, George. *A Dictionary of Egyptian Gods and Goddesses.* London and New York: Routledge, 1996.

Hartmann, F. *Magic White and Black.* 3d ed. Boston: Occult Publishing Company, 1893.

Hartmann, Günther. *Masken südamerikanischer Naturvölker.* Veröffentlichungen des Museums für Völkerkunde N.F. 13. Berlin, 1967.

Haskins, James. *Witchcraft, Mysticism and Magic in the Black World.* Garden City, NY: Doubleday, Inc., 1974.

Hatab, Lawrence J. *Myth and Philosophy: A Contest of Truths.* La Salle, IL: Open Court, 1990.

Hauser, Arnold. *The Social History of Art.* Vol. 1. Translated by Stanley Godman. New York: Vintage Books, a division of Random House, 1951.

Helson, Harry. "Adaption-level as Frame of Reference for Prediction, etc." in *American Journal of Psychology.* Vol. 60, pp. 1–29, 1947.

Herskovits, Melville J. *Man and His Works.* New York: Alfred A. Knopf, 1948.

Hertz, Robert. *Death and the Right Hand.* Translated by Rodney Needham and Claudia Needham. Glencoe, IL: Free Press, 1960.

Hiler, Hilaire. *From Nudity to Raiment.* London: Simpkin Marshall, Ltd. 1929.

Hill, Douglas, and Pat Williams. *The Supernatural.* New York: Hawthorn Books, 1966.

Hiller, Susan, ed. *The Myth of Primitivism: Perspectives on Art.* New York and London: Routledge, 1991.

Hirn, Yrjö. *The Origins of Art.* New York: B. Blom, 1971.

Hitchcock, John T., and Rex L. Jones, eds. *Spirit Possession in the Nepal Himalayas.* New Delhi: Vikas Publishing House, 1976.

Hocart, A. M. *The Life-giving Myth.* Edited and Introduced by Lord Raglan. New York: Grove Press, n.d.

Hoebel, Edward Adamson. *Man in the Primitive World.* 2d ed. New York, Toronto, London: McGraw-Hill, 1958.

Hogarth, William. *The Analysis of Beauty.* New York: Garland Publishing, 1973.

Holden, William C., et al. "Studies of the Yaqui Indians in Sonora, Mexico." In Texas Technological College *Bulletin* vol. 12. No.1. Lubbock: Texas Technological College, 1936.

Holm, Jean, and John Bowker, eds. *Myth and History.* London and New York: Pinter, 1994.

Holy, Ladislav. *Masks and Figures from Eastern and Southern Africa.* Translated by T. Gottheiner. London: Paul Hamlyn, 1967.

Hori, Ichiro. *Folk Religion in Japan.* Chicago: University of Chicago Press, 1968.

Howells, William. *The Heathens: Primitive Man and His Religions.* Garden City, NY: Doubleday, 1949.

Huizinga, J. *Homo Ludens: A Study of the Play-Element in Culture.* London, Boston, and Henley: Routledge & Kegan Paul, 1949.

Hyman, John. *The Imitation of Nature.* New York and Oxford: Basil Blackwell Ltd., 1989.

Ingold, Tim, ed. *Companion Encyclopedia of Anthropology: Humanity, Culture, and Social Life.* New York and London: Routledge, 1994.

Inhaber, Herbert. *Masks From Antiquity to the Modern Era: An Annotated Bibliography.* Lanham, MD and London: Scarecrow Press, 1997.

Irwin, Lee. *Visionary Worlds: The Making and Unmaking of Reality.* Albany, NY: State University of New York Press, 1996.

Isaacson, Robert L., Max L. Hutt, and Milton L. Blum. *Psychology: The Science of Behavior.* New York: Harper and Row, 1965.

Ivanoff, Pierre. *Headhunters of Borneo.* Translated by Edward Fitzgerald. London: Jarrolds, 1958.

Jacobsen, Thorkild. *The Treasures of Darkness.* New Haven and London: Yale University Press, 1976.

Jacobson, Lori, and Donald Fritz. *Changing Faces: Mexican Masks in Transition.* McAllen, TX: McAllen International Museum, 1985.

James, E. O. *Prehistoric Religion: A Study of Prehistoric Archaeology.* London: Thames and Hudson, 1957.

James, William. *Varieties of Religious Experience.* Cambridge, MA: Harvard University Press, 1941.

Jenkins, Iredell. *Art and the Human Enterprise.* Cambridge, MA: Harvard University Press, 1958.

Jennings, H. *The Biological Basis of Human Nature.* New York: W. W. Norton, 1930.

Jensen, Adolf E. *Myth and Cult Among Primitive Peoples.* Translated by Marianna Tax Choldin and Wolfgang Weissleder. Chicago and London: University of Chicago Press, 1963.

Jessup, Helen. *Court Arts of Indonesia.* New York: Asia Society Galleries in association with Harry N. Abrams, 1990.

Jevons, Frank Byron. *Masks and Acting.* Cambridge: University Press, 1916.

Jopling, C. F., ed. *Art and Aesthetics in Primitive Societies: A Critical Anthology.* New York: E. P. Dutton, 1971.

Jordan, David K. *Gods, Ghosts and Ancestors: Folk Religion in a Taiwanese Village.* Berkeley: University of California Press, 1972.

Jung, C. G. *The Integration of the Personality.* Translated by Stanley M. Dell. London: Routledge & Kegan Paul, 1940.

_____. *Symbols of Transformation.* Vol. 5. Translated by R.F.C. Hull. Bollingen Series XX, New York: Pantheon Books, a Division of Random House, 1956.

_____. *The Spirit in Man, Art, and Literature.* Vol. 15. Translated by R.F.C. Hull. Bollingen Series XX, New York: Pantheon Books, a Division of Random House, Inc., 1966.

_____, ed. *Man and His Symbols.* New York: A Laurel Book published by Dell, 1968.

Kaigh, Frederick. *Witchcraft and Magic of Africa.* London: R. Lesley, 1947.

Kandinsky, Wassily. *Concerning the Spiritual in Art.* New York: Dover Publications, 1947.

Kapferer, Bruce. *A Celebration of Demons: Exorcism and the Aesthetics of Healing in Sri Lanka.* Bloomington: Indiana University Press, 1983.

Karp, Ivan, and Steven Lavine, eds. *Exhibiting Cultures: The Poetics and Politics of Museum Display.* Washington and London: Smithsonian Institution Press, 1991.

Kendall, L. *The Life and Hard Times of a Korean Shaman.* Honolulu: University of Hawaii Press, 1988.

Kerstetter, Josie, ed. *Colorado Springs Fine Arts Center: A History and Selections from the Permanent Collections.* Colorado Springs, Colorado Springs Fine Arts Center, 1986.

Kim, Chewon, "Korea." In: Alexander B. Grinswold, Chewon Kim, and Peter H. Pott. *The Art of Burma, Korea, Tibet.* New York, Toronto, London: Greystone Press, 1968.

King, John H. *The Supernatural: Its Origin, Nature, and Evolution.* London: Williams and Norgate; New York: G. P. Putnam's Sons, 1892.

Kirk, G. S. *Myth: Its Meaning and Functions in Ancient and Other Cultures.* Berkeley and Los Angeles: University of California Press, 1970.

Klinger, Eric. *Structure and Functions of Fantasy.* New York: Wiley Interscience, 1971.

Kluckhohn, C. *Navaho Witchcraft.* Boston: Beacon Press, 1944.

Kolbe, G. *Undying Faces: A Collection of Death Masks.* Translated by M. M. Green. New York: W. W. Norton, 1927.

Kress, Gunther, and van Leeuwen, Theo. *Reading Images.* London and New York: Routledge, 1996.

Kreitler, Hans and Kreitler Shulamith. *Psychology of the Arts.* Durham, NC: Duke University Press, 1972.

_____. *Psychoanalytic Explorations in Art.* New York: International Universities Press, 1952.

Kris, Ernst, and Otto Kurz. *Legend, Myth, and Magic in the Image of the Artist.* New Haven and London: Yale University Press, 1979.

Küchler, Susanne, and Walter, Melion, eds. *Images of Memory: On Remembering and Representation.* Washington, D.C. and London: Smithsonian Institution Press, 1991.

Kuper, Adam. *The Invention of Primitive Society.* London and New York: Routledge, 1988.

Labbé, Armond J. *Religion, Art, and Iconography: Man and Cosmos in Prehispanic Mesoamerica.* Santa Ana, CA: Bowers Museum Foundation, 1982.

_____. *Colombia Before Columbus: The People, Culture, and Ceramic Art of Prehispanic Colombia.* New York: Rizzoli International Publications, 1986.

Laing, John, and Wire, David. *The Encyclopedia of Signs and Symbols.* London: Studio Editions, 1993.

Lambek, Michael. *Knowledge and Practice in Mayotte: Local Discourses of Islam, Sorcery, and Spirit Possession.* Toronto, Buffalo, and London: University of Toronto Press, 1993.

Lang, Andrew. *Magic and Religion.* New York and Bombay: Longmans, 1901.

_____. *Myth, Ritual and Religion.* Vols. I and II. London, New York, Bombay, and Calcutta: Longmans, Green, 1913.

_____. *The Making of Religion.* New York: AMS Press, 1968.

Larner, Christina L. *Witchcraft and Religion: The Politics of Popular Belief.* Oxford: Basil Blackwell, 1984.

Larsen, Stephen. *The Shaman's Doorway.* Barrytown, NY: Station Hill Press, 1976.

Lawrence, P., and M. J. Meggitt, eds. *Gods, Ghosts, and Men in Melanesia.* London, Wellington, New York, and Melbourne: Oxford University Press, 1965.

Lawton, Thomas; Fu Shen, Lowry Glenn, Yonemura Ann, and Beach, Milo. *Asian Art in the Arthur M. Sackler Gallery.* Washington, D.C.: Arthur M. Sackler Gallery, Smithsonian Institution, 1987.

Layard, Berthold. "Origin of the Word "Shaman."" *American Anthropologist* 19: 361–71, 1971.

Layton, Robert. "Art and Visual Communication." In Michael Greenhalgh and Vincent Megaw, eds. *Art in Society.* London: Gerald Ducksworth, 1978.

Leakey, Richard. *The Origin of Humankind.* New York: Basic Books, A Division of HarperCollins, 1994.

Lechuga, Ruth D., and Chloë Sayer. *Mask Arts of Mexico.* San Francisco: Chronicle Books, 1994.

Lee, Duhyun. *Masks of Korea.* Seoul: Korean Overseas Information Service, Ministry of Culture and Information, 1981.

Lee, Sherman. *The History of Far Eastern Art.* Englewood Cliffs and New York: Prentice-Hall, and Harry N. Abrams, 1973.

Leeming, David A. *The World of Myth.* New York and Oxford: Oxford University Press, 1990.

Leenhardt, Maurice. *Folk Art of Oceania.* Translated by M. Heron. New York: Tudor, 1950.

Lévi-Strauss, Claude. *Structural Anthropology.* Translated by C. Johnson and B. G. Schoepf. New York: Basic Books, A Division of HarperCollins, 1963.

_____. *The Savage Mind.* Chicago: University of Chicago Press, 1966.

_____. *The Raw and the Cooked.* Translated by John and Doreen Weightman. New York and Evanston: Harper and Row, 1969.

_____. *The Way of the Masks.* Translated by Sylvia Modelski. Seattle: University of Washington Press, 1988.

Lévy-Bruhl, Lucien. *Primitives and the Supernatural.* Translated by Lilian A. Clare. New York: E.P. Dutton, 1935.

_____. *The "Soul" of the Primitive.* New York, Macmillan, 1928.

_____. *How Natives Think.* Translated by Lilian A. Clare. Princeton, NJ: Princeton University Press, 1985.

Lewin, Roger. *The Origin of Modern Humans.* New York: Scientific American Library, a Division of HPHLP, 1993.

Lewis, Ioan, ed. *Symbols and Sentiments: Cross-*

cultural Studies in Symbolism. London, New York, and San Francisco: Academic Press, a subsidiary of Harcourt Brace Jovanovich, 1977.

Lewis, I. M. *Ecstatic Religion: An Anthropological Study of Spirit Possession and Shamanism*. 2d ed. London: Routledge, 1989.

Lincoln, Louise. *Assemblage of Spirits: Idea and Image in New Ireland*. New York: George Braziller in association with the Minneapolis Institute of Arts, 1987.

Lindsay, Jack. *A Short History of Culture*. New York: Citadel Press, 1963.

Linton, Ralph. *The Tree of Culture*. New York: Alfred A. Knopf, 1957.

Lissner, Ivar. *Man, God and Magic*. Translated by J. Maxwell Brownjohn. New York: G. P. Putnam's Sons, 1961.

Lommel, Andreas. *Prehistroic and Primitive Man*. London: Paul Hamlyn, 1966.

_____. *The World of the Early Hunters*. Translated by M. Bullock. London: Evelyn, Adams and Mackay Ltd., 1967.

_____. *Masks: Their Meaning and Function*. Translated by N. Fowler. New York and Toronto: McGraw-Hill, 1972.

Lopatin, Ivan A. *The Cult of the Dead Among the Natives of the Amur Basin*. The Hague: Mouton, 1960.

Lowie, Robert H. *Primitive Religion*. New York: Liveright Publishing Corporation, 1970.

Lü, Tung-pin. *The Secret of the Golden Flower*. Translated by Richard Wilhelm with commentary by C. G. Jung. New York: Causeway Books, 1975.

Maccoby, Hyam. *The Sacred Executioner: Human Sacrifice and the Legacy of Guilt*. London: Thames and Hudson, 1982.

MacGowan K., and H. Rosse. *Masks and Demons*. London: Martin Hopkinson and Company, Ltd., 1923.

Mackenzie, Donald A. *Myths and Legends Series: China and Japan*. London: Bracken Books, 1986.

Maddox, J. L. *The Medicine Man: A Sociological Study of the Character and Evolution of Shamanism*. New York: Macmillan Publishing Co., 1923.

Madsen, W. "Shamanism in Mexico." In *Southwestern Journal of Anthropology*. Vol. II, pp. 48–57, 1955.

Mair, Lucy. *Witchcraft*. New York and Toronto: McGraw-Hill Book Company, 1969.

Maksic, Sava, and Paul Meskil. *Primitive Art of New Guinea Sepik River Basin*. Worcester, MA: Davis Publications, 1973.

Malin, Edward. *A World of Faces*. Portland, OR: Timber Press, 1978.

Malinowski, Bronislaw. *Myth in Primitive Society*. New York: Norton, 1926.

_____. *A Scientific Theory of Culture and Other Essays*. Chapel Hill: University of North Carolina Press, 1944.

_____. *Magic, Science and Religion*. Glencoe, IL: Free Press, 1948.

_____. *Myth in Primitive Psychology*. Westport, CT: Negro Universities Press, 1971.

Malraux, André. *The Psychology of Art: The Creative Act*. Translated by Stuart Gilbert. Bollingen Series XXIV. New York: Pantheon Books, 1949.

_____. *Twilight of the Absolute*. New York: Pantheon Books, 1950.

_____. *The Voices of Silence*. London: Secker and Warburg, 1954.

Markman, Roberta H., and Markman, Peter T. *The Flayed God: The Mesoamerican Mythological Tradition*. New York: HarperCollins, 1992.

Maringer, Johannes. *The Gods of Prehistoric Man*. Edited and translated by Mary Ilford. New York: Alfred A. Knopf, 1960.

Marshack, A. *The Roots of Civilization*. New York and Dusseldorf: McGraw-Hill Book Company, 1972.

Marshall, Richard. *Witchcraft: The History and Mythology*. New York and Avenel, NJ: Crescent Books, 1995.

Martland, T. R. *Religion as Art: An Interpretation*. Albany: State University of New York Press, 1981.

Maschner, Herbert, ed. *Darwinian Archaeologies*. New York and London: Plenum Press, 1996.

Mbiti, John S. *African Religions and Philosophy*. New York and Washington: Praeger, 1969.

McFarren, Peter, ed. *Mascaras de los Andes Bolivianos*. La Paz, Bolivia: Editorial Quipus/ Banco Mercantil S.A., 1993.

McGill, Ormond. *The Mysticism and Magic of India*. South Brunswick and New York: A. S. Barnes, 1977.

McLeod, Malcolm, and Mack, John. *Ethnic Sculpture*. Cambridge, MA: Harvard University Press, 1985.

Mead, Margaret. *Culture and Commitment: A Study of the Generation Gap*. Garden City, NY: Natural History Press/Doubleday, 1970.

_____, and Nicolas Calas, eds. *Primitive Heritage*. New York: Random House, 1953.

Meier, Norman Charles. *Art in Human Affairs*. New York and London: McGraw-Hill, 1942.

Melody, Michael E. *The Apache*. New York and Philadelphia: Chelsea House Publications, 1989.

Merriam-Webster, eds. *Webster's Dictionary of Word Origins*. New York: Smithmark, 1995.

Meyer, Laure. *Black Africa: Masks, Sculpture, Jewelry*. Translated by H. McPhail in association with First Edition Translations Ltd. Paris: Pierre Terrail, 1992.

Middleton, John, ed. *Gods and Rituals*. American Museum Sourcebooks in Anthropology published for the American Museum of Natural History. Garden City, NY: Natural History Press, 1967a.

_____, ed. *Magic, Witchcraft, and Curing*. American Museum Sourcebooks in Anthropology published for the American Museum of Natural History Garden City, NY: Natural History Press, 1967b.

Miksic, John, ed. *Art of Indonesia*. New York: Vendome Press, 1992.

Mitchell, Leonel L. *The Meaning of Ritual*. New York: Paulist Press, 1977.

Mithen, Steven. "The Origin of Art: Natural Signs, Mental Modularity, and Visual Symbolism." In H.D.G. Maschner, ed. *Darwinian Archaeologies*. New York: Plenum Press, 1996.

Moes, Robert. *Mingei: Japanese Folk Art*. From the Brooklyn Museum Collection. New York: Universe Books, 1985.

Moisés, Rosalio, Jane H. Kelly, and William C. Holden. *A Yaqui Life*. Lincoln and London: University of Nebraska Press, 1971.

Montagu, M. F. Ashley, ed. *Culture: Man's Adaptive Dimension*. New York: Oxford University Press, 1968.

Monter, E. William. *Witchcraft in France and Switzerland*. Ithaca and London: Cornell University Press, 1976.

Monti, Franco. *African Masks*. Translated by A. Hale. London, New York, Sydney, Toronto: Hamlyn Publishing Group Limited, 1968.

Montreal Museum of Fine Arts. *The Tokugawa Collection: The Japan of the Shoguns*. Montreal: Montreal Museum of Fine Arts, 1989.

Moss, Rosalind. *The Life After Death in Oceania and the Malay Archipelago*. London: Oxford University Press, 1925.

Munsterberg, Hugo. *The Arts of Japan: An Illustrated History*. Rutland, VT, and Tokyo: Charles E. Tuttle, 1957.

_____. *Symbolism in Ancient Chinese Art*. New York: Hacker Art Books, 1986.

Murray, Henry A., ed. *Myth and Mythmaking*. New York: George Braziller, 1960.

Napier, A. D. *Masks, Transformation, and Paradox*. Berkeley and London: University of California Press, 1986.

National Museum of African Art. *Selected Works*, Vol. 1. Washington, DC: National Museum of African Art, 1999.

National Museum of American Art. *Celebration: A World of Art and Ritual*. Washington, D.C.: Smithsonian Institution Press, 1982.

Needham, Rodney. *Symbolic Classification*. Santa Monica, CA: Goodyear, 1979.

Neihardt, John G. *Black Elk Speaks*. Lincoln: University of Nebraska Press, 1961.

Nelson, Geoffrey R. *Spiritualism and Society*. New York: Schocken Books, 1969.

Newton, Douglas. *Crocodile and Cassowary*. New York: Museum of Primitive Art, 1971.

Nishikawa, Kyōtarō. *Bugaku Masks*. Translated and adapted by Monica Bethe. Tokyo, New York, and San Francisco: Kodansha International Ltd., 1978.

Noel, Daniel C., ed. *Paths to the Power of Myth: Joseph Campbell and the Study of Religion*. New York: Crossroad, 1990.

Nogami, Toyoichiro. *Noh Masks: Classification and Explanation*. Tokyo: Iwanami Press, 1938.

Nooter, Mary. "Secrecy: African Art that Conceals and Reveals." Los Angeles: *African Arts*. Vol XXVI –No. 1, pp. 55–69, 1993.

Norman, Dorothy. *The Hero: Myth/Image/Symbol*. New York and Cleveland: World, 1969.

Nunley, John, W. *Moving with the Face of the Devil*. Urbana and Chicago: University of Illinois Press, 1987.

Oettinger, Marion, Jr., and Suzanne Kenagy. "The Many Faces of Mexico: Masks in Cultural Context." In *Masterkey*. Los Angeles: Southwest Museum, vol. 62, Nos. 2 and 3, Summer/Fall 1988.

Ogden, Robert Morris. *The Psychology of Art*. New York and Chicago: Charles Scribner's Sons, 1938.

O'Keefe, D. L. *Stolen Lightning: The Social Theory of Magic*. New York: Continuum, 1982.

Opler, Morris Edward. "The Curative Role of Shamanism in Mescalero Apache Mythology." *Journal of American Folklore* 59:268–81, 1946.

Ornstein, Robert E. *The Psychology of Consciousness*. 2d ed. New York: Harcourt Brace Jovanovich, 1977.

Osborn, Harold. *South American Mythology*. London: Hamlyn Publishing Group Ltd., 1968.

Ottenburg, Simon. *Masked Rituals of Afikpo: The Context of an African Art*. Seattle: University of Washington Press, 1975.

Pace, David. *Claude Lévi-Strauss: The Bearer of Ashes*. London: ARK Paperbacks, 1986.

Painter, Muriel, T. *A Yaqui Easter*. Tucson: University of Arizona Press, 1971.

Pal, Pratapaditya. *Art of Tibet*. Berkeley and London: University of California Press, 1983.

Palmer, Jerry. "Need and Function: The Terms of a Debate." In Jerry Palmer and Mo Dodson, eds. *Design and Aesthetics*. pp. 110–122, London and New York: Routledge, 1996.

______, and Mo Dodson, eds. *Design and Aesthetics*. London and New York: Routledge, 1996.

Palmer, Spencer J., ed. *Deity and Death*. Vol. 2. Religious Studies Monograph Series, Religious Studies Center: Brigham Young University, 1978.

Pani, Jiwan. *World of Other Faces: Indian Masks*. New Delhi: Publications Division, Ministry of Information and Broadcasting, Government of India, 1986.

Paolucci, Henry. *Hegel: On The Arts*. Abridged and translated with an introduction by H. Paolucci. New York: Frederick Unger, 1979.

Park, Willard Z. *Shamanism in Western North America*. New York: Cooper Square, 1975.

Parrinder, Geoffrey. *African Mythology*. London: Hamlyn Publishing Group Ltd., 1967.

Paulme, Denise. *African Sculpture*. Translated by M. Ross. New York: Viking Press, 1962.

Pernet, Henry. *Ritual Masks: Descriptions and Revelations*. Translated by Laura Grillo. Columbia, SC: University of South Carolina Press, 1992.

Perrin, Olivier. *Masques*. Paris: Musée Guimet in collaboration with the l'École pratique de Hautes Études et son Centre documentaire d'Histoire des Religions, 1959.

Peters, Larry. *Ecstasy and Healing in Nepal*. Malibu, CA: Undena Publications, 1981.

Pfeiffer, John E. *The Emergence of Man*. New York and London: Harper and Row, 1969.

Piggott, Juliet. *Japanese Mythology*. London: Hamlyn Publishing Group Limited, 1969.

Pike, E. Royston. *The Strange Ways of Man: Rites and Rituals and The Incredible Origins*. New York: Hart, 1967.

Pinch, Geraldine. *Magic in Ancient Egypt*. Avon: The Bath Press, 1994.

Poignant, Roslyn. *Oceanic Mythology*. London: Paul Hamlyn, 1967.

Pott, Peter H., "Tibet." In Alexander B. Griswold, Chewon Kim, and Peter H. Pott. *The Art of Burma, Korea, Tibet*. New York, Toronto, London: Greystone Press, 1968.

Potter, Jack M. "Cantonese Shamanism." In Arthur P. Wolf, ed. *Religion and Ritual in Chinese Society*. Stanford: Stanford University Press, 1974.

Pratt, Carroll, C. "The Role of Past Experience in Visual Perception." *Journal of Psychology* Vol. 30, pp. 85–107, 1950.

Radcliffe-Brown, A. R. *The Andaman Islanders*. 2d printing. London: Cambridge University Press, 1933.

______. *Structure and Function in Primitive Society*. New York: Free Press, 1952.

Radin, Paul. *Primitive Religion: Its Nature and Origin*. 2d ed. New York: Dover Publications, 1957.

Ray, Dorothy Jean. *Eskimo Masks: Art and Ceremony*. Seattle: University of Washington Press, 1961.

Read, Herbert. *Icon and Idea*. London: Faber and Faber, 1955.

______. *The Forms of Things Unknown*. London: Faber and Faber, 1960.

______. "A Personal Point of View: Summary of Proceedings." In M. W. Smith, ed. *The Artist in Tribal Society*. pp. 124–127, London: Routledge and Kegan Paul, 1960.

______. *The Origins of Form in Art*. New York: Horizon Press, 1965.

Redfield, Robert. *The Folk Culture of Yucatán*. Chicago: University of Chicago Press, 1941.

Reichel-Eolmatoff, Gerardo. *The Shaman and the Jaguar*. Philadelphia: Temple University Press, 1975.

Reik, T. *Ritual: Psycho-analytic Studies*. Translated by D. Bryan. New York: International Universities Press, 1958.

Reynolds, Barrie. *Magic, Divination and Witchcraft Among the Barotse of Northern Rhodesia*. Berkeley and Los Angeles: University of California Press, 1963.

Riley, Olive L. *Masks and Magic*. New York: Studio Publications and Thomas Y. Crowell, 1955.

Rockhill, William Woodville. "On the Use of Skulls in Lamaist Ceremonies." *Proceedings of the American Oriental Society* (New Haven), XL (pub. 1890), xxiv–xxxi, 1988.

Roediger, V. M. *Ceremonial Costumes of the Pueblo Indians*. Berkeley and Los Angeles: University of California Press, 1961.

Rowland, Benjamin. *The Art and Architecture of India*. 2d ed. Baltimore: Penguin, 1959.

Royce, Anya Peterson. *Ethic Identity*. Bloomington: Indiana University Press, 1982.

Saarinen, Eliel. *Search for Form*. New York: Reinhold Publishing Corporation, 1948.

Sahagún, Fr. Bernardion de. Florentine Codex: General History of the Things in New Spain. Translated from the Nahuatl by Arthur J. O. Anderson and Charles E. Dibble. 13 vols. Monographs of the School of American, 1950–71.

Salmony, Alfred. *Antler and Tongue: An Essay on Ancient Chinese Symbolism and Its Implications*. Ascona: Artibus Asiæ, 1954.

Santayana, George. *The Sense of Beauty.* New York: Random House, 1955.

Sargent, Denny. *Global Ritualism: Myth and Magic Around the World.* St. Paul, MN: Llewellyn Publications, 1994.

Sartre, Jean-Paul. *Words.* Translated by Bernard Frechtman. New York: George Braziller, 1964.

_____. *Being and Nothingness: An Essay on Phenomenological Ontology.* Translated by Hazel Barnes. New York: Philosophical Library, 1965.

Sasser, Elizabeth S. *The World of Spirits and Ancestors in the Art of Western Sub-Saharan Africa.* Lubbock: Texas Tech University Press, 1995.

Schachtel, Ernest G. "On Color and Affect." In *Psychiatry.* Vol. 6. pp. 303–409, 1943.

Schildkrout, Enid, ed. *Wild Spirits, Strong Medicine: African Art and the Wilderness.* New York: Center for African Art, 1989.

Schmalenbach, Werner, ed. *African Art from the Barbier-Mueller Collection.* Munich: Prestel-Verlag, 1988.

Schmidt, P. *Superstition and Magic.* Westminster: Newman Press, 1963.

Schusky, Ernest, and Culbert, Patrick. *Introducing Culture.* 3d ed. Englewood Cliffs, NJ: Prentice-Hall, 1978.

Secor, James L., and Stephen Addiss. "The Male Ghost in Kabuki and Ukiyo-e." In Stephen Addiss, ed. *Japanese Ghosts and Demons.* pp. 49–55, New York: George Braziller in association with the Spencer Museum of Art, University of Kansas, 1985.

Segall, Marshall H., et al. *The Influence of Culture on Visual Perception.* Indianapolis: Bobbs-Merrill, 1966.

Segy, Ladislas. *African Sculpture Speaks.* 4th ed. New York: Da Capo Press, 1975.

_____. *Masks of Black Africa.* New York: Dover Publications, 1976.

Seligmann, K. *History of Magic.* New York: Pantheon Books, 1948.

Shafer, Harry. *Ancient Texans.* Austin: Texas Monthly Press, 1986.

Shah, Sayed Idries. *Oriental Magic.* New York: Philosophical Library, 1957.

Shalleck, J. *Masks.* New York: Viking Press, 1973.

Sharghnessy, J. D., ed. *The Roots of Ritual.* Grand Rapids, MI: William B. Eerdmans, 1973.

Sharon, Douglas. *Wizard of the Four Winds.* New York: Free Press, 1978.

Shirokogoroff, Sergei. *Psychomental Complex of the Tungus.* London: Routledge & Kegan Paul Ltd., 1935.

Sieber, Roy, and Arnold Rubin. *Sculpture of Black Africa: The Paul Tishman Collection.* Washington, D.C.: International Exhibitions Foundation, 1970.

Skorupski, John. *Symbol and Theory: A Philosophical Study of Theories of Religion in Social Anthropology.* Cambridge and New York: Cambridge University Press, 1976.

Slattum, Judy. *Masks of Bali: Spirits of an Ancient Drama.* San Francisco: Chronicle Books, 1992.

Smith, Huston. *Forgotten Truth: The Primordial Tradition.* New York: Harper and Row, 1976.

Smith, Marion W., ed. *The Artist in Tribal Society: Proceedings of a Symposium Held at the Royal Anthropological Institute.* London: Routledge & Kegan Paul, 1961.

Smith, Susan V. H. *Masks in Modern Drama.* Berkeley, Los Angeles, and London: University of California Press, 1984.

Snow, Dean. *The Archaeology of North America.* New York: Viking, 1976.

Sorell, Walter. *The Other Face: The Mask in the Arts.* London: Thames and Hudson, 1973.

Sorokin, Pitirim. *Social and Cultural Dynamics.* Boston: Porter Sargent, 1957.

Southwest Museum. *Masterkey.* Vol. 62, Nos. 2 & 3, Summer/Fall. Los Angeles: Southwest Museum, 1988.

Sperber, Dan. *Rethinking Symbolism.* Translated by Alice L. Morton. Cambridge and New York: Cambridge University Press, 1975.

Spicer, Edward H. *The Yaqui: A Cultural History.* Tucson: University of Arizona Press, 1980.

Staaf, Frits. *Exploring Mysticism.* Berkeley: University of California Press, 1975.

Stafford, Barbara M. *Symbol and Myth.* Cranbury, NJ, and London: Associated University Presses, 1979.

Stein, Gertrude, *Selected Writings of Gertrude Stein.* Edited and introduced by Carl Van Vechten. New York: Modern Library published by Random House, 1962.

Strathern, Andrew. *Body Thoughts.* Ann Arbor: University of Michigan Press, 1996.

_____, and Strathern, Marilyn. *Self-decoration in Mount Hagen.* Toronto and Buffalo: University of Toronto Press, 1971.

Stroup, Herbert. *Four Religions of Asia.* New York and London: Harper and Row, 1968.

Summers, Montague. *The History of Witchcraft.* New York: University Books, 1956.

Swanson, Guy E. *The Birth of the Gods: The Origin of Primitive Beliefs.* Ann Arbor: University of Michigan Press, 1960.

Tambiah, S. J. *Buddhism and the Spirit Cult in North-East Thailand.* London: Cambridge University Press, 1970.

Taussig, M. *Shamanism, Colonialism and the*

Wild Man: A Study in Terror and Healing. Chicago: University of Chicago Press, 1987.

Taylor, Paul, and Lorraine Aragon. *Beyond the Java Sea: Art of Indonesia's Outer Islands*. Washington, DC: The National Museum of Natural History, Smithsonian Institution in association with Harry N. Abrams, New York, 1991.

Teuten, Timothy. *The Letts Guide to Collecting Masks*. London: Studio Editions Ltd., 1991.

Thomas, Julian. *Time, Culture and Identity: An Interpretive Archaeology*. London and New York: Routledge, 1999.

Thomas, Keith. *Religion and the Decline of Magic*. Oxford and New York: Oxford University Press, 1997.

Thompson, Robert Farris. *African Art in Motion*. Berkeley: University of California Press, 1974.

_____. *Flash of the Spirit*. New York: Vintage Books, 1984.

Thorburn, John M. *Art and the Unconscious*. London: K. Paul, Trench, Trubner and Company, Ltd., 1925.

Thorndike, Lynn, A. *A History of Magic and Experimental Science*. 6 vols. New York: Columbia University Press, 1923.

Three Initiates. *The Kybalion: A Study of the Hermetic Philosophy of Ancient Egypt and Greece*. Chicago: Yogi Publication Society, 1908.

Tolstoy, A. *Tolstoy: A Life of My Father*. New York: Harper and Brothers, 1953.

Tolstoy, I. What is Art? Translated by Aylmer Maude. London and New York: Oxford University Press, 1932.

Torrance, Robert M. *The Spiritual Quest: Transcendence in Myth, Religion, and Science*. Berkeley and London: University of California Press, 1994.

Trigg, Elwood B. *Gypsy Demons and Divinities*. Secaucus, NJ: Citadel Press, 1973.

Tsultem, N. *Mongolian Sculpture*. Ulan-Bator: State Publishing House, 1989.

Turnbull, Colin M. *The Human Cycle*. New York: A Touchstone Book published by Simon & Schuster, 1983.

Turner, Victor. *The Forest of Symbols: Aspects of Ndembu Ritual*. Ithaca and London: Cornell University Press, 1967.

_____. *The Ritual Process*. Chicago, IL: Aldine, 1969.

_____. *Dramas, Fields and Metaphors: Symbolic Action in Human Society*. Ithaca and London: Cornell University Press, 1974.

Twycross, Meg, and Sarah *Carpenter. Masks and Masking in Medieval and Early Tudor England*. Aldershot, England: Ashgate Publishing Ltd., 2002.

UCLA Museum of Cultural History. *Image and Identity: The Role of The Mask in Various Cultures*. Los Angeles: University of California, 1972.

Underhill, E. *Mysticism: A Study of the Nature and Development of Man's Spiritual Consciousness*. New York: Noonday Press, 1955.

Underwood, Leon. *Masks of West Africa*. London: Alec Tiranti Ltd., 1952.

Urban, G., and Janet W. Hendricks. "Signal Functions of Masking in Amerindian Brazil." in *Semiotica* 47-1/4:181–218, 1983. Mouton, Amsterdam. Reprinted: Offprint Series No. 255, Institute of Latin American Studies, University of Texas at Austin.

Valéry, Paul. *Aesthetics*. London: Routledge & Kegan Paul, 1964.

Van der Leeuw, Gerardus. *Religion in Essence and Manifestation*. Translated by J. E. Turner. Princeton, NJ: Princeton University Press, 1986.

Van Gennep, Arnold. *The Rites of Passage*. Translated by M. Vizedom and Gabrielle Caffee. Chicago: University of Chicago Press, 1960.

Van Vechten, Carl, ed. *Selected Writings of Gertrude Stein*. New York: Random House, 1946.

Vernon, Glenn M. *The Sociology of Death: An Analysis of Death-Related Behavior*. New York: Ronald Press, 1970.

Vetter, George B. *Magic and Religion*. New York: Philosophical Library and Bonanza Book a division of Crown Publishers, 1973.

Vitersky, Piers. *The Shaman*. Boston and London: Little, Brown, 1995.

Vlahos, Olivia. *Body, The Ultimate Symbol*. New York: J. B. Lippincott, 1979.

von Wonning, Hasso. *Pre-Columbian Art of Mexico and Central America*. New York: Harry N. Abrams, 1968.

Wade, Edwin L., ed. *The Arts of the North American Indian: Native Traditions in Evolution*. New York: Hudson Hills Press in association with Philbrook Art Center, 1986.

Waite, Arthur E. *The Book of Ceremonial Magic*. New York: University Books, 1961.

Walens, Stanley. "Analogic Causality and the Power of Masks." In N. Ross Crumrine and Margorie Halpin, eds. *The Power of Symbols: Masks and Masquerade in the Americas*. pp. 70–78. Vancouver: University of British Columbia Press, 1983.

Wales, H. G. Quaritch. *The Mountain of God: A Study in Early Religion and Kingship*. London: B. Quatrich, 1953.

_____. *Prehistory and Religion in South-East Asia*, London: Quaritch, 1957.

Walker, Barbara G. *The Woman's Dictionary of Symbols and Sacred Objects*. Edison, NJ: Castle Books, 1988.

Wallis, Wilson, D. *Religion in Primitive Society*. New York: F. S. Crofts, 1939.

Walsh, R. N. *The Spirit of Shamanism*. Los Angeles: Tarcher, 1990.

Waters, Frank. *Masked Gods*. Chicago: Swallow Press, 1950.

_____. *Book of the Hopi*. New York: Viking Press, 1963.

_____. *The Ritual Process*. Chicago, IL: Aldine, 1969.

Weber, Max. *The Sociology of Religion*. Boston: Beacon Press, 1922.

Webster, Hutton. *Primitive Secret Societies: A Study of Early Politics and Religion*. 2d ed. New York: Macmillan, 1932.

_____. *Magic: A Sociological Study*. Stanford, CA: Stanford University Press, 1948.

Weitz, Morris. *Problems in Aesthetics*. New York: Macmillan, 1964.

Werbner, Richard P. *Ritual Passage, Sacred Journey: The Form, Process and Organization of Religious Movement*. Washington, D.C.: Smithsonian Institution Press, 1989.

Werner, E. T. C. *Myths and Legends of China*. London, Toronto, and Sydney: George G. Harrap and Company, Ltd., 1958.

Whitehead, Alfred North. *Process and Reality*. Cambridge: University Press, 1929.

_____. *Symbolism: Its Meaning and Effect*. New York: Macmillan, 1958.

Wiles, David. *The Masks of Menander*. Cambridge and New York: Cambridge University Press, 1991.

Willett, Frank. *Ife in the History of West African Sculpture*. New York: McGraw-Hill, 1978.

_____. *African Art*. New York: Thames and Hudson, 1991.

Williams, Denis. *Icon and Image: A Study of Sacred and Secular Forms of African Classical Art*. New York: New York University Press, 1974.

Williams, Joseph J. *Voodoos and Obeahs: Phases of West India Witchcraft*. New York: AMS Books, 1970.

Wilson, Colin. *The Occult: A History*. New York: Vintage Books/Random House, 1973.

Wilson, Frank Avray. *Art into Life*. London: Centaur Press, 1958.

_____. *Alchemy as a Way of Life*. London: Daniel, 1976.

_____. *Art as Revelation*. Fontwell, Sussex: Centaur Press Ltd., 1981.

Wingert, P. S. *Primitive Art: Its Traditions and Styles*. New York: Oxford University Press, 1962.

Winner, Ellen. *Invented Worlds: The Psychology of the Arts*. Cambridge, MA: Harvard University Press, 1982.

Wirz, Paul. *Exorcism and the Art of Healing in Ceylon*. Leiden: E. J. Brill, 1954.

Wissler, Clark. "Masks." In *Guide Leaflet Series* of the American Museum of Natural History No. 96, New York. Reprinted from *Natural History*. Vol. XXVIII, No. 4, 1938, pp. 339–352.

Witherspoon, Gary. *Language and Art in the Navajo Universe*. Ann Arbor: University of Michigan Press, 1977.

Wolf, Eric R. *Sons of the Shaking Earth*. Chicago: University of Chicago Press, 1959.

Wreschner, Ernst E. "Red Ochre and Human Evolution: A Case for Discussion." *Current Anthropology*. Vol. 21, No. 5, pp 631–33, 1980.

Yates, Frances A. *The Art of Memory*. Chicago: University of Chicago Press, 1966.

_____. *Theatre of the World*. Chicago: University of Chicago Press, 1969.

Young, Dudley. *Origins of the Sacred*. New York: St. Martin's Press, 1991.

Young, Frank Wilbur. *Initiation Ceremonies: A Cross-cultural Study of Status Dramatization*. Indianapolis: Bobbs-Merrill, 1965.

Young, J. Z. *An Introduction to the Study of Man*. Oxford: Oxford University Press, 1974.

Yuille, John, C., ed. *Imagery, Memory and Cognition*. Hillsdale NJ and London: Lawrence Erlbaum Associates, 1983.

Zimmer, Heinrich. *Myths and Symbols in Indian Art and Civilization*. Princeton, NJ: Bollingen Series VI, Princeton University Press, 1972.

Zuidema, R. T. "Masks in the Incan Solstice and Equinoctial Ritual." In N. Ross Crumrine and Majorie Halpin, eds. *The Power of Symbols, Masks and Masquerade in the Americas*. pp. 149–56, Vancouver: University of British Columbia Press, 1983.

About the Drawings

1.1—After an illustration in Hiler 1929, figure 45 and H.G. Robley in Lévi-Strauss 1963, plate VII.

1.2 — After an illustration in Leenhardt 1950, plate 94. This artifact was in the Musée de l'Homme, Paris, in 1950; the current location has not been verified.

1.3 — After an illustration in von Winning 1968: 246, figure 334. The current location of this artifact is reported to be a private collection.

1.4 — After an illustration in Leenhardt 1950, plate 33. The artifact was in the Musée de l'Homme, Paris, in 1950. The current location has not been verified.

1.5 — After an illustration in Dockstader 1964, plate 236. The current location of this artifact is reported to be the Museum of the American Indian, The Smithsonian Institution.

1.6 — After an illustration in Lee 1981:13. The current location of this artifact has not been verified.

1.7 — From the artifact. The piece is included in Sasser 1995:98, figure 59. A similar mask is shown in Sieber and Rubin 1970:130, figure 148; Dwyer and Dwyer 1973:29; and Segy 1976, plate 227. The current location of this artifact is the Museum of Texas Tech University, Lubbock, Texas.

1.8 — After an illustration in Wissler 1939:30, figure 60. The current location of this artifact is reported to be the American Museum of Natural History, New York.

1.9 — After an illustration in Cordry 1980:54, plate 69. The current location of this artifact is reported to be the International Folk Art Museum, Santa Fe, New Mexico.

1.10 — After an illustration in the Baltimore Museum of Art 1956:13. The current location of this artifact is unknown.

1.11—After an illustration in Underwood 1952, figure 18. The current location of this artifact has not been verified.

1.12 — After an illustration in Maringer 1960, figure 1 in Lissner 1961, plate 113; Lommel 1972:199; Marshack 1972:272; Campbell 1976:309; Halifax 1982:82; Campbell 1988b:156, figure 269; Larsen 1988:9; Walker 1988:390; Gimbutas 1991: 176, figure 275; Laing and Wire 1993:38; and Leakey 1994:116.

2.1—After an illustration in Markman and Markman 1992:52, image 4; Bushnell 1967:34, figure 25; and Cordry 1980:160, plate 203. A similar image is shown in Halifax 1982:77. The current location of this artifact is reported to be the Museo Nacional de Antropologia, Mexico D.F.

2.2 — From the artifact. The current location of this artifact is the Museum of Texas Tech University, Lubbock, Texas.

2.3 — After an illustration in Leenhardt 1950, plate 41. The artifact was in the Musée de l'Homme, Paris, in 1950; the current location has not been verified.

2.4 — After an illustration in MacGowan and Rosse 1924: 26. The current location of this mask is unknown.

2.5 — After an illustration in Burns 1980:65. The current location of this artifact has not been verified.

2.6 — After an illustration in Cordry 1980:16, plate 19. The current location of this artifact has not been verified.

2.7 — After an illustration in Napier 1986:121, plate 57 and from the mask. The current location of this artifact is the Musée du Bardo, Tunis.

2.8 — After an illustration in de Barradas 1954, figure 1, number 28. The current location of this artifact has not been verified.

2.9 — After an illustration in Cordry 1980:45, plate 55 and from a mask owned by the author. A similar mask is shown in Jacobson and Fritz 1985:64, figure 95. The current location of this artifact is reported to be the University of Arizona.

2.10 — After an illustration in Lommel 1967:115, plate 31 and Lommel 1972:134, plate 82. The current location of this artifact is reported to be the Museum of the American Indian, New York.

2.11— After an illustration in Lissner 1961, plates 114 and 115; Lindsay 1963:21; Marshack 1972:273; Campbell 1976:287; Halifax 1982:54; Campbell 1988b:156, figure 270; Gimbutas 1991:176, figure 275; and Laing and Wire 1993:242.

2.12 — From the artifact. The current location of this artifact is the Museum of Texas Tech University, Lubbock, Texas.

3.1— From the artifact. The mask is in Sasser 1995: figures 43–46. The current location of this artifact is the Museum of Texas Tech University, Lubbock, Texas.

3.2 — After an illustration in Riley 1955:56, plate 19 and Bushnell 1965:131, figure 126. The same mask is included in Campbell 1983:218, plate 285 and Campbell 1988b:218, figure 385. The current location of this artifact is reported to be the University Museum, Philadelphia.

3.3 — After an illustration in Taylor and Aragon 1991:161. The current location of this artifact is reported to be the Barbier-Mueller Museum, Geneva.

3.4— After an illustration in Cole and Aniakor 1984:217, figure 332. The mask is thought to have been made by Ekezi Ngwo of Awkuzu, ca. 1940–1950. The current location of this artifact is reported to be the Museum of Cultural History, University of California, Los Angeles

3.5— After an illustration in Lincoln 1987:110, figure 16. The current location of this artifact is reported to be the Fine Arts Museum of San Francisco.

3.6— After an illustration in the Metropolitan Museum of Art exhibition catalog, 1969, plate 439. A similar mask is shown in Willett 1971:191, figure 185; Bascom 1973:156, figure 111; Segy 1976, figure 223; Schmalenbach 1988:254, figure 161; Meyer 1992:95, figure 78; and Hahner-Herzog, Kecskési, and Vajda 1998:273, figure 212. The current location of this artifact is reported to be the Museum of Primitive Art, New York.

3.7 — From the artifact. A similar mask is shown in Segy 1976, figure 103; Fagg 1968: figure 31; Segy 1976, figure 102; and Huet 1978:164. The piece is part of the Walker/ICASALS collection and the current location of this artifact is the Museum of Texas Tech University, Lubbock, Texas.

3.8 — After an illustration in Melody 1989, cover image. The current location of this artifact has not been verified.

3.9 — After an illustration in Furst and Furst 1982:110, plate 94. The same mask is included in Malin 1978, plate 13. The current location of this artifact is reported to be the Denver Art Museum.

3.10— After an image published in *Arts Quarterly*, New Orleans Museum of Art, vol. XXI issue 4. The mask is in the New Orleans Museum of Art.

3.11— From the object. The piece is included in Sasser 1995:110, figure 79. A similar mask is shown in Segy 1976, figure 102; and Huet 1978:164. The piece is part of the Walker/ICASALS collection and the current location of this artifact is the Museum of Texas Tech University, Lubbock, Texas.

4.1— After an illustration in Greub 1985:113. The current location of this artifact is reported to be the Museum für Volkskunde, Basel, Switzerland.

4.2 — After an illustration in Piggott 1973:32. The current location of the mask is reported to be the Seattle Art Museum.

4.3 — From the artifact. The piece is included in Sasser 1995:103, figure 67. A similar mask is shown in Riley 1955:58, figure 20; Fagg 1968, figure 73a; Monti 1969:51, figure 22; Segy 1976, figure 97; Huet 1978, figure 59; Schmalenbach 1988:120, figure 56; and Willett 1991:99, figure 81. The current location of this artifact is the Museum of Texas Tech University, Lubbock, Texas.

4.4— After an illustration in Greub 1985, plate 34. A similar mask is shown in Newton 1971:42, figure 67. The current location of this artifact is reported to be the Übersee-Museum in Breman, Switzerland.

4.5— After an illustration in the National Museum of American Art 1982:137, figure 180. The current location of this artifact is reported to be the National Museum of African Art, the Smithsonian.

4.6— After an illustration in Fitzhugh and Kaplan 1982:195, plate 243. The current location of this artifact has not been verified.

4.7 — From the artifact. A similar mask is in Segy 1976, figure 227. The current location of this artifact is the Museum of Texas Tech University, Lubbock, Texas.

4.8— After an illustration in Slattum 1992:80. The current location of this artifact has not been verified.

4.9 — From the artifact. The piece is included in Sasser 1995:100, figures 61–63. The current location of this artifact is the Museum of Texas Tech University, Lubbock, Texas.

4.10 — From the artifact. The piece is included in Sasser 1995:60 and 86, figures 12 and 37, and a similar piece is in Hahner-Herzog et al. 1998, plate 27. The current location of this artifact is the Museum of Texas Tech University, Lubbock, Texas.

4.11— After an illustration in Segy 1976, figure 236. The current location of this artifact is reported to be the Museum of Primitive Art, New York.

4.12 — After an illustration in Teuten 1990:26. The current location of the mask is unknown.

4.13 — From the artifact. The current location of this artifact is the Museum of Texas Tech University, Lubbock, Texas.

5.1— After an illustration in the National Museum of American Art 1982:62, figure 21. Similar masks are shown in Campbell 1983:207, plate 341; Campbell 1988b:207, figure 341; and Campbell 1989:174, figure 261. The current location of this artifact is reported to be the National Museum of Natural History, the Smithsonian.

5.2 — After an illustration in Maksic and Meskil 1973:23, plate 10. The current location of this artifact has not been verified.

5.3 — From the artifact. The piece is included in Sasser 1995:110, figure 80. A similar mask is included in Dagan 1987: 33, plate 39. The current location of this artifact is the Museum of Texas Tech University, Lubbock, Texas.

5.4 — After an illustration in MacGowan and Rosse 1923:68. The current location of this artifact has not been verified.

5.5 — After an illustration in Fitzhugh and Crowell 1988:272, figure 372. The current location of this artifact is reported to be the Museum of Anthropology and Ethnography in St. Petersburg, but the location has not been verified.

5.6 — From the artifact. The current location of this mask is the Museum of Texas Tech University, Lubbock, Texas.

5.7 — After an illustration in Dockstader 1967, figure 211. The current location of the mask is reported to be the Museum of American Indians, the Smithsonian.

5.8 — After an illustration in Dockstader 1967, figure 135. The current location of the mask is reported to be the Museum of American Indians, the Smithsonian.

5.9 — After an illustration in Riley 1955:112, plate 48. The current location of the mask has not been verified.

5.10 — After an illustration in Fitzhugh and Kaplan 1982:145, plate 166. The current location of this artifact has not been verified.

5.11 — After an illustration in Chaussonnet 1995:70, plate 71. The current location of the mask is reported to be the Khabarovsk Regional Museum, but the location has not been verified.

6.1 — After an illustration in Cordry 1980:250, plate 310. The current location of this artifact has not been verified.

6.2 — After an illustration in Wingert 1962:213, plate 55. This piece is said to be in the Routenstrauch-Joset-Museum für Volkenkunde, Cologne, but the location has not been confirmed.

6.3 — After an illustration in Halifax 1982:50 of rock painting from Monsell site, Salish, Nanaimo River, British Colombia.

6.4 — After an illustration in Burland 1968:114; Haberland 1968:204, figure 85; Snow 1976:76; Halifax 1982:83; Corbin 1988:103; Campbell 1983:11 and 157; Campbell 1988b:157, figure 274; Walker 1988:370; and others. The current location of this artifact has not been verified.

6.5 — After an illustration in McFarren 1993:56. The current location of this artifact has not been verified.

6.6 — After an illustration in Marshack 1972:272.

6.7 — After an illustration in Hartmann 1967:

250, plate 2. The same mask is in Urban and Hendricks 1983, plate 6 and Teuten 1991:71. The current location of this artifact is reported to be the Museum für Volkerkunde, Berlin.

6.8 — After an illustration in Jessup 1990:179, figure 138/no. 130. A similar mask is in Soebadio 1992:169. The current location of this artifact has not been verified.

6.9 — After an illustration in von Winning 1968:59, plate 56. The current location of the artifact is reported to be the Museum of Primitive Art, New York.

6.10 — After an illustration in von Winning 1955:52, plate 16. The current location of this artifact has not been verified.

6.11 — After an illustration in Lee 1981:33. The current location of this artifact has not been verified.

7.1 — After an illustration in von Winning 1968:247, plate 339. The same piece is included in Kubler 1954. The current location of the artifact is reported to be in the Philadelphia Museum of Art.

7.2 — After an illustration in Leenhardt 1950, figure 13. A similar piece is in the Metropolitan Museum of Art 1969, figure 161 and National Museum of American Art 1982:143, figure 193. The artifact was in the Musée de l'Homme, Paris, in 1950; the current location has not been verified.

7.3 — After an illustration in Kerstetter 1986:108. The current location of this artifact is reported to be the Colorado Springs Fine Arts Center.

7.4 — After an illustration in Lindsay 1963:203, Campbell 1974:120, and Lawton et al. 1987:320 and with reference to Campbell 1988b:194, figure 322 and a diagram at the Palace Museum in Taipei, Taiwan.

7.5 — After an illustration in Gimbutas 1991, figure 225. The current location of this artifact has not been verified.

7.6 — After an illustration in Slattum 1992:106. The current location of this artifact has not been verified.

7.7 — From the artifact. The piece is included in Sasser 1995:98, figure 60. The current location of this artifact is the Museum of Texas Tech University, Lubbock, Texas.

7.8 — After an illustration in Hartmann 1967, figure 98 and Urban and Hendricks 1983:187, plate 4. The current location of this artifact is reported to be the Museum für Völkerkunde, Berlin, Germany.

7.9 — From the artifact. The piece is in Sasser 1995, figure 29. A similar mask is in Segy 1976, figure 227. The current location of this artifact is the Museum of Texas Tech University, Lubbock, Texas.

7.10 — After an illustration in Wissler 1938:12, figure 21. A similar mask is shown in the Montreal

Museum of Fine Arts catalog 1989:191, figure 178. The current location of this artifact is reported to be the American Museum of Natural History, New York.

7.11— After an illustration in Colombino 1989. The current location of this artifact has not been verified.

8.1— After an illustration in McLeod and Mack 1985:44. The current location of this artifact is reported to be the British Museum, London.

8.2 — After an illustration in Napier 1986:112, plate 47; Walker 1988:308; and Laing and Wire 1993:235. The current location of this artifact is reported to be the British Museum, London.

8.3 — After an illustration in Pierre 1959:85. A similar mask is shown in Wissler 1938:25, figure 55. This artifact was in the Musée de l'Homme in Paris.

8.4 — After an illustration in Underwood 1976, figure 20. The current location of this artifact is reported to be the British Museum, London.

8.5 — After an illustration in Moes 1985, figure 15. The current location of the mask has not been verified.

8.6 — From the artifact. The mask is in Sasser 1995:79, figure 28. Similar masks are in Hahner-Herzog, I., Kecskési, M., and Vajda. L. 1998:22 and Meyer 1992:74. The current location of this artifact is the Museum of Texas Tech University, Lubbock, Texas.

8.7 — After an illustration in Smith 1984. A similar piece is in Wissler, 1928, figure 20, and Riley, 1955, figure 51. The current location of the mask has not been verified.

8.8 — After an illustration in Poignant 1967:103. The current location of the mask is reported to be the Pitt Rivers Museum, Oxford.

8.9 — After an illustration in Cole and Aniakor 1984:191, figure 305. The mask was made by Anozie, ca. 1948. The current location of this artifact is reported to be the National Museum, Lagos, Nigeria.

8.10 — After an illustration in MacGowan and Rosse 1924:156. The current location of the mask has not been verified.

8.11— After an illustration in Gardner: 1986:195. The current location of this artifact is unknown.

9.1— After an illustration in McFarren 1993:147. The current location of this artifact has not been verified.

9.2 — After an illustration in Labbé 1986:56, figure 49. The current location of this artifact has not been verified.

9.3 — After an illustration in Meyer 1995:172, plate 177. The current location of this artifact has not been verified.

9.4 — After an illustration in Campbell 1983:202, plate 336. The same mask is illustrated in Halifax 1982:33; Campbell 1988:202, plate 336; and on the cover of Campbell 1988. A similar piece is included in Holm 1989:233, plate 98. The current location of this artifact is reported to be the American Museum of Natural History.

9.5 — After an illustration in Hartmann 1967, figure 42. The same mask is included in Urban and Hendricks 1983:190, plate 7. The current location of this artifact is reported to be the Museum für Völkerkunde, Berlin, Germany.

9.6 — After an illustration in McFarren 1993:109. The current location of this artifact has not been verified.

9.7 — After an illustration in MacGowan and Rosse 1923:105. The current location of this artifact has not been verified.

9.8 — After an illustration in Waite in Fraser 1966:280, figure 9a. A similar mask is in Perrin 1959:27. The current location of this artifact is reported to be the Provincial Museum, Victoria, BC.

9.9 — From the artifact. The current location of this artifact is the Museum of Texas Tech University, Lubbock, Texas.

9.10 — From the artifact. The current location of this artifact is the Museum of Texas Tech University, Lubbock, Texas.

9.11— After an illustration in Lee 1981:22. The current location of this artifact has not been verified.

9.12 — From the artifact. A similar mask is in Segy 1976, figure 22. The current location of this artifact is the Museum of Texas Tech University, Lubbock, Texas).

10.1— From the artifact. The same mask is in Sasser 1995:101, figure 64. The current location of this artifact is the Museum of Texas Tech University, Lubbock, Texas.

10.2 — After an illustration in Dockstader 1967, figure 49. The current location of the artifact is reported to be the Museum of American Indians, the Smithsonian.

10.3 — After an illustration in Berger and Bartholomew 1995:169, figure 40; see also Lommel 1970:114, figure 70. Similar pieces are illustrated in Tsultem 1989, figures 178 and 180. The current location of this artifact is the Choijin-Lama Temple Museum.

10.4 — After an illustration in McFarren 1993:36. The current location of this artifact has not been verified.

10.5 — After an illustration in Cordry 1980:130, figure 180. The current location of this artifact has not been verified.

10.6 — After an illustration in Wade 1986, figure 213. This mask is reportedly in the Philbrook Art Center, but the location has not been verified.

10.7 — From the artifact. The current location of this artifact is the collection of the author in Lubbock, Texas.

10.8 — After an illustration in Holm 1987, plate 36. The current location of the mask has not been verified.

10.9 — From the artifact. The current location of this artifact is the Museum of Texas Tech University, Lubbock, Texas.

10.10 — From the artifact. A similar piece is in Segy 1952:99; Willett 1991, figure 183; and Schmalenbach 1988: 212. The current location of this artifact is the Museum of Texas Tech University, Lubbock, Texas.

10.11— After an illustration in *Masterkey,* vol. 62, No. 2 & 3 Summer/Fall 1988, figure 59. The current location of the mask is reported to be the Southwest Museum, Los Angeles, CA.

11.1— After an illustration in Moes 1986:45, plate 16. The current location of the mask has not been verified.

11.2 — After an illustration in Wissler 1938:9, figure 18 and Riley 1955:115, plate 50. A similar mask is in Jessup 1990, figure 139. The current location of this artifact is reported to be the American Museum of Natural History, New York.

11.3 — After an illustration in Lommel 1972: 119.

11.4 — After an illustration in Marion and Kenagy 1988:23, figure 31. The current location of the mask has not been verified.

11.5 — After an illustration in Lee 1973:334. The current location of the mask has not been verified.

11.6 — After an illustration in MacGowan and Rosse 1924:120. The current location of the mask has not been verified.

11.7 — After an illustration in Burland 1968:45. The current location of this artifact has not been verified.

11.8 — After an illustration in Hartmann 1967, figure 328. The current location of this artifact has not been verified.

11.9 — After an illustration in Lommel 1970:204, figure 143 and Smith 1984; figure 21. The current location of this artifact is reported to be the Festungsmuseum, Salzburg, Austria.

11.10 — After an illustration in MacGowan and Rosse 1924, plate 70; see also Twycross and Carpenter 2002:203, figure 7. The current location of the mask has not been verified.

11.11— From the artifact. The current location of this artifact is the collection of the author in Lubbock, Texas.

Index

www.ingramcontent.com/pod-product-compliance
Ingram Content Group UK Ltd.
Pitfield, Milton Keynes, MK11 3LW, UK
UKHW051853150726
7214IPUK00021B/399